A DICTIONARY OF QUOTATIONS FROM THE BIBLE

A DICTIONARY OF QUOTATIONS FROM THE BIBLE

Selected by
Margaret Miner
and
Hugh Rawson

NAL BOOKS
NEW AMERICAN LIBRARY
NEW YORK
PUBLISHED IN CANADA BY
PENGUIN BOOKS CANADA LIMITED, MARKHAM, ONTARIO

Published simultaneously in Canada by Penguin Books Canada Limited.

NAL BOOKS TRADEMARK REG. U.S. PAT. OFF. AND FOREIGN COUNTRIES
REGISTERED TRADEMARK—MARCA REGISTRADA
HECHO EN CHICAGO, U.S.A.

SIGNET, SIGNET CLASSIC, MENTOR, ONYX, PLUME, MERIDIAN
and NAL BOOKS are published *in the United States* by NAL PENGUIN INC.,
1633 Broadway, New York, New York 10019, *in Canada* by
Penguin Books Canada Limited, 2801 John Street,
Markham, Ontario L3R 1B4

Library of Congress Cataloging-in-Publication Data

Miner, Margaret.
A dictionary of quotations from the Bible/selected by Margaret Miner and Hugh Rawson.
p. cm.
ISBN 0-453-00631-0
1. Bible—~~Quotations, maxims, etc~~. I. Rawson, Hugh.
II. Title Indexes, Topical.
BS416.R39 1988
220.3—dc19 88-21046
CIP

First Printing, November, 1988

1 2 3 4 5 6 7 8 9

PRINTED IN THE UNITED STATES OF AMERICA

To Mary E. Miner,
who lived through it all,
with only one ten-minute break

The names and order of the books of the Old Testament and the New Testament and the Apocrypha

We have listed quotations according to the sequence in which books of the Bible traditionally are printed. That is, we begin with *Genesis* and end with *Revelation*. The Apocrypha appear between the Old and New Testaments. The sequence is as follows:

OLD TESTAMENT

Genesis	II Chronicles	Daniel
Exodus	Ezra	Hosea
Leviticus	Nehemiah	Joel
Numbers	Esther	Amos
Deuteronomy	Job	Obadiah
Joshua	Psalms	Jonah
Judges	Proverbs	Micah
Ruth	Ecclesiastes	Nahum
I Samuel	Song of Solomon	Habakkuk
II Samuel	Isaiah	Zephaniah
I Kings	Jeremiah	Haggai
II Kings	Lamentations	Zechariah
I Chronicles	Ezekiel	Malachi

APOCRYPHA

I Esdras	Ecclesiasticus	Susanna
II Esdras	Baruch	Manasses
Tobit	Song of the Three Holy Children	I Maccabees
Judith		II Maccabees
Wisdom of Solomon		

NEW TESTAMENT

Matthew	Ephesians	Hebrews
Mark	Philippians	James
Luke	Colossians	I Peter
John	I Thessalonians	II Peter
Acts	II Thessalonians	I John
Romans	I Timothy	II John
I Corinthians	II Timothy	III John
II Corinthians	Titus	Jude
Galatians	Philemon	Revelation

Introduction

We designed this book for writers and speakers who are looking for pertinent Biblical quotations, as well as for readers who would like to have at hand great passages of the Bible, such as the twenty-third psalm (listed under GOD'S PROVIDENCE); the flight from Egypt (under EXODUS); the Christmas story from the gospel of St. Luke (at JESUS: BIRTH AND CHILDHOOD); and the opening of the gospel of John ("In the beginning was the Word . . . ," listed under JESUS).

We settled on this combination of succinct quotations and longer passages because this type of selection is what we ourselves find most useful and satisfying; other books generally do not provide this balance. This book, as well as being a compilation of quotes, serves also as a reader's guide to the Bible.

Beyond the traditional categories and famous verses, we have included certain quotes and passages that strike a modern reader with particular urgency or in a new way. Some of these are listed under CITIES ("I have seen violence and strife in the city," *Psalms* 55:9); COVERUP ("You whitewash with lies," *Job* 13:4, Revised Standard Version); ENVIRONMENT ("Hurt not the earth, neither the sea, nor the trees," *Revelation* 7:3); POPULATION ("There is no end of all the people," *Ecclesiastes* 4:16; or, "Thou hast multiplied the nation, and not increased the joy," *Isaiah* 9:3); and PHYSICAL FITNESS ("The race is not to the swift, nor the battle to the strong," *Ecclesiastes* 9:11, but on the other hand we are advised, "Strengthen ye the weak hands, and confirm the feeble knees," *Isaiah* 35:3).

Some verses have been included primarily because they give a picture of life in biblical times. The harsh wilderness (see EXODUS) contrasted dramatically with the opulence of the great courts and trading cities (see RICHES). Wine was essential to the good life (see WINE AND DRINKING); alcoholism and excess took their toll then as now ("The priest and the prophet have erred through strong drink . . . they err in vision, they stumble in judgment," *Isaiah* 28:7; cited under CLERGY). Fathers worried about their daughters ("The father waketh for the daughter, when no man knoweth; and the care for her taketh away sleep," *Ecclesiasticus* 42:9); and daughters sometimes took advantage ("The horseleach [veterinarian] hath two daughters, crying, Give, give," *Proverbs* 30:15); both quotes are cited under CHILDREN.

From time to time, we have included notes and comments when we thought these might interest readers: Did John the Baptist really eat locusts? Probably yes (see JOHN THE BAPTIST). Where did the Israelites cross the Red Sea? There are several possibilities (see EXODUS). What flower was really meant in the verse "The desert shall rejoice, and blossom as the rose" (*Isaiah* 35:1)? See the note under NATURE. Was Pilate an historical figure? Probably yes (see under PONTIUS PILATE).

Again, in offering notes and explanation, we followed our own feelings about what we like to see in a reference work. Pages of quotations without comment tend to lose focus. Moreover knowing the context and original sense of a quote are important to understanding its meaning and associations.

In making selections and comments we have tried to reflect Jewish as well as Christian beliefs and religious practices. Christians, for example, see most of the quotes that we have listed under IMMANUEL, MESSIAH, and SERVANT OF GOD as straightforward references to Jesus Christ as Saviour. Jews, naturally, interpret these passages very differently.

Using the Book

We hope that each quote is placed under an entirely logical heading, but inevitably people's ideas of where quotes should be filed vary widely. In searching for a quote, the reader can either look for a category in the main text (the categories are given alphabetically) or use the key word index in the back of the book, which lists quotes alphabetically according to the most important or memorable word or words in the quote. The categories are also cross-referenced to lead the reader to related subjects; the quote one is seeking under GOVERNMENT, for example, may possibly be found under OPPRESSION; it is important therefore to check the cross-references at the end of each category.

Occasionally an entire quote is given under two categories when it seemed to fit equally well in both places; but space did not allow for much of this. More frequently, a small part of a quote is given under one category, with the reader being advised that more of the quote can be found in a different category.

Within categories, quotes are listed according to the sequence of the books of the Bible. This gives the most satisfactory thematic organization of quotes on any subject. Readers who know what books they are searching for, but cannot remember where in the Bible they fall, will find a list of the books in traditional sequence given on page vii.

We have used The King's James Version as our basic text, with occasional help from the Revised Standard Version to clarify obscure terminology. Other translations have many virtues, but for purposes of quotation this is the most widely used in literature.

Acknowledgments

We have been asked many times recently how one goes about making a volume of Biblical quotes. Our method was to begin reading in *Genesis* and continue on to *Revelation*, marking quotes as we progressed. We also kept a file of clippings and notes on interesting Biblical quotes.

After making an initial collection of quotes, the next step was to consult histories and critical studies of the Bible for a better understanding of the passages we had selected. Finally, we turned to other major reference works to try to be sure that we had not missed anything incredibly obvious.

We are indebted to numerous authors, but we must mention three indispensable works: the multi-volume *Interpreter's Concise Commentary* (Abingdon Press, 1971); *Harper's Bible Dictionary* (Harper & Row, 1985); and *Familiar Quotations* by John Bartlett (edited by Emily Morison Beck, Little, Brown, 1980).

We thank our wonderfully responsible and patient copy editor, Nancy F. Shiner, and our good proofreader Jerold Kappes. Mary E. Miner's work on the index was invaluable. Our publishers extended extra time when we needed it, and then worked hard to keep the book on schedule. Reverend Bruce M. Shipman of Christ Church, Roxbury, Connecticut, directed us to some valuable reference materials.

ABEL

See CAIN AND ABEL

ABILITY

1 Neglect not the gift that is in thee. *I Timothy* 4:14.

ABRAHAM

2 I will bless them that bless thee, and curse him that curseth thee; and in thee shall all families of the earth be blessed. *Genesis* 12:3. (God to Abraham, the first patriarch, founder of the Jewish nation. Abraham is a major figure not only in the Bible, but also in the Koran, where he is called *El-Khalil,* "the Friend of God.")

3 Abram dwelled in the land of Canaan, and Lot dwelled in the cities of the plain, and pitched his tent toward Sodom. *Genesis* 13:12. (Lot was Abraham's nephew.)

4 Thou shalt be a father of many nations. *Genesis* 17:4.

5 Thy name shall be Abraham; for a father of many nations have I made thee. *Genesis* 17:5. (*Abraham* means "father of a multitude." The name *Abraham* and the term *Hebrew* appear to be related and to be derived from the word *Habiru*—there are several variant spellings—used in Mesopotamia and Egypt to refer to certain tribes of seminomadic people.)

See also CHOSEN PEOPLE; COVENANT; ISAAC; SODOM AND GOMORRAH.

ABSENCE

6 Absent in body, but present in spirit. *I Corinthians* 5:3.

ACCUSATIONS

7 Accuse not a servant unto his master, lest he curse thee, and thou be found guilty. *Proverbs* 30:10. (In other words, accusers may end up in trouble themselves.)

8 Where are those thine accusers? *John* 8:10. (Jesus to the woman taken in adultery. See under JUDGING OTHERS.)

See also GUILT; JUDGING OTHERS; TOLERANCE.

ACHIEVEMENT

See GREATNESS; SUCCESS; WORK

ACTIONS

1 Even a child is known by his doings, whether his work be pure, and whether it be right. *Proverbs* 20:11.

2 Whoso diggeth a pit shall fall therein: and he that rolleth a stone, it will return upon him. *Proverbs* 26:27. (Also, "Whoso diggeth a pit shall fall therein: and he that setteth a trap shall be taken therein." *Ecclesiasticus* 27:26.)

3 They have sown the wind, and they shall reap the whirlwind. *Hosea* 8:7.

4 Glorious is the fruit of good labors. *Wisdom of Solomon* 3:15.

5 Be not hasty in thy tongue, and in thy deeds slack and remiss. *Ecclesiasticus* 4:29.

6 Do nothing without advice; and when thou hast once done, repent not. *Ecclesiasticus* 32:19.

7 Whatsoever a man soweth, that shall he also reap. *Galatians* 6:7. (More at GOD'S KNOWLEDGE OF HUMANS.)

8 The Lord reward him according to his works. *II Timothy* 4:14. (St. Paul might more frankly have asked, "The Lord punish him . . ." The verse begins, "Alexander the coppersmith did me much evil.")

9 Be ye doers of the word, and not hearers only. *James* 1:22.

See also GOD'S WORKS; RESPONSIBILITY; RESULTS; SPEED; WORK.

ADAM AND EVE

10 And God said, Let us make man in our image, after our likeness: and let them have dominion over the fish of the sea, and over the fowl of the air, and over the cattle, and over all the earth, and over every creeping thing that creepeth upon the earth.

So God created man in his own image, in the image God created he him; male and female created he them.

And God blessed them, and God said unto them, Be fruitful, and multiply, and replenish the earth, and subdue it. *Genesis* 1:26–28.

11 And the Lord God formed man of the dust of the ground, and breathed into his nostrils the breath of life; and man became a living soul. *Genesis* 2:7.

12 Of every tree of the garden thou mayest freely eat:

But of the tree of the knowledge of good and evil, thou shalt not eat of it: for in the day that thou eatest thereof thou shalt surely die. *Genesis* 2:16–17.

13 It is not good that the man should be alone; I will make him an help meet for him. *Genesis* 2:18.

1 And the Lord God caused a deep sleep to fall upon Adam, and he slept: and he took one of his ribs, and closed up the flesh instead thereof.

And the rib, which the Lord God had taken from man, made he a woman, and brought her unto the man.

And Adam said, This is now bone of my bones, and flesh of my flesh: she shall be called Woman, because she was taken out of Man.

Therefore shall a man leave his father and his mother, and shall cleave unto his wife: and they shall be one flesh.

And they were both naked, the man and his wife, and were not ashamed. *Genesis* 2:21–25.

2 And the serpent said unto the woman, Ye shall not surely die:

For God doth know that in the day ye eat thereof [the tree of the knowledge of good and evil], then your eyes shall be opened, and ye shall be as gods, knowing good and evil. *Genesis* 3:4–5.

3 She took of the fruit thereof, and did eat, and gave also unto her husband with her; and he did eat.

And the eyes of them both were opened, and they knew that they were naked; and they sewed fig leaves together, and made themselves aprons. *Genesis* 3:6–7. (The exact garment fashioned from these leaves is not known. The Geneva Bible [1560] refers to *britches* rather than *aprons,* and is therefore sometimes called the "Breeches Bible." It is indeed possible to sew fig leaves together. This is still done in the Middle East to make wrappings for fresh fruit.)

4 And the Lord God called unto Adam, and said unto him, Where art thou?

And he said, I heard thy voice in the garden, and I was afraid, because I was naked; and I hid myself.

And he said, Who told thee that thou wast naked? *Genesis* 3:9–11.

5 And the man said, The woman whom thou gavest to be with me, she gave me of the tree, and I did eat. *Genesis* 3:12.

6 The woman said, The serpent beguiled me, and I did eat. *Genesis* 3:13.

7 Unto the woman he [God] said, I will greatly multiply thy sorrow and thy conception; in sorrow thou shalt bring forth children; and thy desire shall be to thy husband, and he shall rule over thee. *Genesis* 3:16.

8 In the sweat of thy face shalt thou [Adam] eat bread, till thou return unto the ground; for out of it wast thou taken: for dust thou art, and unto dust shalt thou return. *Genesis* 3:19.

9 And Adam called his wife's name Eve; because she was the mother of all living. *Genesis* 3:20. (*Eve* is probably related to the Hebrew *chava,* which means "life." *Adam* derives from *adamah,* meaning "earth.")

10 And the Lord God said, Behold, the man is become as one of us, to know good and evil: and now, lest he put forth his hand, and take also of the tree of life, and eat, and live for ever:

Therefore the Lord God sent him forth from the garden of Eden, to till the ground from whence he was taken.

So he drove out the man; and he placed at the east of the garden of Eden Cherubims, and a flaming sword which turned every way, to keep the way of the tree of life. *Genesis* 3:22–24.

See also CREATION; DEVIL; EDEN.

ADVERSITY

See DESTRUCTION; IRRITATIONS; MISFORTUNE; POVERTY AND HUNGER; TROUBLE

ADVICE

1 Take advice, and speak your minds. *Judges* 19:30.

2 Reprove not a scorner, lest he hate thee: rebuke a wise man, and he will love thee. *Proverbs* 9:8.

3 He who heeds instruction is on the path to life. *Proverbs* 10:17, RSV.

4 In multitude of counselors there is safety. *Proverbs* 24:6.

5 Have not I written to thee excellent things in counsels and knowledge. *Proverbs* 22:20.

6 Open rebuke is better than secret love. *Proverbs* 27:5.

7 Ask counsel of all that are wise. *Tobit* 4:18.

8 Do nothing without advice. *Ecclesiasticus* 32:19. (More at ACTIONS.)

AGE

See OLD AGE

AGRICULTURE

See FARMING; SHEPHERDS

AHAB AND JEZEBEL

9 Hast thou found me, O mine enemy? *I Kings* 21:20. (Ahab to the prophet Elijah.)

10 There was none like unto Ahab, which did sell himself to work wickedness in the sight of the Lord, whom Jezebel his wife stirred up. *I Kings* 21:25.

11 In the place where dogs licked the blood of Naboth shall dogs lick thy blood, even thine. *I Kings* 21:19. (Elijah to Ahab. Naboth, who owned a fine vineyard, was unjustly executed in a conspiracy engineered by Jezebel and Ahab. Jezebel, too, was cursed for the crime: "The dogs shall eat Jezebel by the wall of Jezreel." *I Kings* 21:23.)

1 When Jehu was come to Jezreel, Jezebel heard of it; and she painted her face, and tired her head, and looked out at a window. *II Kings* 9:30. (Thus Jezebel, daughter of the Phoenician king of Sidon, awaited her death with dignity. Incidentally, her name means "chaste." Her people followed the cult of Baal.)

See also MARRIAGE.

ALCOHOL

See DISSIPATION; FOOD AND DRINK; WINE AND DRINKING

ALIENATION

2 One born out of due time. *I Corinthians* 15:8. (For more see under PAUL.)

See also STRANGERS AND TRAVELERS.

ALMS

See GIVING

AMBITION

3 And seekest thou great things for thyself? seek them not. *Jeremiah* 45:5.

4 I shall set the people in order, and the nations shall be subject unto me. *Wisdom of Solomon* 8:14. (One of the few passages in the Bible in which ambition is accepted approvingly. The speaker is Solomon, and it is the wisdom granted by God that empowers him to rule.)

5 Seek not out the things that are too hard for thee, neither search the things that are above thy strength. *Ecclesiasticus* 3:21.

6 Set your affection on things above, not on things on the earth. *Colossians* 3.2.

See also GREATNESS; POWER.

ANGELS

7 Alas, O Lord God! For now I have seen the angel of the Lord face to face. *Judges* 6:22, RSV. (Gideon is speaking. Direct encounters with God or his angels were greatly feared, but God assures Gideon that no harm will come to him.)

8 He shall give his angels charge over thee, to keep thee in all thy ways.
They shall bear thee up in their hands, lest thou dash thy foot against a stone. *Psalms* 91:11–12. (See also *Matthew* 4:6, below.)

9 I [Isaiah] saw also the Lord sitting upon a throne, high and lifted up, and his train filled the temple.

Above it stood the seraphims: each one had six wings; with twain he covered his face, and with twain he covered his feet; and with twain he did fly.

And one cried unto another, and said, Holy, holy, holy, is the Lord of hosts: the whole earth is full of his glory. *Isaiah* 6:1–3. (See also GOD, ENCOUNTERS WITH.)

1 He shall give his angels charge concerning thee: and in their hands they shall bear thee up, lest at any time thou dash thy foot against a stone. *Matthew* 4:6. (The devil to Jesus in the wilderness, tempting him to throw himself from the pinnacle so that angels will save him, thereby proving his identity. The devil is quoting Psalm 91; see above.)

2 Behold, angels came and ministered unto him. *Matthew* 4:11. (The angels came to Jesus in the wilderness, after he had resisted the devil's temptations.)

3 He shall send his angels with a great sound of a trumpet. *Matthew* 24:31. (These angels shall gather the elect on JUDGMENT DAY.)

4 There is joy in the presence of the angels. *Luke* 15:10.

5 Who maketh his angels spirits, and his ministers a flame of fire. *Hebrews* 1:7.

6 The first beast was like a lion, and the second beast like a calf, and the third beast had a face as a man, and the fourth beast was like a flying eagle.

And the four beasts had each of them six wings about him; and they were full of eyes within: and they rest not day and night, saying, Holy, holy, holy, Lord God Almighty, which was, and is, and is to come. *Revelation* 4:7–8. (These angels, seen in a vision by JOHN OF PATMOS, somewhat resemble the angels described by Isaiah. See above. They are even more closely related to the four angels, each with four faces, that appear in *Ezekiel* 1. See also SCIENCE. The four faces are associated with signs of the zodiac in Babylonian mythology.)

7 I saw four angels standing on the four corners of the earth, holding the four winds of the earth. *Revelation* 7:1.

8 I beheld, and heard an angel flying through the midst of heaven, saying with a loud voice, Woe, woe, woe. *Revelation* 8:13.

9 There was a war in heaven: Michael and his angels fought against the dragon; and the dragon fought and his angels,

And prevailed not. *Revelation* 12:7–8.

See also JESUS; BIRTH AND CHILDHOOD (the Christmas story from *Luke*).

ANGER

10 A fire is kindled in mine anger, and shall burn unto the lowest hell, and shall consume the earth with her increase, and set on fire the foundations of the mountains. *Deuteronomy* 32:22. (God, speaking through Moses. See also DESTRUCTION.)

1 Wrath killeth the foolish man. *Job* 5:2.

2 Wrath brings the punishment of the sword. *Job* 19:29, RSV.

3 His anger endureth but a moment. *Psalms* 30:5.

4 A man of quick temper acts foolishly. *Proverbs* 14:17, RSV.

5 He that is slow to wrath is of great understanding. *Proverbs* 14:29.

6 A soft answer turneth away wrath. *Proverbs* 15:1.

7 Make no friendship with an angry man . . . lest thou learn his ways. *Proverbs* 22:24–25.

8 Wrath is cruel, anger is overwhelming. *Proverbs* 27:4, RSV. (More at ENVY.)

9 Fury is not in me. *Isaiah* 27:4.

10 A furious man cannot be justified; for the sway of his fury shall be his destruction. *Ecclesiasticus* 1:22

11 Strive not with an angry man, and go not with him into a solitary place. *Ecclesiasticus* 8:16.

12 Envy and wrath shorten the life. *Ecclesiasticus* 30:24. (More at SICKNESS.)

13 Whosoever is angry with his brother without a cause shall be in danger of the judgment: and whosoever shall say to his brother, Raca, shall be in danger of the council: but whosoever shall say, Thou fool, shall be in danger of hell fire. *Matthew* 5:22. (From the Sermon on the Mount. One of the many instances in which Jesus urged his followers to go beyond the requirements of the Law in their behavior toward each other. Before coming to the altar with a sacrifice, Jesus said, "first be reconciled to thy brother." *Matthew* 5:24. *Raca* is believed to be an Aramaic term meaning "empty-headed one.")

14 Let not the sun go down upon your wrath. *Ephesians* 4:26.

15 The wrath of man worketh not the righteousness of God. *James* 1:20.

See also EMOTIONS; VIOLENCE.

ANIMALS

16 And God created great whales, and every living creature that moveth. *Genesis* 1:21. (More at CREATION.)

17 And out of the ground the Lord God formed every beast of the field, and every fowl of the air; and brought them unto Adam to see what he would call them: and whatsoever Adam called every living creature, that was the name thereof. *Genesis* 2:19

1 The ass saw the angel of the Lord standing in the way, and his sword drawn in his hand: and the ass turned aside out of the way. *Numbers* 22:23 (This is Balaam's ass, which Balaam is riding to meet King Balak. The ass was a respected animal in biblical culture, often associated with peace. Thus, Jesus entered Jerusalem riding an ass. *Matthew* 21:2–7.)

2 The Lord opened the mouth of the ass, and she said unto Balaam, What have I done unto thee, that thou hast smitten me these three times? *Numbers* 22:28.

3 Then loud beat the horses' hoofs with the galloping, galloping of his steeds. *Judges* 5:22, RSV. (These are the war horses of the Canaanite commander Sisera, in flight from the armies of Deborah and Barak. See also SISERA AND JAEL. While the ass was associated with peace [see above] horses were associated with war. Owning horses in large numbers was generally forbidden as being tantamount to starting up an army—"The horse is prepared against the day of battle." *Proverbs* 21:31. The early Israelites fought without chariots or horses, but King Solomon had stables for thousands of horses, and imported them from Egypt. He was something of an arms merchant, dealing in horses and chariots. See *I Kings* 4:26, *II Chronicles* 1:16 and 9:28.)

4 He [the wild ass] scorns the tumult of the city; he hears not the shouts of the driver.
He ranges the mountains as his pasture, and he searches after every green thing. *Job* 39:7–8, RSV. (See also Jeremiah 14:6, below.)

5 Hast thou given the horse strength? hast thou clothed his neck with thunder? *Job* 39:19. (God to Job. The quote continues below.)

6 He [the war horse] paweth in the valley, and rejoiceth in his strength: he goeth on to meet the armed men.
He mocketh at fear, and is not affrighted; neither turneth he back from the sword. *Job* 39:21–22.

7 He [the war horse] saith among the trumpets, Ha ha; and he smelleth the battle afar off, the thunder of the captains, and the shouting. *Job* 39:25.

8 Doth the eagle mount up at thy command, and make her nest on high?
She dwelleth and abideth on the rock, upon the crag of the rock, and the strong place.
From thence she seeketh the prey, and her eyes behold afar off. *Job* 39:27–29.

9 Behold now behemoth. *Job* 40:15. (Behemoth is believed to be the hippopotamus, much magnified. It represents the greatest of the land animals, while leviathan, below, rules the sea.)

10 Canst thou draw out leviathan with a hook? *Job* 41:1. (Leviathan, here evidently based on the crocodile, is a huge sea monster, associated in

Ugaritic mythology with the God of the underworld. Leviathan appears again in *Job* 41:31–34: "He maketh the deep to boil like a pot," and "upon earth there is not his like, who is made without fear." The passage ends, "He is a king over all the children of pride." At *Psalms* 74:14, God is said to have killed leviathan to feed the Hebrews in the wilderness. In *Isaiah* 27:1, the predicted destruction of leviathan is the equivalent of the destruction of evil, and the animal is called a "crooked serpent," "the dragon that is in the sea." In his book *Leviathan,* Thomas Hobbes applied the term to the "multitude" united to form a commonwealth.)

1 Some trust in chariots, and some in horses. *Psalms* 20:7.

2 The young lions suffer want and hunger, RSV. *Psalms* 34:10. (See also Psalm 104, below.)

3 They [the wicked] are like the deaf adder that stoppeth her ear;
Which will not hearken to the voice of charmers, charming never so wisely. *Psalms* 58:4–5. (According to ancient legend an adder could resist the call of a snake charmer by putting one ear to the ground and sticking its tail in the other.)

4 The young lions roar after their prey, and seek their meat from God. *Psalms* 104:21. (See also Psalm 34, above.)

5 Go to the ant, thou sluggard; consider her ways, and be wise:
Which having no guide, overseer, or ruler,
Provideth her meat in the summer, and gathereth her food in the harvest. *Proverbs* 6:6–8.

6 A righteous man regardeth the life of his beast: but the tender mercies of the wicked are cruel. *Proverbs* 12:10.

7 The way of an eagle in the air; the way of a serpent upon a rock. *Proverbs* 30:19. (The whole passage is at LIFE'S WONDERS.]

8 There be four things which are little upon the earth, but they are exceeding wise.
The ants are a people not strong, yet they prepare their meat in the summer;
The conies [rabbits] are but a feeble folk, yet make they their houses in the rocks;
The locusts have no king, yet go they forth all of them by bands;
The spider taketh hold with her hands, and is in kings' palaces. *Proverbs* 30:24–28.

9 That which befalleth the sons of men befalleth beasts . . . as the one dieth, so dieth the other . . . a man hath no preeminence above a beast. *Ecclesiastes* 3:19.

10 Take us the foxes, the little foxes, that spoil the vines: for our vines have tender grapes. *Song of Solomon* 2:15. (This verse is believed to be an

interposed fragment from another work, and its meaning is not clear. Harriet Beecher Stowe, in her book *Little Foxes,* explained that the title referred to "those unsuspected, unwatched, insignificant *little* causes that nibble away domesticated happiness." Lillian Hellman used the same title for her play about an unpleasant family in the Civil War era.)

1 The ox knoweth his owner, and the ass his master's crib. *Isaiah* 1:3.

2 The wolf also shall dwell with the lamb, and the leopard shall lie down with the kid. *Isaiah* 11:6. (More of this passage on the great Davidic kingdom prophesied by Isaiah is given at PEACE.)

3 An habitation of dragons, and a court for owls. *Isaiah* 34:13. (One of the passages in *Isaiah* prophesying destruction and desolution. The reference here is to palaces and fortresses, perhaps in Edom, which will be taken over by wild animals. See also CITIES.)

4 The stork in the heaven knoweth her appointed times; and the turtle [dove] and the crane and the swallow observe the time of their coming. *Jeremiah* 8:7.

5 The wild asses did stand in the high places, they snuffed up the wind like dragons. *Jeremiah* 14:6.

6 As the partridge sitteth on eggs, and hatcheth them not; so he that getteth riches, and not by right, shall leave them in the midst of his days, and at his end shall be a fool. *Jeremiah* 17:11. (The implication that the partridge takes over other birds' eggs is a canard, so to speak.)

7 The lion hath roared, who will not fear? *Amos* 3:8.

See also CREATION; NATURE.

ANXIETY See WORRY

APOSTLES AND DISCIPLES

8 Follow me, and I will make you fishers of men.

And they straightway left their nets, and followed him. *Matthew* 4:19–20. (Thus Jesus gathers his first apostles: Simon, called Peter, and his brother Andrew, who were fishing in the Sea of Galilee.)

9 The names of the twelve apostles are these; The first, Simon, who is called Peter, and Andrew his brother; James the son of Zebedee, and John his brother;

Philip, and Bartholomew; Thomas, and Matthew the publican; James the son of Alphaeus, and Lebbaeus, whose surname was Thaddaeus;

Simon the Canaanite, and Judas Iscariot, who also betrayed him. *Matthew* 10:2–4. (There are variations in the lists of apostles, but the number is always twelve—the number of the tribes of Israel. After the

Resurrection, Matthias was elected to replace Judas, and apostleship is said to require that one have seen the risen Christ, *Acts* 1:21–26. But Paul and sometimes others are also referred to as apostles. The term means "one who is sent out," as with a mission.)

1 Heal the sick, cleanse the lepers, raise the dead, cast out devils: freely ye have received, freely give. *Matthew* 10:8.

2 He that receiveth you receiveth me, and he that receiveth me receiveth him that sent me. *Matthew* 10:40.

3 Many prophets and righteous men have desired to see those things which ye see, and have not seen them; and to hear those things which ye hear, and have not heard them. *Matthew* 13:17. (At *Luke* 10:24, the quote begins, "Many prophets and kings have desired . . .")

4 Whatsoever ye shall bind on earth shall be bound in heaven: and whatsoever ye shall loose on earth shall be loosed in heaven. *Matthew* 18:18. (Here Jesus extends to the apostles the spiritual authority he earlier vested in Peter.)

5 Go ye into all the world, and preach the gospel to every creature. *Mark* 16:15. (The term *gospel* is a translation of the Greek *euangelion,* meaning "good news." The good news that the resurrected Christ bids his disciples to preach is that salvation is at hand for those who believe.)

6 Carry neither purse, not scrip, nor shoes. *Luke* 10:4.

7 By this shall all men know that ye are my disciples, if ye have love one to another. *John* 13:35.

8 Ye have not chosen me, but I have chosen you. *John* 15:16.

9 Receive ye the Holy Ghost:
Whose soever sins ye remit, they are remitted unto them; and whose soever sins ye retain, they are retained. *John* 20:22–23. (The risen Jesus to his disciples.)

10 The gods are come down to us in the likeness of men. *Acts* 14:11. (The apostles quickly deny any claims to divinity; see below.)

11 We also are men of like passions with you. *Acts* 14:15. (Paul and Barnabas protest against the tendency of the crowds to deify them rather than worship God.)

12 We are made a spectacle unto the world, and to angels, and to men. *I Corinthians* 4:9.

See also PENTECOST; PETER.

APPEARANCES

13 Man looketh on the outward appearance, but the Lord looketh on the heart. *I Samuel* 16:7.

1 Commend not a man for his beauty, neither abhor a man for his outward appearance. *Ecclesiasticus* 11:2.

2 A man's attire, and excessive laughter, and gait, show what he is. *Ecclesiasticus* 19:30.

3 The countenance is a sign of changing of the heart. *Ecclesiasticus* 37:17.

4 Judge not according to the appearance. *John* 7:24.

See also BEAUTY.

ARK

See NOAH AND THE ARK

ARK OF THE COVENANT

5 Let them make me a sanctuary; that I may dwell among them. *Exodus* 25:8. (The Ark contained the two tablets of the law given to Moses on Mount Sinai; it signified God's presence. The Israelites carried it with them in their wanderings and eventually enclosed it in the Temple at Jerusalem. See also TEMPLE.)

6 The glory of the Lord filled the tabernacle. *Exodus* 40:34.

7 The cloud of the Lord was upon the tabernacle by day, and fire was on it by night, in the sight of all the house of Israel, throughout all their journeys. *Exodus* 40:38.

8 The glory is departed from Israel: for the ark of God is taken. *I Samuel* 4:22. (It was captured by the Philistines, but rescued by David.)

See also COVENANT.

ARMAGEDDON

See TO WORLD, END OF

ASKING

See INITIATIVE; PRAYER

ATHEISM

9 The fool hath said in his heart, There is no God. *Psalms* 14:1 (and 53:1).

10 He is antichrist, that denieth the Father and the Son. *I John* 2:22.

See also GOD, DOUBTING.

ATONEMENT

11 The goat, on which the lot fell to be the scapegoat, shall be presented alive before the Lord, to make an atonement with him, and to let him go for a scapegoat into the wilderness. *Leviticus* 16:10. (Here God gives Moses instruction to be passed on to his brother Aaron, the first high priest, regarding rites of atonement. See also YOM KIPPUR.)

[1] The Lord hath laid on him [God's servant] the iniquity of us all.
He was oppressed, and he was afflicted, yet he opened not his mouth: he is brought as a lamb to the slaughter. *Isaiah* 53:6–7. (To Jews, the suffering of God's servant described by Isaiah refers to the suffering of the chosen people. To Christians, it is a prophetic vision of Christ's suffering and death in atonement of mankind's sin. See MESSIAH; SERVANT OF GOD.)

See also GUILT.

ATONEMENT, DAY OF

See YOM KIPPUR

BABEL

1 Let us build us a city and a tower, whose top may reach unto heaven. *Genesis* 11:4.

2 Therefore is the name of it called Babel; because the Lord did there confound the language of all the earth: and from thence did the Lord scatter them abroad upon the face of all the earth. *Genesis* 11:9. (*Babel,* which means "gate of God," was the Hebrew name for Bab-ilu, or Babylon.)

See also LANGUAGE.

BABYLON

See CITIES

BAPTISM

3 I indeed baptize you with water unto repentance: but he that cometh after me is mightier than I, whose shoes I am not worthy to bear: he shall baptize you with the Holy Ghost, and with fire. *Matthew* 3:11. (John the Baptist speaking of the coming of Jesus.)

4 I indeed have baptized you with water: but he shall baptize you with the Holy Ghost. *Mark* 1:8. (The same passage as above, characteristically simpler in Mark, who was probably the first evangelist. See also *Acts* 1:5.)

5 We have not so much as heard whether there be any Holy Ghost. *Acts* 19:2. (Certain semi-informed disciples in Ephesus. Paul rebaptizes them in the name of the Lord Jesus, and lays his hands on them. Then the Holy Ghost inspires them, and "they spake with tongues, and prophesied." *Acts* 19:6.)

See also RELIGION; SPIRITUAL BIRTH.

BEATITUDES

6 Blessed are the poor in spirit: for theirs is the kingdom of heaven.

Blessed are they that mourn: for they shall be comforted.

Blessed are the meek: for they shall inherit the earth.

Blessed are they which do hunger and thirst after righteousness: for they shall be filled.

Blessed are the merciful: for they shall obtain mercy.

Blessed are the pure in heart: for they shall see God.

Blessed are the peacemakers: for they shall be called the children of God.

Blessed are they which are persecuted for righteousness' sake: for theirs is the kingdom of heaven.

Blessed are ye, when men shall revile you, and persecute you, and shall say all manner of evil against you falsely, for my sake.

Rejoice, and be exceeding glad: for great is your reward in heaven: for so persecuted they the prophets which were before you. *Matthew* 5:3–12. (These are the Beatitudes from the Sermon the Mount, which runs from *Matthew* 5:1 to 7:27. The concept that the meek and persecuted eventually will triumph is found also in the Old Testament, often with revolutionary overtones. See REVOLUTION. The phrase "poor in spirit" means dependent on and trusting in God. While the Beatitudes address personal qualities valued by God, much of what follows is a discussion of the law and right behavior. Famous passages reject retaliation [turn the other cheek, *Matthew* 5:39] and urge love [even of one's enemies, *Matthew* 5:43–48.] The Lord's Prayer begins at 6:9. The sermon is one of the great passages of world literature and contains the heart of the Christian message.)

See also BLESSINGS.

BEAUTY

1 The sons of God saw the daughters of men that they were fair. *Genesis* 6:2.

2 Let the beauty of the Lord our God be upon us. *Psalms* 90:17.

3 He [God] hath made every thing beautiful in his time. *Ecclesiastes* 3:11. The Revised Standard Version reads, "He has made everything beautiful in its time." More at CREATION.)

4 I am black, but comely, O ye daughters of Jerusalem, as the tents of Kedar, as the curtains of Solomon. *Song of Solomon* 1:5. (In the next verse, the speaker explains, "I am black, because the sun hath looked upon me: my mother's children . . . made me the keeper of the vineyards." The tents of Kedar are black goatshair tents of the Kedar tribes of the northern Arabian deserts. Kedar is one of the sons of Ishmael. The reference to the curtains of Solomon is unclear.)

5 Thou art all fair, my love; there is no spot in thee. *Song of Solomon* 4:7.

6 Thou didst trust in thine own beauty. *Ezekiel* 16:15.

7 Many have been deceived by the beauty of a woman. *Ecclesiasticus* 9:8. (And many more will be, given the facts set out in the next quote.)

8 The beauty of a woman cheereth the countenance, and a man loveth nothing better. *Ecclesiasticus* 36:22.

See also APPEARANCES; LIFE'S WONDERS.

BEGINNING AND ENDING

1 When I begin, I will also make an end. *I Samuel* 3:12.

2 Though your beginning was small, your latter days will be very great. *Job* 8:7, RSV.

3 Better is the end of a thing than the beginning thereof. *Ecclesiastes* 7:8.

4 Whatsoever thou takest in hand, remember the end, and thou shall never do amiss. *Ecclesiasticus* 7:36.

5 He that endureth to the end shall be saved. *Matthew* 10:22.

See also PERSEVERANCE.

BETRAYAL

6 They weighed for my price thirty pieces of silver. *Zechariah* 11:12. (This is from one of the most ominous and mysterious passages in the Bible, in which God appears as a destructive shepherd, turning on his own animals. The correct interpretation is not clear, but the verse has of course become associated with the thirty pieces of silver taken by Judas.)

7 One of you shall betray me. *Matthew* 26:21. (Jesus to the disciples at the Last Supper. Judas has already arranged the betrayal for thirty pieces of silver.)

8 Before the cock crow, thou shalt deny me thrice. *Matthew* 26:34. (More at PETER.)

9 He is at hand that doth betray me. *Matthew* 26:46. (Jesus referring to Judas. See also JESUS: PASSION AND DEATH.)

See also JESUS; PASSION AND DEATH; JUDAS ISCARIOT.

BIBLE STUDY

10 Search the scriptures. *John* 5:39. (See also CLERGY, *Acts* 18:24.)

BIRTH, SPIRITUAL

See SPIRITUAL BIRTH

BLESSINGS

11 God give thee of the dew of heaven, and of the fatness of the earth, and plenty of corn and wine. *Genesis* 27:28.

12 I will not let thee go, except thou bless me. *Genesis* 32:26. (Jacob here addresses the stranger—actually God—with whom he has wrestled all the night. See also JACOB.)

1 Consecrate yourselves today to the Lord . . . that he may bestow upon you a blessing this day. *Exodus* 32:29.

2 The Lord bless thee, and keep thee:
The Lord make his face shine upon thee, and be gracious unto thee:
The Lord lift up his countenance upon thee, and give thee peace. *Numbers* 6:24–26.

3 Blessed shalt thou be in the city, and blessed shalt thou be in the field. *Deuteronomy* 28:3.

4 Blessed shalt thou be when thou comest in, and blessed shalt thou be when thou goest out. *Deuteronomy* 28:6.

5 The Lord deal kindly with you. *Ruth* 1:8.

6 Go, and the Lord be with thee. *I Samuel* 17:37.

7 Go in peace . . . The Lord be between me and thee. *I Samuel* 20:42. (Jonathan's loving farewell to David.)

8 Blessed be he that cometh in the name of the Lord. *Psalms* 118:26.

9 Peace be within thy walls, and prosperity within thy palaces. *Psalms* 122:7.

10 He who blesses his neighbor with a loud voice, rising early in the morning, will be counted as cursing. *Proverbs* 27:14, RSV.

11 Peace be to this house. *Luke* 10:5.

12 The God of peace be with you all. Amen. *Romans* 15:33.

13 The grace of the Lord Jesus Christ be with you all. Amen. *Revelation* 22:21. (The last words in the Bible.)

See also BEATITUDES.

BLINDNESS

See BODY; IGNORANCE; MIRACLES OF JESUS; VISION

BOASTING

14 Let another man praise thee, and not thine own mouth. *Proverbs* 27:2.

15 The tongue is a little matter, and boasteth great things. *James* 3:5.

BODY

16 Eyes have they, but they see not. *Psalms* 115:5. (More at IDOLS.)

17 The hearing ear, and the seeing eye, the Lord hath made even both of them. *Proverbs* 20:12.

1 All flesh is grass, and all the goodliness thereof is as the flower of the field. *Isaiah* 40:6. (In the Revised Standard Version, this passage runs, "All flesh is grass, and all its beauty is like the flower of the field. / The grass withers, the flower fades, when the breath of the Lord blows upon it." *Isaiah* 40:6–7. See also *Peter* 1:24.)

2 Mine eye affecteth mine heart. *Lamentations* 3:51.

3 Can these bones live? *Ezekiel* 37:3. (God brings Ezekiel to a valley full of bones, representing the people of Israel slain by the Chaldeans, and asks this question. See below and also RESURRECTION OF THE DEAD.)

4 O ye dry bones, hear the word of the Lord. *Ezekiel* 37:4.

5 The light of the body is the eye. *Matthew* 6:22.

6 The spirit indeed is willing, but the flesh is weak. *Matthew* 26:41. (Jesus to Peter the night before the crucifixion. He had asked Peter, James, and John to keep him company, but they fell asleep. More at TEMPTATION. See also JESUS: PASSION AND DEATH.)

7 Wretched man that I am! who shall deliver me from this body of this death? *Romans* 7:24.

8 I beseech you therefore, brethren, by the mercies of God, that ye present your bodies a living sacrifice, holy, acceptable unto God, which is your reasonable service. *Romans* 12:1.

9 Know ye not that your body is the temple of the Holy Ghost which is in you, which ye have of God, and ye are not your own? *I Corinthians* 6:19.

10 If a woman have long hair, it is a glory to her. *I Corinthians* 11:15.

11 The flesh lusteth against the Spirit, and the Spirit against the flesh: and these are contrary the one to the other: so that ye cannot do the things that ye would. *Galatians* 5:17.

See also APPEARANCES; BEAUTY; HEALTH; HEARING; SEX; SICKNESS; VISION.

BODY IN (OR OF) CHRIST

See RELIGION

BOOKS

See WRITING

BOREDOM

See ENNUI

BORN AGAIN

See SPIRITUAL BIRTH

BORROWING AND LENDING

12 The wicked borroweth, and payeth not again. *Psalms* 37:21.

1 Lend not unto him that is mightier than thyself: for if thou lendest to him, count it but lost. *Ecclesiasticus* 8:12.

2 Be not made a beggar by banqueting upon borrowing. *Ecclesiasticus* 18:33.

3 Today he lendeth, and tomorrow will he ask it [back] again: such a one is to be hated of God and man. *Ecclesiasticus* 20:15.

4 Give to him that asketh thee, and from him that would borrow of thee turn not away. *Matthew* 5:42. (From the Sermon on the Mount—one of the more difficult injunctions in Christian ethics.)

See also MONEY.

BRIBERY

5 Thou shalt take no gift: for the gift blindeth the wise, and perverteth the words of the righteous. *Exodus* 23:8. (See also *Deuteronomy* 16:19 and *Ecclesiasticus* 20:29.)

6 He who is greedy for unjust gain makes trouble for his household, but he who hates bribes will live. *Proverbs* 15:27, RSV.

7 That they may do evil with both hands earnestly, the prince asketh, and the judge asketh for a reward; and the great man, he uttereth his mischievous desire: so they wrap it up. *Micah* 7:3.

See also JUDGES; LAW AND JUSTICE.

BUSINESS

8 It is naught, it is naught, saith the buyer: but when he is gone his way, then he boasteth. *Proverbs* 20:14.

9 Tyre, the crowning city, whose merchants are princes. *Isaiah* 23:8. (The Revised Standard Version reads, "Tyre, the bestower of crowns, whose merchants were princes, whose traders were the honored of the earth.")

10 Let not the buyer rejoice, nor the seller mourn: for wrath is upon all the multitude thereof. *Ezekiel* 7:12.

11 Ye shall have just balances. *Ezekiel* 45:10. (One of many passages in the Bible on the importance of fair scales and measures. See also HONESTY.)

12 He is a merchant, the balances of deceit are in his hand: he loveth to oppress. *Hosea* 12:7.

13 They sold the righteous for silver, and the poor for a pair of shoes. *Amos* 2:6.

14 Thou hast multiplied thy merchants above the stars of heaven. *Nahum* 3:16.

1 Be not overwise in doing thy business. *Ecclesiasticus* 10:26.

2 Deliver all things in number and weight; and put all in writing that thou givest out, or receivest in. *Ecclesiasticus* 42:7.

3 Jesus went into the temple of God, and cast out all them that sold and bought in the temple, and overthrew the tables of the moneychangers, and the seats of them that sold doves. *Matthew* 21:12. (Jesus asserts that they have made the temple into "a den of thieves." *Matthew* 21:13.)

4 Cast ye the unprofitable servant into outer darkness. *Matthew* 25:30.

5 Which of you, intending to build a tower, sitteth not down first, and counteth the cost, whether he have sufficient to finish it? *Luke* 14:28.

6 What shall I do? . . . I cannot dig; to beg I am ashamed. *Luke* 16:3. (This is a steward who is about to be fired. His solution is to call in his lord's debtors and reduce their debts by half, so that they will take him in. "And the Lord commended the unjust steward, because he had done wisely." *Luke* 16:8.)

7 No man might buy or sell, save that he had the mark, or the name of the beast. *Revelation* 13:17. (A rigid form of economic oppression. The perpetrators were overthrown by the forces of good.)

See also MONEY.

BUSINESS, MINDING ONE'S OWN

See BUSYBODIES

BUSYBODIES

8 Every fool will be meddling. *Proverbs* 20:3.

9 He who meddles in a quarrel not his own is like one who takes a passing dog by the ears. *Proverbs* 26:17, RSV.

10 Study to be quiet, and to do your own business. *I Thessalonians* 4:11.

11 They [young widows] learn to be idle, wandering about from house to house; and not only idle, but tattlers also and busybodies, speaking things which they ought not. *I Timothy* 5:13.

BUYING AND SELLING

See BUSINESS

CAIN AND ABEL

1 Abel was a keeper of sheep, but Cain was a tiller of the ground. *Genesis* 4:2. (In the ancient Middle East, there was a long history of conflict between nomads, who kept herds, and farmers. Scholars relate the enmity between Cain and Abel to that tradition.)

2 And Cain talked with Abel his brother: and it came to pass when they were in the field, that Cain rose up against Abel his brother, and slew him.

And the Lord God said unto Cain, Where is Abel thy brother? And he said, I know not: Am I my brother's keeper?

And he said, What hast thou done? the voice of thy brother's blood crieth unto me from the ground.

And now art thou cursed from the earth. *Genesis* 4:8–11.

3 A fugitive and a vagabond shalt thou be in the earth. *Genesis* 4:12.

4 My punishment is greater than I can bear. *Genesis* 4:13.

5 The Lord set a mark upon Cain, lest any finding him should kill him. *Genesis* 4:15. (Note that the mark was a protection, not part of Cain's punishment as is sometimes supposed.)

CANAAN

6 I am come down to deliver them [the people of Israel] out of the hand of the Egyptians, and to bring them up out of that land unto a good land and a large, unto a land flowing with milk and honey. *Exodus* 3:8. (The phrase "a land flowing with milk and honey" appears at *Exodus* 33:3, *Leviticus* 20:24, and in passing throughout the Bible. The land is Canaan, promised by God to Abraham's descendants, *Genesis* 12:7.)

7 The Lord thy God bringeth thee into a good land, a land of brooks of water, of fountains and depths that spring out of valleys and hills;

A land of wheat, and barley, and vines, and fig trees, and pomegranates; a land of oil olive, and honey;

A land wherein thou shalt eat bread without scarceness . . . a land whose stones are iron, and out of those hills thou mayest dig brass. *Deuteronomy* 8:7–9. (In ancient times, iron was derived from meteorites.)

8 Israel then shall dwell in safety alone: the fountain of Jacob shall be upon a land of corn and wine; also his heavens shall drop down dew. *Deuteronomy* 33:28.

See also JOSHUA AND THE CONQUEST OF CANAAN; ZION.

CAUTION

1 Trust ye not in a friend, put ye not confidence in a guide: keep the doors of thy mouth from her that lieth in thy bosom. *Micah* 7:5.

2 Go not in a way wherein thou mayest fall. *Ecclesiasticus* 32:20.

See also DANGER; PRUDENCE; TRUST, MISPLACED.

CELEBRATIONS

See FEASTS AND FESTIVITY; JUBILEE YEAR; SABBATICAL YEAR

CHANCE

See FATE; LUCK

CHANGE

3 Can the Ethiopian change his skin, or the leopard his spots? *Jeremiah* 13:23.

CHARITY

See CHARITY, CHRISTIAN; GIVING

CHARITY, CHRISTIAN

4 (*Charity* in the biblical sense combines the meanings of *love* and *brotherly love,* and implies concern for and generosity toward others, especially those in need. It is one of the translations used for the Greek *agape,* meaning "love.")

5 Knowledge puffeth up, but charity edifieth. *I Corinthians* 8:1.

6 Though I speak with the tongues of men and angels, and have not charity, I am become as sounding brass, or a tinkling cymbal.

And though I have the gift of prophecy, and understand all mysteries, and all knowledge; and though I have all faith, so that I could remove mountains, and have not charity, I am nothing.

And though I bestow all my goods to feed the poor, and though I give my body to be burned, and have not charity, it profiteth me nothing.

Charity suffereth long, and is kind; charity envieth not; charity vaunteth not itself, is not puffed up,

Doth not behave itself unseemly, seeketh not her own, is not easily provoked, thinketh no evil;

Rejoiceth not in iniquity, but rejoiceth in the truth;

Beareth all things, believeth all things, hopeth all things, endureth all things.

Charity never faileth. *I Corinthians* 13:1–8.

7 And now abideth faith, hope, charity, these three; but the greatest of these is charity. *I Corinthians* 13:13.

1 Follow after charity, and desire spiritual gifts. *I Corinthians* 14:1.

2 Charity shall cover the multitude of sins. *I Peter* 4:8.

See also LOVE.

CHILDREN

3 Be ye fruitful, and multiply. *Genesis* 9:7. (See also *Genesis* 1:28.)

4 Give me children, or else I die. *Genesis* 30:1. (Rachel to her husband, Jacob.)

5 I will go down into the grave unto my son mourning. Thus his father wept for him. *Genesis* 37:35. (Jacob grieving over the apparent death of Joseph.)

6 The lad cannot leave his father: for if he should leave his father, his father would die. *Genesis* 44:22. (The lad is Benjamin, the father, Jacob.)

7 They are a perverse generation, children in whom there is no faithfulness. *Deuteronomy* 32:20, RSV.

8 They would not listen to the voice of their father. *I Samuel* 2:25 RSV. (These are the sons of the high priest Eli, who raised Samuel. They meet an untimely death.)

9 O my son Absalom, my son, my son Absalom! *II Samuel* 18:33. (More at DAVID.)

10 I go the way of all the earth: be thou strong therefore, and shew thyself a man. *I Kings* 2:2. (David, near death, to his son Solomon.)

11 They send forth their little ones like a flock, and their children dance. *Job* 21:11. (See also *Matthew* 21:16.)

12 Out of the mouths of babes and sucklings hast thou ordained strength. *Psalms* 8:2.

13 Instead of thy fathers shall be thy children. *Psalms* 45:16. (In this wedding poem, probably written for Ahab and Jezebel, the bride is reminded that now her concerns must turn from her own parents and family to the next generation.)

14 Children are an heritage of the Lord. *Psalms* 127:3.

15 As arrows are in the hand of a mighty man; so are children of the youth. *Psalms* 127:4.

16 A wise son makes a glad father, but a foolish son is a sorrow to his mother. *Proverbs* 10:1, RSV.

17 A wise son hears his father's instruction. *Proverbs* 13:1, RSV.

1 He who spares the rod hates his son, but he who loves him is diligent to discipline him. *Proverbs* 13:24, RSV. (Also, "Withhold not correction from the child: for if thou beatest him with the rod, he shall not die." *Proverbs* 23:13. Similar verses are at *Proverbs* 29:15 and 29:17.)

2 The father of a fool hath no joy. *Proverbs* 17:11.

3 Train up a child in the way he should go: and when he is old, he will not depart from it. *Proverbs* 22:6.

4 My son, be wise, and make my heart glad. *Proverbs* 27:11.

5 The horseleach [veterinarian] hath two daughters, crying, Give, give. *Proverbs* 30:15.

6 I have nourished and brought up children, and they have rebelled against me. *Isaiah* 1:2.

7 A little child shall lead them. *Isaiah* 11:6. (This is from the description of the great Davidic kingdom prophesied by Isaiah. See under PEACE.)

8 Woe to the rebellious children, saith the Lord. *Isaiah* 30:1.

9 I care for nothing, my son, since I have let thee go, the light of mine eyes. *Tobit* 10:5. (The lament of a mother whose son is late returning from a journey. Naturally, she fears the worst. Actually the young man, Tobias, has made an excellent marriage and soon comes home with a fortune.)

10 Desire not a multitude of unprofitable children. *Ecclesiasticus* 16:1.

11 A horse not broken becometh headstrong: and a child left to himself will be wilful. *Ecclesiasticus* 30:8.

12 Beware of thy own children. *Ecclesiasticus* 32:22. (This book is unsympathetic to children. See the quotes above, for example. Chapter 31 urges strict discipline and corporal punishment.)

13 The father waketh for the daughter, when no man knoweth; and the care for her taketh away sleep. *Ecclesiasticus* 42:9.

14 Jesus called a little child unto him, and set him in the midst of them [the disciples],

And said, . . . Except ye be converted, and become as little children, ye shall not enter into the kingdom of heaven.

Whosoever therefore shall humble himself as this little child, the same is greatest in the kingdom of heaven.

And whoso shall receive one such little child in my name receiveth me.

But whoso shall offend one of these little ones which believe in me, it were better for him that a millstone were hanged about his neck, and that he were drowned in the depth of the sea. *Matthew* 18:2–6. (Also at *Luke* 17:2, in slightly different words.)

1 Take heed that ye despise not one of these little ones; for I say unto you, That in heaven their angels do always behold the face of my Father. *Matthew* 18:10.

2 Suffer the little children to come unto me, and forbid them not: for of such is the kingdom of God. *Mark* 10:14.

3 Thou shalt have joy and gladness; and many shall rejoice at his birth. *Luke* 1:14. (An angel telling Zacharias that he and his wife will have a child. This child will be John the Baptist.)

4 Son, thou art ever with me, and all I have is thine. *Luke* 15:31. (The father to his oldest son at the conclusion of the parable of the PRODIGAL SON.)

5 When a woman is in travail she has sorrow, because her hour has come; but when she is delivered of the child, she no longer remembers the anguish, for joy that a child is born into the world. *John* 16:21, RSV. (One of several instances in which the Revised Standard Version of the Bible corrects a masculine bias in the King James translation. In the latter, the wording is ". . . joy that a son is born . . ." But the Greek term translated here as "son" refers more correctly to a human being than to a male.)

6 When I was a child, I spake as a child, I understood as a child, I thought as a child: but when I became a man, I put away childish things. *I Corinthians* 13:11. (From the chapter in praise of charity. See CHARITY, CHRISTIAN and VISION.)

7 Fathers, provoke not your children to anger, lest they be discouraged. *Colossians* 3:21.

8 Let them [young people] learn first to show piety at home. *I Timothy* 5:4.

See also CHOSEN PEOPLE; FAMILIES; GENERATIONS; PARENTS.

CHOICE

9 See, I have set before thee this day life and good, and death and evil. *Deuteronomy* 30:15. (Here Moses explains to the Israelites the fundamental choice that lies before them now that they have been given God's law. The passage is then repeated in slightly different words, with the conclusion, "Choose life, that both thou and thy seed may live." *Deuteronomy* 30:19.)

10 I set before you the way of life, and the way of death. *Jeremiah* 21:8. (The same choice as above, but in a different context. The prophet is warning that those who stay in Jerusalem to fight off the Chaldeans [Babylonians] will die; those who go out and surrender will live. This defeatist posture made Jeremiah extremely unpopular, but he was right.)

1 Multitudes, multitudes in the valley of decision. *Joel* 3:14. (More at JUDGMENT DAY.)

See also DIRECTION; INDECISION.

CHOSEN PEOPLE

2 I will make of thee a great nation, and I will bless thee, and make thy name great. *Genesis* 12:2. (God to Abraham.)

3 Unto thy seed will I give this land. *Genesis* 12:7.

4 For all the land which thou seest, to thee will I give it, and to thy seed for ever.

And I will make thy seed as the dust of the earth: so that if a man can number the dust of the earth, then shall thy seed also be numbered. *Genesis* 13:15–16. (In *Genesis* 15:5, Abraham's offspring are likened to the number of stars, and in *Genesis* 22:17, to stars and to sand on the shore. This theme is repeated many times.)

5 I will take you to me for a people, and I will be to you a God: and ye shall know that I am the Lord your God. *Exodus* 6:7. (See also *Deuteronomy* 7:6)

6 Ye shall be unto me a kingdom of priests, and a holy nation. *Exodus* 19:6.

7 I will dwell among the children of Israel, and will be their God. *Exodus* 29:45.

8 The Lord said unto Moses, I have seen this people, and, behold, it is a stiffnecked people. *Exodus* 32:9.

9 I will walk among you, and will be your God, and ye shall be my people. *Leviticus* 26:12.

10 The Lord said unto Moses, How long will this people provoke me? *Numbers* 14:11.

11 It shall be said of Jacob and of Israel, what hath God wrought!

Behold the people shall rise up as a great lion. *Numbers* 23:23–24. (Balaam is prophesying the triumph of Israel, to the great displeasure of Balak, king of Moab, who wants Balaam to curse the Israelites. See under GOD'S WORKS for Samuel Morse's use of the passage.)

12 How goodly are thy tents, O Jacob, and thy tabernacles, O Israel! *Numbers* 24:5.

13 There shall come a Star out of Jacob, and a Sceptre shall rise out of Israel. *Numbers* 24:17.

14 Surely this great nation is a wise and understanding people. *Deuteronomy* 4:6. (With these words, Moses states what he believes will be the reaction of other nations to the Israelite system of sacred and secular laws.)

1 Thou shalt be blessed above all people. *Deuteronomy* 7:14.

2 Thou shalt become an astonishment, a proverb, and a byword, among all the nations. *Deuteronomy* 28:37.

3 The Lord shall scatter thee among all people, from the one end of the earth even unto the other. *Deuteronomy* 28:64. (Moses is speaking.)

4 He found him in a desert land, and in the waste howling wilderness; he led him about, he instructed him, he kept him as the apple of his eye. *Deuteronomy* 32:10. (In the first line, *him* refers to the people of Israel collectively; *he* is God. This is part of a song that Moses speaks shortly before his death to remind the Israelites of all that God has done for them. The apple, incidentally, was probably not an apple, but perhaps an apricot or orange. Apples grew poorly in the Middle East. Most scholars believe that the "apples of gold" referred to by Solomon were most likely apricots.)

5 The Lord shall smite Israel, as a reed is shaken in the water, and he shall root up Israel out of this good land [Canaan], which he gave to their fathers, and shall scatter them beyond the river. *I Kings* 14:15. (The prophet Ahijah is speaking.)

6 The people that walked in darkness have seen a great light: they that dwell in the land of the shadow of death, upon them hath the light shined. *Isaiah* 9:2. (The light is the great king of the house of David prophesied by Isaiah. See *Isaiah* 9:6 under MESSIAH. This passage is recalled with a Christian reference in *Matthew* 4:16. See REVELATION.)

7 For though thy people Israel be as the sand of the sea, yet a remnant of them shall return. *Isaiah* 10:22. (Here the prophet promises that despite devastation at the hands of the Assyrians, a remnant of the people of Israel will survive to begin again. The survival is specifically likened to the Israelites' earlier survival under slavery to the Egyptians.)

8 Fear not: for I have redeemed thee, I have called thee by thy name; thou art mine. *Isaiah* 43:1. (Another pledge for God that some, at least, will be saved.)

9 Thy people also shall be all righteous: they shall inherit the land for ever, the branch of my planting, the work of my hands, that I may be glorified. *Isaiah* 60:21.

10 This people has a stubborn and a rebellious heart. *Jeremiah* 5:23, RSV. (This conveys the sense of the passage better than the King James Version, which reads, "This people hath a revolting and rebellious heart." *Revolting,* of course, means "inclined to revolution.")

11 I have loved you with an everlasting love. *Jeremiah* 31:3, RSV. (God, speaking of his faithfulness to his people.)

1 They shall be my people, and I will be their God. *Jeremiah* 32:38. (Also, "I will put my law . . . in their hearts; and will be their God, and they shall be my people. *Jeremiah* 31:33.)

2 Ye are the sons of the living God. *Hosea* 1:10.

See also CANAAN; COVENANT; GOVERNMENT; MESSIAH.

CHRIST

See JESUS

CHRIST, BODY IN (OR OF)

See RELIGION

CHRISTIANITY

See RELIGION

CHRISTMAS

See JESUS: BIRTH AND CHILDHOOD

CHURCH

3 Let us go into the house of the Lord. *Psalms* 122:1.

4 Guard your steps when you go to the house of God; to draw near to listen is better than to offer the sacrifice of fools. *Ecclesiastes* 5:1, RSV.

5 My house shall be called a house of prayer for all peoples. *Isaiah* 56:7, RSV. (Here God specifically welcomes all who keep his commandments.)

6 The Lord is in his holy temple: let all the earth keep silence before him. *Habakkuk* 2:20. (This recalls Emerson: "I like the silent church before the service begins, better than any preaching." *Self-Reliance.*)

7 My house shall be called the house of prayer; but ye have made it a den of thieves. *Matthew* 21:13. (Jesus as he drove the moneychangers out of the temple. See also BUSINESS.)

8 Make not my Father's house an house of merchandise. *John* 2:16. (In *John* there is a detail in this scene, repeated in many paintings: "When he had made a scourge of small cords, he drove them all out of the temple." *John* 2:15.)

9 The temple of God is holy, which temple ye are. *I Corinthians* 3:17.

See also CLERGY; RELIGION; TEMPLE.

CIRCUMCISION

10 Every man child among you shall be circumcised.

And ye shall circumise the flesh of your foreskin; and it shall be a token of the covenant betwixt me and you. *Genesis* 17:10–11. (God to Abraham. *Leviticus* 12:3 specifies circumcision on the eighth day after birth.)

See also COVENANT.

CITIES

1 I have seen violence and strife in the city. *Psalms* 55:9.

2 Pray for the peace of Jerusalem: they shall prosper that love thee. *Psalms* 122:6.

3 How is the faithful city become a harlot! it was full of judgment; righteousness lodged in it; but now murderers. *Isaiah* 1:21. (The city is ancient Jerusalem. The process is familiar today. In the Revised Standard Version, the passage continues, "Your silver has become dross, your wine mixed with water. / Your princes are rebels and companions of thieves. Every one loves a bribe and runs after gifts. They do not defend the fatherless, and the widow's cause does not come to them.")

4 Wild beasts of the desert shall lie there [in Babylon]; and their houses shall be full of doleful creatures; and owls shall dwell there, and satyrs shall dance there

And the wild beasts of the islands shall cry in their desolate houses, and dragons in their pleasant palaces: and her time is near to come, and her days shall not be prolonged. *Isaiah* 13:21–22. (In the Revised Standard Version, the animals are identified differently: "Wild beasts will lie down there, and its houses will be full of howling creatures; there ostriches will dwell, and there satyrs will dance. / Hyenas will cry in its towers, and jackals in the pleasant palaces." There is a similar passage in *Isaiah* 34.)

5 Babylon is fallen, is fallen. *Isaiah* 21:9. (From the mysterious, troubling chapter in *Isaiah* in which the prophet, unnamed, is likened to a watchman in the night. The vision of the destruction of the enemies of Israel is recounted in a mood of fear and sadness. In the New Testament, the theme is repeated at *Revelation* 14:8: "Babylon is fallen, is fallen that great city.")

6 The city of confusion is broken down: every house is shut up, that no man may come in. *Isaiah* 24:10 (One of many biblical passages describing urban desolation in almost modern terms. In the Revised Standard Version the quote runs, "The city of chaos is broken down, every house is shut up so that none can enter." The particular city is not identified, and the *Interpreter's Commentary* suggests that the reference may be to city life in general.)

7 In the city is left desolation. *Isaiah* 24:12.

8 They shall raise up the former desolations, they shall repair the waste cities, the desolations of many generations. *Isaiah* 61:4. (Urban renewal: the remnant of the people who survive the era of destruction will rebuild the cities.)

9 I will rejoice in Jerusalem, and joy in my people: and the voice of weeping shall be no more heard in her, nor the voice of crying. *Isaiah* 65:19. (God is speaking.)

[1] This city [Jerusalem] shall remain for ever. *Jeremiah* 17:25.

[2] How doth the city sit solitary, that was full of people! how is she become as a widow! *Lamentations* 1:1 (Jerusalem after the Babylonian conquest.)

[3] This city is the caldron, and we be the flesh. *Ezekiel* 11:3.

[4] Look not around thee in the streets of the city, neither wander thou in the solitary places thereof. *Ecclesiasticus* 9:7.

[5] A city that is set on an hill cannot be hid. *Matthew* 5:14. (From the Sermon on the Mount. More of the quote is at GREATNESS.)

[6] When he was come near, he beheld the city, and wept over it. *Luke* 19:41. (Jesus entering Jerusalem.)

[7] What city is like unto this great city! *Revelation* 18:18. (The people mourning over Babylon during the destruction of the world.)

See also ZION.

CLERGY

[8] They are given as a gift for the Lord. *Numbers* 18:6. (God speaking of the Levites, the first priests.)

[9] I will raise me up a faithful priest, that shall do according to that which is in mine heart and in my mind: and I will build him a sure house; and he shall walk before mine anointed for ever. *I Samuel* 2:35.

[10] Touch not mine anointed, and do my prophets no harm. *Psalms* 105:15.

[11] The priest and the prophet have erred through strong drink, they are swallowed up of wine, they are out of the way through strong drink; they err in vision, they stumble in judgment. *Isaiah* 28:7.

[12] The spirit of the Lord God is upon me; because the Lord hath anointed me to preach good tidings unto the meek; he hath sent me to bind up the brokenhearted. *Isaiah* 61:1. (The prophet speaks of his mission. It includes freeing captives and prisoners. See under LAW: PUNISHMENTS AND PENALTIES. This passage is quoted by Jesus. See *Luke* 4:18 under JESUS.)

[13] I [God] will give you pastors according to mine heart, which shall feed you with knowledge and understanding. *Jeremiah* 3:15.

[14] Like people, like priest. *Hosea* 4:9.

[15] [Apollos was] an eloquent man, and mighty in the scriptures. *Acts* 18:24.

[16] Revilest thou God's high priest? *Acts* 23:4. (A question put to Paul after he had said to the high priest Ananias, "God shall smite thee, thou whited wall." *Acts* 23:3. Paul apologizes.)

[17] I am made all things to all men, that I might by all means save some. *I Corinthians* 9:22. (Paul describing his role as a preacher and missionary.)

1 Poor, yet making many rich; as having nothing, and yet possessing all things. *II Corinthians* 6:10. (From Paul's description of ministers of God.)

2 If a man desire the office of a bishop, he desireth a good work. *I Timothy* 3:1.

3 [A bishop must be] Not given to wine, no striker, not greedy of filthy lucre. *I Timothy* 3:3. (From a list of qualifications for bishops and deacons.)

4 If a man know not how to rule his own house, how shall he take care of the church of God! *I Timothy* 3:5. (Then as now, some ministers of the faith were distracted by domestic concerns.)

See also APOSTLES AND DISCIPLES; PAUL; PETER; RELIGION.

CLOTHING

5 Put on her garments of gladness. *Judith* 10:3.

6 Beware of the scribes, which love to go in long clothing, and love salutations in the marketplaces. *Mark* 12:38.

See also FASHION.

COMMANDMENTS

See TEN COMMANDMENTS

COMMERCE

See BUSINESS; RICHES

COMMITMENT

7 No one who puts his hand to the plow and looks back is fit for the kingdom of God. *Luke* 9:62, RSV.

8 Be no more children, tossed to and fro, and carried about with every wind of doctrine. *Ephesians* 4:14.

9 This one thing I do, forgetting those things which are behind, and reaching forth into those things which are before,
I press toward the mark. *Philippians* 3:13–14.

See also PERSEVERANCE; RELIABILITY.

COMMUNION

See LAST SUPPER

COMPANIONS

See FRIENDS AND COMPANIONS

COMPETITION

See PHYSICAL FITNESS; WINNING

COMPLAINT

See FRANKNESS; TALK

CONDEMNING OTHERS

See JUDGING OTHERS

CONFLICT

1 Every man's sword was against his fellow. *I Samuel* 14:20. (Also, "Every man's sword shall be against his brother." *Ezekiel* 38:21.)

2 I am for peace: but when I speak, they are for war. *Psalms* 120:7.

3 Strive not with a man without cause, if he have done thee no harm. *Proverbs* 3:30.

4 Go not forth hastily to strive. . . . Debate thy cause with thy neighbor himself. *Proverbs* 25:8–9. (The advice is to settle quarrels privately, and especially without going to court.)

5 They shall fight every one against his brother, and every one against his neighbor; city against city, and kingdom against kingdom. *Isaiah* 19:2.

6 How agree the kettle and the earthen pot together? *Ecclesiasticus* 13:2.

7 Every kingdom divided against itself is brought to desolation; and every city or house divided against itself shall not stand. *Matthew* 12:25. (See also *Mark* 3:25, which reads, "If a house be divided against itself, that house cannot stand." Used by Abraham Lincoln in a speech on June 16, 1858: " 'A house divided against itself cannot stand.' I believe this government cannot endure permanently half slave and half free.")

See also PEACE; UNITY; WAR.

CONFUSION

8 Thou shalt grope at noonday, as the blind gropeth in darkness. *Deuteronomy* 28:29.

CONSCIENCE

9 After the fire a still small voice. *I Kings* 19:12. (The voice is the manifestation of God to Elijah, and sometimes identified as the voice of conscience. For more on this passage, see GOD, ENCOUNTERS WITH.)

See also GUILT.

CONVICTION

10 Let every man be fully persuaded in his own mind. *Romans* 14:5.

COURAGE

1 Be ye of good courage. *Numbers* 13:20.

2 Fear not, neither be discouraged. *Deuteronomy* 1:21.

3 Be strong and of a good courage. *Deuteronomy* 31:23. (Moses to Joshua, passing on the message of God. The phrase is repeated a number of times in this part of the Old Testament.)

4 Be of good courage, and he [God] shall strengthen your heart. *Psalms* 31:24.

5 The Lord is my helper, and I will not fear what man shall do unto me. *Hebrews* 13:6.

See also FEAR.

COVENANT

6 I will establish my covenant between me and thee and thy seed after thee in their generations for an everlasting covenant. *Genesis* 17:7. (God to Abraham.)

7 I have made a covenant with thee and with Israel. *Exodus* 34:27. (God to Moses. While the concept of the Convenant begins in God's relationship with Abraham, the term usually refers to this "Sinai Convenant," given by God to Moses. It includes the Ten Commandments.)

See also ARK OF THE COVENANT; CHOSEN PEOPLE; CIRCUMCISION; TEN COMMANDMENTS.

COVERUP

8 You whitewash with lies. *Job* 13:4, RSV.

9 There is nothing covered, that shall not be revealed; and hid, that shall not be known. *Matthew* 10:26.

See also DECEIT AND LIES.

CRAFTINESS

See PRUDENCE

CREATION

10 In the beginning God created the heaven and the earth.
And the earth was without form, and void; and darkness was upon the face of the deep. And the Spirit of God moved upon the face of the waters.
And God said, Let there be light; and there was light. *Genesis* 1:1–3.

1 And God said, Let there be a firmament in the midst of the waters, and let it divide the waters from the waters.

And God made the firmament, and divided the waters which were under the firmament from the waters which were above the firmament; and it was so. *Genesis* 1:6–7. (The firmament is a vault over the earth, holding back the waters of chaos, the unformed universe.)

2 And God said, let the waters under the heaven be gathered together unto one place, and let the dry land appear: and it was so.

And God called the dry land Earth; and the gathering together of the waters called he Seas: and God saw that it was good. *Genesis* 1:9–10.

3 And God said, Let the waters bring forth abundantly the moving creature that hath life, and fowl that may fly above the earth in the open firmament of heaven.

And God created great whales, and every living creature that moveth. *Genesis* 1:20–21.

4 And God blessed them, saying, Be fruitful and multiply. *Genesis* 1:22. (Also at many other places throughout *Genesis*.)

5 And God said, Let the earth bring forth the living creature after his kind, cattle, and creeping thing, and beast of the earth after his kind: and it was so. *Genesis* 1:24.

6 So God created man in his own image, in the image of God created he him; male and female created he them. *Genesis* 1:27. (More under ADAM AND EVE.)

7 And God saw everything that he had made, and, behold it was very good. *Genesis* 1:31.

8 He stretcheth out the north over the empty place, and hangeth the earth upon nothing. *Job* 26:7.

9 Where wast thou when I laid the foundations of the earth? *Job* 38:4. (God to Job.)

10 Hath the rain a father? or who hath begotten the drops of dew? *Job* 38:28.

11 Thou hast set all the borders of the earth: thou hast made summer and winter. *Psalms* 74:17.

12 He hath made every thing beautiful in his time; also he hath set the world in their heart, so that no man can find out the work that God maketh from the beginning to the end. *Ecclesiastes* 3:11. (The Revised Standard Version reads, "He has made everything beautiful in its time; also he has put eternity into man's mind, yet so that he cannot find out what God has done from the beginning to the end.")

1 Who hath measured the waters in the hollow of his hand, and meted out heaven with the span, and comprehended the dust of the earth in a measure, and weighed the mountains in scales, and the hills in a balance? *Isaiah* 40:12.

2 I form the light and create darkness: I make peace, and create evil: I the Lord do all these things. *Isaiah* 45:7.

3 All things were made by him; and without him was not any thing made that was made. *John* 1:3. (The whole of this hymn opening the gospel of John is given at JESUS.)

4 By him were all things created, that are in heaven, and that are in earth, visible and invisible, whether they be thrones, or dominions, or principalities, or powers: all things were created by him, and for him:

And he is before all things, and by him all things consist. *Colossians* 1:16–17.

5 Thou hast created all things, and for thy pleasure they are and were created. *Revelation* 4:11.

See also GOD'S WORKS; NATURE.

CREATION OF ADAM AND EVE See ADAM AND EVE

CRIME

6 Cain rose up against Abel his brother, and slew him. *Genesis* 4:8. (More at CAIN AND ABEL.)

7 Whoso sheddeth man's blood, by man shall his blood be shed; for in the image of God made he man. *Genesis* 9:6. (See also the LAW categories.)

8 He [Moses] spied an Egyptian smiting a Hebrew, one of his brethren.

And he looked this way and that way, and when he saw that there was no man, he slew the Egyptian, and hid him in the sand. *Exodus* 2:11–12. (See also MOSES AND THE EGYPTIANS.)

9 Thou shalt not kill. *Exodus* 20:13.

10 Thou shalt not steal. *Exodus* 20:15.

11 Then Jael Heber's wife took a nail of the tent, and took a hammer in her hand, and went softly unto him, and smote the nail into his temples, and fastened it into the ground: for he was fast asleep and weary. So he died. *Judges* 4:21. (More at SISERA AND JAEL.)

12 He took a knife, and laid hold on his [dead] concubine, and divided her, together with her bones, into twelve pieces, and sent her into all the coasts of Israel. *Judges* 19:29. (The concubine, consort of a Levite, had died after having been abused by Benjamites. Here her lover makes a dramatic appeal for vengeance, an appeal that leads to war against the Benjamites.)

1 The tabernacles of robbers prosper, and they that provoke God are secure. *Job* 12:6. (Job observes that crime pays.)

2 The murderer rising with the light killeth the poor and needy, and in the night is as a thief. *Job* 24:14.

3 In the dark they dig through houses, which they had marked for themselves in the daytime. *Job* 24:16.

4 From heaven did the Lord behold the earth;
To hear the groaning of the prisoner; to loose those that are appointed to death. *Psalms* 102:19–20.

5 Men do not despise a thief, if he steal to satisfy his soul when he is hungry. *Proverbs* 6:30.

6 Woe is me now! for my soul is wearied because of murderers. *Jeremiah* 4:31. (The murderers here are in the armies of Babylon that Jeremiah predicts will conquer Jerusalem.)

7 The land is full of bloody crimes, and the city is full of violence. *Ezekiel* 7:23.

8 She came to the pillar of the bed which was at Holofernes' head, and took down his falchion [a curved sword] from thence,
And approached to his bed, and took hold of the hair of his head, and said, Strengthen me, O Lord God of Israel, this day.
And she smote twice upon his neck with all her might, and she took away his head from him. *Judith* 13:6–8. (A well-planned assassination by a resourceful heroine. Judith had already established a pattern of leaving Holofernes's camp every night to pray. She and her maid also carried their own kosher food with them. After killing the commander, Judith covered the body with the canopy of the bed and put his head in the bag of meat carried by her maid; then they left the camp as usual. Thus Judith was able to escape and inspire her people to counterattack Holofernes' army.)

9 He was a murderer from the beginning . . . there is no truth in him. *John* 8:44. (Said of the devil. More at EVIL.)

10 A thief in the night. *I Thessalonians* 5:2. (Not usually used in its original context: "The day of the Lord so cometh as a thief in the night.")

See also BRIBERY; CAIN AND ABEL; COVERUP; DARKNESS; EVIL; GOOD SAMARITAN; LAW AND JUSTICE; SECRETS.

CURIOSITY

11 Be not curious in unnecessary matters. *Ecclesiasticus* 3:23.

DANCE

See DAVID

DANGER

1 My soul is among lions. *Psalms* 57:4.

2 We went through fire and through water. *Psalms* 66:12.

3 Watchman, what of the night? *Isaiah* 21:11.

4 A prudent man sees danger and hides himself; but the simple go on, and suffer for it. *Proverbs* 27:12, RSV.

DANIEL

5 They brought Daniel, and cast him into the den of lions. *Daniel* 6:16. (King Darius appointed Daniel his second in command in the civil government. Jealous princes and officials, knowing that Daniel prayed three times a day, tricked the king into decreeing that, for one month, any person who petitioned any king or person other than Darius would be thrown to the lions.)

6 The king arose very early in the morning, and went in haste unto the den of lions. *Daniel* 6:19.

7 O Daniel, servant of the living God, is thy God, whom thou servest continually, able to deliver thee from the lions?

Then said Daniel unto the king, O king, live for ever.

My God hath sent his angel, and hath shut the lions' mouths, that they have not hurt me. *Daniel* 6:20–22.

8 So Daniel was taken up out of the den, and no manner of hurt was found upon him, because he believed in his God. *Daniel* 6:23. (As for Daniel's unlucky enemies, "They brought those men which had accused Daniel, and they cast them into the den of lions, them, their children, and their wives, and the lions had the mastery of them, and brake all their bones in pieces or ever they came at the bottom of the den." *Daniel* 6:24.)

See also DESTRUCTION; MIRACLES IN THE OLD TESTAMENT.

DARKNESS

9 Darkness was upon the face of the deep. *Genesis* 1:2. (For more, see CREATION.)

10 Darkness which may be felt. *Exodus* 10:21. (For more, see MOSES AND THE EGYPTIANS. The ninth plague was three days of darkness.)

1 Moses drew near unto the thick darkness where God was. *Exodus* 20:21. (More at GOD, ENCOUNTERS WITH.)

2 He [God] made darkness pavilions round about him, dark waters, and thick clouds of the skies. *II Samuel* 22:12.

3 The Lord said that he would dwell in the thick darkness. *I Kings* 8:12.

4 He [God] discovereth deep things out of darkness, and bringeth out to light the shadow of death. *Job* 12:22.

5 They are friends with the terrors of deep darkness. *Job* 24:17, RSV. (Darkness is both sacred and frightening, the cloak of God and the habitation of evil.)

6 The dark places of the earth are full of the habitations of cruelty. *Psalms* 74:20.

7 I will give thee the treasures of darkness, and hidden riches of secret places. *Isaiah* 45:3.

DAVID

8 There remaineth yet the youngest, and, behold, he keepeth the sheep. *I Samuel* 16:11. (The high priest Samuel, guided by the Lord, is seeking a successor to King Saul among the sons of Jesse the Bethlehemite. He has met seven of the sons, but has asked if there is not another. This is Jesse's answer.)

9 He [David] was ruddy, and had beautiful eyes, and was handsome. And the Lord said, Arise, anoint him; for this is he. *I Samuel* 16:12, RSV. (The name *David* is probably, more precisely, a title rather than a name, deriving from *Davidum,* meaning "commander," or "general.")

10 I have seen a son of Jesse the Bethlehemite, that is cunning in playing [music], and a mighty valiant man, and a man of war, and prudent in matters, and a comely person, and the Lord is with him. *I Samuel* 16:18. (A servant of King Saul describing David—with considerable prescience, for David is still a young boy at this time.)

11 David came to Saul, and stood before him: and he loved him greatly; and he became his armor-bearer. *I Samuel* 16:21.

12 Whenever the evil spirit from God was upon Saul, David took the lyre and played it with his hand; so Saul was refreshed, and was well, and the evil spirit departed from him. *I Samuel* 16:23, RSV. (Saul suffered from depressions that only David's playing could soothe. David is the most famous musician of ancient times, "the sweet psalmist of Israel." *II Samuel* 23:1.)

1 I know thy pride, and the naughtiness of thine heart. *I Samuel* 17:28. (David's brother Eliab is berating him for leaving his sheep and coming down to see fighting between the Philistines and the Israelites. For more on the Philistines, see under WAR.)

2 Saul said to David, Thou art not able to go against this Philistine [Goliath] to fight with him: for thou art but a youth. *I Samuel* 17:33.

3 David put his hand in his bag, and took thence a stone, and slang it, and smote the Philistine in his forehead, that the stone sunk into his forehead; and he fell upon his face to the earth. *I Samuel* 17:49. (In ancient times, slings were used by shepherds to chase away predators, and also in warfare. Many armies had regular units of slingmen. The most famous were the left-handed slingmen of the tribe of Benjamin: "There were seven hundred chosen men lefthanded; every one could sling stones at a hairbreadth and not miss. *Judges* 20:16.)

4 David ran and stood over the Philistine, and took his [Goliath's] sword and drew it out of its sheath, and killed him, and cut off his head with it. When the Philistines saw that their champion was dead, they fled. *I Samuel* 17:51, RSV.

5 The women answered one another as they played, and said, Saul hath slain his thousands, and David his ten thousands. *I Samuel* 18:7. (These women came out of the cities and sang and danced to celebrate the Israelite victory. See MUSIC. The "answering" was a chanting back and forth. King Saul naturally was alarmed by this acclaim for his young armor bearer, and wondered, "What can he have more but the kingdom?" *I Samuel* 18:8. See also below.)

6 Saul eyed David from that day and forward. *I Samuel* 18:9.

7 Saul was afraid of David, because the Lord was with him, and was departed from Saul. *I Samuel* 18:12.

8 Thy glory, O Israel, is slain upon thy high places! How are the mighty fallen!
Tell it not in Gath, publish it not in the streets of Ashkelon; lest the daughters of the Philistines rejoice. *II Samuel* 1:19–20, RSV. (The opening of David's lament at the death of Saul and Jonathan. See also SAUL AND JONATHAN.)

9 David danced before the Lord with all his might. *II Samuel* 6:14. (David and the men of Israel honored the Lord, present in the Ark of the Covenant, with music and dancing. See also MUSIC. One of David's wives, Saul's daughter Michal, who had earlier saved her husband from one of Saul's attempts on his life, did not approve of this gaiety. When she saw "King David leaping and dancing before the Lord," she "despised him in her heart." *II Samuel* 6:16. She spoke up, and as a result David evidently had nothing more to do with her, for in his very fertile household, she remained childless.)

1 It came to pass in an eveningtide, that David arose from off his bed, and walked upon the roof of the king's house: and from the roof he saw a woman washing herself; and the woman was very beautiful to look upon. *II Samuel* 11:2. (The woman is Bathsheba, wife of Uriah the Hittite, whom David arranges to have killed. With her, David fathers Solomon.)

2 O my son Absalom, my son, my son Absalom! would God I had died for thee, O Absalom, my son, my son! *II Samuel* 18:33. (David mourning the death of his talented but rebellious son, who had led a revolt against him and taken over his throne. The refrain is repeated in the next chapter, "O my son Absalom, O Absalom, my son, my son." *II Samuel* 19:4. William Faulkner used the title *Absalom, Absalom* for a novel about a troubled family at the time of the Civil War.)

3 King David was old and stricken in years; and they covered him with warm clothes, but he gat no heat. *I Kings* 1:1. (A young virgin was chosen to lie by the king and warm him; their affection was chaste and she became his nurse.)

4 He [David] died in a good old age, full of days, riches, and honor. *I Chronicles* 29:28. (For his last words to Solomon, see CHILDREN.)

See also DAVID AND JONATHAN; MUSIC; SAUL AND JONATHAN; WAR.

DAVID AND JONATHAN

5 The soul of Jonathan was knit with the soul of David, and Jonathan loved him as his own soul. *I Samuel* 18:1.

6 Jonathan stripped himself of the robe that was upon him, and gave it to David, and his garments, even to his sword, and to his bow, and to his girdle. *I Samuel* 18:4. (The value of this generosity may be judged by the paucity of weapons among the Israelites. The Philistines allowed no smiths among the Israelites, "lest the Hebrews make them swords or spears." *I Samuel* 13:19. Most of the Jews were fighting with farm tools.)

7 My brother Jonathan: very pleasant hast thou been unto me: thy love to me was wonderful, passing the love of women. *II Samuel* 1:26. (David's lamentation upon hearing of the death of Jonathan. See also DEATH; SAUL AND JONATHAN; and WAR.)

DEATH

8 Let me die the death of the righteous. *Numbers* 23:10. (Balaam is speaking to the Moab king, Balak.)

9 This day I am going the way of all the earth. *Joshua* 23:14. (Joshua, near death, speaking to the Israelites. See also *I Kings* 2:2.)

1 There is but a step between me and death. *I Samuel* 20:3. (David is speaking to Jonathan; he has just escaped death at the hands of men sent by King Saul, Jonathan's father.)

2 The beauty of Israel is slain upon thy high places: how are the mighty fallen! *II Samuel* 1:19. (David's lamentation over the death of Saul and Jonathan in battle. See also SAUL AND JONATHAN.)

3 We must needs die, and are as water spilt upon the ground, which cannot be gathered up again. *II Samuel* 14:14. (In the most ancient Old Testament books, death is seen as the end of the person. Later, the concept of an enduring soul emerges. See below.)

4 Wherefore should I fast? Can I bring him back again? I shall go to him, but he shall not return to me. *II Samuel* 12:23. (King David speaking of the pointlessness of mourning after the death of his beloved first son by Bathsheba.)

5 Set thine house in order; for thou shalt die. *II Kings* 20:1. (See also *Isaiah* 38:1.)

6 There the wicked cease from troubling; and there the weary be at rest. *Job* 3:17.

7 You shall come to your grave in ripe old age, as a shock of grain comes up to the threshing floor in its season. *Job* 5:26, RSV.

8 As the cloud fades and vanishes, so he who goes down to Sheol [the underworld] does not come up. *Job* 7:9, RSV.

9 Man dieth, and wasteth away: yea, man giveth up the ghost, and where is he? *Job* 14:10.

10 If a man die, shall he live again? *Job* 14:14.

11 I have said to corruption, Thou art my father: to the worm, Thou art my mother, and my sister. *Job* 17:14.

12 Yea, though I walk through the valley of the shadow of death, I will fear no evil. *Psalms* 23:4. (The entire Psalm is given at GOD'S PROVIDENCE.)

13 Lord, let me know my end, and what is the measure of my days. *Psalms* 39:4, RSV.

14 But ye shall die like men, and fall like one of the princes. *Psalms* 82:7.

15 How dieth the wise man? as the fool. *Ecclesiastes* 2:16.

16 All go unto one place; all are of the dust, and all turn to dust again. *Ecclesiastes* 3:20.

17 There is no man that hath power over the spirit to retain the spirit; neither hath he power in the day of death; and there is no discharge in that war. *Ecclesiastes* 8:8.

1 Man does not know his time. *Ecclesiastes* 9:12, RSV.

2 Man goeth to his long home, and the mourners go about the streets:
[Remember God in your youth before] the silver cord be loosed, or the golden bowl be broken, or the pitcher be broken at the fountain, or the wheel be broken at the cistern.
Then shall the dust return to the earth as it was: and the spirit shall return unto God who gave it. *Ecclesiastes* 12:5–7. (The idea of the spirit that endures after the death of the body, arose relatively late in Old Testament thought. It was more common among the Greeks.)

3 He [the Lord of Hosts] will swallow up death in victory; and the Lord God will wipe away tears from off all faces. *Isaiah* 25:8.

4 She hath given up the ghost; her sun is gone down while it was yet day. *Jeremiah* 15:9.

5 Thou shalt die in peace. *Jeremiah* 34:5.

6 I will ransom them from the power of the grave; I will redeem them from death: Oh death, I will be thy plagues; O grave, I will be thy destruction. *Hosea* 13:14.

7 God made not death: neither hath he pleasure in the destruction of the living. *Wisdom of Solomon* 1:13. (In this book, probably written in the late first century B.C., the concept of the immortality of the soul is first clearly introduced.)

8 Through envy of the devil came death into the world. *Wisdom of Solomon* 2:24. (Again, as in the quote above, the author is clear that it is not God, but evil and sin, that brought death into the world.)

9 Death is better than bitter life or continual sickness. *Ecclesiasticus* 30:17. (Here, and in the quote below, death is seen not so much as an evil but as a natural and necessary conclusion to life.)

10 When the dead is at rest, let his remembrance rest; and be comforted for him, when his spirit is departed from him. *Ecclesiasticus* 38:23.

11 Some there be, which have no memorial; who are perished, as though they had never been; and are become as though they had never been born; and their children after them. *Ecclesiasticus* 44:9. (This grim verse is from the passage that begins, "Let us now praise famous men," *Ecclesiasticus* 44:1.)

12 Follow me; and let the dead bury their dead. *Matthew* 8:22. (Jesus to a disciple whose father had died. The demands of faith may override even profound obligations.)

13 My time is at hand. *Matthew* 26:18.

14 Lord, now lettest thou thy servant depart in peace. *Luke* 2:29. (Simeon in the temple. More at SALVATION.)

1 Death hath no more dominion over him. *Romans* 6:9 (Paul speaking of Christ.)

2 The last enemy that shall be destroyed is death. *I Corinthians* 15:26.

3 Death is swallowed up in victory.
O death, where is thy sting? O grave where is thy victory? *I Corinthians* 15:54–55.

4 Behold a pale horse: and his name that sat on him was Death, and Hell followed with him. *Revelation* 6:8.

5 Blessed are the dead which die in the Lord . . . that they may rest from their labors. *Revelation* 14:13.

See also DESTRUCTION; MARTYRDOM; RESURRECTION OF THE DEAD.

DEBORAH

See MUSIC; WAR

DECEIT AND LIES

6 No man who practices deceit shall dwell in my house; no man who utters lies shall continue in my presence. *Psalms* 101:7, RSV.

7 I hate and abhor lying. *Psalms* 119:163.

8 A false balance is abomination to the Lord: but a just weight is his delight. *Proverbs* 11:1. (See also *Proverbs* 20:10 and 20:23.)

9 Lying lips are abomination to the Lord. *Proverbs* 12:22.

10 Bread of deceit is sweet to a man; but afterwards his mouth shall be filled with gravel. *Proverbs* 20:17.

11 The heart is deceitful above all things. *Jeremiah* 17:9. (More at HUMAN BEINGS.)

12 With lies ye have made the heart of the righteous sad. *Ezekiel* 13:22.

13 A thief is better than a man that is accustomed to lie. *Ecclesiasticus* 20:25.

See also COVERUP; EVIL.

DECISION

See CHOICE; INDECISION

DESOLATION

14 We grope for the wall like the blind, and we grope as if we had no eyes: we stumble at noon day as in the night; we are in desolate places as dead men. *Isaiah* 59:10.

See also CITIES; DESPAIR; DESTRUCTION; TROUBLE.

DESPAIR

1 Let the day perish wherein I was born, and the night in which it was said, There is a man child conceived. *Job* 3:3. (Spoken by Job in despair, but yet not the curse that his wife had urged on him: "Doest thou still retain thine integrity? curse God, and die." *Job* 2:9. A similar despair is voiced in *Jeremiah* 20:14–15. "Cursed be the day wherein I was born . . . Cursed be the man who brought tidings to my father, saying, A man child is born unto thee.")

2 What is my strength, that I should hope? and what is mine end, that I should prolong my life? *Job* 6:11.

3 My God, my God, why hast thou forsaken me? *Psalms* 22:1. (The psalm Christ spoke on the cross.)

4 My days are consumed like smoke. *Psalms* 102:3.

See also DESOLATION; EMOTIONS; GOD, DOUBTING; UNHAPPINESS.

DESTRUCTION

5 Wilt thou also destroy the righteous with the wicked? *Genesis* 18:23 (Abraham questioning God, trying to persuade him to spare Sodom and Gomorrah.)

6 The sword without, and terror within, shall destroy both the young man and the virgin, the suckling also with the man of gray hairs. *Deuteronomy* 32:25. (See also ANGER, the first quote.)

7 The day of their calamity is at hand. *Deuteronomy* 32:35.

8 Thy glory, O Israel, is slain upon thy high places! How are the mighty fallen! *II Samuel* 1:19 RSV. (The beginning of David's lamentation upon hearing of the death of King Saul and Jonathan in battle on Mount Gilboa.)

9 He [God] destroys both the blameless and the wicked. *Job* 9:22, RSV.

10 Through the wrath of the Lord of hosts is the land darkened, and the people shall be as the fuel of the fire: no man shall spare his brother. *Isaiah* 9:19.

11 All the host of heaven shall be dissolved, and the heavens shall be rolled together as a scroll: and all their host shall fall down, as the leaf falleth off from the vine. *Isaiah* 34:4. (This horrific picture appears to represent the end of the world, although the writer speaks of the survival of some and eventual salvation.)

12 I will send the sword, the famine, and the pestilence, among them, till they be consumed. *Jeremiah* 24:10.

1 Destruction cometh. *Ezekiel* 7:25.

2 This is the writing that was written, MENE, MENE, TEKEL, UPHARSIN. *Daniel* 5:25. (The writing on the wall. See also MIRACLES IN THE OLD TESTAMENT. King Belshazzar's astrologers and soothsayers could not read or interpret it, but Daniel understood it. *MENE:* "God hath numbered [the days of] thy kingdom, and finished it." *TEKEL:* "Thou art weighed in the balances and art found wanting." *PERES* (singular of *parsin*): "Thy kingdom is divided, and given to the Medes and Persians." The terms are believed to be Babylonian terms for certain monetary weights. *Peres* is Aramaic for "division.")

3 There shall not be left here one stone upon another, that shall not be thrown down. *Matthew* 24:2. (Jesus referring to the buildings of the temple. He goes on to speak of the last days of the world. See WORLD, END OF.)

4 Remember Lot's wife. *Luke* 17:32. (Part of a warning not to look back during the destruction that will accompany the return of the Son of man.)

See also ANGER; CITIES; DESOLATION; JUDGMENT DAY; WAR; WORLD, END OF.

DETAILS

See SMALL THINGS

DETERMINATION

See PERSEVERANCE

DEVIL

5 Now the serpent was more subtil than any beast of the field. *Genesis* 3:1.

6 God said unto the serpent, Because thou hast done this, thou art cursed above all cattle, and above every beast of the field; upon thy belly shalt thou go, and dust shalt thou eat all the days of thy life.

And I will put enmity between thee and the woman and between thy seed and her seed; it shall bruise thy head, and thou shalt bruise his heel. *Genesis* 3:14–15.

7 The Lord said unto Satan, Whence comest thou? Then Satan answered . . . From going to and fro in the earth, and from walking up and down in it. *Job* 1:7.

8 Get thee hence, Satan. *Matthew* 4:10. (Jesus to the devil. See also TEMPTATION.)

9 Fear not them which kill the body, but are not able to kill the soul: but rather fear him which is able to destroy both soul and body in hell. *Matthew* 10:28.

1 The devil . . . showed unto him all the kingdoms of the world in a moment of time.
And the devil said unto him, All this power will I give thee . . .
If thou therefore wilt worship me, all shall be thine. *Luke* 4:5–7.

2 I saw Satan fall like lightning from heaven. *Luke* 10:18, RSV. (This has become popularly associated with the fall of Lucifer described in *Isaiah*. That passage, however, does not actually refer to the devil. See LUCIFER.)

3 He was a murderer from the beginning . . . there is no truth in him. *John* 8:44. (More at EVIL.)

4 Put on the whole armor of God, that ye may be able to stand against the wiles of the devil. *Ephesians* 6:11. (More at EVIL.)

5 Resist the devil, and he will flee from you. *James* 4:7.

6 Be sober, be vigilant; because your adversary the devil, as a roaring lion, walketh about, seeking whom he may devour. *I Peter* 5:8.

7 The great dragon was cast out, that old serpent, called the Devil, and Satan, which deceiveth the whole world. *Revelation* 12:9. (Michael and his angels did this. See ANGELS.)

See also DEVILS; LUCIFER.

DEVILS

8 The devils besought him [Jesus], saying, If thou cast us out, suffer us to go away into the herd of swine. *Matthew* 8:31. (A case of demonic possession, is described at greater length and somewhat differently at *Mark* 5:1–20. It did the devils little good to enter the swine, for the whole herd "ran violently down a steep place into the sea, and perished in the waters." *Matthew* 8:32. Later, following another exorcism by Jesus, the Pharisees commented, "He casteth out devils through the prince of devils," *Matthew* 9:34. A similar accusation appears at *Matthew* 12:24. See also EVIL.)

9 My name is Legion: for we are many. *Mark* 5:9. (The unclean spirit possessing a man in the land of the Gadarenes; the same story as that in *Matthew* above.)

See also EVIL.

DIASPORA

See CHOSEN PEOPLE; ZION

DIRECTION

10 Quo Vadis? *John* 16:5, Vulgate. (In the King James Version, "Whither goest thou?")

DISCIPLES OF JESUS See APOSTLES AND DISCIPLES

DISEASE See SICKNESS

DISHONESTY See BUSINESS; COVERUP; DECEIT AND LIES; HONESTY; HYPOCRISY

DISSIPATION

1 He who follows worthless pursuits has no sense. *Proverbs* 12:11, RSV.

2 The drunkard and the glutton shall come to poverty: and drowsiness shall clothe a man with rags. *Proverbs* 23:21.

3 Be not over much wicked, neither be thou foolish: why shouldest thou die before thy time? *Ecclesiastes* 7:17.

4 Whoredom and wine and new wine take away the heart. *Hosea* 4:11.

5 The bewitching of naughtiness doth obscure things that are honest; and the wandering of concupiscence doth undermine the simple mind. *Wisdom of Solomon* 4:12.

See also HEDONISM; SEX; WINE AND DRINKING.

DOCTORS AND MEDICINE

6 Worthless physicians are you all. *Job* 13:4, RSV.

7 Is there no balm in Gilead; is there no physician there? *Jeremiah* 8:22. (The Gilead region, east of Jordan, produced an ointment, a resinous gum, used to treat wounds. The reference here is metaphorical—Israel is deeply wounded.)

8 Honor a physician with the honor due unto him for the uses which ye may have of him: for the Lord hath created him. *Ecclesiasticus* 38:1.

9 The Lord hath created medicines out of the earth; and he that is wise will not abhor them. *Ecclesiasticus* 38:4.

10 He that sinneth before his Maker, let him fall into the hand of the physician. *Ecclesiasticus* 38:15.

11 They that be whole need not a physician, but they that are sick. *Matthew* 9:12.

12 Physician, heal thyself. *Luke* 4:23. (Identified as a proverb.)

Luke, the beloved physician, *Colossians* 4:14. (This is the only place in which this apostle is identified as a physician.)

See also HEALTH; MIDWIVES; SICKNESS.

DOUBT See GOD, DOUBTING

DOUBTING THOMAS See JESUS, RESURRECTION OF

DREAMS AND DREAMERS

1 Behold, this dreamer cometh. *Genesis* 37:19. (See also under JOSEPH.)

2 Do not interpretations belong to God? *Genesis* 40:8. (Joseph, on interpreting dreams. In the ancient Middle East, the power to interpret dreams was considered God-given. Another famous reader of dreams was Daniel. See under FAILINGS for interpretation of the image with feet of iron and clay.)

3 A dream cometh through the multitude of business. *Ecclesiastes* 5:3.

4 The prophet that hath a dream, let him tell a dream. *Jeremiah* 23:28.

5 I saw a dream which made me afraid, and the thoughts upon my bed and the visions of my head troubled me. *Daniel* 4:5. (Nebuchadnezzar speaking of his vision of the great figure with feet of iron and clay. See under FAILINGS.)

6 Your old men shall dream dreams, your young men shall see visions. *Joel* 2:28.

See also HOPE.

DRINKING See FOOD AND DRINK; HEDONISM; WINE AND DRINKING

EARS

See BODY; HEARING

EARTH

See CREATION; ENVIRONMENT; FARMING; WORLD

EDEN

1 And the Lord God planted a garden eastward in Eden; and there he put the man whom he had formed. *Genesis* 2:8. (From the rivers mentioned in *Genesis*, we know that this was somewhere in Mesopotamia, between the Tigris and the Euphrates. The name *Eden* may derive from the Babylonian *edinu*, a "plain," "steppe," or "oasis in the desert."

2 And out of the ground made the Lord God to grow every tree that is pleasant to the sight, and good for food; the tree of life also in the midst of the garden, and the tree of knowledge of good and evil. *Genesis* 2:9.

See also ADAM AND EVE.

EDUCATION

See CHILDREN; LEARNING

EGYPT

See EXODUS; MOSES AND THE EGYPTIANS

ELIJAH

3 The ravens brought him [Elijah] bread and flesh in the morning, and bread and flesh in the evening; and he drank of the brook. *I Kings* 17:6.

4 Behold, there appeared a chariot of fire, and horses of fire . . . and Elijah went up by a whirlwind into heaven. *II Kings* 2:11. (Chariots of fire appear again in connection with Elisha, Elijah's successor as prophet. Elisha is surrounded by the horses and chariots of the king of Syria, but he has on his side the horses and chariots of God: "Behold, the mountain was full of horses and chariots of fire round about Elisha." *II Kings* 6:17.)

5 He [Elisha] took up also the mantle of Elijah. *II Kings* 2:13.

6 I will send you Elijah the prophet before the coming of the great and dreadful day of the Lord. *Malachi* 4:5.

7 His word burned like a lamp. *Ecclesiasticus* 48:1.

EMOTIONS

8 Why does your heart carry you away? *Job* 15:12, RSV.

1 My heart was hot within me, while I was musing the fire burned. *Psalms* 39:3.

2 Keep your heart with all vigilance; for from it flow the springs of life. *Proverbs* 4:23, RSV.

3 Anxiety in a man's heart weighs him down, but a good word makes him glad. *Proverbs* 12:25, RSV.

4 A merry heart maketh a cheerful countenance: but by the sorrow of the heart the spirit is broken. *Proverbs* 15:13.

5 He that is slow to anger is better than the mighty; and he that ruleth his spirit than he that taketh a city. *Proverbs* 16:32.

6 As he thinketh in his heart, so is he. *Proverbs* 23:7.

7 He that trusteth in his own heart is a fool. *Proverbs* 28:26.

8 The heart of a man changeth his countenance, whether it be for good or evil. *Ecclesiasticus* 13:25.

9 Envy and wrath shorten the life, and carefulness [worry] bringeth age before the time. *Ecclesiasticus* 30:24.

10 God hath not given us the spirit of fear; but of power, and of love, and of a sound mind. *II Timothy* 1:7.

See also ANGER; DESPAIR; ENVY; FEAR; HAPPINESS; HATE; HOPE; LOVE; MADNESS; categories at SELF; UNHAPPINESS; VIOLENCE.

ENDING

See BEGINNING AND ENDING

ENEMIES

11 Hast thou found me, O mine enemy? *I Kings 21:20.* (Ahab to Elijah.)

12 Many are they that rise up against me. *Psalms* 3:1.

13 Let them [enemies] be as chaff before the wind: and let the angel of the Lord chase them.

Let their way be dark and slippery: and let the angel of the Lord persecute them. *Psalms* 35:5–6.

14 His enemies shall lick the dust. *Psalms* 72:9.

15 Do not rejoice when your enemy falls, and let not your heart be glad when he stumbles;

Lest the Lord see it and be displeased, and turn away his anger from him. *Proverbs* 24:17–18, RSV.

16 If thine enemy be hungry, give him bread to eat; and if he be thirsty, give him water to drink.

For thou shalt heap coals of fire upon his head. *Proverbs* 25:21. (Repeated in essence at *Romans* 12:20.)

1 A man's enemies are the men of his own house. *Micah* 7:6.

2 A friend cannot be known in prosperity: and an enemy cannot be hid in adversity. *Ecclesiasticus* 12:8.

3 If adversity come upon thee, thou shalt find him [an enemy] there first; and though he pretend to help thee, yet shall be undermine thee.
He will shake his head, and clap his hands, and whisper much, and change his countenance. *Ecclesiasticus* 12:17–18.

4 Remember thy end, and let enmity cease. *Ecclesiasticus* 28:6.

5 I say unto you, Love your enemies, bless them that curse you, do good to them that hate you, and pray for them which despitefully use you, and persecute you. *Matthew* 5:44. (From the Sermon on the Mount. Jesus goes on to say that in loving all people, even one's enemies, one is like God. This is the heart of the Christian message.)

See also GOD, ENEMIES AND WAR; HATE.

ENNUI

6 The thing that hath been, is that which shall be; and that which is done is that which shall be done: and there is no new thing under the sun. *Ecclesiastes* 1:9.

ENVIRONMENT

7 The land is defiled. *Leviticus* 18:25. (The reference is to moral defilement, but today it is natural to read such passages more literally. See also the quote from *Numbers* below.)

8 The land is mine. *Leviticus* 25:23. (God is speaking. For more, see under STRANGERS AND TRAVELERS.)

9 Ye shall not pollute the land wherein ye are. *Numbers* 35:33.

10 I have healed these waters; there shall not be from thence any more death or barren land. *II Kings* 2:21. (The speaker is Elisha, successor to Elijah. Using salt, he has purified the spring at Jericho in the Jordan valley.)

11 The land mourns and languishes. *Isaiah* 33:9, RSV.

12 From generation to generation it [the land] shall lie waste; none shall pass through it for ever and ever.*Isaiah* 34:10. (Here the land is laid waste by burning pitch, part of the worldwide destruction prophesied by Isaiah.)

13 Hurt not the earth; neither the sea, nor the trees. *Revelation* 7:3.

See also FARMING; NATURE; POPULATION.

ENVY

1 Wrath killeth the foolish man, and envy slayeth the silly one. *Job* 5:2. (Also, "Envy and wrath shorten the life." *Ecclesiasticus* 30:24.)

2 Who is able to stand before envy? *Proverbs* 27:4. (The meaning is that envy is an emotion that overwhelms a person. In the Revised Standard Version, the translation is "jealousy" rather than "envy.")

See also EMOTIONS; JEALOUSY.

EQUALITY

3 They shall see eye to eye, when the Lord shall bring again Zion. *Isaiah* 52:8.

4 Have we not all one father? hath not one God created us? *Malachi* 2:10.

5 When I was born, I drew in the common air, and fell upon the earth, which is of like nature, and the first voice which I uttered was crying, as all others do.

. . . There is no king that had any other beginning. *Wisdom of Solomon* 7:3–5. (King Solomon makes the point that it is not noble birth, but wisdom, which leads to greatness.)

6 All men have one entrance into life, and the like going out. *Wisdom of Solomon* 7:6.

7 [God] hath made of one blood all nations of men for to dwell on all the face of the earth. *Acts* 17:26.

ESAU

See JACOB AND ESAU

ESCAPE

8 I am escaped with the skin of my teeth. *Job* 19:20.

9 He shall fly away as a dream, and shall not be found. *Job* 20:8.

10 Flee as a bird to your mountain. *Psalms* 11:1.

11 Oh that I had wings like a dove! for then would I fly away, and be at rest. *Psalms* 55:6.

12 I would hasten my escape from the windy storm and tempest. *Psalms* 55:8.

13 Oh that I had in the wilderness a lodging place of wayfaring men; that I might leave my people, and go from them! *Jeremiah* 9:2.

See also FLIGHT.

ETERNAL LIFE

See HEAVEN; SALVATION

ETERNITY

See HEAVEN; TIME AND ETERNITY

EVE

See ADAM AND EVE

EVENING

1 The day goeth away, for the shadows of the evening are stretched out. *Jeremiah* 6:4.

EVIDENCE

See LAW; WITNESSES AND EVIDENCE

EVIL

2 And God saw that the wickedness of man was great in the earth, and that every imagination of the thoughts of his heart was only evil continually. *Genesis* 6:5.

3 The earth also was corrupt before God, and the earth was filled with violence.

And God looked upon the earth, and, behold, it was corrupt; for all flesh had corrupted his way upon the earth. *Genesis* 6:11–12.

4 Thou shalt not follow a multitude to do evil. *Exodus* 23:2.

5 What wickedness is this that is done among you? *Judges* 20:12.

6 The wicked shall be cut off in darkness. *I Samuel* 2:9, RSV.

7 Wickedness proceedeth from the wicked. *I Samuel* 24:13. (Identified as a "proverb of the ancients.")

8 The earth is given into the hand of the wicked. *Job* 9:24, RSV.

9 Who can bring a clean thing out of an unclean? *Job* 14:4.

10 The triumphing of the wicked is short, and the joy of the hypocrite but for a moment. *Job* 20:5. (Job does not accept this optimistic claim, put forth by one of his so-called friends. In response, he poses the following question.)

11 Why do the wicked live, reach old age, and grow mighty in power? *Job* 21:7, RSV.

12 God is angry with the wicked every day. *Psalms* 7:11.

1 His mouth is filled with cursing and deceit and oppression; under his tongue are mischief and iniquity.
He sits in ambush in the villages; in hiding places he murders the innocent.
His eyes stealthily watch for the hapless. *Psalms* 10:7–8, RSV. (This Psalm paints a vivid portrait of the"wicked" man, the "man greedy for gain." *Psalms* 10:3.

2 I have seen the wicked in great power, and spreading himself like a green bay tree. *Psalms* 37:35.

3 The wicked are estranged from the womb: they go astray as soon as they be born, speaking lies. *Psalms* 58:3.

4 They [prosperous and wicked people] have no pangs; their bodies are sound and sleek.
They are not in trouble as other men are; they are not stricken like other men. *Psalms* 73:4–5, RSV. (Verses 3–12 of this Psalm focus on ruthless, amoral, arrogant—and successful—people. Frustration at the complacency and power of the wicked is a common theme in the Old Testament.)

5 They eat the bread of wickedness, and drink the wine of violence. *Proverbs* 4:17.

6 A worthless person, a wicked man, goes about with crooked speech,
Winks with his eyes, scrapes with his feet, points with his finger,
With perverted heart devises evil, continually sowing discord;
Therefore calamity will come upon him suddenly; in a moment he will be broken beyond healing. *Proverbs* 6:12–15, RSV.

7 These six things doth the Lord hate: yea, seven are an abomination unto him:
A proud look, a lying tongue, and hands that shed innocent blood,
A heart that deviseth wicked imaginations, feet that be swift in running to mischief,
A false witness that speaketh lies, and he that soweth discord among brethren. *Proverbs* 6:16–19.

8 A cruel man hurts himself. *Proverbs* 11:17, RSV. (More at GENTLENESS AND KINDNESS.)

9 The wicked shall not be unpunished. *Proverbs* 11:21.

10 The tender mercies of the wicked are cruel. *Proverbs* 12:10. (More at ANIMALS.)

11 Woe unto them that call evil good, and good evil. *Isaiah* 5:20.

12 We have made a convenant with death, and with hell are we in agreement. *Isaiah* 28:15.

1 There is no peace, saith the Lord, unto the wicked. *Isaiah* 48:22. (Repeated in nearly the same words at *Isaiah* 57:21.)

2 Ye have plowed wickedness, ye have reaped iniquity. *Hosea* 10:13.

3 Hate the evil, and love the good. *Amos* 5:15.

4 He that toucheth pitch shall be defiled therewith. *Ecclesiasticus* 13:1.

5 How great is that darkness! *Matthew* 6:23. (From the Sermon on the Mount. The reference is to inner evil.)

6 When the unclean spirit is gone out of a man, he walketh through dry places, seeking rest, and findeth none.

. . . when he is come [to his house] he findeth it empty, swept, and garnished.

Then goeth he, and taketh with himself seven other spirits more wicked than himself, and they enter in and dwell there: and the last state of that man is worse than the first. *Matthew* 12:43–45. (Often quoted to illustrate the psychoanalytic concept of repression: The person who heroically overcomes one evil habit or inclination may find that the repressed behavior emerges in a far worse form. Whether or not one agrees with the theory, this pattern of behavior is curiously common.)

7 My name is Legion: for we are many. *Mark* 5:9. (For more, see under DEVILS.)

8 If they do these things in a green tree, what shall be done in the dry? *Luke* 23:31.

9 Men loved darkness rather than light, because their deeds were evil. *John* 3:19.

10 Ye are of your father the devil, and the lusts of your father ye will do. He was a murderer from the beginning. *John* 8:44. (More at CRIME.)

11 Certain lewd fellows of the baser sort [instigators] . . . set all the city on an uproar. *Acts* 17:5.

12 Be not overcome of evil, but overcome evil with good. *Romans* 12:21.

13 Put on the whole armor of God, that ye may be able to stand against the wiles of the devil.

For we wrestle not against flesh and blood, but against principalities, against powers, against the rulers of the darkness of this world, against spiritual wickedness in high places.

Wherefore take unto you the whole armor of God, that ye may be able to withstand in the evil day, and having done all, to stand. *Ephesians* 6:11–13.

See also CRIME; DECEIT AND LIES; DISSIPATION; GENERATIONS (for "generation of vipers"); GREED; HYPOCRISY; MADNESS; OPPRESSION; PRIDE; SIN AND SINNERS; VIOLENCE; WAR.

EXCELLENCE

1 [Thou] approvest the things that are more excellent. *Romans* 2:18.

2 I show unto you a more excellent way. *I Corinthians* 12:31.

EXODUS

3 The Lord brought us forth out of Egypt. *Exodus* 13:16.

4 The Lord went before them by day in a pillar of a cloud, to lead them the way; and by night in a pillar of fire, to give them light; to go by day and night. *Exodus* 13:21. (At *Psalms* 78:14, "In the daytime also he led them with a cloud, and all the night with a light of fire.")

5 Moses stretched out his hand over the sea; and the Lord caused the sea to go back by a strong east wind all that night, and made the sea dry land, and the waters were divided.

And the children of Israel went into the midst of the sea upon the dry ground: and the waters were a wall unto them on their right hand, and on their left. *Exodus* 14:21–22. (There are several theories regarding the location of this passage across the "*Sea of Reeds,*" to use the correct translation from the Hebrew. One possible passage is in the north, at the Bardawil Lake, which is very shallow in places, and separated from the Mediterranean only by a narrow strip of land that is frequently flooded over; the lake is also swept by strong winds. The Egyptian chariots could well have become mired in mud, and with a change of winds, the water would have risen over them. In the south, a passage might have been effected via the two Bitter Lakes, which lie between Ismalia and Suez. In the past, prior to the construction of the Suez Canal, the straits between them often became dry when the water level fell in the Gulf of Suez. When the level rose, the straits would first become muddy and then, with a rush of water, the straits would be obliterated, the two lakes becoming one body of water. A possible central route would cross the marshes of Lake Timsah, now part of the Suez Canal.)

6 The Lord said unto Moses, Stretch out thine hand over the sea, that the waters may come again upon the Egyptians, upon their chariots, and upon their horsemen. *Exodus* 14:26.

7 The Lord overthrew the Egyptians in the midst of the sea. *Exodus* 14:27.

8 There remained not so much as one of them. *Exodus* 14:28.

9 Then sang Moses and the children of Israel this song unto the Lord, and spake, saying, I will sing unto the Lord for he hath triumphed gloriously: the horse and his rider hath he thrown into the sea.

The Lord is my strength and song, and he is become my salvation. He is my God, and I will prepare him a habitation; my father's God, and I will exalt him. *Exodus* 15:1, 2. (This is the beginning of the famous song in praise of God which constitutes the first eighteen verses of this chapter of *Exodus*. The rebellion and escape of a captive people was indeed extraordinary, the only event of its kind recorded in the ancient world.)

1 With the blast of thy nostrils the waters were gathered together, the floods stood upright as a heap, and the depths were congealed in the heart of the sea. *Exodus* 15:8.

2 The people murmured against Moses. *Exodus* 15:24. (The first of many complaints as the people of Israel discover the difficulty of life in the wilderness.)

3 Would to God we had died by the hand of the Lord in the land of Egypt, when we sat by the flesh pots, and when we did eat bread to the full; for ye have brought us forth into this wilderness, to kill this whole assembly with hunger. *Exodus* 16:3. (Flesh pots were slaughterhouses, or butcher shops.)

4 I will rain bread from heaven for you. *Exodus* 16:4.

5 At even [evening] the quails came up, and covered the camp. *Exodus* 16:13. (God feeds the Israelites with characteristic resources of the Sinai desert, quail and manna [see below]. At sundown, migrating quail sometimes land in the Sinai in great numbers, often so exhausted that they are easily caught. See *Numbers* 11:31 for a longer description of the arrival of quail.)

6 This [manna] is the bread which the Lord hath given you to eat. *Exodus* 16:15. (Manna is often identified with the resinlike secretions of tamarisk trees and bushes; small cochineal insects pierce the stems of the tamarisk, and drops of this substance form and fall to the ground in the early morning. Its appearance and taste fit well with the biblical description: "It was like coriander seed, white; and the taste of it was like wafers made with honey."*Exodus* 16:31. More detail is given at *Numbers* 11:7–9. At *Psalms* 78:24–25, Revised Standard Version translation, manna is called "the grain of heaven" and "the bread of angels;" See the quote from *Psalms* 78 below.)

7 The children of Israel did eat manna forty years, until they came to a land inhabited; they did eat manna, until they came unto the borders of the land of Canaan. *Exodus* 16:35.

8 Moses cried unto the Lord, saying, What shall I do unto this people? they be almost ready to stone me. *Exodus* 17:4.

9 Thou shalt smite the rock, and there shall come water out of it, that the people may drink. *Exodus* 17:6. (God guiding Moses. In the Sinai, limestone rock can contain an abundance of water held in under pressure by the crust that forms on the surface of the rock. If the crust is suddenly cracked apart, the water may gush out.)

[1] Moses lifted up his hand, and with his rod he smote the rock twice: and the water came out abundantly. *Numbers* 20:11. (In the early Christian era, St. Paul likened Christ to the rock and his life-giving grace to the flow of water.)

[2] The Lord's anger was kindled against Israel, and he made them wander in the wilderness forty years. *Numbers* 32:13. (See also *Numbers* 14:33.)

[3] Thou [Moses] shalt see the land before thee; but thou shalt not go thither unto the land which I give to the children of Israel. *Deuteronomy* 32:52.

[4] The children of Israel walked forty years in the wilderness. *Joshua* 5:6.

[5] Man did eat angels' food. *Psalms* 78:25.

See also ARK OF THE COVENANT; CANAAN; CHOSEN PEOPLE; GOVERNMENT; JOSHUA AND THE CONQUEST OF CANAAN; MOSES; TEN COMMANDMENTS.

EXPERIENCE

[6] I gave my heart to know wisdom, and to know madness and folly. *Ecclesiastes* 1:17.

EYES

See BODY; VISION

FAILINGS

[1] Who can understand his [own] errors? cleanse thou me from secret faults. *Psalms* 19:12.

[2] That which is crooked cannot be made straight: and that which is wanting cannot be numbered. *Ecclesiastes* 1:15. (A similar verse is *Ecclesiastes* 7:13.)

[3] His feet part of iron and part of clay. *Daniel* 2:33. (The feet of iron and clay are the weakness in the great image that appeared to King Nebuchadnezzar in a dream. Daniel interpreted the dream for the king. The image had a head of gold; this represented Nebuchadnezzar's Babylonian kingdom. The other parts of the image represented succeeding kingdoms, the last of which, being weak as well as strong, would break apart.)

[4] Thou art weighed in the balances, and art found wanting. *Daniel* 5:27.

[5] Why beholdest thou the mote that is in thy brother's eye, but considerest not the beam that is in thine own eye? *Matthew* 7:3.

[6] Thou hypocrite, first cast out the beam out of thine own eye; and then shalt thou see clearly to cast out the mote out of thy brother's eye. *Matthew* 7:5.

[7] The good that I would I do not: but the evil which I would not, that I do. *Romans* 7:19.

See also SIN AND SINNERS; STRENGTH.

FAILURE

[8] Some seeds fell by the way side. *Matthew* 13:4.

See also REJECTION.

FAIRNESS

See JUSTICE AND FAIRNESS

FAITH

[9] Believe in the Lord your God, so shall ye be established; believe in his prophets, so shall ye prosper. *II Chronicles* 20:20.

[10] Believe in him [God], and he will help thee. *Ecclesiasticus* 2:6.

1 I have not found so great faith, no, not in Israel. *Matthew* 8:10. (Jesus to the centurion who humbly asks him to heal his servant who is deathly sick. See MIRACLES OF JESUS. It is the centurion's faith that wins him divine favor. This passage continues, "Go thy way; and as thou hast believed, so be it done unto thee. And his servant was healed in the selfsame hour." *Matthew* 8:13.)

2 Why are ye fearful, O ye of little faith? *Matthew* 8:26. (Jesus to his disciples during the storm on the Sea of Galilee. See MIRACLES OF JESUS.)

3 Thy faith hath made thee whole. *Matthew* 9:22. (Jesus to the woman suffering from bleeding, who wanted to touch his garment in order to be cured.)

4 Oh thou of little faith, wherefore didst thou doubt? *Matthew* 14:31. (Jesus as he reaches out to save Peter, who miraculously had been walking on the water of the Sea of Galilee until he had become fearful and then began to sink.)

5 If ye have faith as a grain of mustard seed, ye shall say unto this mountain, Remove hence to yonder place; and it shall remove; and nothing shall be impossible unto you. *Matthew* 17:20. (See also *Matthew* 21:21.)

6 Lord, I believe; help thou mine unbelief. *Mark* 9:24.

7 Thy faith hath saved thee; go in peace. *Luke* 7:50. (Jesus to the woman who washed his feet with tears and anointed them with ointment.)

8 Whosoever believeth in him [Jesus Christ] should not perish, but have everlasting life. *John* 3:16 (More at JESUS.)

9 I am the resurrection, and the life: he that believeth in me, though he were dead, yet shall he live:

And whoso liveth and believeth in me shall never die. *John* 11:25–26. (From the story of the resurrection of Lazarus. See MIRACLES OF JESUS.)

10 Be not faithless, but believing. *John* 20:27. (The risen Jesus to the skeptical apostle, Thomas. More at JESUS, RESURRECTION OF. See also below.)

11 Blessed are they that have not seen, and yet have believed. *John* 20:29.

12 These [events] are written, that ye might believe that Jesus is the Christ, the Son of God; and that believing ye might have life through his name. *John* 20:31. (The events written down concern the Resurrection. John writes that there were many other signs as well that were not recorded.)

13 Watch ye, stand fast in the faith, quit you like men, be strong. *I Corinthians* 16:13.

14 We walk by faith, not by sight. *II Corinthians* 5:7.

1 Fight the good fight of faith, lay hold on eternal life. *I Timothy* 6:12.

2 I have kept the faith. *II Timothy* 4:7. (More at PERSEVERANCE.)

3 Faith is the substance of things hoped for, the evidence of things not seen. *Hebrews* 11:1.

4 As the body without the spirit is dead, so faith without works is dead also. *James* 2:26.

See also GOD; GOD, TRUST IN; JESUS; MIRACLES OF JESUS; SALVATION; SPIRITUAL BIRTH.

FALSE FRIENDS See FRIENDS, FALSE

FALSE GODS See IDOLS

FAME See GREATNESS; PUBLIC OPINION; SUCCESS

FAMILIES

5 Thou shalt not hate thy brother in thine heart. *Leviticus* 19:17.

6 Whither thou goest, I will go; and where thou lodgest, I will lodge: thy people shall be my people. *Ruth* 1:16. (Ruth to Naomi, her mother-in-law. More at LOVE.)

7 Go not empty unto thy mother in law. *Ruth* 3:17.

8 Yea, I have a goodly heritage. *Psalms* 16:6.

9 Your wife will be like a fruitful vine within your house; your children will be like olive shoots around your table. *Psalms* 128:3, RSV.

10 How good and pleasant it is when brothers dwell in unity! *Psalms* 133:1, RSV.

11 Grandchildren are the crown of the aged, and the glory of sons is their father. *Proverbs* 17:6, RSV

12 A brother is born for adversity. *Proverbs* 17:17.

13 A brother offended is harder to be won than a strong city. *Proverbs* 18:19.

14 A foolish son is ruin to his father, and a wife's quarreling is a continual dripping of rain. *Proverbs* 19:13, RSV.

15 A man's enemies are the men of his own house. *Micah* 7:6. (Also, "A man's foes shall be they of his own household." *Matthew* 10:36.)

16 Let us now praise famous men, and our fathers that begat us. *Ecclesiasticus* 44:1.

1 Whosoever shall say [to a brother], Thou fool, shall be in danger of hell fire. *Matthew* 5:22. For more, see under ANGER.)

2 Who is my mother? and who are my brethren? *Matthew* 12:48. (Jesus to his disciples. He goes on to say that those who do the will of God are his family. See GOD AS FATHER.)

See also ADAM AND EVE; CAIN AND ABEL; CHILDREN; GENERATIONS; HOME; JACOB AND ESAU; MARRIAGE; PARENTS.

FARMING

3 The Lord God sent him [Adam] forth from the garden of Eden, to till the ground from whence he was taken. *Genesis* 3:23.

4 Six years thou shalt sow thy land, and shalt gather in the fruits thereof:

But the seventh year thou shalt let it rest and lie still. *Exodus* 23:10–11. (This was part of the observance of the sabbatical year. It was an opportunity for the poor to gather free food, but the practice also rested the land. In another example of agricultural discipline, *Leviticus* 19:23–25, RSV, specifies that after planting trees, the fruit should not be eaten until the fifth year, and then it must be eaten so that the trees may "yield more richly." Also, in the jubilee year, the land was to lie fallow.)

5 When ye reap the harvest of your land, thou shalt not wholly reap the corners of thy field, neither shalt thou gather the gleanings of thy harvest. *Leviticus* 19:9. (Naomi takes advantage of this charitable practice when she asks, "I pray you, let me glean and gather after the reapers among the sheaves." *Ruth* 2:7. See also below.)

6 And thou shalt not glean thy vineyard, neither shalt thou gather every grape of thy vineyard; thou shalt leave them for the poor and stranger. *Leviticus* 19:10. (For more detail, see *Deuteronomy* 24:19–21.)

7 Thou shalt not sow thy vineyard with divers seeds. *Deuteronomy* 22:9.

8 When thou comest into the standing corn of thy neighbor, then thou mayest pluck the ears with thine hand; but thou shalt not move a sickle unto thy neighbor's standing corn. *Deuteronomy* 23:25.

9 The Lord will give what is good, and our land will yield its increase. *Psalms* 85:12, RSV.

10 He [God] causeth the grass to grow for the cattle, and herb for the service of man: that he may bring forth food out of the earth;

And wine that maketh glad the heart of man, and oil to make his face to shine, and bread which strengtheneth man's heart. *Psalms* 104:14–15.

11 He who tills his land will have plenty of bread. *Proverbs* 12:11, RSV.

1 Be thou diligent to know the state of thy flocks, and look well to thy herds.

For riches are not for ever: and doth the crown endure to every generation?

The hay appeareth, and the tender grass showeth itself, and herbs of the mountains are gathered.

The lambs are for thy clothing, and the goats are the price of the field.

And thou shalt have goats' milk enough for thy food, for the food of thy household, and for the maintenance for thy maidens. *Proverbs* 27:23–27.

2 In the morning sow thy seed, and in the evening withhold not thine hand. *Ecclesiastes* 11:6.

3 My wellbeloved hath a vineyard in a very fruitful hill. *Isaiah* 5:1.

4 Blessed are ye that sow beside all waters, that send forth thither the feet of the ox and the ass. *Isaiah* 32:20.

5 That which the palmerworm hath left hath the locust eaten; and that which the locust hath left hath the cankerworm eaten; and that which the cankerworm hath left hath the caterpillar eaten. *Joel* 1:4. (This ruinous famine prompts the prophet Joel to call upon the Jews to repent. The main cause was a plague of locusts. The palmerworm is a type of caterpillar, not specifically identified. For more, see below.)

6 The seed is rotten under their clods, the garners are laid desolate, the barns are broken down; for the corn is withered.

How do the beasts groan! the herds of cattle are perplexed, because they have no pasture; yea, the flocks of sheep are made desolate. *Joel* 1:17–18. (A plague of locusts, drought, and famine opens the book of *Joel,* a scene reminiscent of the American drought in the 1930s, and again in 1988.)

7 The harvest truly is plenteous, but the laborers are few. *Matthew* 9:37. (Matching labor to harvest, a familiar problem in all farming communities, here symbolizes of the need for representatives of God to work among the multitude.)

8 I have planted, Apollos watered, but God gave the increase. *I Corinthians* 3:6. (St. Paul is speaking metaphorically of his mission. Apollos was a colleague.)

9 The husbandman waiteth for the precious fruit of the earth, and hath long patience for it, until he receive the early and latter rain. *James* 5:7.

See also FOOD AND DRINK; SHEPHERDS.

FASHION

10 The fashion of this world passeth away. *I Corinthians* 7:31.

See also CLOTHES.

FATE

1 One event happeneth to them all [wise and foolish alike]. *Ecclesiastes* 2:14. (The Revised Standard Version reads, "One fate comes to all of them.")

2 All things come alike to all [the virtuous and wicked alike]. *Ecclesiastes* 9:2.

3 Who can think what the will of the Lord is? *Wisdom of Solomon* 9:13.

4 A book . . . sealed with seven seals. *Revelation* 5:1. (The passage continues below.)

5 And no man in heaven, nor in earth, neither under the earth, was able to open the book, neither to look thereon. *Revelation* 5:3.

See also LUCK.

FATHER

See GOD AS FATHER; PARENTS

FAULTS

See FAILINGS

FEAR

6 Thou shalt fear day and night. *Deuteronomy* 28:66.

7 Fear came upon me, and trembling. *Job* 4:14.

8 Fear and trembling come upon me, and horror overwhelms me. *Psalms* 55:5, RSV.

9 You will not fear the terror of the night, nor the arrow that flies by day,
Nor the pestilence that stalks in darkness, nor the destruction that wastes at noonday.
A thousand may fall at your side, ten thousand at your right hand; but it will not come near you. *Psalms* 91:5–7, RSV.

10 Do not be afraid of sudden panic. *Proverbs* 3:25, RSV.

11 Fears shall be in the way. *Ecclesiastes* 12:5. (From the poignant description of old age at the conclusion of this book of the Bible.)

12 My heart panted, fearfulness affrighted me: the night of my pleasure hath he turned into fear unto me. *Isaiah* 21:4. (An unnamed prophet reacts in horror to a vision of destruction, evidently the destruction of Babylon.)

13 Thou hast drunken the dregs of the cup of trembling, and wrung them out. *Isaiah* 51:17.

1 Let not your heart be troubled, neither let it be afraid. *John* 14:27. (More at PEACE.)

See also COURAGE; EMOTIONS; GOD, FEARING AND RESPECTING; INDECISION; PARANOIA.

FEASTS

See FEASTS, RELIGIOUS; FOOD AND DRINK; HOSPITALITY

FEASTS, RELIGIOUS

2 We must hold a feast unto the Lord. *Exodus* 10:9.

3 Ye shall keep it [Passover] a feast to the Lord throughout your generations; ye shall keep it a feast by an ordinance for ever. *Exodus* 12:14. (More on this at PASSOVER.)

4 Three times thou shalt keep a feast unto me in the year.
Thou shall keep the feast of unleavened bread . . .
And the feast of harvest, the firstfruits of thy labors, which thou hast sown in the field; and the feast of ingathering, which is in the end of the year, when thou hast gathered in thy labors out of the field. *Exodus* 23:14–16. (Similar instruction is given in other passages in *Exodus* and elsewhere. These agricultural feasts in time became associated with memorable events in the history of the Israelites. The feast of unleavened bread became part of PASSOVER. The Feast of Weeks—also called Shavuot and PENTECOST—comes seven weeks after Passover at the closing of the spring grain harvest; it became a commemoration of God's giving the commandments to Moses on Mount Sinai. The fall harvest festival, the feast of ingathering, is also called SUCCOTH, or the Feast of Booths, or Feast of Tabernacles. For this happy, nine-day festival, booths are built with thatched roofs in memory of life in the wilderness.)

See also JUBILEE YEAR; PASSOVER; PURIM; SABBATH; SABBATICAL YEAR; SUCCOTH; YOM KIPPUR.

FLATTERY

5 Meddle not with him that flattereth with his lips. *Proverbs* 20:19.

FLIGHT

6 He [God] rode upon a cherub, and did fly: and he was seen upon the wings of the wind. *II Samuel* 22:11. (From the aged King David's song in praise of the Lord. Also at *Psalms* 18:10.)

7 Who maketh the clouds his chariot: who walketh upon the wings of the wind. *Psalms* 104:3.

1 The Lord rideth upon a swift cloud. *Isaiah* 19:1.

2 Who are these that fly as a cloud, and as the doves to their windows? *Isaiah* 60:8.

See also ESCAPE.

FLIGHT OUT OF EGYPT

See EXODUS

FLOOD

See NOAH AND THE ARK

FLOWERS

See GARDENS AND FLOWERS

FOOD AND DRINK

3 We remember the fish, which we did eat in Egypt freely; the cucumbers, and the melons, and the leeks, and the onions, and the garlick. *Numbers* 11:5. (The people of Israel complaining to Moses. Life in the wilderness was harsh. See also EXODUS.)

4 Our soul loatheth this light bread. *Numbers* 21:5. (The Revised Standard Version reads, "We loathe this worthless food." The Hebrew word for "bread," *lekhem,* also means food in general. A chief item in the Israelite diet at this time was manna, which could be eaten several ways, including cooked in cake form. *Numbers* 11:8. Evidently it became monotonous after a time. For more on manna, see EXDOUS.)

5 When thou hast eaten and art full, then thou shalt bless the Lord thy God for the good land which he hath given thee. *Deuteronomy* 8:10. (The land is Canaan, a land of "wheat, and barley, and vines, and fig trees, and pomegranates; a land of oil olive, and honey." *Deuteronomy* 8:8.)

6 He made him [Israel] ride on the high places of the earth, that he might eat the increase of the fields; and he made him to suck honey out of the rock, and oil out of the flinty rock;

Butter of kine, and milk of sheep, with fat of lambs, and rams of the breed of Bashan, and goats, with the fat of kidneys of wheat; and thou didst drink the pure blood of the grape.

But Jeshurun waxed fat, and kicked: thou art waxen fat, thou art grown thick, thou art covered with fatness; then he forsook God which made him. *Deuteronomy* 32:13–15. (In the Revised Standard Version, "the fat of kidneys of wheat" is translated "the finest wheat." *Jeshurun* is a poetic name for the people of Israel. In this famous song, spoken shortly before his death, Moses describes how God cared for the people of Israel and how little gratitude they returned.)

1 There is death in the pot. *II Kings* 4:40. (By accident, poisonous gourds have been used in a pottage prepared for Elijah and other prophets; Elijah counteracts the poison by throwing in good meal. The poison may have been colocynth, the bitter apple, a member of the gourd family and a strong cathartic.)

2 Can that which is unsavory be eaten without salt? or is there any taste in the white of an egg? *Job* 6:6. (The Revised Standard Version reads, "or is there any taste in the slime of the purslane?" The correct translation is not known.)

3 The people curse him who holds back grain, but a blessing is on the head of him who sells it. *Proverbs* 11:26, RSV.

4 Put a knife to thy throat, if thou be a man given to appetite. *Proverbs* 23:2. (This advice is given to the person who sits down to eat with a ruler: There may be a high price to pay for the delicacies at that table. Similarly, the reader is warned that a stingy person will keep a mental reckoning of what a guest eats and later a price may be exacted.)

5 Eat your bread with enjoyment, and drink your wine with a merry heart. *Ecclesiastes* 9:7, RSV.

6 A feast is made for laughter, and wine maketh merry. *Ecclesiastes* 10:19.

7 Sustain me with raisins, refresh me with apples; for I am sick with love. *Song of Solomon* 2:5, RSV. (These healthy foods were reputed to be aphrodisiacs.)

8 A feast of fat things, a feast of wines on the lees, of fat things full of marrow, of wines on the lees well refined. *Isaiah* 25:6. (A victory feast prepared by the Lord.)

9 Corn shall make the young men cheerful, and new wine the maids. *Zechariah* 9:17. (The Revised Standard Version reads: "Grain shall make the young men flourish, and new wine the maidens.")

10 A cheerful and good heart will have a care of his meat and diet. *Ecclesiasticus* 30:25.

11 A very little [food] is sufficient for a man well nurtured. *Ecclesiasticus* 31:19. (In this passage, the writer warns against the gastric pain that follows overeating. See also below.)

12 Sound sleep cometh of moderate eating. *Ecclesiasticus* 31:20.

13 If thou hast been forced to eat, arise, go forth, vomit, and thou shalt have rest. *Ecclesiasticus* 31:21. (At a time when famine was rightly feared, it was impolite not to eat enthusiastically at a feast.)

14 Excess of meats bringeth sickness. *Ecclesiasticus* 37:30. (An observation we have had to make anew in recent years. The average person in the ancient world could not afford meat every day.)

1 Bring hither the fatted calf. *Luke* 15:23. (More at PRODIGAL SON.)

2 A little leaven leaveneth the whole lump. *I Corinthians* 5:6.

3 Strong meat belongeth to them that are of full age. *Hebrews* 5:14. (In the Revised Standard Version, the reference is to "solid food.")

See also CANAAN; DISSIPATION; FARMING; FEASTS, RELIGIOUS; FOOD LAWS; HEDONISM; HOSPITALITY; WINE AND DRINKING.

FOOD LAWS

4 Whatsoever parteth the hoof, and is clovenfooted, and cheweth the cud, among the beasts, that shall ye eat. *Leviticus* 11:3. (The pig is the most famous of the unclean animals—it *is* cloven-hooved but does *not* chew a cud. See below. References to the camel and rabbit in this chapter are somewhat confusing, for the camel is actually clovenfooted, although it is described as not so, and hares do not chew cuds. Birds of prey are also generally forbidden.)

5 The swine . . . is unclean unto you.
Of their flesh shall ye not eat. *Leviticus* 11:7–8.

6 Whatsoever hath fins and scales in the waters, in the seas, and in the rivers, them shall ye eat. *Leviticus* 11:9. (Shellfish and eels are forbidden.)

7 Ye shall eat the blood of no manner of flesh. *Leviticus* 17:14. (The blood, which is seen as the sacred source of life, is to be a sacrifice in atonement for sins. *Leviticus* 17:11. Note that in *Deuteronomy* 12, where temporary exemptions are granted from the food laws, the rule against blood stands. Kosher meat is prepared by draining out the blood.)

8 Thou shalt not seethe a kid in his mother's milk. *Deuteronomy* 14:21. (This injunction is the basis of the kosher proscription against eating meat and dairy products at the same meal.)

9 What God hath cleansed, that call not thou common. *Acts* 10:15. (God to Peter, who has had a vision of all manner of creatures being lowered from heaven in a sheet. Peter hears a command, "Rise, Peter; kill and eat." *Acts* 10:13. See also Matthew 15:11 under TALK.)

FOOLS

See STUPIDITY

FOREIGNERS

See STRANGERS AND TRAVELERS

FORGIVENESS

10 Joseph said unto them, Fear not; for am I in the place of God? *Genesis* 50:19. (Thus Joseph forgave his brothers who had sold him into slavery. See also JOSEPH.)

1 Forgive thy neighbor the hurt that he hath unto thee, so shall thy sins also be forgiven when thou prayest. *Ecclesiasticus* 28:2.

2 Son, be of good cheer; thy sins be forgiven thee. *Matthew* 9:2. (Jesus to a paralyzed man. Certain scribes said that Jesus blasphemed when claiming to have the power to forgive sins. To prove that his powers were indeed unique, Jesus cured the young man. See also MIRACLES OF JESUS.)

3 How oft shall my brother sin against me, and I forgive him? till seven times?

Jesus saith unto him, I say not unto thee, Until seven times: but, Until seventy times seven. *Matthew* 18:21–22. (It is Peter who poses the question.)

4 Forgive, and ye shall be forgiven. *Luke* 6:37. (More at TOLERANCE.)

5 Father, forgive them; for they know not what they do. *Luke* 23:34.

6 Be ye kind to one another, tenderhearted, forgiving one another, even as God for Christ's sake hath forgiven you. *Ephesians* 4:32.

7 Without the shedding of blood there is no forgiveness of sins. *Hebrews* 9:22, RSV. (This refers both to Christ's role and to Old Testament law regarding sacrifices. It is a reminder that wrongdoing is serious, and forgiveness not to be taken for granted.)

See also JUDGING OTHERS; MERCY; TOLERANCE.

FRANKNESS

8 I will speak in the anguish of my spirit; I will complain in the bitterness of my soul. *Job* 7:11.

9 It is much better to reprove, than to be angry secretly. *Ecclesiasticus* 20:2.

See also SINCERITY; TALK.

FREEDOM

10 The chief captain answered, With a great sum obtained I this freedom. And Paul said, But I was free born. *Acts* 22:28. (Paul here asserts his status and rights as a Roman citizen. The officer, who evidently purchased his citizenship, releases him from custody. See also PAUL.)

See also INDEPENDENCE.

FRIENDS AND COMPANIONS

11 He who withholds kindness from a friend forsakes the fear of the Almighty. *Job* 6:14, RSV.

12 He that walketh with wise men shall be wise: but a companion of fools shall be destroyed. *Proverbs* 13:20.

1 A friend loveth at all times. *Proverbs* 17:17.

2 A man that hath friends must show himself friendly: and there is a friend that sticketh closer than a brother. *Proverbs* 18:24.

3 If thou wouldest get a friend, prove him first, and be not hasty to credit him. *Ecclesiasticus* 6:7.

4 A faithful friend is a strong defense: and he that hath found such an one hath found a treasure. *Ecclesiasticus* 6:14.

5 A faithful friend is the medicine of life. *Ecclesiasticus* 6:16.

6 Forsake not an old friend; for the new is not comparable to him: a new friend is as new wine; when it is old, thou shalt drink it with pleasure. *Ecclesiasticus.* 9:10.

7 A friend cannot be known in prosperity; and an enemy cannot be hid in adversity. *Ecclesiasticus* 12:8.

8 I will not be ashamed to defend a friend. *Ecclesiasticus* 22:25.

9 Greater love hath no man than this, that a man lay down his life for his friends. *John* 15:13.

10 Bad company ruins good morals. *I Corinthians* 15:33, RSV. (The King James Version reads, "Evil communications corrupt good manners.")

See also DAVID AND JONATHAN; FRIENDS, FALSE.

FRIENDS, FALSE

11 Miserable comforters are ye all. *Job* 16:2. (Not the least of Job's afflictions were the comments of his three self-righteous "friends.")

12 There is a friend which is only a friend in name. *Ecclesiasticus* 37:1.

FUTURE

13 Boast not thyself of tomorrow; for thou knowest not what a day may bring forth. *Proverbs* 27:1.

14 What is past I know, but what is for to come I know not. *II Esdras* 4:46.

15 Take therefore no thought for the morrow; for the morrow shall take thought for the things of itself. Sufficient unto the day is the evil thereof. *Matthew* 6:34.

GARDENS AND FLOWERS

1 I went down into the garden of nuts to see the fruits of the valley, and to see whether the vine flourished, and the pomegranates budded. *Song of Solomon* 6:11. (Garden imagery runs through this book, sometimes as a metaphor for the body. Thus, "A garden inclosed is my sister, my spouse." *Song of Solomon* 4:12. The cherished gardens of the Near East were typically enclosed, with a central fountain, and planted with spices, fruit, and flowers.)

2 Consider the lilies of the field, how they grow; they toil not, neither do they spin:

And yet I say unto you, That even Solomon in all his glory was not arrayed like one of these. *Matthew* 6:28–29. (Part of the passage in the Sermon on the Mount in which Jesus urges his listeners to serve God and abandon anxiety and worry over wordly cares. The full passage runs from *Matthew* 6:25 to 6:34.).

See also EDEN.

GENERATIONS

3 A stubborn and rebellious generation. *Psalms* 78:8.

4 One generation passeth away, and another generation cometh: but the earth abideth for ever. *Ecclesiastes* 1:4. (The passage is given in full at VANITY.)

5 As of the green leaves on a thick tree, some fall, and some grow; so is the generation of flesh and blood, one cometh to an end, and another is born. *Ecclesiasticus* 14:18.

6 O generation of vipers. *Matthew* 3:7. (John the Baptist, accosting the Pharisees and Sadducees. These two religious groups evidently were hostile to each other, but in the New Testament are linked without much distinction. The pious Pharisees were by far the more influential. The phrase is used again at *Matthew* 12:34; and at 23:33, Jesus asks the scribes and Pharisees, "Ye serpents, ye generation of vipers, how can ye escape the damnation of hell?")

7 An evil and adulterous generation seeketh after a sign. *Matthew* 12:39. (Jesus' answer to certain scribes and Pharisees who ask him for a sign. The sign he promises refers to his resurrection.)

8 O faithless and perverse generation. *Matthew* 17:17.

1 This is an evil generation; they seek a sign. *Luke* 11:29. (Jesus is warning his followers not to look for signs, but to listen to his message. The only sign they will receive, he tells them, is the sign of Jonah. At *Matthew* 12:40, this is interpreted to be Christ's resurrection. Here, however, the reference appears to be to Jonah's mission to preach repentance. See JONAH.)

See also CHILDREN; FAMILIES; PARENTS.

GENEROSITY

See GIVING; HOSPITALITY

GENESIS

See CREATION

GENTLENESS AND KINDNESS

2 Thy gentleness hath made me great. *II Samuel* 22:36. (King David to God.)

3 A man who is kind benefits himself, but a cruel man hurts himself. *Proverbs* 11:17, RSV.

4 A soft answer turneth away wrath. *Proverbs* 15:1.

5 In her tongue is the law of kindness. *Proverbs* 31:26. (Used in 1872 on the memorial tablet for Jane Austen—although her tongue was in fact rather sharp. The verse is from the famous portrait of the virtuous woman. See WOMEN.)

GIDEON

See ANGELS; HUMILITY; MUSIC

GIVING

6 One man gives freely, yet grows all the richer; another withholds what he should give, and only suffers want.
A liberal man will be enriched. *Proverbs* 11:24–25, RSV.

7 Cast thy bread upon the waters: for thou shalt find it after many days. *Ecclesiastes* 11:1.

8 Ho, every one that thirsteth, come ye to the waters, and he that hath no money; come ye, buy, and eat. *Isaiah* 55:1.

9 If thou hast abundance, give alms accordingly: if thou have but a little, be not afraid to give according to that little. *Tobit* 4:8.

10 Give of thy bread to the hungry, and of thy garments to them that are naked. *Tobit* 4:16.

1 It is better to give alms than to lay up gold. *Tobit* 12:8. (The angel Raphael is speaking.)

2 Take heed that ye do not your alms before men, to be seen of them: otherwise ye have no reward of your Father which is in heaven.

Therefore when thou doest thine alms, do not sound a trumpet before thee, as the hypocrites do in the synagogues and in the streets, that they may have glory of men. Verily I say unto you, They have their reward.

But when thou doest alms, let not thy left hand know what thy right hand doeth:

That thine alms may be in secret: and thy Father which seeth in secret himself shall reward thee openly. *Matthew* 6:1–4.

3 Freely ye have received, freely give. *Matthew* 10:8.

I was hungry and you gave me food, I was thirsty and you gave me drink, I was a stranger and you welcomed me,

I was naked and you clothed me, I was sick and you visited me, I was in prison and you came to me. *Matthew* 25:35–36, RSV. (Jesus to the saved at the Last Judgment. See also JUDGMENT DAY. When they ask how they had done these things without knowing him, Jesus answers that what they have done for the needy they have done for him. See also JESUS.)

4 There came a certain poor widow, and she threw in two mites. *Mark* 12:42, RSV. (Jesus and his disciples were watching people make donations to the offering boxes outside the Temple. The mites were leptons, the smallest Greek coins, a fraction of a cent. Jesus comments that the widow's gift was worth more than all those of the rich, because they had abundance from which to give, but she gave all that she had.)

5 When thou makest a feast, call the poor, the maimed, the lame, the blind:

And thou shalt be blessed. *Luke* 14:13–14. (See also HOSPITALITY.)

6 Silver and gold have I none; but such as I have give I thee. *Acts* 3:6.

7 It is more blessed to give than to receive. *Acts* 20:35.

8 God loveth a cheerful giver. *II Corinthians* 9:7.

9 If any one has the world's goods and sees his brother in need, yet closes his heart against him, how does God's love abide in him? Little children, let us not love in word or speech but in deed and in truth. *I John* 3:17–18, RSV.

See also CHARITY, CHRISTIAN; HOSPITALITY; MISFORTUNE (for one's responsibilities to the poor, afflicted, and unlucky.)

GLORY

See GOD'S GLORY; GREATNESS; SUCCESS

GOD

1 The Lord shall reign for ever and ever. *Exodus* 15:18.

2 The Lord God, merciful and gracious, longsuffering, and abundant in goodness and truth. *Exodus* 34:6. (See also *Psalms* 103:8.)

3 The Lord thy God is a consuming fire. *Deuteronomy* 4:24.

4 Hear, O Israel: The Lord our God is one Lord.

And thou shalt love the Lord thy God with all thine heart, and with all thy soul, and with all thy might.

And these words, which I command thee this day, shall be in thine heart:

And thou shalt teach them diligently unto thy children, and shalt talk of them when thou sittest in thine house, and when thou walkest by the way, and when thou liest down, and when thou risest up. *Deuteronomy* 6:4–7. (In Jewish liturgy, this is the beginning of the uniquely important prayer *Shema Yisrael.* A more literal translation of the first verse is: "Hear, O Israel, Yaweh our God, Yahweh alone." In the New Testament, the first two verses are identified by Jesus as "the first of all the commandments." *Mark* 12:29–30.)

5 Man doth not live by bread only, but by every word that proceedeth out of the mouth of the Lord doth man live. *Deuteronomy* 8:3. (See also *Matthew* 4:4, which reads, "Man shall not live by bread alone.")

6 The Lord your God is God of gods, and Lord of lords, a great God, a mighty, and a terrible, which regardeth not persons, nor taketh reward. *Deuteronomy* 10:17.

7 He is the Rock, his work is perfect: for all his ways are judgment: a God of truth and without iniquity, just and right is he. *Deuteronomy* 32:4.

8 He is a holy God; he is a jealous God; he will not forgive your transgressions or your sins. *Joshua* 24:19, RSV.

9 Jehovah-shalom. *Judges* 6:24. ("The Lord is peace"—the name of the altar built by Gideon.)

10 The Lord is my rock, and my fortress, and my deliverer. *II Samuel* 22:2. (The beginning of King David's song of thanks to the Lord for delivering him from his enemies. In many passages God is likened to a rock, for in the Middle East, the flat plains offer little protection and few firm building sites. Fortresses and cities were built on rocky cliffs and hills. Thus, another familiar passage runs, "The Lord is my defence; and my God is the rock of my refuge." *Psalms* 94:22. Rocks represented strength, majesty, and endurance.)

11 The Lord is righteous. *II Chronicles* 12:6.

1 Thou art a God ready to pardon, gracious and merciful, slow to anger, and of great kindness. *Nehemiah* 9:17.

2 He wounds, but he binds up; he smites, but his hands heal. *Job* 5:18, RSV.

3 He is wise in heart, and mighty in strength. *Job* 9:4.

4 With him is wisdom and strength, he hath counsel and understanding. *Job* 12:13.

5 In thy [God's] presence is fulness of joy; at thy right hand there are pleasures for evermore. *Psalms* 16:11.

6 His anger endureth but a moment. *Psalms* 30:5.

7 God is our refuge and strength, a very present help in trouble.
Therefore will not we fear, though the earth be removed, and though the mountains be carried into the midst of the sea. *Psalms* 46:1–2.

8 He only is my rock and my salvation; he is my defense; I shall not be moved. *Psalms* 62:6.

9 Thou crownest the year with thy goodness. *Psalms* 65:11.

10 A day in thy courts is better than a thousand. I had rather be a door-keeper in the house of my God than to dwell in the tents of wickedness.
For the Lord God is a sun and shield: the Lord will give grace and glory. *Psalms* 84:10–11.

11 Lord, thou hast been our dwelling place in all generations.
Before the mountains were brought forth, or ever thou hadst formed the earth and the world, even from everlasting to everlasting, thou art God. *Psalms* 90:1–2.

12 I will say of the Lord, He is my refuge and my fortress: my God; in him will I trust. *Psalms* 91:2. (See also *Jeremiah* 16:19 below.)

13 The Lord reigneth; let the earth rejoice. *Psalms* 97:1.

14 The Lord is good; his mercy is everlasting; and his truth endureth to all generations. *Psalms* 100:5.

15 Who layeth the beams of his chambers in the waters: who maketh the clouds his chariot: who walketh upon the wings of the wind. *Psalms* 104:3.

16 A man's heart deviseth his way: but the Lord directeth his steps. *Proverbs* 16:9.

17 The fining pot is for silver, and the furnace for gold: but the Lord trieth hearts. *Proverbs* 17:3.

18 Behold, God is my salvation; I will trust, and not be afraid: for the Lord Jehovah is my strength and my song; he also is become my salvation. *Isaiah* 12:2.

1 The Lord rideth upon a swift cloud. *Isaiah* 19:1. (For similar quotes, see FLIGHT.)

2 For thou hast been a strength to the poor, a strength to the needy in his distress, a refuge from the storm, a shadow from the heat. *Isaiah* 25:4.

3 Behold, the Lord God will come with strong hand. *Isaiah* 40:10.

4 O Lord, my strength, and my fortress, and my refuge in the day of affliction. *Jeremiah* 16:19.

5 Behold, a whirlwind of the Lord is gone forth in fury. *Jeremiah* 23:19.

6 Thou hast made the heaven and the earth by thy great power and stretched out arm, and there is nothing too hard for thee. *Jeremiah* 32:17.

7 He is the living God, and steadfast for ever, and his kingdom that which shall not be destroyed, and his dominion shall be even unto the end. *Daniel* 6:26.

8 He shall come unto us as the rain. *Hosea* 6:3.

9 Thou art a God of the afflicted, a helper of the oppressed, an upholder of the weak, a protector of the forlorn, a saviour of them that are without hope. *Judith* 9:11. (From the prayer of the beautiful and pious widow Judith, asking God for help in the dangerous mission she has undertaken: the assassination of Holofernes.)

10 The Lord is full of compassion and mercy, longsuffering, and very pitiful, and forgiveth sins, and saveth in time of affliction. *Ecclesiasticus* 2:11.

11 Prosperity and adversity, life and death, poverty and riches, come of the Lord. *Ecclesiasticus* 11:14.

12 There is none good but one, that is, God. *Matthew* 19:17. (Jesus to the young man who addressed him as "Good Master.")

13 With God all things are possible. *Matthew* 19:26. (*Luke* 1:37 reads, "With God nothing shall be impossible.")

14 The kingdom of God is within you. *Luke* 17:21.

15 He is not a God of the dead, but of the living. *Luke* 20:38.

16 No man hath seen God at any time. *John* 1:18.

17 A man can receive nothing, except it be given him from heaven. *John* 3:27.

18 God is no respecter of persons. *Acts* 10:34. (See also *Ecclesiasticus* 35:12 and *Romans* 2:11 for similar sayings. Also, "The Father, who without respect of persons judgeth according to every man's work." *I Peter* 1:17.)

19 In him [God] we live, and move, and have our being; as certain also of your own poets have said, For we are also his offspring. *Acts* 17:28. (From Paul's sermon to the Athenians. See also EQUALITY and RELIGION.)

1 If God be for us, who can be against us? *Romans* 8:31.

2 Who hath known the mind of the Lord? *Romans* 11:34.

3 And he is before all things, and by him all things consist. *Colossians* 1:17. (More at CREATION.)

4 Every good gift and every perfect gift is from above, and cometh down from the Father of lights, with whom is no variableness, neither shadow of turning. *James* 1:17.

5 God is love. *I John* 4:8. (More at LOVE.)

See also BLESSINGS; CREATION; DARKNESS; DESTRUCTION; FAITH; HEAVEN; PRAYERS; SALVATION.

GOD AS A SHEPHERD

See GOD'S PROVIDENCE

GOD AS A SOURCE OF STRENGTH

6 God is my strength and power. *II Samuel* 22:33.

7 Seek the Lord and his strength. *I Chronicles* 16:11. (Also at *Psalms* 105:4.)

8 The Lord is my strength and my shield. *Psalms* 28:7.

9 In the Lord JEHOVAH is everlasting strength. *Isaiah* 26:4.

10 They that wait upon the Lord shall renew their strength; they shall mount up with wings as eagles; they shall run, and not be weary; and they shall walk, and not faint. *Isaiah* 40:31.

11 Fear thou not; for I am with thee: be not dismayed; for I am thy God: I will strengthen thee; yea, I will help thee. *Isaiah* 41:10.

See also GOD; STRENGTH.

GOD AS DESCRIBED BY HIMSELF

12 I am thy shield, and thy exceeding great reward. *Genesis* 15:1. (God to Abraham.)

13 Is any thing too hard for the Lord? *Genesis* 18:14. (God to Abraham.)

14 God said unto Moses, I AM THAT I AM. *Exodus* 3:14. (God's words in Hebrew are *Eyeh Asher Eyeh.* Among the other translations suggested by scholars are: "I will be what I will be" and "I will be there when I will be there.")

1 God spoke unto Moses, and said unto him, I am the Lord.

And I appeared unto Abraham, unto Isaac, and unto Jacob, by the name of God Almighty, but by my name JEHOVAH was I not known to them. *Exodus* 6:2–3. (*Jehovah* derives from *Yahweh,* the most sacred name of God, which, to avoid sacrilege, traditionally is abbreviated YHWH, or YHVH, the *w* and *v* being interchangeable. These consonants combined with the vowels of *Adonai,* meaning "Lord," gave rise *Jehovah.* Martin Buber wrote that the name *Yahweh* may derive from *hu,* Arabic for "he"; the cry *Ya-hu* means "Oh He!,"" and was used in the ancient world to refer to "the One," or God.)

2 I the Lord thy God am a jealous God, visiting the iniquity of the fathers upon the children unto the third and fourth generation of them that hate me;

And showing mercy unto thousands of them that love me, and keep my commandments. *Exodus* 20:5–6.

3 I, even I, am he, and there is no god with me: I kill and I make alive; I wound, and I heal . . .

I live for ever. *Deuteronomy* 32:39–40. (This is very close to an absolute monotheism, although the quotes from *Isaiah* 44:6 and 45:5 below usually are taken as the verses first establishing monotheism unequivocally.)

4 Be still, and know that I am God, *Psalms* 46:10.

5 I am the Lord: that is my name: and my glory will I not give to another, neither my praise to graven images. *Isaiah* 42:8.

6 Before the day was I am he. *Isaiah* 43:13.

7 I am the first, and I am the last; and beside me there is no God. *Isaiah* 44:6. (This and the variant below are often cited as the most absolute statements of monotheism in the Old Testament. Also: "I am he; I am the first, I also am the last." *Isaiah* 48:12.)

8 I am the Lord, and there is none else, there is no God beside me. *Isaiah* 45:5. (Similar words at *Isaiah* 45:22).

9 My thoughts are not your thoughts, neither are your ways my ways, saith the Lord. *Isaiah* 55:8.

10 I have trodden the winepress alone. *Isaiah* 63:3. (More at VIOLENCE.)

11 The cities that are inhabited shall be laid waste, and the land shall be desolate; and ye shall know that I am the Lord. *Ezekiel* 12:20.

12 I desired mercy, and not sacrifice; and the knowledge of God more than burnt offerings. *Hosea* 6:6. (For more on the Lord's impatience with shallow religiosity, see RELIGION.)

13 I am Alpha and Omega, the beginning and the end, the first and the last. *Revelation* 22:13.

GOD AS FATHER

1 Thou, O Lord, art our father, our redeemer. *Isaiah* 63:16.

2 Whosoever shall do the will of my Father which is in heaven, the same is my brother, and sister, and mother. *Matthew* 12:50. (Jesus to his disciples.)

3 Call no man your father upon the earth: for one is your Father, which is in heaven. *Matthew* 23:9.

See also LORD'S PRAYER.

GOD AS LAWGIVER AND JUDGE

4 The Lord is a God of knowledge, and by him actions are weighed. *I Samuel* 2:3.

5 The Lord shall judge the ends of the earth. *I Samuel* 2:10.

6 The judgments of the Lord are true and righteous altogether.
More to be desired are they than gold, yea, than much fine gold: sweeter also than honey and the honeycomb. *Psalms* 19:9–10.

7 All the ways of a man are clean in his own eyes: but the Lord weigheth the spirits. *Proverbs* 16:2. (See also *Proverbs* 21:2.)

8 God shall bring every work into judgment, with every secret thing, whether it be good, or whether it be evil. *Ecclesiastes* 12:14.

9 He shall judge among the nations, and shall rebuke many people: and they shall beat their swords into plowshares. *Isaiah* 2:4. (More at PEACE. Passages from *Isaiah* are especially familiar to music lovers, for they were used by Handel as the basis of *Messiah.*)

GOD AS LIGHT

10 Thou art my lamp, O Lord; and the Lord will lighten my darkness. *II Samuel* 22:29. (A similar passage is at *Psalms* 18:28.)

11 The Lord is my light and my salvation. *Psalms* 27:1.

12 Thy word is a lamp unto my feet, and a light unto my path. *Psalms* 119:105.

13 The people that walked in darkness have seen a great light: they that dwell in the land of the shadow of death, upon them hath the light shined. *Isaiah* 9:2. (This is one of the verses introducing the concept of a great king to come from the house of David. See MESSIAH.)

14 Arise, shine; for thy light is come, and the glory of the Lord is risen upon thee. *Isaiah* 60:1.

15 The Lord shall be thine everlasting light. *Isaiah* 60:20.

1 God is light, and in him is no darkness at all. *I John* 1:5.

See also JESUS.

GOD AS SHEPHERD

See GOD'S PROVIDENCE

GOD, DOUBTING

2 If the Lord be with us, why then is all this befallen us? and where be all his miracles? *Judges* 6:13. (Gideon is speaking to an angel of the Lord at a time when the Israelites were suffering under the Midianites.)

3 Curse God, and die. *Job* 2:9. (Job's wife to Job.)

See also ATHEISM; DESPAIR; GOD, QUESTIONING; JOB.

GOD, ENCOUNTERS WITH

4 I have seen God face to face, and my life is preserved. *Genesis* 32:30. (More is given under JACOB.)

5 God spoke unto Israel in the visions of the night, and said, Jacob, Jacob. And he said, Here am I.

And he said, I am God, the God of thy father. *Genesis* 46:3. (Israel is the name God gave to Jacob. See under JACOB.)

6 Moses hid his face; for he was afraid to look upon God. *Exodus* 3:6.

7 This is the finger of God. *Exodus* 8:19.

8 Let not God speak with us, lest we die. [The people of Israel are imploring Moses to approach God for them.]

And Moses said unto the people, Fear not: for God is come to prove you, and that his fear may be before your faces, that ye sin not.

And the people stood afar off, and Moses drew near unto the thick darkness where God was. *Exodus* 20:19–21. (The scene is Mount Sinai. See also TEN COMMANDMENTS.)

9 They saw the God of Israel: and there was under his feet as it were a paved work of a sapphire stone, and as it were the body of heaven in his clearness. *Exodus* 24:10.

10 The Lord spake unto Moses face to face, as a man speaketh unto his friend. *Exodus* 33:11.

11 Thou canst not see my face: for there shall be no man see me, and live. *Exodus* 33:20. (There is danger in encountering God face to face. See also the next quote below.)

12 We shall surely die, because we have seen God. *Judges* 13:22. (The father of Samson is speaking.)

1 The Lord came, and stood, and called as at other times, Samuel, Samuel. Then Samuel answered, Speak; for thy servant heareth. *I Samuel* 3:10. (Three times the Lord had called the young Samuel, and each time the boy had run to his master, the high priest Eli, believing it was he who had called. Finally, Eli instructed Samuel to answer in this manner.)

2 The Lord thundered from heaven. *II Samuel* 22:14.

3 And after the fire a still small voice. *I Kings* 19:12. (One of God's most dramatic manifestations. The prophet Elijah is awaiting the Lord on a mountain top, and a wind comes that shatters rocks in pieces, "but the Lord was not in the wind." Nor is God in the earthquake or fire that follow. But then Elijah hears this "still small voice." The voice is also sometimes identified as the voice of conscience.)

4 He passes me by, and I see him not; he moves on, but I do not perceive him. *Job* 9:11, RSV.

5 Thou art near, O Lord. *Psalms* 119:151.

6 Woe is me! for I am undone; because I am a man of unclean lips . . . for mine eyes have seen the King, the Lord of hosts. *Isaiah* 6:5. (Isaiah's reaction to the vision of God on his throne surrounded by seraphim. See under ANGELS. One of the angels then puts a live coal on Isaiah's mouth, purging his sins. Then the Lord calls upon him to become a prophet, a messenger of God.)

7 The heavens were opened, and I saw visions of God. *Ezekiel* 1:1.

See also DARKNESS; JACOB'S LADDER.

GOD, ENEMIES AND WAR

8 Blessed be the most high God, which hath delivered thine enemies into thy hand. *Genesis* 14:20.

9 The Lord is a man of war. *Exodus* 15:3.

10 Thy right hand, O Lord, is become glorious in powers: thy right hand, O Lord, hath dashed in pieces the enemy. *Exodus* 15:6.

11 The Lord your God is he that goeth with you, to fight for you against your enemies, to save you. *Deuteronomy* 20:4.

12 I will call upon the Lord, who is worthy to be praised: so shall I be saved from mine enemies. *II Samuel* 22:4. (This entire chapter of *II Samuel* is a song by King David in praise of God for delivering him from his powerful enemies.)

13 The Lord said unto my Lord, Sit thou at my right hand, until I make thine enemies thy footstool. *Psalms* 110:1.

See also PEACE; WAR.

GOD, FAITH IN

See FAITH; GOD, TRUST IN

GOD, FEARING AND RESPECTING

1 Ye shall not tempt the Lord your God. *Deuteronomy* 6:16. (Also at *Matthew* 4:7.)

2 Thou shalt fear the Lord thy God. *Deuteronomy* 10:20. (See also *II Kings* 17:39.)

3 Fear the Lord, and serve him in sincerity and in truth. *Joshua* 24:14. (The Revised Standard Version reads, "serve him in sincerity and in faithfulness.")

4 Fear of the Lord, that is wisdom. *Job* 28:28. (More at WISDOM. Also, "The fear of the Lord is beginning of wisdom."' *Psalms* 111:10.)

5 The secret of the Lord is with them that fear him. *Psalms* 25:14.

6 Let all the earth fear the Lord. *Psalms* 33:8.

7 Blessed is the man that feareth the Lord. *Psalms* 112:1.

8 Unto you that fear my name shall the Sun of righteousness arise with healing in his wings. *Malachi* 4:2.

9 Thou hast much wealth, if thou fear God, and depart from all sin, and do that which is pleasing in his sight. *Tobit* 4:21.

10 The fear of the Lord is a crown of wisdom. *Ecclesiasticus* 1:18. (This is the theme of this opening chapter, and the idea is repeated several times in different words; see also WISDOM.)

11 The fear of the Lord driveth away sins. *Ecclesiasticus* 1:21.

12 The fear of the Lord is the beginning of his love. *Ecclesiasticus* 25:12.

13 Whoso feareth the Lord shall not fear or be afraid. *Ecclesiasticus* 34:14.

See also WISDOM.

GOD, LOVING

14 Thou shalt love the Lord thy God with all thine heart, and with all thy soul, and with all thy might. *Deuteronomy* 6:5.

15 Let them that love him [the Lord] be as the sun when he goeth forth in his might. *Judges* 5:31.

16 My heart rejoiceth in the Lord. *I Samuel* 2:1.

17 Love the Lord all thy life, and call upon him for thy salvation. *Ecclesiasticus* 13:14.

18 All things work together for good to them that love God. *Romans* 8:28.

[1] Eye hath not seen, nor ear heard, neither have entered into the heart of man, the things which God hath prepared for them that love him. *I Corinthians* 2:9.

GOD, LOYALTY TO

[2] Who is on the Lord's side? let him come unto me. *Exodus* 32:26. (Moses after finding the people of Israel worshiping the golden calf.)

[3] Cleave unto the Lord your God. *Joshua* 23:8.

[4] The Lord is with you while ye be with him; and if ye seek him, he will be found of you; but if ye forsake him, he will forsake you. *II Chronicles* 15:2.

[5] This God is our God for ever and ever: he will be our guide even unto death. *Psalms* 48:14.

See also GOD, OBEYING AND SERVING.

GOD, OBEYING AND SERVING

[6] Whatsoever God hath said unto thee, do. *Genesis* 31:16.

[7] All that the Lord hath spoken we will do. *Exodus* 19:8.

[8] What the Lord saith, that will I speak. *Numbers* 24:13. (Balaam to Balak, king of Moab. Balaam is explaining why he has repeatedly blessed the people of Israel when Balak has asked him to curse them.)

[9] God will we serve, and his voice will we obey. *Joshua* 24:24.

[10] Serve the Lord with all your heart. *I Samuel* 12:20. (Also "Serve him with a perfect heart." *I Chronicles* 28:9.)

[11] To obey is better than sacrifice. *I Samuel* 15:22.

[12] Serve the Lord with gladness: come before his presence with singing. *Psalms* 100:2.

[13] Obey my voice, and I will be your God. *Jeremiah* 7:23.

[14] Ye cannot serve God and mammon. *Matthew* 6:24.(Mammon is Aramaic for "money.")

[15] Not my will, but thine, be done. *Luke* 22:42. (Jesus accepts his fate after praying, "If thou be willing, remove this cup from me." See also JESUS: PASSION AND DEATH.)

See also ISAAC; SERVANT OF GOD.

GOD, PRAISING

1 I will sing unto the Lord, for he hath triumphed gloriously. *Exodus* 15:1.

2 The Lord is my strength and song, and he is become my salvation: he is my God, and I will prepare him a habitation; my father's God, and I will exalt him. *Exodus* 15:2.

3 Who is like thee, O Lord, among the gods? Who is like thee, majestic in holiness, terrible in glorious deeds, doing wonders? *Exodus* 15:11, RSV.

4 Give ear, O heavens, and I will speak; and let the earth hear the words of my mouth.

May my teaching drop as the rain, my speech distil as the dew, as the gentle rain upon the tender grass, and as the showers upon the herb.

For I will proclaim the name of the Lord. Ascribe greatness to our God! *Deuteronomy* 32:1–3, RSV.

5 Hear, O kings; give ear, O princes; to the Lord I will sing, I will make melody to the Lord, the God of Israel. *Judges* 5:3, RSV. (From the song of Deborah and Barak celebrating victory over the Canaanite commander Sisera.)

6 Sing unto him, sing psalms unto him, talk ye of all his wondrous works. *I Chronicles* 16:9. (A psalm sung by David before the ark of the covenant; similar to *Psalms* 105).

7 O Lord, there is none like thee. *I Chronicles* 17:20. (Similar to *II Samuel* 7:22.)

8 O Lord our Lord, how excellent is thy name in all the earth! *Psalms* 8:1 and 8:9.

9 I will praise thee, O Lord, with my whole heart; I will show forth all thy marvellous works. *Psalms* 9:1.

10 O magnify the Lord with me, and let us exalt his name together. *Psalms* 34:3.

11 Sing praises unto God, sing praises: sing praises unto our King, sing praises.

For God is the King of all the earth: sing ye praises with understanding. *Psalms* 47:6–7.

12 Who is so great a God as our God? *Psalms* 77:13.

13 Make a joyful noise unto the Lord, all ye lands. *Psalms* 100:1.

14 Oh that men would praise the Lord for his goodness! *Psalms* 107:31.

15 Praise ye the Lord from the heavens: praise him in the heights.
Praise ye him, all his angels: praise ye him, all his hosts.
Praise ye him, sun and moon: praise him, all ye stars of light.
Praise him, ye heavens of heavens. *Psalms* 148:1–4.

1 Praise him with the sound of the trumpet: praise him with the psaltery and harp.

Praise him with the timbrel and dance: praise him with stringed instruments and organs.

Praise him upon the loud cymbals: praise him on the high sounding cymbals.

Let everything that hath breath praise the Lord. *Psalms* 150:3–6.

2 Holy, holy, holy, is the Lord of hosts: the whole earth is full of his glory. *Isaiah* 6:3.

3 It is good to praise God, and exalt his name. *Tobit* 12:6. (The angel Raphael is speaking. In this happy book of the Bible, the point is made several times that prayers should praise God before asking for favors.)

4 O all ye works of the Lord, bless ye the Lord: praise him and exalt him above all for ever. *Song of Three Holy Children* 35. (Most of this book is a song of praise, offered by Shadrach, Meshach, and Abednego upon their escape from death in the fiery furnace. See DANIEL and MIRACLES IN THE OLD TESTAMENT.)

5 Glory to God in the highest. *Luke* 2:14. (More at JESUS: BIRTH AND CHILDHOOD.)

See also GOD'S GLORY; GOD, WORSHIPING; MUSIC; PRAYERS.

GOD, QUESTIONING

6 Why dost thou stand afar off, O Lord? Why dost thou hide thyself in times of trouble? *Psalms* 10:1, RSV.

7 O Lord, why dost thou cast me off? Why dost thou hide thy face from me? *Psalms* 88:14, RSV.

8 Then said I, Lord how long? *Isaiah* 6:11. (The prophet asks God how long the era of desolation will last. God answers that it will last until all but a tenth of his people are destroyed. But this remnant will flourish and be saved.)

9 Shall the clay say to him that fashioneth it, What makest thou? *Isaiah* 45:9.

10 Oh man, who art thou that repliest against God? Shall the thing formed say to him that formed it, Why hast thou made me thus?

Hath not the potter power over the clay, of the same lump to make one vessel unto honor, and another unto dishonor? *Romans* 9:20–21.

See also GOD, DOUBTING.

GOD, SEEKING

11 I would seek unto God, and unto God would I commit my cause. *Job* 5:8.

12 Canst thou by searching find out God? *Job* 11:7.

1 Prepare thine heart, and stretch out thine hands toward him. *Job* 11:13.

2 As the hart longs for flowing streams, so longs my soul for thee, O God. My soul thirsts for God, for the living God. *Psalms* 42, 1–2, RSV.

3 Ye shall seek me, and find me, when ye shall search for me with all your heart. *Jeremiah* 29:13.

4 The Lord is good unto them that wait for him, to the soul that seeketh him. *Lamentations* 3:25.

GOD, SERVANT OF

See SERVANT OF GOD

GODS, FALSE

See IDOLS

GOD'S GLORY

5 Thine, O Lord, is the greatness, and the power, and the glory, and the victory, and the majesty: for all that is in the heaven and in the earth is thine; thine is the kingdom, O Lord, and thou art exalted as head above all. *I Chronicles* 29:11.

6 Who is this King of glory? The Lord of hosts, he is the King of glory. *Psalms* 24:10.

7 The glory of the Lord shall endure for ever. *Psalms* 104:31.

8 The glory of the Lord shall be revealed, and all flesh shall see it together. *Isaiah* 40:5.

GOD, SILENT

9 O my God, I cry by day, but thou dost not answer; and by night, but find no rest. *Psalms* 22:2, RSV.

GOD'S KNOWLEDGE OF HUMANS

10 I know thy abode, and thy going out, and thy coming in, and thy rage against me. *II Kings* 19:27. (God speaking through Isaiah to the Assyrians. He warns, "I will put my hook in thy nose, and my bridle in thy lips, and I will turn thee back by the way by which thou camest." Thereafter the Assyrians were stricken by the plague. See under SICKNESS.)

11 The Lord searches all hearts, and understands every plan and thought. *I Chronicles* 28:9, RSV.

12 He [God] knoweth vain men: he seeth wickedness also. *Job* 11:11.

13 The Lord knoweth the thoughts of man. *Psalms* 94:11.

14 O Lord, thou hast searched me, and known me.
Thou knowest my downsitting and mine uprising, thou understandest my thought afar off. *Psalms* 139:1–2.

1 I know the things that come into your mind, every one of them. *Ezekiel* 11:5.

2 The eyes of the Lord are ten thousand times brighter than the sun, beholding all the ways of men. *Ecclesiasticus* 23:19.

3 The very hairs of your head are all numbered. *Matthew* 10:30.

4 Be not deceived; God is not mocked; for whatsoever a man soweth, that shall he also reap. *Galatians* 6:7.

GOD'S LOVE

5 Neither death, nor life, nor angels, nor principalities, nor powers, nor things present, nor things to come,
Nor height, nor depth, nor any other creature, shall be able to separate us from the love of God, which is in Christ Jesus our Lord. *Romans* 8:38–39.

GOD'S MERCY

6 The Lord thy God is a merciful God. *Deuteronomy* 4:31.

7 His mercy endureth forever. *I Chronicles* 16:34. (Repeated many times, especially in *Psalms*. *Psalms* 136 has this line in every verse. In the Revised Standard Version, the translation is, "His steadfast love endures for ever.")

8 I am like a green olive tree in the house of God: I trust in the mercy of God for ever and ever. *Psalms* 52:8.

9 As the heaven is high above the earth, so great is his mercy toward them that fear him. *Psalms* 103:11.

10 The mercy of the Lord is from everlasting to everlasting. *Psalms* 103:17.

11 Thou sparest all: for they are thine, O Lord, thou lover of souls. *Wisdom of Solomon* 11:26.

GOD'S PROVIDENCE

12 God is with thee in all that thou doest. *Genesis* 21:22.

13 I bore you on eagles' wings, and brought you unto myself. *Exodus* 19:4. (God to Moses on Mount Sinai.)

14 I sent an Angel before thee. *Exodus* 23:20.

15 My presence shall go with thee, and I will give thee rest. *Exodus* 33:14.

16 The Lord thy God hath blessed thee in all the works of thy hand. *Deuteronomy* 2:7.

1 Like an eagle that stirs up its nest, that flutters over its young, spreading out its wings, catching them, bearing them on its pinions, the Lord alone did lead him [the people of Israel]. *Deuteronomy* 32:11–12, RSV.

2 The Lord shall cover him all the day long. *Deuteronomy* 33:12. (Thus Moses describes God's care of Benjamin.)

3 The eternal God is thy refuge, and underneath are the everlasting arms. *Deuteronomy* 33:27.

4 I will be with thee: I will not fail thee, nor forsake thee. *Joshua* 1:5.

5 I will be his father, and he shall be my son. *II Samuel* 7:14. (God to the prophet Nathan, telling him to convey this message to King David.)

6 The Lord also will be a refuge for the oppressed, a refuge in times of trouble. *Psalms* 9:9.

7 The Lord is my shepherd; I shall not want.

He maketh me to lie down in green pastures: he leadeth me beside the still waters.

He restoreth my soul: he leadeth me in the paths of righteousness for his name's sake.

Yea, though I walk through the valley of the shadow of death, I will fear no evil: for thou art with me; thy rod and thy staff comfort me.

Thou preparest a table before me in the presence of mine enemies: thou anointest my head with oil; my cup runneth over.

Surely goodness and mercy shall follow me all the days of my life: and I will dwell in the house of the Lord for ever. *Psalms* 23.

8 The Lord shall preserve thee from all evil: he shall preserve thy soul.

The Lord shall preserve thy going out and thy coming in from this time forth, and even for evermore. *Psalms* 121:7–8.

9 If I take the wings of morning, and dwell in the uttermost parts of the sea;

Even there shall thy hand lead me, and thy right hand shall hold me. *Psalms* 139:9–10.

10 He shall feed his flock like a shepherd: he shall gather the lambs with his arm, and carry them in his bosom, and shall gently lead those that are with young. *Isaiah* 40:11. (This loving picture of the good shepherd is from a chapter prophesying the return of God's presence and guidance on earth after an era of war and destruction.)

11 As one whom his mother comforteth, so will I comfort you. *Isaiah* 66:13.

12 Thou art my hope in the day of evil. *Jeremiah* 17:17.

13 I will seek out my sheep, and will deliver them out of all places where they have been scattered in the cloudy and dark day. *Ezekiel* 34:12.

1 I will feed my flock, and I will cause them to lie down, saith the Lord God.

I will seek that which was lost . . . and will bind up that which was broken, and will strengthen that which was sick. *Ezekiel* 34:15–16.

2 Ye my flock, the flock of my pasture, are men, and I am your God. *Ezekiel* 34:31.

See also CHOSEN PEOPLE; SALVATION.

GOD'S VISION

3 Even the darkness is not dark to thee; the light is bright as the day; for darkness is as light with thee. *Psalms* 139:12, RSV.

4 He seeth from everlasting to everlasting. *Ecclesiasticus* 39:20.

See also GOD'S KNOWLEDGE OF HUMANS.

GOD'S WORD

5 The grass withereth, the flower fadeth: but the word of our God shall stand for ever. *Isaiah* 40:8.

6 O earth, earth, earth, hear the word of the Lord. *Jeremiah* 22:29.

7 Man shall not live by bread alone, but by every word that proceedeth out of the mouth of God. *Matthew* 4:4.

8 The word of God grew and multiplied. *Acts* 12:24.

9 The word of God is quick, and powerful, and sharper than any two-edged sword, piercing even to the dividing asunder of soul and spirit, and of the joints and marrow, and is a discerner of the thoughts and intents of the heart. *Hebrews* 4:12. (The passage helps to clarify the meaning of "word of God," which does not refer to a text, but rather to the spirit and power of God. In the opening hymn of the gospel of John—"In the beginning was the Word"—and elsewhere, the Word is identified with Christ. See under JESUS.)

10 The word of the Lord endureth for ever. *I Peter* 1:25.

GOD'S WORKS

11 What hath God wrought! *Numbers* 23:23. (Balaam is prophesying: "It shall be said of Jacob and of Israel, What hath God wrought!" This passage was suggested to Samuel Morse by Annie Ellsworth, daughter of the United States Commissioner of Patents, when he was looking for a text for the first telegraph message.)

1 The Lord gave, and the Lord hath taken away, blessed be the name of the Lord. *Job* 1:21.

2 Whatsoever God doeth, it shall be for ever: nothing can be put to it, nor any thing taken from it: and God doeth it, that men should fear before him. *Ecclesiastes* 3:14.

3 All the works of the Lord are exceeding good. *Ecclesiasticus* 39:16.

4 If this counsel or this work be of men, it will come to nought:
But if it be of God, ye cannot overthrow it. *Acts* 5:38–39.

See also CREATION.

GOD, TEMPTING

5 Thou shalt not tempt the Lord thy God. *Luke* 4:12. (Jesus to the devil in the wilderness.)

GOD, TRUST IN

6 Though he slay me, yet will I trust in him. *Job* 13:15.

7 I know that my Redeemer lives, and at last he will stand upon the earth;
And after my skin has been thus destroyed, then from my flesh I shall see God. *Job* 19:25–26, RSV.

8 Blessed are all they that put their trust in him. *Psalms* 2:12.

9 Trust in the Lord, and do good. *Psalms* 37:3, RSV.

10 O Lord of hosts, blessed is the man that trusteth in thee. *Psalms* 84:12.

11 Trust ye in the Lord for ever: for in the Lord JEHOVAH is everlasting strength. *Isaiah* 26:4.

12 Blessed is the man that trusteth in the Lord, and whose hope the Lord is.
For he shall be as a tree planted by the waters, and that spreadeth out her roots by the river, and shall not see when heat cometh, but her leaf shall be green; and shall not be careful in the year of drought, neither shall cease from yielding fruit. *Jeremiah* 17:7–8.

13 They that put their trust in him shall understand the truth: and such as be faithful in love shall abide with him. *Wisdom of Solomon* 3:9. (This book offers the first explicit promises of an immortal life with God for the righteous.)

See also FAITH.

GOD, WORSHIPING

1 O come, let us worship and bow down: let us kneel before the Lord our maker.

For he is our God; and we are the people of his pasture, and the sheep of his hand. *Psalms* 95:6–7.

2 Get thee hence, Satan: for it is written, Thou shalt worship the Lord thy God, and him only shalt thou serve. *Matthew* 4:10. (Jesus to the devil, who has tried to tempt him in the wilderness. The same injunction appears in *Luke*; see below.)

3 Thou shalt worship the Lord thy God, and him only shalt thou serve. *Luke* 4:8.

4 The hour cometh, and now is, when the true worshipers shall worship the Father in spirit and in truth: for the Father seeketh such to worship him.

God is a Spirit: and they that worship him must worship him in spirit and in truth. *John* 4:23–24.

GOODNESS

See VIRTUE

GOOD SAMARITAN

5 A certain man went down from Jerusalem to Jericho, and fell among thieves, which stripped him of his raiment, and wounded him, and departed, leaving him half dead. *Luke* 10:30. (In this parable, the victim is ignored by a priest and a Levite, but rescued by a Samaritan. The Samaritans were related to the Jews, but held somewhat different beliefs, and were despised as aliens and heretics. The priests and Levites were religious leaders.)

6 A certain Samaritan, as he journeyed, came where he was: and when he saw him, he had compassion on him. *Luke* 10:33.

7 Which now of these three, thinkest thou, was neighbor unto him that fell among the thieves?

And he said, He that showed mercy on him. Then said Jesus unto him, Go, and do thou likewise. *Luke* 10:36–37. (Jesus tells the parable of the Good Samaritan in answer to a lawyer who, referring to the commandment to love one's neighbor, asks: "Who is my neighbor?" *Luke* 10:29. Now Jesus asks him the same question, and the lawyer identifies the good Samaritan, who showed mercy.)

GOLDEN RULE

8 Do that to no man which thou hatest. *Tobit* 4:15. (The Golden Rule in an inverted form.)

1 All things whatsoever ye would that men should do to you, do ye even so to them. *Matthew* 7:12.

GOSSIP

2 Thou shalt not go up and down as a talebearer among thy people. *Leviticus* 19:16.

3 He that repeateth a matter separateth very friends. *Proverbs* 17:9.

4 The words of a talebearer are as wounds, and they go down into the innermost parts of the belly. *Proverbs* 18:8.

5 Whether it be to friend or foe, talk not of other men's lives. *Ecclesiasticus* 19:8.

See also TALK.

GOVERNMENT

6 Thou shalt provide out of all the people able men, such as fear God, men of truth, hating covetousness; and place such over them [the people of Israel], to be rulers of thousands, and rulers of hundreds, rulers of fifties, and rulers of tens. *Exodus* 18:21. (Jethro, the father-in-law of Moses, advising him to delegate authority in governing the Israelites. More is below.)

7 Every great matter they shall bring unto thee, but every small matter they shall judge: so shall it be easier for thyself, and they shall bear the burden with thee. *Exodus* 18:22.

8 Thou shalt not revile the gods, nor curse the ruler of thy people. *Exodus* 22:28.

9 I will not rule over you, neither shall my son rule over you: the Lord shall rule over you. *Judges* 8:23. (Gideon refusing an invitation to become king.)

10 In those days there was no king in Israel: every man did that which was right in his own eyes. *Judges* 21:25.

11 We will have a king over us;
That we also may be like all the nations; and that our king may judge us, and go out before us, and fight our battles. *I Samuel* 8:19–20. (The people of Israel importune Samuel, the last of the judges, to appoint a king. He has warned that a king will be oppressive, but they insist. The danger that inspired this insistence and that drew the tribes together was the presence of the Philistines. See also under WAR.)

12 All the people shouted, and said, God save the king. *I Samuel* 10:24. (The king is Saul. Under his rule, the tribes of Israel united, not to divide again until after the death of Solomon.)

1 He that ruleth over men must be just, ruling in the fear of God.

And he shall be as the light of the morning, when the sun riseth, even a morning without clouds; as the tender grass springing out of the earth by clear shining after rain. *II Samuel* 23:3–4. (Spoken by David near the end of his life. The Revised Standard Version reads, "When one rules justly over men, ruling in the fear of God, he dawns on them like the morning light, like the sun shining forth upon a cloudless morning, like rain that makes grass to sprout from the earth." Psalm 72 contains a similar passage.)

2 He [the king] shall judge the poor of the people, he shall save the children of the needy, and shall break in pieces the oppressor. *Psalms* 72:4. (This is from a royal coronation hymn, designated in the King James Version as "A Psalm for Solomon." The phrase "he shall judge the poor" means that he shall bring justice to the poor. A similar verse is at *Proverbs* 29:14: "The king that faithfully judgeth the poor, his throne shall be established for ever.")

3 Where there is no guidance, a people falls; but in an abundance of counselors there is safety. *Proverbs* 11:14, RSV.

4 A wise king scattereth the wicked, and bringeth the wheel over them. *Proverbs* 20:26. (For the king who assaulted the good as well as the wicked—with whips and scorpions—see under OPPRESSION.)

5 When the righteous are in authority, the people rejoice. *Proverbs* 29:2.

6 Where there is no vision, the people perish. *Proverbs* 29:18.

7 If it be a question of words and names . . . I will be no judge of such matters. *Acts* 18:15. (Gallio, proconsul of Achaia in Corinth, declining to involve himself in religious arguments and feuds, for "Gallio cared for none of those things." *Acts* 18:17. He was the brother of the philosopher Seneca.)

8 He shall rule them with a rod of iron. *Revelation* 2:27. (*He* refers to the faithful in general, sharing in the final triumph of Christ over the nations of the world.)

See also BRIBERY; JUDGES; LAW AND JUSTICE; OPPRESSION; PEOPLE, THE; POWER; TAXES.

GRACE

9 Where sin abounded, grace did much more abound. *Romans* 5:20.

GREATNESS

10 Great men are not always wise. *Job.* 32:9.

1 Let us now praise famous men. *Ecclesiasticus* 44:1. (Those to be praised are the great figures of the Old Testament, described as wise rulers and leaders; musicians and writers; and rich men who lived peacefully. In Hebrew a single phrase represents the English translations "famous men," "our fathers," and "men of mercy"; a more literal translation would be "men of piety.")

2 All these were honored in their generations, and were the glory of their times. *Ecclesiasticus* 44:7.

3 Ye are the light of the world. A city that is set on a hill cannot be hid.
Neither do men light a candle, and put it under a bushel, but on a candlestick; and it giveth light unto all that are in the house.
Let your light so shine before men, that they may see your good works, and glorify your Father, which is in heaven. *Matthew* 5:14–16. (From the Sermon on the Mount. In American history, the first verse is the source of John Winthrop's inspirational remarks at the founding of the Massachusetts Bay Colony in 1630: "For we must consider that we shall be a city upon a hill. The eyes of all people are upon us.")

4 One star differeth from another star in glory. *I Corinthians* 15:41.

5 Let us not be desirous of vain glory. *Galatians* 5:26.

See also AMBITION; SUCCESS.

GREED

6 He who is greedy for unjust gain makes trouble for his household. *Proverbs* 15:27, RSV.

7 Let not thy hand be stretched out to receive, and shut when thou shouldest pay. *Ecclesiasticus* 4:31.

8 Wheresoever the carcass is, there will the eagles be gathered together. *Matthew* 24:28.

9 Greedy of filthy lucre. *I Timothy* 3:8. (More at CLERGY.)

See also EVIL; MONEY; OPPRESSION; PROPERTY.

GUILT

10 Thou art the man. *II Samuel* 12:7. (With these words, the prophet Nathan, guided by God, accused King David of the murder of Uriah the Hittite, husband of Bathsheba. Nathan had told David a story of a rich man who owned many flocks and herds, and a poor man who "had nothing, save one little ewe lamb." *II Samuel* 12:3. The rich man, merely to feed a traveler, killed the cherished lamb. David, outraged, said that the rich man should die, for "he had no pity." *II Samuel* 12:6. Nathan then spoke the accusation.)

[1] Your own mouth condemns you, and not I; your own lips testify against you. *Job* 15:6, RSV

[2] The wicked flee when no man pursueth. *Proverbs* 28:1. (Often misquoted as "The guilty flee . . ." for example, by Robert Bork in his Supreme Court nomination confirmation hearings, 1987. More at VIRTUE.)

See also ATONEMENT.

HAIL MARY

See MARY

HAPPINESS

1 Thou shalt rejoice in every good thing which the Lord thy God hath given unto thee. *Deuteronomy* 26:11.

2 Rejoice, O ye nations. *Deuteronomy* 32:43.

3 Let the heart of them rejoice that seek the Lord. *I Chronicles* 16:10. (Also at *Psalms* 105:3.)

4 Let the heavens be glad, and let the earth rejoice. *I Chronicles* 16:31.

5 The morning stars sang together, and all the sons of God shouted for joy. *Job* 38:7.

6 Thou hast given him his heart's desire. *Psalms* 21:2.

7 Weeping may endure for a night, but joy cometh in the morning. *Psalms* 30:5.

8 Be glad in the Lord, and rejoice, ye righteous: and shout for joy, all ye that are upright in heart. *Psalms* 32:11.

9 Let the heavens be glad, and let the earth rejoice; let the sea roar, and all that fills it;

Let the field exult, and everything in it! Then shall all the trees of the wood sing for joy. *Psalms* 96:11–12, RSV.

10 I will be glad in the Lord. *Psalms* 104:34.

11 He that is of a merry heart hath a continual feast. *Proverbs* 15:15.

12 A merry heart doeth good like a medicine. *Proverbs* 17:22.

13 Sorrow and sighing shall flee away. *Isaiah* 35:10.

14 Sing, O heavens; and be joyful, O earth. *Isaiah* 49:13.

15 Judge none blessed before his death. *Ecclesiasticus* 11:28. (A common ancient saying. For example, "Call no man happy until he dies." Solon, quoted in Herodotus, *Histories*.)

16 I have learned, in whatsoever state I am, therewith to be content. *Philippians* 4:11.

See also EMOTIONS; HEDONISM; LAUGHTER; UNHAPPINESS.

HATE

[1] I hate them with perfect hatred: I count them mine enemies. *Psalms* 139:22.

[2] Hatred stirs up strife, but love covers all offenses. *Proverbs* 10:12, RSV.

[3] He that hideth hatred with lying lips, and he that uttereth a slander, is a fool. *Proverbs* 10:18.

[4] The bloodthirsty hate the upright. *Proverbs* 29:10.

See also EMOTIONS.

HAVES AND HAVE NOTS

[5] Unto every one that hath shall be given, and he shall have abundance: but from him that hath not shall be taken away even that which he hath. *Matthew* 25:29. (The same statement by Jesus is also at *Matthew* 13:12. This widely quoted verse reflects a universal tendency in human affairs, but not one usually associated with Christianity. In the earlier passage, the explanation is that those prepared to hear Christ's message will understand and benefit from his parables. In Chapter 25, this verse concludes the parable of the servants who were given money to care for while their master was gone. The one who fails to make more money with what he was given is cast into outer darkness. Far more typical of the biblical message is the quote below. See also REVOLUTION; RICH AND POOR.)

[6] He hath put down the mighty from their seats, and exalted them of low degree.

He hath filled the hungry with good things; and the rich he hath sent empty away. *Luke* 1:52–53. (Part of the Magnificat. See under MARY.)

See also RICH AND POOR.

HEALTH

[7] I will take sickness away from the midst of thee . . .

The number of thy days I will fulfill. *Exodus* 23:25–26.

[8] The Lord will take away from thee all sickness. *Deuteronomy* 7:15.

[9] Thou shalt conceive, and bear a son.

Now therefore beware, I pray thee, and drink not wine nor strong drink, and eat not any unclean thing. *Judges* 13:4–5. (An angel is speaking to the mother of Samson, giving advice that today we recognize as medically well-founded.)

[10] He keepeth all his bones: not one of them is broken. *Psalms* 34:20.

1 A sound heart is the life of the flesh. *Proverbs* 14:30.

2 Health and good estate of body are above all gold, and a strong body above infinite wealth. *Ecclesiasticus* 30:15.

3 There is no riches above a sound body. *Ecclesiasticus* 30:16.

4 The joyfulness of a man prolongeth his days. *Ecclesiasticus* 30:22.

See also BODY; DOCTORS AND MEDICINE; SICKNESS.

HEARING

5 Who hath ears to hear, let him hear. *Matthew* 13:9 and 13:43. (Jesus to his disciples. The meaning is that those who have not hardened themselves with worldly and sinful concerns will understand what Jesus says. See also PARABLES.)

6 Be swift to hear, slow to speak. *James* 1:19. (More at ANGER.)

See also BODY.

HEART

See EMOTIONS

HEAVEN

7 How lovely is thy dwelling place, O Lord of hosts!
My soul longs, yea, faints for the courts of the Lord. *Psalms* 84:1–2, RSV.

8 I had rather be a doorkeeper in the house of my God, than to dwell in the tents of wickedness. *Psalms* 84:10. (More at GOD.)

9 Sorrows are passed, and in the end is shewed the treasure of immortality. *II Esdras* 8:54.

10 The souls of the righteous are in the hand of God, and there shall no torment touch them.
In the sight of the unwise they seemed to die: and their departure is taken for misery,
And their going from us to be utter destruction: but they are in peace.
. . . having been a little chastised, they shall be greatly rewarded: for God proved them and found them worthy for himself. *Wisdom of Solomon* 3:1–3, 5. (The first clear statement of an eternal, God-given reward for the righteous.)

1 Except your righteousness shall exceed the righteousness of the scribes and the Pharisees, ye shall in no case enter into the kingdom of heaven. *Matthew* 5:20. (From the Sermon on the Mount. The scribes, who were learned in the law, are often associated in the New Testament with the priests and the Pharisees. The scribes represented a legalistic approach to religion. The Pharisees, a highly influential and popular religious group, also adhered strictly to sectarian rules. They are usually shown in to the New Testament as rigid and hypocritical, although in doctrine they were quite close to Christ's teachings. For example, they believed that the soul survives the death of the body, and is punished or rewarded according to the life the person led.)

2 Lay up for yourselves treasures in heaven, where neither moth nor rust doth corrupt, and where thieves do not break through nor steal.
For where your treasure is, there will your heart be also. *Matthew* 6:20–21. (See also VALUE.)

3 Not every one that saith unto me, Lord, Lord, shall enter into the kingdom of heaven; but he that doeth the will of my Father which is in heaven. *Matthew* 7:21.

4 The kingdom of heaven is at hand. *Matthew* 10:7.

5 The kingdom of heaven is like to a grain of mustard seed, which a man took, and sowed in his field:
Which indeed is the least of all seeds: but when it is grown, it is the greatest among herbs, and becometh a tree, so that the birds of the air come and lodge in the branches thereof. *Matthew* 13:31–32.

6 The kingdom of heaven is like unto treasure hid in a field. *Matthew* 13:44.

7 So the last shall be first, and the first last: for many be called, but few chosen. *Matthew* 20:16. (This concludes the parable of the householder who pays the same wage to laborers who began work at the end of the day as to those who started in the morning. See also *Matthew* 22:14.)

8 Well done, thou good and faithful servant . . . enter thou into the joy of thy lord. *Matthew* 25:21.

9 Today shalt thou be with me in paradise. *Luke* 23:43. (More at JESUS: PASSION AND DEATH.)

10 In my Father's house are many mansions: if it were not so, I would have told you. I go to prepare a place for you. *John* 14:2. (Jesus in farewell to the apostles. More below.)

11 I will come again, and receive you unto myself; that where I am, there ye may be also. *John* 14:3.

12 The wages of sin is death; but the gift of God is eternal life through Jesus Christ our Lord. *Romans* 6:23.

1 Here have we no continuing city, but we seek one to come. *Hebrews* 13:14.

2 Ye shall receive a crown of glory that fadeth not away. *I Peter* 5:4.

3 To him that overcometh will I give to eat of the tree of life, which is in the midst of the paradise of God. *Revelation* 2:7. (At *Revelation* 3:5, God promises, "I will not blot out his name out of the book of life.")

4 There shall be no night there. *Revelation* 22:5.

See also SALVATION.

HEAVENS AND SKY

5 And God said, let there be lights in the firmament of the heaven to divide the day from the night; and let them be for signs, and for seasons, and for days, and years. *Genesis* 1:14.

6 I do set my bow in the cloud. *Genesis* 9:13. (More on the rainbow at NOAH AND THE ARK.)

7 The heavens declare the glory of God; and the firmament showeth his handywork. *Psalms* 19:1.

8 In them [the heavens, the stars] hath he set a tabernacle for the sun,
Which is as a bridegroom coming out of his chamber, and rejoiceth as strong man to run a race.
His going forth is from the end of the heaven, and his circuit unto the ends of it: and there is nothing hid from the heat thereof. *Psalms* 19:4–6.

9 The sun also ariseth. *Ecclesiastes* 1:5. (The entire passage is given at VANITY.)

10 Truly the light is sweet, and a pleasant thing it is for the eyes to behold the sun. *Ecclesiastes* 11:7.

See also STARS.

HEDONISM

11 He that loveth pleasure shall be a poor man: he that loveth wine and oil shall not be rich. *Proverbs* 21:17.

12 I said to myself, "Come now, I will make a test of pleasure; enjoy yourself." But behold, this also was vanity. *Ecclesiastes* 2:1, RSV. (See also VANITY and the quotes from *Ecclesiastes* below.)

13 Every man should eat and drink, and enjoy the good of all his labor, it is the gift of God. *Ecclesiastes* 3:13.

1 The heart of fools is in the house of mirth. *Ecclesiastes* 7:4. (Nevertheless, the author ultimately recommends enjoyment of life as the best course in a sorrowful world. See below.)

2 Then I commended mirth, because a man hath no better thing under the sun, than to eat, and to drink, and to be merry. *Ecclesiastes* 8:15. (The somewhat contradictory statements in *Ecclesiastes* result from the tension between the writer's intellectual conviction that there is no lasting worth to be found in life, and his emotional enjoyment of life, both work and play. He concludes that life and pleasure are gifts of God and we should accept them as such. See also VANITY.)

3 Let us eat and drink; for to morrow we shall die. *Isaiah* 22:13. (The classic statement of hedonism, repeated almost exactly at *I Corinthians* 15:32.)

4 Woe to them that are at ease in Zion. *Amos* 6:1. (Amos, the simple shepherd-prophet, warned the pleasure-loving people of Israel that God would destroy them. The people he meant were "[Those] who lie upon beds of ivory, and stretch themselves upon their couches, and eat the lambs out of the flock, and the calves out of the midst of the stall." *Amos* 6:4.)

5 Let no flower of spring pass by us.
Let us crown ourselves with rosebuds, before they be withered. *Wisdom of Solomon* 2:7–8. (The ultimate source for Robert Herrick's "Gather ye rosebuds while ye may,/ Old Time is still a-flying; And this same flower that smiles today,/ Tomorrow will be dying." *To the Virgins, To Make Much of Time.* Here, however, the view is rejected as "ungodly" and unduly pessimistic. This book of the Bible is directed toward answering the doubts and pessimism expressed in *Ecclesiastes.* See above.)

See also DISSIPATION.

HELL

6 Hell hath enlarged herself, and opened her mouth without measure: and their glory, and their multitude, and their pomp, and he that rejoiceth, shall descend into it. *Isaiah* 5:14.

7 The axe is laid unto the root of the trees: therefore every tree which bringeth not forth good fruit is hewn down, and cast into the fire. *Matthew* 3:10.

8 Wide is the gate, and broad is the way, that leadeth to destruction, and many there be which go in thereat. *Matthew* 7:13.

9 The children of the kingdom shall be cast out into outer darkness: there shall be weeping and gnashing of teeth. *Matthew* 8:12. (See also the quote below, where the phrase is repeated.)

[1] At the end of the world: the angels shall come forth, and sever the wicked from among the just,

And shall cast them into the furnace of fire: there shall be wailing and gnashing of teeth. *Matthew* 13:49–50.

[2] Between us and you there is a great gulf fixed. *Luke* 16:26. (Abraham, representing God, to the rich man in hell. From the parable of the rich man and the beggar Lazarus.)

[3] I saw a star fall from heaven unto the earth: and to him was given the key of the bottomless pit. *Revelation* 9:1.

See also DEVIL.

HISTORY

[4] There is no enduring remembrance, seeing that in the days to come all will have been long forgotten. *Ecclesiastes* 2:16, RSV.

[5] Till heaven and earth pass, one jot or one tittle shall in no wise pass from the law, till all be fulfilled. *Matthew* 5:18.

See also PAST.

HOLY GHOST

See BAPTISM; PENTECOST; SPIRIT; SPIRITUAL BIRTH

HOME

[6] God gives the desolate a home to dwell in. *Psalms* 68:6, RSV. (In the King James Version, the reading is: "God setteth the solitary in families.")

[7] He that troubleth his own house shall inherit the wind. *Proverbs* 11:29.

[8] Better is a dry morsel with quiet than a house full of feasting with strife. *Proverbs* 17:1, RSV. (Also, "It is better to dwell in a corner of the housetop; than with a brawling woman in a wide house." *Proverbs* 21:9.)

[9] By wisdom a house is built, and by understanding it is established;

By knowledge the rooms are filled with all precious and pleasant riches. *Proverbs* 24:3–4, RSV.

[10] Like a bird that strays from its nest, is a man who strays from his home. *Proverbs* 27:8, RSV.

[11] Build ye houses, and dwell in them; and plant gardens, and eat the fruit of them. *Jeremiah* 29:5, RSV. (Also *Jeremiah* 29:28).

[12] Be not as a lion in thy house, nor frantic among thy servants. *Ecclesiasticus* 4:30.

HONESTY

1 Thou shalt not raise a false report. *Exodus* 23:1 (More in LAW categories.)

2 Ye shall not steal, neither deal falsely, neither lie one to another. *Leviticus* 19:11.

3 How forceful are honest words! *Job* 6:25, RSV.

4 He that hath clean hands shall be stronger and stronger. *Job* 17:9.

5 A just weight and balance are the Lord's. *Proverbs* 16:11.

See also COVERUP; DECEIT AND LIES; JUSTICE AND FAIRNESS.

HONOR

6 Honor shall uphold the humble in spirit. *Proverbs* 29:23.

7 Leave not a stain in thine honor. *Ecclesiasticus* 33:22.

See also REPUTATION.

HOPE

8 Hope deferred makes the heart sick, but a desire fulfilled is a tree of life. *Proverbs* 13:12, RSV.

9 Ye prisoners of hope. *Zechariah* 9:12.

10 The hope of the ungodly is like dust that is blown away with the wind . . . and passeth away as the remembrance of a guest that tarrieth but a day. *Wisdom of Solomon* 5:14.

11 Dreams lift up fools. *Ecclesiasticus* 34:1.

12 Who against hope believed in hope. *Romans* 4:18.

13 We are saved by hope. *Romans* 8:24.

14 Hope to the end. *I Peter* 1:13.

See also EMOTIONS.

HOSPITALITY

15 Be content, I pray thee, and tarry all night, and let thine heart be merry. *Judges* 19:6.

16 The king made a feast unto all the people that were present in Shushan the palace, both unto great and small, seven days, in the court of the garden of the king's palace;

Where were white, green, and blue hangings, fastened with cords of fine linen and purple to silver rings and pillars of marble: the beds [couches] were of gold and silver, upon a pavement of red, and blue, and white, and black, marble.

And they gave them drink in vessels of gold . . .

And the drinking was according to the law; none did compel. *Esther* 1:5–8. (Ahasuerus, or Xerxes I, is the king. The palace is the winter residence built by his father, Darius I, at Susa. The description is quite accurate. In the Revised Standard Version, the pavement is described in more detail as "a mosiac pavement or porphyry, marble, mother-of-pearl, and precious stones.")

1 Eat, O friends; drink, yea, drink abundantly, O beloved. *Song of Solomon* 5:1.

2 Go ye therefore into the highways, and as many as ye shall find, bid to the marriage. *Matthew* 22:9.

3 Bring in hither the poor, and the maimed, and the halt, and the blind. *Luke* 14:21. (From the parable of the man who prepared a banquet, but all those invited were too busy to come. So he sent his servant to bring others. The banquet represents the kingdom of heaven, which Christ is offering to mankind.)

4 Go out into the highways and hedges, and compel them to come in. *Luke* 14:23.

5 [Be] given to hospitality. *Romans* 12:13.

6 Be not forgetful to entertain strangers: for thereby some have entertained angels unawares. *Hebrews* 13:2.

HUMAN BEINGS

7 Dust thou art, and unto dust shalt thou return. *Genesis* 3:19. (For more of this passage, see under ADAM AND EVE.)

8 In the day that God created man, in the likeness of God made he him. *Genesis* 5:1.

9 There were giants in the earth in those days. *Genesis* 6:4.

10 The imagination of man's heart is evil from his youth. *Genesis* 8:21.

11 What is man that thou dost make so much of him? *Job* 7:17, RSV. (Job to God. See also *Psalms* 144:3.)

12 Man that is born of a woman is of few days, and full of trouble.
He cometh forth like a flower, and is cut down. *Job* 14:1–2.

13 Yea, the stars are not pure in his [God's] sight. How much less man, that is a worm? and the son of man, which is a worm? *Job* 25:5–6.

[1] What is man that thou [God] art mindful of him, and the son of man that thou dost care for him?
Yet thou hast made him little less than God, and dost crown him with glory and honor.
Thou hast given him dominion over the works of thy hands. *Psalms* 8:4–6, RSV.

[2] His soul shall dwell at ease; and his seed shall inherit the earth. *Psalms* 25:13.

[3] They were but flesh; a wind that passeth away, and cometh not again. *Psalms* 78:39.

[4] As for man, his days are like grass; he flourishes like a flower of the field;
For the wind passes over it, and it is gone, and its place knows it no more. *Psalms* 103:15–16, RSV.

[5] I said in my haste, All men are liars. *Psalms* 116:11.

[6] I am fearfully and wonderfully made. *Psalms* 139:14.

[7] The glory of young men is their strength: and the beauty of old men is the gray head. *Proverbs* 20:29.

[8] As he came forth of his mother's womb, naked shall he return to go as he came, and shall take nothing of his labor. *Ecclesiastes* 5:15. (A similar passage, from *Job,* is given under LIFE.)

[9] All our righteousnesses are as filthy rags; and we all do fade as a leaf. *Isaiah* 64:6.

[10] We are the clay, and thou [God] our potter; and we are all the work of thy hand. *Isaiah* 64:8.

[11] The heart is deceitful above all things, and desperately wicked: who can know it? *Jeremiah* 17:9.

[12] Ye are the sons of the living God. *Hosea* 1:10.

[13] Have we not all one father? hath not one God created us? *Malachi* 2:10.

[14] God created man to be immortal, and made him to be an image of his own eternity. *Wisdom of Solomon* 2:23. (In the next verse, the existence of death is attributed to sin—the "envy of the devil." The righteous are promised eternal life with God.)

[15] All flesh consorteth according to kind, and a man will cleave to his like. *Ecclesiasticus* 13:16.

[16] Ye are the salt of the earth. *Matthew* 5:13. (In the Revised Standard Version, the quote continues, "But if the salt has lost its taste, how shall its saltness be restored? It is no longer good for anything." This is a warning to those who are not meeting the mission God has set for them. The passage is from the Sermon on the Mount.)

1 We are the children of God:
And if children, then heirs; heirs of God, and joint-heirs with Christ. *Romans* 8:16–17.

2 The first man is of the earth, earthy. *I Corinthians* 15:47. (St. Paul on human nature. The second man is the person resurrected in Christ.)

3 Speak every man truth with his neighbor: for we are members one of another. *Ephesians* 4:25.

See also EMOTIONS; GOD'S KNOWLEDGE OF HUMANS; LIFE; PEOPLE.

HUMILITY

4 I am the least in my father's house. *Judges* 6:15. (Gideon to an angel sent by God.)

5 Before honor is humility. *Proverbs* 15:33.

6 The greater thou art, the more humble thyself. *Ecclesiasticus* 3:18.

7 The prayer of the humble pierceth the clouds. *Ecclesiasticus* 35:17.

8 Do not be haughty, but associate with the lowly; never be conceited. *Romans* 12:16, RSV. (In the King James Version, the last phrase is translated, "Be not wise in your own conceits.")

9 [Desire the] ornament of a meek and quiet spirit. *I Peter* 3:4.

See also MEEK, THE; MOSES.

HUNGER

See POVERTY AND HUNGER

HYPOCRISY

10 What is the hope of the hypocrite, though he hath gained, when God taketh away his soul? *Job* 27:8.

11 [Prophets] that bite with their teeth, and cry, Peace. *Micah* 3:5. (God does not intend to answer the prayers of such people.)

12 Woe unto you, scribes and Pharisees, hypocrites! for ye are like unto whited sepulchres, which indeed appear beautiful outward, but are within full of dead men's bones, and of all uncleanness. *Matthew* 23:27. (The Pharisees were widely respected for their piety, but are remembered now primarily from this verse.)

13 Beware of the scribes . . . which devour widows' houses, and for a pretense make long prayers. *Mark* 12:38–40.

IDENTITY

1 I am what I am. *I Corinthians* 15:10. (More at PAUL.)

IDLENESS

2 Idleness teacheth much evil. *Ecclesiasticus* 33:27.

See also LAZINESS; LEISURE.

IDOLS

3 Their idols are like scarecrows in a cucumber field, and they cannot speak; they have to be carried, for they cannot walk. Be not afraid of them, for they cannot do evil; neither is it in them to do good. *Jeremiah* 10:5, RSV.

4 They have mouths, but they speak not; eyes have they, but they see not.
They have ears, but they hear not. *Psalms* 115:5–6. (Also at *Psalms* 135:16.

5 The idols of the heathen are silver and gold, the work of men's hands. *Psalms* 135:15.

6 In that day a man shall cast his idols of silver, and his idols of gold . . . to the moles and to the bats. *Isaiah* 2:20. (The day is the era when the Lord will come to judge the nations of the world.)

IGNORANCE

7 If the blind lead the blind, both shall fall into the ditch. *Matthew* 15:14. (Later, Jesus speaks of "blind guides, which strain at a gnat, but swallow a camel." *Matthew* 23:24.)

See also INFORMATION; LEARNING.

ILLNESS

See SICKNESS

IMMANUEL

8 The Lord himself shall give you [the house of David] a sign; Behold, a virgin shall conceive, and bear a son, and shall call his name Immanuel. *Isaiah* 7:14. (*Immanuel* means "God is with us." In the New Testament,

this prophecy became associated with the person of Jesus. See *Matthew* 1:23, 7:14. However, although Isaiah wrote of a great king to come from the house of David—see MESSIAH—the Immanuel prophecy in its original context is believed by scholars to refer to a more immediate sign of God's presence and providence. The prophecy arises in a conversation between Isaiah and King Ahaz, a skeptic who refused to ask God for a sign, but who nevertheless was given this rather obscure one. The child, according to the prophecy, is someone who will be born and mature in the course of the events described in this book of the Bible.)

IMMORTALITY

See HEAVEN; RESURRECTION OF THE DEAD

INDECISION

1 How long halt ye between two opinions? *I Kings* 18:21. (The Revised Standard Version reads, "How long will you go limping with two different opinions?")

2 Their heart is divided; now shall they be found faulty. *Hosea* 10:2.

3 Woe be to fearful hearts, and faint hands, and the sinner that goeth two ways! *Ecclesiasticus* 2:12.

See also CHOICE.

INDEPENDENCE

4 Better is the life of a poor man in a mean cottage, than delicate fare in another man's house. *Ecclesiasticus* 29:22.

5 Give not thy son and wife, thy brother and friend, power over thee while thou livest, and give not thy goods to another: lest it repent thee, and thou entreat for the same again. *Ecclesiasticus* 33:19.

See also FREEDOM; SELF-RELIANCE.

INFORMATION

6 Be not ignorant of any thing in a great matter or small. *Ecclesiasticus* 5:15.

See also IGNORANCE; LEARNING.

INGRATITUDE

7 Wherefore have ye rewarded evil for good? *Genesis* 44:4.

INITIATIVE

1 Ask, and it shall be given you; seek, and ye shall find; knock, and it shall be opened unto you:

For every one that asketh receiveth; and he that seeketh findeth; and to him that knocketh it shall be opened. *Matthew* 7:7–8.

INJUSTICE

2 I cry out of wrong, but I am not heard: I cry aloud, but there is no judgment. *Job* 19:7.

See also JUSTICE AND FAIRNESS; LAW AND JUSTICE.

INNOCENCE

3 Deliver not the soul of thy turtledove unto the multitude of the wicked. *Psalms* 74:19.

4 Blessed are the pure in heart: for they shall see God. *Matthew* 5:8.

5 A conscience void of offense toward God and toward men. *Acts* 24:16.

6 Unto the pure all things are pure. *Titus* 1:15.

See also VIRTUE.

INSOMNIA

See SLEEP AND SLEEPLESSNESS

IRRITATIONS

7 They shall be as thorns in your sides. *Judges* 2:3. (The Lord is speaking to the Israelites about the Canaanites. In the New Testament a "thorn in the flesh" afflicting St. Paul is mentioned at *II Corinthians* 12:7.)

8 Lord, how are they increased that trouble me! *Psalms* 3:1.

ISAAC

9 Behold the fire and the wood: but where is the lamb for a burnt offering? [Isaac is speaking to his father, Abraham.]

And Abraham said, My son, God will provide himself a lamb for a burnt offering. *Genesis* 22:7–8. (Abraham, believing he is obeying God's wish, intends to sacrifice Isaac.)

1 Now I know that thou fearest God, seeing thou hast not withheld thy son, thine only son from me. *Genesis* 22:12. (This troubling story has been interpreted in varying ways by biblical scholars. Historically, it represents a rejection of human sacrifice. For the Jewish philosopher Maimonides, the story represents the extreme of loyalty and faith that God can rightfully demand. Similarly, the Christian philosopher Kierkegaard, in *Fear and Trembling,* spoke of Abraham as a "knight of faith," prepared to give up not only his son but his moral convictions for love and fear of God.)

ISHMAEL

2 He will be a wild man; his hand will be against every man, and every man's hand against him. *Genesis* 16:12. ("Call me Ishmael" are the opening words of *Moby Dick.* For his hero Melville chose a name suggesting a man alienated from the world, but also blessed. The biblical Ishmael was watched over by an angel of the Lord, lived to a venerable age, and was survived by the prosperous and powerful family he founded. He appears in the Koran, in which it is said that Ishmael and Abraham established the shrine of Kaaba at Mecca, and that Ishmael is the forefather of the Arabs.)

ISRAEL

See CANAAN; CHOSEN PEOPLE; JACOB

JACOB

1 Leah was tender eyed [her eyes were weak]; but Rachel was beautiful and well favored.

And Jacob loved Rachel; and said, I will serve thee seven years for Rachel thy younger daughter. *Genesis* 29:17–18. (He is speaking to his uncle Laban.)

2 Jacob served seven years for Rachel; and they seemed unto him but a few days, for the love he had to her. *Genesis* 29:20. (He had to serve another seven years, though, for Laban tricked him into marrying Rachel's older sister, Leah, first.)

3 Jacob was left alone; and there wrestled a man with him until the breaking of the day. *Genesis* 32:24.

4 Thy name shall be called no more Jacob, but Israel: for as a prince hast thou power with God and with men, and hast prevailed. *Genesis* 32:28. (*Israel* means "contender with God"; it is now apparent that the stranger with whom Jacob has wrestled is God. In this mysterious episode, the nation of Israel is born; Jacob/Israel's twelve sons correspond to the twelve tribes of Israel.)

5 And Jacob called the name of the place Peniel: for I have seen God face to face, and my life is preserved. *Genesis* 32:30. (*Peniel* means "face of God.")

6 God spake unto Israel in the visions of the night, and said, Jacob, Jacob. And he said, Here am I.

And he said, I am God, the God of thy father: fear not to go down into Egypt; for I will make of thee a great nation. *Genesis* 46:2–3.

7 When Jacob had made an end of commanding his sons, he gathered up his feet into the bed and yielded up the ghost, and was gathered unto his people. *Genesis* 49:33.

JACOB AND ESAU

8 And the boys grew: and Esau was a cunning hunter, a man of the field; and Jacob was a plain man, dwelling in tents.

And Isaac loved Esau, because he did eat of his venison: but Rebekah loved Jacob. *Genesis* 25:27–28. (*Esau* is also called *Edom;* traditionally there was enmity between the Hebrews and the Edomites, who lived in Edom, or Seir, semi-desert land south of the Dead Sea.)

9 Esau said to Jacob, Feed me, I pray thee, with that same red pottage; for I am faint. *Genesis* 25:30.

1 Jacob said, Sell me this day thy birthright. *Genesis* 25:31.

2 Then Jacob gave Esau bread and pottage of lentiles; and he did eat and drink, and rose up, and went his way: thus Esau despised his birthright. *Genesis* 25:34. (The lentil plant, related to the weed vetch, grew well in the Middle East, and was especially prized in Alexandria in Egypt. The lentils were used in bread and to make porridge.)

3 Thy brother came with subtilty, and hath taken away thy blessing. *Genesis* 27:35.

JACOB'S LADDER

4 He took of the stones of that place, and put them for his pillows, and lay down in that place to sleep.

And he dreamed, and behold a ladder set up on the earth, and the top of it reached to heaven; and behold the angels of God ascending and descending on it.

And, behold, the Lord stood above it. *Genesis* 28:11–13.

5 I am with thee, and will keep thee in all places whither thou goest. *Genesis* 28:15.

6 Surely the Lord is in this place; and I knew it not. *Genesis* 28:16.

7 This is none other but the house of God, and this is the gate of heaven. *Genesis* 28:17.

8 This stone, which I have set for a pillar, shall be God's house; and of all that thou shalt give me I surely give the tenth unto thee. *Genesis* 28:22.

JAEL

See SISERA AND JAEL

JEALOUSY

9 Jealousy is the rage of a man: therefore he will not spare in the day of vengeance. *Proverbs* 6:34.

10 The ear of jealousy heareth all things. *Wisdom of Solomon* 1:10.

See also ENVY.

JEREMIAH

11 A man of strife and a man of contention. *Jeremiah* 15:10. (Jeremiah's description of himself, an outcast among his own people for prophesying the destruction of Judah. Jeremiah warned that the alliance with Egypt and the revolt against Babylon would end in disaster. After the Babylonians overran Jerusalem in 586 B.C., survivors fled to Egypt. They took with them Jeremiah and Baruch, his scribe, disciple, and friend.)

JERUSALEM

See CITIES; ZION

JESUS

1 Lo, the heavens were opened unto him, and he [Jesus] saw the Spirit of God descending like a dove, and lighting upon him:

And lo a voice from heaven, saying, This is my beloved Son, in whom I am well pleased. *Matthew* 3:16–17. (This revelation of the identity of Jesus occurs immediately following his baptism by John the Baptist. See also BAPTISM. God speaks the same words again at the Transfiguration, at *Matthew* 17:5.)

2 I am not come to destroy, but to fulfill. *Matthew* 5:17.

3 The foxes have holes, and the birds of the air have nests; but the Son of man hath not where to lay his head. *Matthew* 8:20.

4 Follow me; and let the dead bury their dead. *Matthew* 8:22. (Jesus to the disciple who wanted to follow him but asked, "Suffer me first to go and bury my father.")

5 What manner of man is this, that even the winds and the sea obey him! *Matthew* 8:27. (The disciples after Jesus calmed the tempest on the Sea of Galilee. Also at *Mark* 4:41. See MIRACLES OF JESUS.)

6 He that receiveth me receiveth him that sent me. *Matthew* 10:40.

7 Every one who acknowledges me before men, I also will acknowledge before my Father who is in heaven; but whoever denies me before men, I also will deny before my Father who is in heaven. *Matthew* 10:32–33, RSV.

8 He that taketh not his cross, and followeth after me is not worthy of me.

He that findeth his life shall lose it: and he that loseth his life for my sake shall find it. *Matthew* 10:38–39. (This follows closely on the disturbing "I came not to send peace, but a sword," at *Matthew* 10:34. It is one of a series of warnings by Jesus in this chapter of the gospel that, while he brings new life and a new religious vision to the world, to follow him is difficult and dangerous. The passage is closely repeated at *Matthew* 16:24–25).

9 All things are delivered unto me of my Father: and no man knoweth the Son, but the Father; neither knoweth any man the Father, save the Son, and he to whomsoever the Son will reveal him. *Matthew* 11:27. (The first fully explicit statement by Jesus describing himself as the intermediary between humankind and God the Father.)

10 I am meek and lowly in heart. *Matthew* 11:29.

11 Is not this the carpenter's son? *Matthew* 13:55.

1 Be of a good cheer; it is I; be not afraid. *Matthew* 14:27. (Jesus reassuring his disciples, who are frightened when they see him walking on the Sea of Galilee. See also MIRACLES OF JESUS.)

2 They . . . worshiped him, saying, Of a truth thou art the Son of God. *Matthew* 14:33. (The first complete acknowledgment by the disciples of the divinity of Jesus. It follows the miracle of walking on the water. See above and MIRACLES OF JESUS.)

3 I am not sent but unto the lost sheep of the house of Israel. *Matthew* 15:24. (Jesus, refusing to help the woman of Canaan. He quickly relents.)

4 Jesus taketh Peter, James, and John his brother, and bringeth them up into a high mountain apart,

And was transfigured before them: and his face did shine as the sun, and his raiment was white as the light. *Matthew* 17:1–2. (Moses and Elijah appear with Jesus. When Peter suggests building a tabernacle to each, a voice from heaven says, "This is my beloved Son, in whom I am well pleased." *Matthew* 17:5. The divine voice and the words are the same as at the baptism of Jesus by John the Baptist.)

5 The Son of man is come to save that which was lost. *Matthew* 18:11.

6 Thy King cometh unto thee, meek, and sitting upon an ass. *Matthew* 21:5. (The ass symbolized peace. See also ANIMALS.)

7 Heaven and earth shall pass away, but my words shall not pass away. *Matthew* 24:35.

8 Inasmuch as ye have done it unto one of the least of these my brethren, ye have done it unto me. *Matthew* 25:40. (Jesus identifies himself with the hungry, the sick, the stranger, the prisoner. See also GIVING.)

9 There cometh one mightier than I after me, the latchet of whose shoes I am not worthy to stoop down and unloose. *Mark* 1:7. (John the Baptist, speaking of Jesus.)

10 The Spirit of the Lord is upon me, because he hath anointed me to preach the gospel to the poor. *Luke* 4:18. (Jesus at the outset of his ministry, quoting *Isaiah* 61:1.)

11 Blessed be the King that cometh in the name of the Lord: peace in heaven and glory in the highest. *Luke* 19:38. (The followers of Jesus praising him as he enters Jerusalem. When the Pharisees advise Jesus to rebuke them, he answers, "If these should hold their peace, the stones would immediately cry out." *Luke* 19:40.)

12 In the beginning was the Word, and the Word was with God, and the Word was God.

The same was in the beginning with God.

All things were made by him; and without him was not any thing made that was made.

In him was life; and the life was the light of men.
And the light shineth in darkness; and the darkness comprehended it not.
There was a man sent from God, whose name was John.
The same came for a witness, to bear witness of the Light, that all men through him might believe.
He was not that Light, but was sent to bear witness of that Light.
That was the true Light, which lighteth every man that cometh into the world.
He was in the world, and the world was made by him, and the world knew him not.
He came unto his own, and his own received him not.
But as many as received him, to them gave he power to become the sons of God, even to them that believe on his name:
Which were born, not of blood, nor of the will of the flesh, nor of the will of man, but of God.
And the Word was made flesh, and dwelt among us, (and we beheld the glory, the glory as of the only begotten of the Father,) full of grace and truth. *John* 1:1–14.

1 This is he of whom I spoke. *John* 1:15. (John the Baptist, identifying Jesus.)

2 Behold the Lamb of God, which taketh away the sin of the world. *John* 1:29. (John the Baptist, speaking of Jesus.)

3 Hereafter ye shall see heaven open, and the angels of God ascending and descending upon the Son of man. *John* 1:51. (Jesus promises his disciple Nathanael that he will see the divine revelation on JUDGMENT DAY.)

4 God so loved the world, that he gave his only begotten Son, that whosoever believeth in him should not perish, but have everlasting life.
For God sent not his Son into the world to condemn the world; but that the world through him might be saved. *John* 3:16–17.

5 The Father loveth the Son, and hath given all things into his hand.
He that believeth on the Son hath everlasting life. *John* 3:35–36.

6 The Father judgeth no man, but hath committed all judgment unto the Son:
That all men should honor the Son, even as they honor the Father. He that honoreth not the Son honoreth not the Father which hath sent him. *John* 5:22.

7 I seek not mine own will, but the will of the Father which hath sent me. *John* 5:30.

8 I am the bread of life: he that cometh to me shall never hunger; and he that believeth on me shall never thirst. *John* 6:35.

1 If any man thirst, let him come unto me, and drink. *John* 7:37.

2 Never man spoke like this man. *John* 7:46.

3 I am the light of the world: he that followeth me shall not walk in darkness, but shall have the light of life. *John* 8:12.

4 I must work the works of him that sent me. *John* 9:4. (More at WORK.)

5 I am the door: by me if any man enter in, he shall be saved. *John* 10:9.

6 I am come that they might have life, and that they might have it more abundantly. *John* 10:10.

7 I am the good shepherd: the good shepherd giveth his life for the sheep. *John* 10:11. (This is the culmination of the theme of the special role of the shepherd. See also SHEPHERDS.)

8 I am the good shepherd; I know my own and my own know me. *John* 10:14, RSV.

9 As the Father knoweth me, even so know I the Father: and I lay down my life for the sheep. *John* 10:15.

10 Other sheep I have, which are not of this fold. *John* 10:16. (More at RELIGION.)

11 I and my Father are one. *John* 10:30.

12 I am the resurrection, and the life. *John* 11:25. (More at FAITH.)

13 Jesus wept. *John* 11:35. (From the story of the resurrection of Lazarus. See MIRACLES OF JESUS.)

14 When they heard that Jesus was coming to Jerusalem,

[The people] took branches of palm trees, and went forth to meet him, and cried, Hosanna: Blessed is the King of Israel that cometh in the name of the Lord. *John* 12:13.

15 Yet a little while is the light with you. Walk while ye have the light, lest darkness come upon you. *John* 12:35. (Jesus gently urging his disciples to take advantage of the little time that remains in his life.)

16 Having loved his own which were in the world, he loved them unto the end. *John* 13:1. (John, most clearly of all the evangelists, states the virtue of love in Christian life. This passage occurs during the LAST SUPPER. See also *John* 13:34 at LOVE.)

17 I am the way, the truth, and the life: no man cometh unto the Father, but by me. *John* 14:6. (Jesus to the apostles at the LAST SUPPER.)

18 I am the vine, ye are the branches. *John* 15:5.

19 Who shall separate us from the love of Christ? *Romans* 8:35.

1 If any man love not the Lord Jesus Christ, let him be Anathema Marantha. *I Corinthians* 16:22. (*Anathema* means, roughly, "cursed." *Marantha* is a blessing, meaning something on the lines of "Our Lord has come.")

2 Jesus the author and finisher of our faith. *Hebrews* 12:2.

3 Jesus Christ the same yesterday, and today, and for ever. *Hebrews* 13:8.

4 If any man sin, we have an advocate with the Father, Jesus Christ the righteous:
And he is the propitiation for our sins: and not for ours only, but also for the sins of the whole world. *I John* 2:1–2.

5 His eyes were as a flame of fire;
And his feet like unto fine brass, as if they burned in a furnace; and his voice as the sound of many waters. *Revelation* 1:14–15. (The Son of Man as revealed to John on the island of Patmos. Traditionally, this John has been identified with John the son of Zebedee, also traditionally identified as the evangelist John. Scholars do not believe that all three—John the son of Zebedeer, JOHN OF PATMOS, and John the evangelist—could have been the same person.)

6 When I saw him, I fell at his feet as dead. *Revelation* 1:17.

7 Behold, I stand at the door, and knock: if any man hear my voice, and open the door, I will come in to him. *Revelation* 3:20.

8 He is Lord of lords, and King of kings. *Revelation* 17:14.

See also BAPTISM; DEVIL; JESUS categories below; JOHN THE BAPTIST; LAST SUPPER; MESSIAH; MIRACLES OF JESUS; SALVATION; SERVANT OF GOD.

JESUS: BIRTH AND CHILDHOOD

9 She [Mary] shall bring forth a son, and thou shalt call his name JESUS: for he shall save his people from their sins. *Matthew* 1:21. (An angel speaking to Joseph. The angel tells Joseph that his betrothed, Mary, is a virgin and "that which is conceived in her is of the Holy Ghost." *Matthew* 1:20. The name *Jesus* is the Greek version of *Yeshua,* which means "he shall save.")

10 Behold, a virgin shall be with child, and shall bring forth a son, and they shall call his name Emmanuel, which being interpreted is, God with us. *Matthew* 1:23. (See also IMMANUEL.)

11 Now when Jesus was born in Bethlehem of Judæa in the days of Herod the king, behold, there came wise men from the east to Jerusalem,
Saying, Where is he that is born King of the Jews? for we have seen his star in the east, and are come to worship him.
When Herod the king had heard these things, he was troubled, and all Jerusalem with him. *Matthew* 2:1–3. (The classic Christmas story is told in *Luke*. See below.)

Lo, the star, which they saw in the east, went before them, till it came and stood over where the young child was.

When they saw the star, they rejoiced with exceeding great joy. *Matthew* 2:10. (The presence of a new star was a traditional sign of the birth of a great leader. Thus, "There shall come a Star out of Jacob, and a Scepter shall rise out of Israel." *Numbers* 24:17. In 7 B.C., there was a dazzling conjunction of Jupiter and Saturn in the constellation Pisces, considered a constellation of the Jews. This may have been the star of Bethlehem.)

1 They saw the young child with Mary his mother, and fell down, and worshiped him: and . . . they presented unto him gifts; gold, and frankincense, and myrrh.

And being warned of God in a dream that they should not return to Herod, they departed into their own country another way. *Matthew* 2:11–12. (Gold, the richest of metals, was a traditional gift for a king. Frankincense, the fragrant resin exuded by Boswellia trees, was used in religious ceremonies, and reflected the sacred mission of the child Jesus. Myrrh, an aromatic gum that grows in the Middle East, was an ingredient in costly incense and perfume, but was also used in embalming. It signified the early death of Jesus.)

2 The angel of the Lord appeareth to Joseph in a dream, saying, Arise, and take the young child and his mother, and flee into Egypt. *Matthew* 2:13. (In this way, Jesus avoided the massacre of two-year-old boys in which Herod hoped to destroy him. This massacre, although evidently fictionalized or exaggerated, is not inconsistent with the character of the historical Herod the Great, a ruthless, complicated, grandiose ruler. He murdered the first of his ten wives, three of his sons, and various other relatives whom he considered a threat to his throne. On the other hand, he was one of the great builders of the ancient world, not only rebuilding the Temple on a magnificent scale, but constructing at Caeserea an astonishing harbor, the first entirely man-made harbor built in open sea.)

3 Out of Egypt have I called my son. *Matthew* 2:15. (Matthew says that this fulfills the words of the prophet. The reference is to *Hosea* 11:1, which reads, "When Israel was a child, then I loved him, and called my son out of Egypt.")

4 Rachel weeping for her her children, and would not be comforted, because they are not. *Matthew* 2:18. (A reference to the massacre of infants by Herod. The passage mirrors *Jeremiah* 31:15, in which Rachel personifies Israel in mourning.)

5 He shall be called a Nazarene. *Matthew* 2:23. (Returning from Egypt, Joseph, Mary, and Jesus settled in Nazareth in Galilee. According to Matthew, this fulfilled a prophecy, possibly that the Messiah will be a *nétzer,* or shoot, of the tree of David. The emphasis on the ways in which Jesus is said to have fulfilled Old Testament prophecies tended to provoke anti-Semitism among medieval Christians and others who, not being well educated in biblical history, thought that the Jews willfully ignored obvious signs that Jesus was the Messiah.)

1 Joseph also went up from Galilee, out of the town of Nazareth, into Judea, unto the city of David, which is called Bethlehem. *Luke* 2:4.

2 She brought forth her firstborn son, and wrapped him in swaddling clothes, and laid him a manger; because there was no room for them in the inn.

And there were in the same country shepherds abiding in the field, keeping watch over their flock by night.

And, lo, the angel of the Lord came upon them, and the glory of the Lord shone round about them: and they were sore afraid.

And the angel said unto them, Fear not: for, behold, I bring you good tidings of great joy, which shall be to all people.

For unto you is born this day in the City of David a Savior, which is Christ the Lord.

And this shall be a sign unto you; Ye shall find the babe wrapped in swaddling clothes, lying in a manger.

And suddenly there was with the angel a multitude of the heavenly host praising God, and saying,

Glory to God in the highest, and on earth peace, good will toward men. *Luke* 2:7–14. (In the Douay Bible, the last phrase reads, "Peace to men of good will.")

3 The child grew, and waxed strong in spirit, filled with wisdom: and the grace of God was upon him. *Luke* 2:40.

4 Son, why hast thou thus dealt with us? behold, thy father and I have sought thee sorrowing.

And he said unto them, How is it that ye sought me? wist ye not that I must be about my Father's business? *Luke* 2:48–49. (Conversation between Mary and Joseph and the twelve-year-old Jesus, whom they had lost but then find in the Temple.)

5 Jesus increased in wisdom and stature, and in favor with God and man. *Luke* 2:52.

JESUS: PASSION AND DEATH

6 My soul is exceeding sorrowful, even unto death: tarry ye here, and watch with me.

And he went a little farther, and fell on his face, and prayed, saying, O my Father, if it be possible, let this cup pass from me: nevertheless not as I will, but as thou wilt.

And he cometh unto the disciples, and findeth them asleep, and saith unto Peter, What, could ye not watch with me one hour? *Matthew* 26:38–40. (Jesus in Gethsemane on the Mount of Olives the night before his death, with Peter, James, and John.)

1 O my Father, if this cup may not pass away from me, except I drink it, thy will be done. *Matthew* 26:42. (Jesus, praying in Gethsemane.)

2 Behold, the hour is at hand, and the Son of man is betrayed into the hands of sinners. *Matthew* 26:45. (Jesus to his sleeping disciples.)

3 He that betrayed him gave them a sign, saying, Whomsoever I shall kiss, that same is he: hold him fast. *Matthew* 26:48. (Judas preparing to betray Jesus to the chief priests and elders.)

4 He came to Jesus, and said, Hail, Master; and kissed him. *Matthew* 26:49.

5 Art thou the King of the Jews? [Pontius Pilate to Jesus.] And Jesus said unto him, Thou sayest. *Matthew* 27:11. (See also PONTIUS PILATE.)

6 Whom will ye that I release unto you? Barabbas, or Jesus which is called Christ? *Matthew* 27:17. (Pilate asks the crowd if they want Barabbas, "a notable prisoner," or Jesus, to be set free.)

7 They said, Barabbas. *Matthew* 27:21. (At *John* 18:40 we are told, "Now Barabbas was a robber." Lord Byron is believed to have claimed, "Now Barabbas was a publisher," but more likely it was Thomas Campbell who originated this *bon mot.*)

8 What shall I do then with Jesus which is called Christ? They all say unto him, Let him be crucified. *Matthew* 27:22. (After Pilate washes his hands in front of the crowd to demonstrate his innocence of the execution of Christ, the people answer, "His blood be on us, and on our children." *Matthew* 27:25. This verse was cited for centuries in justification of violence against Jews.)

9 When they [the Roman soldiers] had plaited a crown of thorns, they put it upon his head . . . and mocked him, saying, Hail, King of the Jews!

And they spit upon him. *Matthew* 27:29–30.

10 They crucified him, and parted his garments, casting lots. *Matthew* 27:35. (*Psalms* 22:18 refers to dividing garments.)

11 [They] set over his head his accusation written, THIS IS JESUS THE KING OF THE JEWS. *Matthew* 27:37.

12 If thou be the Son of God, come down from the cross. *Matthew* 27:40.

13 He saved others; himself he cannot save. *Matthew* 27:42.

14 From the sixth hour there was darkness all over the land unto the ninth hour.

And about the ninth hour Jesus cried with a loud voice, saying, Eli, Eli, lama sabachthani? that is to say, My God, my God, why hast thou forsaken me? *Matthew* 27:45–46. (These words are from *Psalms* 22:1, transliterated from Hebrew. Mark gives the Aramaic.)

[1] One of them [the people watching] ran, and took a sponge, and filled it with vinegar, and put it on reed, and gave him to drink. *Matthew* 27:48. (Here, and in *Matthew* 27:34, which reads, "They gave him vinegar to drink mingled with gall," are allusions to *Psalms* 69:21, which reads, "They gave me also gall for my meat; and in my thirst they gave me vinegar to drink." *Mark* 15:23, however, refers to Jesus being offered "wine mingled with myrrh," a sedative which would slightly relieve the agony. Jesus does not accept it.)

[2] Jesus, when he had cried again with a loud voice, yielded up the ghost. *Matthew* 27:50. (At this moment the veil of the Temple is torn open, the earth quakes, graves open, and "many bodies of the saints which slept arose." *Matthew* 27:51–52.)

[3] Truly this was the Son of God. *Matthew* 27:54. (An admission by the Roman centurion and those who were watching with him at the foot of the cross.)

[4] When they were come to the place, which is called Calvary, there they crucified him. *Luke* 23:33. (*Matthew* 27:33 refers to "a place called Golgotha, that is to say, a place of a skull." *Golgotha* means "skull," and Mark and John also use the term. *Calvary* is based on the Latin for "skull." It was probably so named because it was used for executions. The exact site is not known.)

[5] Father, forgive them; for they know not what they do. *Luke* 23:34.

[6] Jesus, Lord, remember me when thou comest into thy kingdom.
And Jesus said unto him, Verily I say unto thee, Today shalt thou be with me in paradise. *Luke* 23:42–43. (The first speaker is one of the two thieves who were crucified along with Jesus. Children are sometimes taught that the good thief and the Virgin Mary are the only people we know for certain are in heaven. On the other hand, Judas is said to be the only person we know to be in hell. See JUDAS ISCARIOT. The thief's conversation with Jesus is recorded only in *Luke*.)

[7] Father, into thy hands I commend my spirit: and having said thus, he gave up the ghost. *Luke* 23:46.

[8] Yet a little while I am with you, and then I go unto him that sent me.
Ye shall seek me, and shall not find me: and where I am, thither ye cannot come. *John* 7:33–34. (But at *John* 16:16, Jesus promises: "A little while, and ye shall not see me: and again, a little while, and ye shall see me.")

[9] I lay down my life, that I might take it again.
No man taketh it from me, but I lay it down of myself. *John* 10:17–18. (The conclusion of the "good shepherd" passage. See JESUS above. In this section John establishes that Christ's death was an act of his free will, done in accord with the wishes of the Father.)

1 Greater love hath no man than this, that a man lay down his life for his friends. *John* 15:13. (Jesus to the apostles.)

2 Ecce homo. *John* 19:5, Vulgate. (In the King James Version, "Behold the man!" Said by Pilate to the crowd as he presents Jesus wearing the crown of thorns.)

3 It is finished. *John* 19:30. (Jesus' last words in John's account of his death.)

4 One of the soldiers with a spear pierced his side, and forthwith came there out blood and water. *John* 19:34. (This is said to be in fulfillment of *Zechariah* 12:10, which reads, "They shall look upon me whom they have pierced." The blood and water are sometimes interpreted as symbolic of the sacraments of the Eucharist and Baptism. In legend, Joseph of Arimathaea collected blood from the crucified Christ in the Holy Grail.)

5 For even Christ our Passover is sacrificed for us. *I Corinthians* 5:7. (St. Paul related Christ to the PASSOVER lamb.)

See also JUDAS ISCARIOT; LAST SUPPER; PETER.

JESUS, RESURRECTION OF

6 As Jonas [Jonah] was three days and three nights in the whale's belly, so shall the Son of man be three days and three nights in the heart of the earth. *Matthew* 12:40. (Jesus, in answer to certain scribes and Pharisees, who asked him for a sign. In *Luke* 11:29–32, the reference is to the preaching of Jonah, without mention of resurrection. Note also that Jesus was entombed two nights, and part of three days.)

7 As it began to dawn toward the first day of the week, came Mary Magdalene and the other Mary [the mother of James] to see the sepulchre. *Matthew* 28:1. (The tomb belonged to Joseph of Arimathaea, and in this gospel is said to have been sealed under orders from Pilate. An angel appears and rolls back the stone sealing the tomb.)

8 His [the angel's] countenance was like lightning, and his raiment white as snow. *Matthew* 28:3.

9 Fear not ye: for I know that ye seek Jesus, which was crucified.
He is not here: for he is risen, as he said. *Matthew* 28:5–6. (The angel to the women at the sepulchre. They leave in "fear and great joy," and on their way meet the resurrected Jesus, who tells them to bring the news to the disciples, who should go to Galilee, where they will see him.)

10 The Lord is risen indeed. *Luke* 24:34. (In *Luke,* two disciples meet the risen Jesus at Emmaus, but do not recognize him until he repeats the ritual of the LAST SUPPER, breaking bread. The disciples return to Jerusalem with the message that the Lord is risen. One disciple is named Cleopas; the other is not identified. The location of Emmaus is not known for certain.)

1 Yet a little while, and the world seeth me no more; but ye see me: because I live, ye shall live also. *John* 14:19. (Jesus in farewell to the apostles.)

2 Noli me tangere. *John* 20:17, Vulgate. (The King James Version reads, "Touch me not." Said by the risen Jesus to Mary Magdalene.)

3 Except I shall see in his hands the print of the nails, and put my finger into the print of the nails, and thrust my hand into his side, I will not believe. *John* 20:25. (The apostle Thomas, upon hearing the others report, "We have seen the Lord.")

4 Reach hither thy finger, and behold my hands; and reach hither thy hand, and thrust it into my side: and be not faithless, but believing.

And Thomas answered and said unto him, My Lord and my God.

Jesus saith unto him, Thomas, because thou hast seen me, thou hast believed: blessed are they that have not seen, and yet have believed. *John* 20:27–29.

5 If Christ be not risen, then is our preaching vain, and your faith is also vain. *I Corinthians* 15:14. (A passage that has troubled many Christians who have some degree of doubt concerning the resurrection. Martin Gardner wrote a novel, *The Flight of Peter Fromm,* on a crisis in the life of a young minister who took this passage to heart.)

6 Now is Christ risen from the dead, and become the firstfruits of them that slept.

For since by man came death, by man came also the resurrection of the dead.

For as in Adam all die, even so in Christ shall all be made alive. *I Corinthians* 15:20–22.

7 I am he that liveth, and was dead; and, behold, I am alive for evermore, Amen; and have the keys of hell and of death. *Revelation* 1:18.

JEWS

See CHOSEN PEOPLE

JEZEBEL

See AHAB AND JEZEBEL

JOB

8 There was a man in the land of Uz, whose name was Job; and that man was perfect and upright, and one that feared God, and eschewed evil. *Job* 1:1. (This great story, called by Carlyle "one of the grandest things ever written with pen," poses in starkly dramatic terms the problem of evil: Why must an innocent person suffer?)

1 I am a brother to dragons, and a companion to owls. *Job* 30:29.

2 The Lord answered Job out of the whirlwind. *Job* 38:1.

3 Where wast thou when I laid the foundations of the earth? *Job* 38:4. (God to Job.)

4 So the Lord blessed the latter end of Job more than his beginning. *Job* 42:12.

5 Ye have heard of the patience of Job. *James* 5:11.

JOHN OF PATMOS

6 I John, who also am your brother, and companion in tribulation, and in the kingdom and patience of Jesus Christ, was on the isle that is called Patmos, for the word of God, and for the testimony of Jesus Christ. *Revelation* 1:9. (The identity of the author of *Revelation,* often called "John of Patmos," has long been an issue of scholarly debate. Traditionally, John of Patmos, John the Evangelist, and the apostle John, son of Zebedee, are said to be the same person. Scholars agree, however, that John the Evangelist did not live contemporaneously with Christ and could not have written *Revelation.* But John of Patmos may have been the same person as the apostle John.)

JOHN THE BAPTIST

7 Behold, I will send my messenger, and he shall prepare the way before me. *Malachi* 3:1.

8 In those days came John the Baptist, preaching in the wilderness of Judaea,

And saying, Repent ye: for the kingdom of heaven is at hand.

For this is he that was spoken of by the prophet Esaias [Isaiah], saying, The voice of one crying in the wilderness, Prepare ye the way of the Lord, make his paths straight. *Matthew* 3:1–3. (The Esaias, or Isaiah, quote is under PROPHETS.)

9 John had his raiment of camel's hair, and a leathern girdle about his loins; and his meat was locusts and wild honey. *Matthew* 3:4. (Information that has fascinated readers young and old for centuries. The term *locust* also refers to the carob tree, but *locusts* is probably not a mistranslation. These insects swarmed regularly in the Middle East and Africa—see the plague under EXODUS. They were, and still are, eaten in large numbers. They are a good source of protein.)

10 Then cometh Jesus from Galilee to Jordan unto John, to be baptized of him.

But John forbad him, saying, I have need to be baptized of thee, and comest thou to me? *Matthew* 3:13–14.

1 She [Salome] . . . said, Give me here John Baptist's head in a charger. *Matthew* 14:8. (Salome had danced for Herod Antipas, who was her stepfather and uncle, and won from him a promise to do whatever she asked. She was acting at the instruction of her mother Herodias, a granddaughter of Herod the Great, who had married two half-uncles—Herod [called Philip in *Matthew* 14:3] and Herod Antipas. John the Baptist had preached against the divorce and remarriage, thus earning a deadly enemy.)

2 There was a man sent from God, whose name was John. *John* 1:6. (The whole of the prologue to the gospel of John is given at JESUS.)

3 He was a burning and a shining light. *John* 5:35.

See also PROPHETS.

JONAH

4 Arise, go to Nineveh, that great city. *Jonah* 1:2. (God to Jonah. Nineveh, an ancient and sophisticated city, was the capital of Assyria from 705 B.C. to 612 B.C. The story of Jonah is usually said to be a plea to extend toleration and understanding to all nations. But God's call to go and proselytize in Nineveh was not welcomed by Jonah, who quickly boarded a ship headed in the opposite direction. For the meaning of "the sign of Jonah" see GENERATIONS, *Luke* 11:29, and JESUS, RESURRECTION OF, *Matthew* 12:40.)

5 The Lord had prepared a great fish to swallow up Jonah. And Jonah was in the belly of the fish three days and three nights. *Jonah* 1:17. (*Matthew* 12:40 relates this to Jesus. See JESUS, RESURRECTION OF.)

6 Out of the belly of hell cried I, and thou heardest my voice. *Jonah* 2:2.

7 The Lord spoke unto the fish, and it vomited out Jonah upon the dry land. *Jonah* 2:10. (Thus Jonah is persuaded to undertake the mission to Nineveh, where he is remarkably successful, for the people and the king quickly repent. Jonah, a harsh character, wants God to destroy the city anyway. But God, referring to the more than one hundred thousand innocent citizens—and cattle as well—spares Nineveh.)

JONATHAN

See DAVID AND JONATHAN; SAUL AND JONATHAN

JOSEPH

8 Now Israel [Jacob] loved Joseph more than all his children, because he was the son of his old age: and he made him a coat of many colors. [The coat was probably a long-sleeved robe.]

And when his brethren saw that their father loved him more than all his brethren, they hated him, and could not speak peaceably unto him.

And Joseph dreamed a dream, and he told it his brethren: and they hated him yet the more. *Genesis* 37:3–5. (In the dreams of the sheaves and of the sun, moon, and stars, Joseph envisions his brothers and parents bowing down to him.)

1 They conspired against him to slay him.
And they said to one another, Behold this dreamer cometh. *Genesis* 37:18–19.

2 They stript Joseph out of his coat, his coat of many colors that was on him;
And they took him, and cast him into a pit. *Genesis* 37:23–24.

3 The dream of Pharaoh is one: God hath showed Pharoah what he is about to do.
The seven good kine are seven years; and the seven good ears [of corn] are seven years: the dream is one. *Genesis* 41:25–26.

4 Behold, there come seven years of great plenty throughout all the land of Egypt:
And there shall arise after them seven years of famine. *Genesis* 41:29–30.

5 Joseph knew his brethren, but they knew him not. *Genesis* 42:8.

6 I am Joseph your brother, whom ye sold into Egypt. *Genesis* 45:4.

7 Joseph my son is yet alive: I will go and see him before I die. *Genesis* 45:28.

JOSHUA AND THE CONQUEST OF CANAAN

8 And the priests that bore the ark of the covenant of the Lord stood firm on dry ground in the midst of Jordan, and all the Israelites passed over on dry ground, until all the people were passed clean over Jordan. *Joshua* 3:17.

9 At the seventh time, when the priests blew with the trumpets, Joshua said unto the people, Shout; for the Lord hath given you the city [Jericho]. *Joshua* 6:16. (The name *Joshua* in Hebrew means "the Lord saves.")

10 So the people shouted when the priests blew with the trumpets; and it came to pass, when the people heard the sound of the trumpet, and the people shouted with a great shout, that the wall fell down flat, so that the people went up into the city, every man straight before him, and they took the city. *Joshua* 6:20. (The remains of Jericho indicate that in this period it had double brick walls, the interior walls being twelve feet thick, and the exterior, six feet thick. Whether the walls in *Joshua* were these walls or ones built later is a matter of dispute. There is evidence that the double walls were brought down by an earthquake, but if or how this relates to the biblical account is also not certain.)

1 Sun, stand thou still upon Gibeon; and thou, Moon, in the valley of Ajalon. *Joshua* 10:12. (With this miracle, Joshua is able to halt and destroy the fleeing Amorites at the battle of Gibeon. Verse 14 observes, "There was no day like that before it or after it, that the Lord hearkened unto the voice of a man: for the Lord fought for Israel.")

JOY

See HAPPINESS

JUBILEE YEAR

2 Ye shall hallow the fiftieth year, and proclaim liberty throughout all the land unto all the inhabitants thereof: it shall be a jubilee unto you. *Leviticus* 25:10 (In this year—a sort of grand sabbatical year—Israelite slaves were to be freed, property was to be returned to the original owner, and the land was to lie fallow.)

See also FEASTS, RELIGIOUS.

JUDAS ISCARIOT

3 What will ye give me, and I will deliver him [Jesus] unto you? *Matthew* 26:15. (Judas to the chief priests. They offer thirty pieces of silver.)

4 Woe unto that man by whom the Son of man is betrayed! It had been good for that man if he had not been born.

Then Judas, which betrayed him, answered and said, Master, is it I? He said unto him, Thou hast said. *Matthew* 26:24–25. (Judas is sometimes said to be the only person identified as damned. His worst sin, it is said, was not the betrayal, but his despair and suicide. See below.)

5 He cast down the pieces of silver in the temple, and departed, and went and hanged himself. *Matthew* 27:5. (The chief priests cannot put the silver in the treasury because "it is the price of blood." *Matthew* 27:6. They use the money to buy the Potter's Field in which to bury strangers.)

JUDGES

6 The Lord raised up judges. *Judges* 2:16. (These judges, or *shoftim,* were political and military leaders who rose through merit and charisma. Beginning with the quote from *Samuel* below, *judge* is used in its more traditional sense.)

7 The Lord was with the judge. *Judges* 2:18.

8 Oh that I were made judge. *II Samuel* 15:4. (Absalom is speaking. He uses the position to win allies in his ill-fated rebellion against his father, David.)

1 Give therefore thy servant an understanding heart to judge thy people, that I may discern between good and bad *I Kings* 3:9. (Solomon to God.)

2 Consider what you do, for you judge not for man but for the Lord . . . take heed what you do, for there is no perversion of justice with the Lord our God, or partiality, or taking bribes. *II Chronicles* 19:6–7, RSV. (King Jehoshaphat to newly appointed judges.)

3 Go not to law with a judge, for they will judge for him according to his honor. *Ecclesiasticus* 8:14.

See also GOD AS LAWGIVER AND JUDGE; JUSTICE AND FAIRNESS; LAW AND JUSTICE.

JUDGING OTHERS

4 Judge not, that ye be not judged.

For with what judgment ye judge, ye shall be judged: and with what measure ye mete, it shall be measured to you again. *Matthew* 7:1–2.

5 This woman was taken in adultery, in the very act.

Now Moses in the law commanded us, that such should be stoned: but what sayest thou? *John* 8:4–5.(Scribes and Pharisees questioning Jesus.)

6 He that is without sin among you, let him first cast a stone at her. *John* 8:7.

7 Woman, where are those thine accusers? hath no man condemned thee?

She said, No man, Lord. And Jesus said unto her, Neither do I condemn thee: go, and sin no more. *John* 8:10–11.

8 I judge no man. *John* 8:15.

9 Wherein thou judgest another, thou condemnest thyself; for thou that judgest doeth the same things. *Romans* 2:1.

See also FAILINGS; FORGIVENESS; MERCY; TOLERANCE.

JUDGMENT DAY

10 Howl ye; for the day of the Lord is at hand. *Isaiah* 13:6.

11 Behold the day of the Lord cometh, cruel both with wrath and with fierce anger, to lay the land desolate: and he shall destroy the sinners thereof out of it.

For the stars of heaven and the constellations thereof shall not give their light: the sun shall be darkened in his going forth, and the moon shall not cause her light to shine.

And I will punish the world for their evil, and the wicked for their iniquity; and I will cause the arrogancy of the proud to cease, and will lay low the haughtiness of the terrible. *Isaiah* 13:9–11. (This passage refers in particular to the destruction of Babylon. See also under CITIES. It has come to stand for God's final judgment of the world.)

1 The whole earth is at rest, and is quiet: they [the people] break forth into singing. *Isaiah* 14:7. (One of the few blissful views of the day of judgment. After the destruction of Babylon, God promises the people of Israel freedom in their own land and an era of peace.)

2 Let all the inhabitants of the land tremble: for the day of the Lord cometh, for it is high at hand. *Joel* 2:1.

3 Multitudes, multitudes in the valley of decision: for the day of the Lord is near in the valley of decision. *Joel* 3:14.

4 It shall come to pass in that day, that the mountains shall drop down new wine, and the hills shall flow with milk, and all the rivers of Judah shall flow with waters. *Joel* 3:18. (This is the Golden Age in which "Judah shall dwell forever, and Jerusalem from generation to generation," *Joel* 3:20).

5 Behold, the day cometh, that shall burn as an oven. *Malachi* 4:1.

6 The Son of man shall come in the glory of his Father with his angels; and then he shall reward every man according to his works. *Matthew* 16:27. (See also *Matthew* 25:31. When Jesus repeats this thought to the high priest after his arrest, it becomes important evidence against him.)

7 Watch therefore: for ye know now what hour your Lord doth come. *Matthew* 24:42. (See also *Matthew* 25:13.)

8 Before him [the Son of man] shall be gathered all nations: and he shall separate them one from another, as a shepherd divideth his sheep from the goats.

And he shall set the sheep on his right hand, but the goats on the left. *Matthew* 25:32–33. (To those who are saved Jesus explains that when he was hungry and thirsty, in need of clothes, in prison, they gave to him. See GIVING. When they ask how this could be, for they had never seen him, he explains that what they have done for those in need, they have done for him. See JESUS.)

9 Watch ye therefore: for ye know not when the master of the house cometh, at even, or at midnight, or at the cockcrowing, or in the morning:

Lest coming suddenly he find you sleeping. *Mark* 13:35–36.

10 Then shall they see the Son of man coming in a cloud with power and great glory. *Luke* 21:27.

11 I saw a new heaven and a new earth: for the first heaven and the first earth were passed away; and there was no more sea.

And I John saw the holy city, new Jerusalem, coming down from God out of heaven, prepared as a bride adorned for her husband. *Revelation* 21:1–2. (The speaker is JOHN OF PATMOS.)

1 He that is unjust, let him be unjust still: and he which is filthy, let him be filthy still: and he that is righteous, let him be righteous still: and he that is holy, let him be holy still.

And, behold, I come quickly. *Revelation* 22:11–12.

See also WORLD, END OF.

JUSTICE AND FAIRNESS

2 Shall not the Judge of all the earth do right? *Genesis* 118:25. (Abraham is trying to save Sodom and Gomorrah. Obtaining God's agreement to spare these cities if fifty righteous men can be found there, Abraham continues to press his case, working the number down to ten. Unfortunately, not even ten righteous men were found.)

3 That which is altogether just shalt thou follow. *Deuteronomy* 16:20.

4 The Lord shall judge his people. *Deuteronomy* 32:36.

5 How long will you judge unjustly and show partiality to the wicked? *Psalms* 82:2, RSV. (This is a visionary psalm in which God is addressing the heavenly council and accusing certain rebels there of injustice. The accusation is serious, for God's justice is seen as the basis of order in both nature and society. In the next verse, God demands justice for the weak and unfortunate. See MISFORTUNE.)

6 Blessings are upon the head of the just. *Proverbs* 10:6.

7 Learn to do well; seek judgment [justice], relieve the oppressed, judge the fatherless, plead for the widow. *Isaiah* 1:17. ("Judge the fatherless" means "secure justice for the fatherless.")

8 Shall evil be recompensed for good? *Jeremiah* 18:20.

9 Let judgment run down as waters, and righteousness as a mighty stream. *Amos* 5:24. (Used by Martin Luther King, Jr., June 15, 1963.)

See also CRIME; FORGIVENESS; GOD AS LAWGIVER AND JUDGE; GOVERNMENT; JUDGES; INJUSTICE; LAW AND JUSTICE.

KINDNESS See GENTLENESS AND KINDNESS

KINGS See GOVERNMENT; POWER

KNOWLEDGE See INFORMATION; LEARNING; WISDOM

LAND

See CANAAN; ENVIRONMENT; FARMING; PROPERTY

LANGUAGE

1 And the whole earth was of one language, and of one speech. *Genesis* 11:1.

2 The ear tests words as the palate tastes food. *Job* 34:3, RSV.

3 Death and life are in the power of the tongue. *Proverbs* 18:21, RSV.

4 A word fitly spoken is like apples of gold in pictures of silver. *Proverbs* 25:11.

5 By speech wisdom shall be known *Ecclesiasticus* 4:24.

6 Is not a word better than a gift? *Ecclesiasticus* 18:17.

7 His word burned like a lamp. *Ecclesiasticus* 48:1. (The reference is to the prophet Elijah.)

8 Seeing then that we have such hope, we use great plainness of speech. *II Corinthians* 3:12.

See also BABEL; NAMES; SWEARING; TALK.

LAST SUPPER

9 As they were eating, Jesus took bread, and blessed it, and broke it, and gave it to the disciples, and said, Take, eat; this is my body.

And he took the cup, and gave thanks, and gave it to them, saying, Drink ye all of it;

For this is my blood of the new testament, which is shed for many for the remission of sins.

But I say unto you, I will not drink henceforth of this fruit of the vine, until that day when I drink it new with you in my Father's kingdom. *Matthew* 26:26–29.

10 This is my body which is given for you: this do in remembrance of me. *Luke* 22:19.

11 Take, eat: this is my body, which is broken for you: this do in remembrance of me. *I Corinthians* 11:24.

12 This cup is the new testament in my blood: this do ye, as often as ye drink it, in remembrance of me. *I Corinthians* 11:25.

See also JUDAS ISCARIOT; PETER.

LAUGHTER

1 God hath made me to laugh, so that all that hear will laugh with me. *Genesis* 21:6. (This is Sarah, wife of Abraham, believed to be the first person in history reported to have laughed. She first laughed when God promised her a child in her old age, after a lifetime of infertility. Now, following the birth of her son, she laughs in happiness. The name she chose, *Isaac,* means "he laughed.")

2 He [God] will yet fill your mouth with laughter. *Job* 8:21, RSV.

3 He that sitteth in the heavens shall laugh. *Psalms* 2:4.

4 I said of laughter, It is mad: and of mirth, Who doeth it? *Ecclesiastes* 2:2.

5 The heart of fools is in the house of mirth. *Ecclesiastes* 7:4.

6 For as the crackling of [burning] thorns under a pot, so is the laughter of the fool. *Ecclesiastes* 7:6.

7 A fool lifteth up his voice with laughter; but a wise man doth scarce smile a little. *Ecclesiasticus* 21:20. (The idea that laughter is loutish was expressed particularly peevishly by Lord Chesterfield. "In my mind, there is nothing so illiberal and so ill-bred as audible laughter." Letter to his son, March 9, 1748.)

See also HAPPINESS.

LAW AND JUSTICE

8 Thou shalt not raise a false report: put not thine hand with the wicked to be an unrighteous witness. *Exodus* 23:1. (This covers slander, libel, and perjury.)

9 You shall do no injustice in judgment; you shall not be partial to the poor or defer to the great. *Leviticus* 19:15, RSV. (Impartiality with respect to wealth and poverty is also treated at *Exodus* 23:3 and 23:6.)

10 Ye shall have one manner of law, as well for the stranger, as for one of your own country. *Leviticus* 24:22. (See also *Numbers* 15:15–16, and STRANGERS AND TRAVELERS.)

11 Ye shall not respect persons in judgment; but ye shall hear the small as well as the great. *Deuteronomy* 1:17.

12 You shall not remove your neighbor's landmark. *Deuteronomy* 19:14, RSV. (*Proverbs* 22:28 reads, "Remove not the ancient landmark, which thy fathers have set." Also, "Remove not the old landmark; and enter not into the fields of the fatherless [orphans]," *Proverbs* 23:10.)

13 The law is light. *Proverbs* 6:23.

14 Lawlessness takes away lives. *Proverbs* 11:30, RSV.

1 He who states his case first seems right, until the other comes and examines him. *Proverbs* 18:17, RSV.

2 The Lord . . . will magnify the law, and make it honorable. *Isaiah* 42:21.

3 A man of understanding trusteth in the law. *Ecclesiasticus* 33:3.

4 God forbid that we should forsake the law. *I Maccabees* 2:21.

5 If any man will sue thee at the law, and take away thy coat, let him have thy cloak also.

And whosoever shall compel thee to go a mile, go with him twain. *Matthew* 5:40–41. (This advice, offered by Jesus in the Sermon on the Mount, fits with his general instruction to go beyond the strict requirements of the law and to avoid an-eye-for-an-eye retaliation. See PACIFISM. The kind of generosity urged here would largely obviate the need for lawyers.)

6 Is it not lawful for me to do what I will with mine own? *Matthew* 20:15. (The answer often is no. But in this case, since the speaker represents the Lord, the answer is yes.)

7 I appeal unto Caesar. *Acts* 25:11. (St. Paul asserting his rights under Roman law.)

8 These, having not the law, are a law unto themselves. *Romans* 2:14. (St. Paul referring to the Gentiles.)

9 Where no law is, there is no transgression. *Romans* 4:15.

10 There is utterly a fault among you, because ye go to law one with another. *I Corinthians* 6:7.

11 Touch not; taste not; handle not. *Colossians* 2:21. (A summary of the world's ordinances.)

12 The law is good, if a man use it lawfully. *I Timothy* 1:8.

See also BRIBERY; GOD AS LAWGIVER AND JUDGE; GOVERNMENT; GUILT; INJUSTICE; JUDGES; JUSTICE AND FAIRNESS; LAW entries below.

LAW: PUNISHMENTS AND PENALTIES

13 Whoso sheddeth man's blood, by man shall his blood be shed: for in the image of God made he man. *Genesis* 9:6. (One of the key passages in the Old Testament assuming a unique value for human life. Other ancient societies tended to make little distinction between crimes against property and crimes against persons, often allowing money payments in settlement of murders. The Israelites were unusual in forbidding capital punishment or unusually cruel corporal punishment for crimes against property, while mandating death for murder. See also below.)

1 He that smiteth a man, so that he die, shall be surely put to death. *Exodus* 21:12. (But this does not apply to involuntary manslaughter. At *Deuteronomy* 19:3–6 and *Joshua* 20 provision is made for havens—separate cities—for those who have killed by accident. See also below.)

2 Thou shalt give life for life,
Eye for eye, tooth for tooth, hand for hand, foot for foot,
Burning for burning, wound for wound, stripe for stripe. *Exodus* 21:23–25. (See also *Leviticus* 24:19–20. and *Deuteronomy* 19:21. Scholars point out that this passage was not meant to stimulate a thirst for revenge, but to express a strict and logical approach to justice at a time when laws were inconsistent and punishments often vicious. In the New Testament, Jesus refers to the principle of an eye for an eye, and then says not to retaliate, but to turn the other cheek. See PACIFISM.)

3 For all manner of trespass . . . the cause of both parties shall come before judges; and whom the judges shall condemn, he shall pay double unto his neighbor. *Exodus* 22:9.

4 Forty stripes he may give him, and not exceed: lest . . . thy brother should seem vile unto thee. *Deuteronomy* 25:3. (In this famous passage, judges are empowered to order the beating of a culprit, but the punishment is limited in order not to degrade the wrongdoer.)

5 The fathers shall not be put to death for the children, nor the children be put to death for the fathers; but every man shall be put to death for his own sin. *II Kings* 14:6. (See also *II Chronicles* 25:4.)

6 From heaven did the Lord behold the earth;
To hear the groaning of the prisoner; to loose those that are appointed to death. *Psalms* 102:19–20. (At *Isaiah* 42:7, God calls upon his servant "to open the blind eyes, to bring out the prisoners from prison, and them that sit in the darkness of the prison house." The servant is sometimes identified as the Messiah. See SERVANT OF GOD and the quote from *Isaiah* below.)

7 Because sentence against an evil work is not executed speedily, therefore the heart of the sons of men is fully set in them to do evil. *Ecclesiastes* 8:11.

8 He hath sent me to bind up the brokenhearted, to proclaim liberty to the captives, and the opening of the prison to them that are bound. *Isaiah* 61:1. (Here the prophet speaks as the messenger of God.)

See also FORGIVENESS; JUDGING OTHERS; TOLERANCE.

LAWS, FOOD

See FOOD LAWS

LAW: WITNESSES AND EVIDENCE

9 Put not thine hand with the wicked to be an unrighteous witness. *Exodus* 23:1.

1 The murderer shall be put to death on the evidence of witnesses; but no person shall be put to death on the testimony of one witness. Moreover you shall accept no ransom for the life of a murderer. *Numbers* 35:30–31, RSV. (At *Deuteronomy* 19:15, the requirement of two or more witnesses is extended. See below.)

2 A single witness shall not prevail against a man for any crime or for any wrong . . . only on the evidence of two witnesses, or of three witnesses, shall a charge be sustained. *Deuteronomy* 19:15, RSV.

3 Daniel had convicted them of false witness by their own mouth. *History of Susanna* 61. (In this fictional story, two elders who were rejected by the young and beautiful Susanna falsely accuse her of adultery, an offense punishable by death. The youthful Daniel exposes their treachery with a time-honored interrogatory technique used by police everywhere. Separating the elders, he asked them to be more precise: where did the act take place? One said under a mastic tree; the other specified a holm tree. The outraged populace killed the elders on the spot.)

4 By thy words thou shalt be justified, and by thy words thou shalt be condemned. *Matthew* 12:37. (More at TALK.)

5 Out of thine own mouth will I judge thee. *Luke* 19:22.

LAWYERS

6 Woe to you lawyers also! for you load men with burdens hard to bear, and you yourselves do not touch the burdens with one of your fingers. *Luke* 11:46, RSV.

LAZARUS

See MIRACLES OF JESUS

LAZINESS

7 Go to the ant thou sluggard; consider her ways, and be wise. *Proverbs* 6:6. (More at ANIMALS.)

8 How long wilt thou sleep, O sluggard? when wilt thou arise out of thy sleep?

Yet a little sleep, a little slumber, a little folding of the hands to sleep.

So shall thy poverty come as one that travelleth, and thy want as an armed man. *Proverbs* 6:9–11. (In the RSV, the last verse reads: "And poverty will come upon you like a vagabond, and want like an armed man.")

9 The way of the slothful man is as a hedge of thorns. *Proverbs* 15:19.

10 The sluggard will not plow by reason of the cold; therefore shall he beg in harvest, and have nothing. *Proverbs* 20:4.

1 The slothful man saith, There is a lion in the way; a lion is in the streets. *Proverbs* 26:13.

See also IDLENESS; LEISURE; SLEEP AND SLEEPLESSNESS.

LEADERSHIP

2 If the trumpet give an uncertain sound, who shall prepare himself to the battle? *I Corinthians* 14:8. (This provided the title for Gen. Maxwell Taylor's *The Uncertain Trumpet,* 1960.)

See also GOVERNMENT.

LEARNING

3 Fools despise wisdom and instruction. *Proverbs* 1:7.

4 Wise men lay up knowledge. *Proverbs* 10:14.

5 Poverty and shame shall be to him that refuseth instruction. *Proverbs* 13:18.

6 In much wisdom is much grief: and he that increaseth knowledge increaseth sorrow. *Ecclesiastes* 1:18. (This melancholy view is characteristic of the dominant tone of *Ecclesiastes.* See also VANITY.)

7 Much study is a weariness of the flesh. *Ecclesiastes* 12:12.

8 [In teaching] precept must be upon precept, precept upon precept; line upon line, line upon line; here a little, and there a little. *Isaiah* 28:10.

9 My people are destroyed for lack of knowledge. *Hosea* 4:6.

10 Profess not the knowledge therefore that thou hast not. *Ecclesiasticus* 3:25.

11 Put your neck under the yoke, and let your soul receive instruction. *Ecclesiasticus* 51:26.

12 Do you understand what you are reading?

. . . How can I, unless some one guides me? *Acts* 8:30–31, RSV. (Conversation between Philip and an Ethiopian official, a eunuch, who is reading from *Isaiah.*)

13 Much learning doth make thee mad. *Acts* 26:24.

14 Knowledge puffeth up. *I Corinthians* 8:1. (The rest is at CHARITY, CHRISTIAN.)

See also IGNORANCE; INFORMATION; SCIENCE; WISDOM.

LEISURE

1 The wisdom of a learned man cometh by opportunity of leisure: and he that hath little business shall become wise. *Ecclesiasticus* 38:24.

See also IDLENESS; LAZINESS; WORRY.

LENDING

See BORROWING AND LENDING

LEPROSY

See SICKNESS

LIES

See COVERUP; DECEIT AND LIES

LIFE

2 Few and evil have the days of the years of my life been. *Genesis*. 47:9. (Jacob, just introduced by his son Joseph to Pharoah, gives this answer to the king's polite question regarding his age. The complaint is memorable but hardly justified—Jacob is one hundred and thirty years old.)

3 Our days on the earth are as a shadow. *I Chronicles* 29:15.

4 Naked came I out of my mother's womb, and naked shall I return thither: the Lord gave, and the Lord hath taken away; blessed be the name of the Lord. *Job* 1:21. (The similar passage from *Ecclesiastes* 5:15 is given under HUMAN BEINGS.)

5 All that a man hath will he give for his life. *Job* 2:4.

6 Is there not an appointed time to man upon earth? *Job* 7:1.

7 My days are swifter than a weaver's shuttle, and are spent without hope. *Job* 7:6. (Also, "My days are swifter than a runner." *Job* 9:25, RSV.)

8 I loathe my life; I would not live for ever. *Job* 7:16, RSV. (Also, "My soul is weary of my life." *Job* 10:1.)

9 We spend our years as a tale that is told. *Psalms* 90:9. (The Revised Standard Version reads, "Our years come to an end like a sigh." For more, see under OLD AGE.)

10 All is vanity . . .
One generation passeth away, and another generation cometh. *Ecclesiastes* 1:2 and 1:4. (The entire passage is given at VANITY.)

11 As it happeneth to the fool, so it happeneth even to me. *Ecclesiastes* 2:15. (Life is the same for the wise, the foolish, and every man. "One event happeneth to them all." *Ecclesiastes* 2:14.)

12 Therefore I hated life . . . for all is vanity and vexation of spirit. *Ecclesiastes* 2:17.

1 There is nothing better for a man than that he should eat and drink, and that he should make his soul enjoy good in his labor. *Ecclesiastes* 2:24.

2 To every thing there is a season, and a time to every purpose under the heaven:

A time to be born, and a time to die; a time to plant, and a time to pluck up that which is planted;

A time to kill, and a time to heal; a time to break down, and a time to to build up;

A time to weep, and a time to laugh; a time to mourn, and a time to dance;

A time to cast away stones, and a time to gather stones together; a time to embrace, and a time to refrain from embracing;

A time to get, and a time to lose; a time to keep, and a time to cast away;

A time to rend, and a time to sew; a time to keep silence, and a time to speak;

A time to love, and a time to hate; a time of war, and a time of peace. *Ecclesiastes* 3:1–8. (A favorite passage of John F. Kennedy; also used in the song "Turn! Turn! Turn!")

3 For to him that is joined to all the living there is hope: for a living dog is better than a dead lion. *Ecclesiastes* 9:4.

4 Do not be anxious about your life. *Matthew* 6:25, RSV. (More at WORRY.)

5 He that findeth his life shall lose it: and he that loseth his life for my sake shall find it. *Matthew* 10:39. (A paradoxical statement of the view that the life of faith is more real and of greater value that physical life. More at JESUS.)

6 None of us liveth to himself, and no man dieth to himself.

For whether we live, we live unto the Lord; and whether we die, we die unto the Lord: whether we live therefore, or die, we are the Lord's. *Romans* 14:7–8.

7 To me to live is Christ, and to die is gain. *Philippians* 1:21.

8 What is your life? It is even a vapor, that appeareth for a little time, and then vanisheth away. *James* 4:14.

9 Another book was opened, which is the book of life. *Revelation* 20:12.

See also FATE; HUMAN BEINGS; LUCK; WORLD.

LIFE, ETERNAL See HEAVEN; SALVATION

LIFE'S WONDERS

1 There be three things which are too wonderful for me, yea, four which I know not:
The way of an eagle in the air; the way of a serpent upon a rock; the way of a ship in the midst of the sea; and the way of a man with a maid. *Proverbs* 30:18–19.

LIGHT

See GOD AS LIGHT

LONELINESS

2 Lover and friend hast thou put far from me. *Psalms* 88:18.

3 I am like a lonely bird on the housetop. *Psalms* 102:7, RSV.

4 I looked, and there was none to help. *Isaiah* 63:5.

5 All thy lovers have forgotten thee; they seek thee not. *Jeremiah* 30:14.

6 She weepeth sore in the night, and her tears are on her cheeks: among all her lovers she hath none to comfort her. *Lamentations* 1:2.

See also REJECTION.

LORD'S PRAYER

7 After this manner therefore pray ye: Our Father which art in heaven, Hallowed be thy name.
Thy kingdom come. Thy will be done in earth, as it is in heaven. Give us this day our daily bread.
And forgive us our debts, as we forgive our debtors.
And lead us not into temptation, but deliver us from evil: For thine is the kingdom, and the power, and the glory, for ever. Amen. *Matthew* 6:9–13. (From the Sermon on the Mount.)

LOVE

8 He kept him as the apple of his eye. *Deuteronomy* 32:10. (God keeps the people of Israel as his beloved. More at CHOSEN PEOPLE.)

9 Intreat me not to leave thee, or to return from following after thee: for whither thou goest, I will go; and where thou lodgest, I will lodge: thy people shall be my people, and thy God my God:
Where thou diest, will I die, and there will I be buried. *Ruth* 1:16–17. (Immortal lines, spoken by Ruth to her mother-in-law Naomi.)

10 The Lord is nigh unto them that are of a broken heart. *Psalms* 34:18.

11 Love covers all offenses. *Proverbs* 10:12, RSV.

1 Better is a dinner of herbs where love is, than a stalled ox and hatred therewith. *Proverbs* 15:17. (A stalled ox is an ox that has been kept in to be fattened.)

2 Thy love is better than wine. *Song of Solomon* 1:2. (More below, under LOVE, INVITATIONS TO.)

3 I am the rose of Sharon, and the lily of the valleys.

As the lily among thorns, so is my love among the daughters.

As the apple tree among the trees of the wood, so is my beloved among the sons. I sat down under his shadow with great delight, and his fruit was sweet to my taste. *Song of Solomon* 2:1–3.

4 The voice of my beloved! behold, he cometh leaping upon the mountains, skipping upon the hills.

My beloved is like a roe or a young hart. *Song of Solomon* 2:8–9. (The Revised Standard Version reads, "Behold he comes, leaping upon the mountains, bounding over the hills. My beloved is like a gazelle, or a young stag.")

5 I am my beloved's, and my beloved is mine. *Song of Solomon* 6:3. (Also, "I am my beloved's, and his desire is toward me." 7:10.)

6 I have loved thee with an everlasting love. *Jeremiah* 31:3.

7 I drew them with . . . bands of love. *Hosea* 11:4.

8 Love your enemies. *Matthew* 5:44. (From the Sermon on the Mount, the central principle in the Christian message. It is not enough to love one's friends, neighbors, and allies. One must love all equally, even one's enemies. In doing so, one becomes a child of God, that is, like "your Father which is in heaven: for he maketh his sun to rise on the evil and on the good, and sendeth rain on the just and on the unjust." *Matthew* 5:45. More at ENEMIES.)

9 Thou shalt love thy neighbor as thyself. *Mark* 12:30–31. (More at TEN COMMANDMENTS.)

10 Her sins, which are many, are forgiven; for she loved much. *Luke* 7:47. (Jesus speaking of the woman who washed his feet with tears and anointed them with ointment.)

11 Thou shalt love the Lord thy God with all thy heart, and with all thy soul, and with all thy strength, and with all thy mind; and thy neighbor as thyself. *Luke* 10:27. (Here a lawyer in conversation with Jesus correctly identifies the key commandments. But then the lawyer asks, "Who is my neighbor?" Jesus replies with the parable of the GOOD SAMARITAN.)

12 A new commandment I give unto you, That ye love one another. *John* 13:34. (See also *John* 13:1 at JESUS for more on the theme of love in the gospel of John.)

1 Greater love hath no man than this, that a man lay down his life for his friends. *John* 15:13. (Jesus in farewell to the apostles.)

2 Let love be without dissimulation. *Romans* 12:9.

3 Be kindly affectioned one to another with brotherly love. *Romans* 12:10.

4 Owe no man any thing, but to love one another. *Romans* 13:8.

5 Love is the fulfilling of the law. *Romans* 13:10. (By *law*, St. Paul meant God's law for humankind.)

6 Let brotherly love continue. *Hebrews* 13:1.

7 He that loveth not, knoweth not God; for God is love. *I John* 4:8.

8 There is no fear in love; but perfect love casteth out fear. *I John* 4:18.

9 I have somewhat against thee, because thou hast left thy first love. *Revelation* 2:4.

See also CHARITY, CHRISTIAN; DAVID AND JONATHAN; EMOTIONS; GOD, LOVING; LOVE, INVITATIONS TO; MARRIAGE; SEX; WOMEN.

LOVE, INVITATIONS TO

10 Come, let us take our fill of love until the morning: let us solace ourselves with loves. *Proverbs* 7:18.

11 Let him kiss me with the kisses of his mouth; for thy love is better than wine. *Song of Solomon* 1:2. (The *Song of Solomon,* or *Song of Songs,* became popular through public readings at Passover, and was accepted rather late in the canon. In rabbinical tradition, Rabbi Akiva, early in the Christian era, commented, "In all the world there is nothing to equal the day on which the Song of Songs was given to Israel." He described it as the Holy of Holies, and warned, "He who for the sake of entertainment sings the song as though it were a profane song, will have no place in the next world.")

12 Rise up, my love, my fair one, and come away.
For, lo, the winter is past, the rain is over and gone. *Song of Solomon* 2:10–11. (More at SEASONS.)

See also LOVE; SEX.

LOYALTY

13 Blessed is he that blesseth thee, and cursed is he that curseth thee. *Numbers* 24:9.

14 What is desired in a man is loyalty. *Proverbs* 19:22, RSV.

1 No man can serve two masters: for either he will hate the one, and love the other; or else he will hold to the one, and despise the other. Ye cannot serve God and mammon. *Matthew* 6:24.

2 He that is not with me is against me; and he that gathereth not with me scattereth abroad. *Matthew* 12:30.

3 Could ye not watch with me one hour? *Matthew* 26:40. (Jesus to Peter on the night before his death. See JESUS: PASSION AND DEATH.)

4 Be thou faithful unto death, and I will give thee a crown of life. *Revelation* 2:10.

See also GOD, LOYALTY TO; UNITY.

LUCIFER

5 How art thou fallen from heaven, O Lucifer, son of the morning! *Isaiah* 14:12.

6 Thou [Lucifer] hast said in thine heart, I will ascend into heaven, I will exalt my throne above the stars of God . . .

I will ascend above the heights of the clouds; I will be like the most High.

Yet thou shalt be brought down to hell, to the sides of the pit. *Isaiah* 14:13–15. (Lucifer is popularly taken to be another name for the devil. His fall here is assumed to be the same as that described at Luke 10:18: "I beheld Satan fall as lightning from heaven." This passage from *Isaiah* also fits well with the concept that Satan's sin was essentially a crime of pride. Nevertheless, Isaiah's Lucifer represents the king of Babylon; he is likened to the mythological figure "Day Star, son of Dawn." In the King James Version, this was translated *Lucifer,* which means "light bearer," "shining one.")

7 They that see thee shall narrowly look upon thee . . . saying, Is this the man that made the earth to tremble, that did shake kingdoms? *Isaiah* 14:16.

LUCK

8 The race is not to the swift, nor the battle to the strong, neither yet bread to the wise, nor riches to men of understanding, nor yet favor to men of skill; but time and chance happeneth to them all. *Ecclesiastes* 9:11. (In his column in the *New York Times Magazine* [April 10, 1988], William Safire noted that the use of *happeneth* is not only awkward, but wrong. That form of the verb is correct for the third person singular. But since the subject here is plural, the line should read, "Time and chance happen to them all.")

See also FATE.

LUXURY

See RICHES

LYING

See COVERUP; DECEIT AND LYING

MADNESS

1 The heart of the sons of men is full of evil, and madness is in their heart. *Ecclesiastes* 9:3.

2 Let his portion be with the beasts in the grass of the earth:

Let his heart be changed from man's, and let a beast's heart be given unto him: and let seven times [years] pass over him. *Daniel* 4:15–16. (Ostensibly about King Nebuchadnezzar, but in fact a veiled reference to the Seleucid King Antiochus IV, who ruled from 175–164 B.C. He took the name Antiochus Epiphanes, meaning "Antiochus, the manifested one." The Jews called him Antiochus Epimanes, meaning "Antiochus, the mad." The madness manifested itself when Nebuchadnezzar/Antiochus was "driven from men, and did eat grass as oxen.")

3 I will wail and howl, I will go stripped and naked. *Micah* 1:8.

See also EMOTIONS; PARANOIA.

MAGNIFICAT

See MARY

MANKIND

See HUMAN BEINGS

MARRIAGE

4 When a man hath taken a new wife, he shall not go out to war, neither shall he be charged with any business: but he shall be free at home one year, and shall cheer up his wife which he hath taken. *Deuteronomy* 24:5.

5 Why weepest thou? . . . am not I better to thee than ten sons? *I Samuel* 1:8. (Elkanah is reasoning with his beloved wife Hannah, who is bitterly unhappy because she has no children.)

6 Hearken, O daughter, and consider, and incline thine ear; forget also thine own people, and thy father's house;

So shall the king greatly desire thy beauty: for he is thy Lord; and worship thou him. *Psalms* 45:10–11. (These lines addressing a royal bride are part of a psalm probably written for the wedding of King Ahab and Princess Jezebel.)

7 Let thy fountain be blessed: and rejoice with the wife of thy youth.

Let her be as the loving hind and pleasant roe; let her breasts satisfy thee at all times; and be thou ravished always with her love. *Proverbs* 5:18–19.

[1] A virtuous woman is a crown to her husband. *Proverbs* 12:4.

[2] He who finds a wife finds a good thing, and obtains favor from the Lord. *Proverbs* 18:22, RSV.

[3] Live joyfully with the wife whom thou lovest. *Ecclesiastes* 9:9.

[4] Behold, thou art fair, my beloved, yea pleasant: also our bed is green. *Song of Solomon* 1:16. (The bed is the nuptial couch, decorated with green branches. In the Revised Standard Version, this passage reads: "Behold, you are beautiful, my beloved, truly lovely. Our couch is green.")

[5] A man . . . cleaveth unto his wife. *I Esdras* 4:20.

[6] It is not good that a man should be alone . . .

Mercifully ordain that we may become aged together. *Tobit* 8:6–7. (From the prayer of Tobias on the night of his wedding to his kinswoman Sarah. His plea is granted, for this is one of the happiest books in the Bible.)

[7] The grace of a wife delighteth her husband. *Ecclesiasticus* 26:13.

[8] They [man and wife] are no more twain, but one flesh. What therefore God hath joined together, let not man put asunder. *Matthew* 19:6. (Jesus to the Pharisees. He does, however, allow a man to set aside an unfaithful wife. *Matthew* 19:9.)

[9] Behold, the bridegroom cometh. *Matthew* 25:6.

[10] Whosoever putteth away his wife, and marrieth another, committeth adultery: and whosoever marrieth her that that is put away from her husband committeth adultery. *Luke* 16:18.

[11] It is better to marry than to burn. *I Corinthians* 7:9.

See also FAMILIES.

MARTHA AND MARY

[12] A certain woman named Martha received him [Jesus] into her house.

And she had a sister called Mary, which also sat at at Jesus' feet, and heard his word.

But Martha was cumbered about much serving, and came to him, and said, Lord, dost thou not care that my sister hath left me to serve alone? bid her therefore that she help me.

And Jesus answered and said unto her, Martha, Martha, thou are careful and troubled about many things:

But one thing is needful: and Mary hath chosen that good part, which shall not be taken away from her. *Luke* 10:38–42. (It has been some consolation to the many generations of women who have felt that Martha was rather unfairly slighted here that elsewhere she appears as an important and especially beloved disciple of Jesus. See, for example, *John* 11:5. This assumes that the Martha here is the same as the Martha of Bethany, whose sister is Mary and whose brother is LAZARUS.)

MARTYRDOM

1 He that loseth his life for my sake shall find it. *Matthew* 10:39. (Jesus to his disciples. See also SAINTS.)

MARY

2 The angel came in unto her, and said, Hail, thou that art highly favored, the Lord is with thee: blessed art thou among women. *Luke* 1:28

3 Fear not, Mary: for thou hast found favor with God.
And, behold, thou shalt conceive in thy womb, and bring forth a son, and shalt call his name JESUS. *Luke* 1:30–31.

4 Mary said, Behold the handmaid of the Lord; be it unto me according to thy word. *Luke* 1:38.

5 Blessed art thou among women, and blessed is the fruit of thy womb. *Luke* 1:42. (Mary's cousin Elizabeth greeting her.)

6 Mary said, My soul doth magnify the Lord.
And my spirit hath rejoiced in God my Savior.
For he hath regarded the low estate of his handmaiden: for, behold, from henceforth all generations shall call me blessed. *Luke* 1:46–48. (The beginning of the Magnificat, which goes on through verse 55. It is based on *I Samuel* 2:1–10. More at HAVES AND HAVE NOTS; PRIDE.)

7 Woman, behold thy son! *John* 19:26. (Jesus to his mother at the foot of the cross. He then said to "the disciple whom he loved," "Behold thy mother!" Then we are told that the disciple took her into his own home. This disciple is sometimes identified as John, son of Zebedee, but there is no evidence for this identification.)

MARY AND MARTHA

See MARTHA AND MARY

MEDICINE

See DISEASE; DOCTORS AND MEDICINE; HEALTH; MIDWIVES

MEDDLING

See BUSYBODIES

MEDIOCRITY

8 I know thy works, that thou art neither cold nor hot: I would thou were cold or hot.
So then because thou art lukewarm, and neither cold nor hot, I will spew thee out of my mouth. *Revelation* 3:15–16.

MEEK, THE

1 The meek shall inherit the earth; and shall delight themselves in the abundance of peace. *Psalms* 37:11. (Repeated in part in the Sermon on the Mount, *Matthew* 5:5.)

2 A little one shall become a thousand, and a small one a strong nation. *Isaiah* 60:22.

3 Many are in high place, and of renown: but mysteries are revealed unto the meek. *Ecclesiasticus* 3:19.

4 Blessed are the meek: for they shall inherit the earth. *Matthew* 5:5. (From the Sermon on the Mount.)

See also HUMILITY; JESUS; REVOLUTION.

MENE, MENE, TEKEL UPHARSIN See DESTRUCTION

MERCY

5 Mercy and truth are met together. *Psalms* 85:10. (More at SALVATION.)

6 Mercy is seasonable in the time of affliction, as clouds of rain in the time of drought. *Ecclesiasticus* 35:20. (The source perhaps for Portia's speech in *The Merchant of Venice:* "The quality of mery is not strained,/ It droppeth as the gentle rain from heaven/ Upon the place beneath.")

7 Blessed are the merciful: for they shall obtain mercy. *Matthew* 5:7. (From the Sermon on the Mount.)

8 Be ye therefore merciful, as your Father also is merciful. *Luke* 6:36.

9 Go, and do thou likewise [show mercy]. *Luke* 10:37. (The conclusion of the parable of the GOOD SAMARITAN.)

See also FORGIVENESS; TOLERANCE.

MESSIAH

10 Unto us a child is born, unto us a son is given: and the government shall be upon his shoulder: and his name shall be called Wonderful, Counsellor, The mighty God, The everlasting Father, The Prince of Peace.

Of the increase of his government and peace there shall be no end, upon the throne of David, and upon his kingdom, to order it, and to establish it with judgment and with justice from henceforth even for ever. *Isaiah* 9:6–7. (In the first verse, a more accurate translation is "his name shall be called Wonderful Counsellor," omitting the comma, as is done in the Revised Standard Version. The prophecies of a great king to come from the house of David later became associated with the concept of a Messiah. The term *Messiah* means "anointed one," and it was used in variable and ambiguous ways until the early Christian era, when it took on the more precise sense of savior and Lord.)

1 There shall come forth a rod out of the stem of Jesse, and a branch shall grow out of his roots. [Jesse was the father of King David.]

And the spirit of the Lord shall rest upon him, the spirit of wisdom and understanding, the spirit of counsel and might, the spirit of knowledge and of the fear of the Lord. *Isaiah* 11:1–2. (A similar passage is *Jeremiah* 23:5.)

2 With righteousness shall he judge the poor. *Isaiah* 11:4. (*Judge* here means "bring justice to." For a further description of the kingdom of peace the Davidic king will bring, see *Isaiah* 11:6–9 under PEACE.)

3 [He] shall stand as an ensign to the peoples; him shall the nations seek, and his dwellings shall be glorious. *Isaiah* 11:10, RSV.

4 Behold, a king shall reign in righteousness. *Isaiah* 32:1.

5 Behold, the King cometh unto thee . . . lowly, and riding upon an ass. *Zechariah* 9:9. (In Christian thought, this prophecy was fulfilled as Christ entered Jerusalem five days before his death.)

See also IMMANUEL; JESUS; SALVATION; SERVANT OF GOD.

MIDWIVES

6 It came to pass, because the midwives feared God, that he made them houses. *Exodus* 1:21. (In the Revised Standard Edition, God gives "families," rather than "houses." God rewarded these Egyptian midwives for not obeying Pharaoh's order to kill all sons born to Hebrew women. The midwives told Pharaoh that Hebrew women had their babies so quickly that midwives had no time to get there.)

MIND

See SOUL; SPIRIT; WISDOM

MIRACLES IN THE OLD TESTAMENT

(The Old Testament is full of wonders, a few of which have been selected here. Others appear in quotes from *Genesis, Exodus,* and so on; see the cross-references below. There is a different quality to the miracles of Jesus—see the next section—which are in general less poetic, and more personal and naturalistically detailed.)

7 The mountains skipped like rams, and the little hills like lambs. *Psalms* 114:4. (At the parting of the sea during the flight into Egypt. See also EXODUS.)

8 Then the eyes of the blind shall be opened, and the ears of the deaf shall be unstopped.

Then shall the lame man leap up as an hart, and the tongue of the dumb sing. *Isaiah* 35:5–6

1 Every valley shall be exalted, and every mountain and hill shall be made low. *Isaiah* 40:4. (More of the passage is given at PROPHETS.)

2 Then Shadrach, Meshach, and Abednego, came forth of the midst of the fire. *Daniel* 3:26. (These three Jews, promoted along with Daniel to positions of power by King Nebuchadnezzar, refused the king's order to worship an idol of gold. The king had them thrown into a fiery furnace, but they were rescued unharmed by an angel. Note that in *Isaiah* 43:2 it is promised to Israel, "When thou walkest through the fire, thou shalt not be burned; neither shall the flame kindle upon thee." See also the quote below from *Song of the Three Holy Children,* referring to the same miracle.)

3 In the same hour came forth fingers of a man's hand, and wrote over against the candlestick upon the plaister of the wall of the king's palace. *Daniel* 5:5. (The king is Belshazzar, king of Babylonia, incorrectly identified as a son of Nebuchadnezzar. The words are *Mene, Mene, Tekel, Upharsin.* See under DESTRUCTION.)

4 He [God] worketh signs and wonders in heaven and in earth. *Daniel* 6:27.

5 They walked in the midst of the fire, praising God, and blessing the Lord. *Song of the Three Holy Children 1.* (Another version of the miracle of Shadrach, Meshach, and Abednego. See above.)

See also DANIEL; EXODUS; JONAH; JOSHUA; JUDGMENT DAY; MOSES; NOAH; WAR.

MIRACLES OF JESUS

6 There came a leper and worshiped him, saying, Lord, if thou wilt, thou canst make me clean. *Matthew* 8:2. (This occurs immediately following the Sermon on the Mount. Jesus heals the leper and tells him, "See thou tell no man; but go thy way, show thyself to the priest, and offer the gift that Moses commanded." *Matthew* 8:4. Thus Jesus fulfills his unique mission while honoring the law of the Old Testament. It is the first of the series of miracles that open his ministry. See below.)

7 The centurion answered and said, Lord, I am not worthy that thou shouldest come under my roof: but speak the word only, and my servant shall be healed. *Matthew* 8:8. (Jesus is moved by the centurion's faith and tells him to return home, where he will find his sick servant healed. This miracle is considered particularly significant, because here Jesus extends his grace beyond his own people. See also FAITH.)

8 There arose a great tempest in the sea, insomuch that the ship [bearing Jesus and his disciples] was covered with the waves: but he was asleep.

And his disciples came to him, and awoke him, saying, Lord, save us: we perish.

And he saith unto them, Why are ye fearful, O ye of little faith? Then he arose, and rebuked the winds and the sea; and there was a great calm. *Matthew* 8:24–26.

1 Arise, take up thy bed, and go unto thine house. *Matthew* 9:6. (Jesus curing the young man with palsy. More at FORGIVENESS.)

2 She said within herself, If I may but touch his garment, I shall be whole. *Matthew* 9:21. (The woman with the issue of blood. Her faith moved Jesus, who cured her. See also FAITH.)

3 The maid is not dead, but sleepeth. *Matthew* 9:24. (Jesus to the ruler who came to him to revive his daughter who had died.)

4 The blind receive their sight, and the lame walk, the lepers are cleansed, and the deaf hear, the dead are raised up, and the poor have the gospel preached to them. *Matthew* 11:5.

5 We have here but five loaves, and two fishes.

He said, Bring them hither to me.

And he commanded the multitude to sit down on the grass, and took the five loaves, and the two fishes, and looking up to heaven, he blessed, and broke, and gave the loaves to his disciples, and the disciples to the multitude.

And they did all eat, and were filled: and they took up of the fragments that remained twelve baskets full. *Matthew* 14:17–20. (The size of the multitude was set at 5,000 by Matthew. The breaking and offering of bread prefigures the sacrament of the Eucharist. The fish was an early Christian symbol, for the letters of the Greek term for fish, *ichthus,* were the initials of *Iesous Christos Theou Uios Soter,* meaning, "Jesus Christ God's Son, Savior." The feeding of the multitude is one of the few events mentioned in all four gospels.)

6 And in the fourth watch of the night Jesus went unto them [his disciples], walking on the sea. *Matthew* 14:25. (Peter said to Jesus, "Lord, if it be thou, bid me come unto thee on the water." 14:28. Peter was able to walk on the water until he suddenly became fearful, lost faith, and began to sink. See FAITH. It was this miracle that led the disciples to recognize Jesus as the Son of God and to worship him.)

7 [The sick] besought him that they might only touch the hem of his garment: and as many as touched were made perfectly whole. *Matthew* 14:36.

8 O woman, great is thy faith: be it unto thee even as thou wilt. And her daughter was made whole from that very hour. *Matthew* 15:28 (Jesus to the woman of Canaan whose daughter was "grievously vexed with a devil.")

9 Arise, and take up thy bed, and walk. *Mark* 2:9. (Jesus asserts that just as he has the power to give this command, he has the power to forgive sins. See *Matthew* 9:6 above, where the same story is told, and *Matthew* 9:2 at FORGIVENESS.)

10 My little daughter lieth at the point of death. *Mark* 5:23. (See also above *Matthew* 9:24. In Matthew's version, the little girl is clearly said to be dead.)

1 There was a marriage in Cana of Galilee; and the mother of Jesus was there. *John* 2:1.

2 The mother of Jesus saith unto him, They have no wine.
Jesus saith unto her, Woman, what have I to do with thee? mine hour is not yet come. *John* 2:3–4. (Hour at hand or not, Jesus responded to his mother and changed water into wine for the wedding feast. The story has been interpreted in numerous ways. For example, the wine is symbolic both of Christ's blood and death and the new wine, or grace, that he brings to the world. John states that this is the first of Jesus' miracles; it "manifested forth his glory; and his disciples believed on him." *John* 2:11. See also WINE AND DRINKING.)

3 Rise, take up thy bed, and walk. *John* 5:8. (Jesus to the paralyzed man at the pool at Bethesda.)

4 Whether he be a sinner or no, I know not: one thing I know, that, whereas I was blind, now I see. *John* 9:25. (A blind man cured by Jesus, responding to Pharisees who were trying to establish that Jesus was a blasphemer and sinner.)

5 A certain man was sick, named Lazarus. *John* 11:1. (The raising of Lazarus, the greatest of Christ's miracles, is recorded only in *John*. It introduces the concept that Jesus represents resurrection for all mankind: "I am the resurrection, and the life." *John* 11:25. More under FAITH.)

6 He whom thou lovest is sick. *John* 11:3. (Lazarus's sisters, Martha and Mary, speaking to Jesus.)

7 When Jesus came, he found that he [Lazarus] had lain in the grave four days already. *John* 11:17.

8 Thy brother shall rise again. *John* 11:23. (Jesus to Martha.)

9 Jesus wept.
Then said the Jews, Behold how he loved him [Lazarus]! *John* 11:35–36.

10 He cried with a loud voice, Lazarus come forth. *John* 11:43.

MISFORTUNE

11 Ye shall not afflict any widow, or fatherless child. *Exodus* 22:22. (See also MONEY.)

12 Thou shalt not curse the dead, nor put a stumblingblock before the blind. *Leviticus* 19:14.

13 To him that is afflicted pity should be showed from his friend. *Job* 6:14.

14 In the thought of one who is at ease there is contempt for misfortune. *Job* 12:5, RSV.

1 Give justice to the weak and the fatherless; maintain the right of the afflicted and the destitute.
Rescue the weak and the needy; deliver them from the hand of the wicked. *Psalms* 82:3–4, RSV.

2 Do right to the widow, judge for the fatherless, give to the poor, defend the orphan, clothe the naked,
Heal the broken and weak, laugh not a lame man to scorn, defend the maimed, and let the blind man come into the sight of my clearness.
Keep the old and young within thy walls. *II Esdras* 2:20–22.

See also HAVES AND HAVE NOTS; JUSTICE AND FAIRNESS; LAW AND JUSTICE; OPPRESSION; POVERTY AND HUNGER; UNHAPPINESS.

MONEY

3 If thou lend money to any of my people that is poor by thee, thou shalt not be to him as a usurer, neither shalt thou lay upon him usury. *Exodus* 22:25. (The Revised Standard Version translation is, "If you lend money to any of my people with you who is poor, you shall not be to him as a creditor, and you shall not exact interest from him.")

4 The wages of him that is hired shall not abide with thee all night until the morning. *Leviticus* 19:13.

5 Thou say in thine heart, My power and the might of mine hand hath gotten me this wealth.
But thou shalt remember the Lord thy God: for it is he that giveth thee power to get wealth. *Deuteronomy* 8:17–18.

6 He hath swallowed down riches, and he shall vomit them up again. *Job* 20:15.

7 He heapeth up riches, and knoweth not who shall gather them. *Psalms* 39:6.

8 Be not afraid when one becomes rich, when the glory of his house increases. For when he dies, he will carry nothing away. *Psalms* 49:16–17, RSV.

9 Riches profit not in the day of wrath. *Proverbs* 11:4.

10 He that is surety for a stranger shall smart for it. *Proverbs* 11:15. (*Stranger* is meant in the sense of "outsider" or "foreigner.")

11 He that trusteth in his riches shall fall. *Proverbs* 11:28.

12 One man pretends to be rich, yet has nothing; another pretends to be poor, yet has great wealth. *Proverbs* 13:7, RSV.

13 Wealth hastily gotten will dwindle, but he who gathers little by little will increase it. *Proverbs* 13:11, RSV.

1 A good man leaveth an inheritance to his children's children. *Proverbs* 13:22.

2 Wealth maketh many friends. *Proverbs* 19:4.

3 Be not one of those who give pledges, who become surety for debts.
If you have nothing with which to pay, why should your bed be taken from under you? *Proverbs* 22:26–27, RSV.

4 Riches certainly make themselves wings; they fly away as an eagle toward heaven. *Proverbs* 23:5.

5 Riches are not for ever. *Proverbs* 27:24. (More at FARMING.)

6 He that maketh haste to be rich shall not be innocent. *Proverbs* 28:20.

7 Give me neither poverty nor riches. *Proverbs* 30:8.

8 He that loveth silver shall not be satisfied with silver; nor he that loveth abundance with increase. *Ecclesiastes* 5:10.

9 There is a grievous evil which I have seen under the sun: riches were kept by their owner to his hurt, and those riches were lost in a bad venture. *Ecclesiastes 5:13, RSV.*

10 A feast is made for laughter, and wine maketh merry: but money answereth all things. *Ecclesiastes* 10:19.

11 How is the gold become dim! *Lamentations* 4:1.

12 Neither their silver nor their gold shall be able to deliver them in the day of the Lord's wrath. *Zephaniah* 1:18.

13 The silver is mine, and the gold is mine, saith the Lord hosts. *Haggai* 2:8.

14 Be not greedy to add money to money. *Tobit* 5:18. (This charming book, one of the Apocrypha, urges both commonsense financial prudence and generosity to those in need.)

15 Wisdom that is hid, the treasure that is hoarded up, what profit is in them both? *Ecclesiasticus* 20:30

16 Watching for riches consumeth the flesh, and the care thereof driveth away sleep. *Ecclesiasticus* 31:1.

17 Gold hath been the ruin of many. *Ecclesiasticus* 31:6.

18 Forgive us our debts, as we forgive our debtors. *Matthew* 6:12. (More at LORD'S PRAYER.)

19 A rich man shall hardly enter into the kingdom of heaven.
. . . It is easier for a camel to go through the eye of a needle, than for a rich man to enter into the kingdom of God. *Matthew* 19:23–24. (It is often claimed that the "eye of a needle" refers to a narrow gate where camels had to be unloaded to pass through. Scholars say that this comforting suggestion is not founded in fact.)

1 Thy money perish with thee. *Acts* 8:20. (Peter's curse upon the sorcerer Simon, who tried to buy from him the powers he saw demonstrated by the apostles.)

2 Filthy lucre. *I Timothy* 3:3. (More under CLERGY.)

3 The love of money is the root of all evil. *I Timothy* 6:10.

4 In one hour so great riches is come to nought. *Revelation* 18:17. (This refers to the destruction of Babylon, but might apply to certain days on Wall Street as well.)

See also BORROWING AND LENDING; BUSINESS; GIVING; GREED; POVERTY AND HUNGER; RICH AND POOR; PROPERTY; RICHES; SUCCESS.

MORNING

5 Arise, shine; for thy light is come, and the glory of the Lord is risen upon thee. *Isaiah* 60:1.

6 The night is far spent, the day is at hand. *Romans* 13:12. (More at VIRTUE.)

MORTALITY

See DEATH; LIFE

MOTHER

See PARENTS

MOSES

7 I am slow of speech, and of a slow tongue. *Exodus* 4:10. (Here, speaking to God, Moses expresses doubt that he is capable of fulfilling his mission. God, although displeased, suggests that Aaron, Moses's brother, may act as a spokesman.)

8 Thou hast found grace in my sight, and I know thee by name. *Exodus* 33:17. (God is speaking to Moses.)

9 The man Moses was very meek. *Numbers* 12:3.

10 No man knoweth of his sepulchre unto this day. *Deuteronomy* 34:6.

11 Moses was a hundred and twenty years old when he died: his eye was not dim, nor his natural force abated. *Deuteronomy* 34:7.

12 There arose not a prophet since in Israel like unto Moses, whom the Lord knew face to face. *Deuteronomy* 34:10.

See also EXODUS; GOD, ENCOUNTERS WITH; GOVERNMENT; MOSES AND THE EGYPTIANS; TEN COMMANDMENTS.

MOSES AND THE EGYPTIANS

1 There arose up a new king in Egypt, which knew not Joseph.

And he said unto his people, Behold, the people of the children of Israel are more and mightier than we. *Exodus* 1:8–9. (The king may have been Sethos I, his son, the great Ramses II, or Ramses' son Merneptah. A victory stele from 1220 B.C., in the reign of Merneptah refers to a battle in Canaan, which may have involved the Israelites.)

2 The Egyptians made the children of Israel to serve with rigor:

And they made their lives bitter with hard bondage, in morter, and in brick, and in all manner of service in the field. *Exodus* 1:13–14. (The Hebrews were held as slave laborers, especially for the production of bricks. See *Exodus* 5:7, below.)

3 Every son that is born ye shall cast into the river. *Exodus* 1:22. (Pharaoh ordering the death of sons born to the Hebrews. See also MIDWIVES. Moses' mother set him out among the reeds at the edge of the river in a basket made of bulrushes.)

4 The daughter of the Pharaoh came down to wash herself at the river; and her maidens walked along by the river's side. *Exodus* 2:5.

5 She saw the child: and, behold, the babe wept. And she had compassion on him, and said, This is one of the Hebrews' children. *Exodus* 2:6.

6 She called his name Moses: and she said, Because I drew him out of the water. *Exodus* 2:10. (The Hebrew *Moshe* means "to draw out"; but the name more likely derives from the Egyptian word for "child.")

7 He [Moses] slew the Egyptian, and hid him in the sand. *Exodus* 2:12. (More at CRIME.)

8 Who made thee a prince and a judge over us? intendest thou to kill me, as thou killedst the Egyptian? *Exodus* 2:14. (Moses is challenged by one of his own people, who had seen him kill the Egyptian. Realizing that he was in danger, Moses fled to the household of Jethro, a priest in Midian, in southeast Canaan. He worked as a shepherd, married one of Jethro's daughters, and here, in the wilderness, was first called by God. See below.)

9 The bush burned with fire, and the bush was not consumed. *Exodus* 3:2.

10 God called unto him out of the midst of the bush, and said Moses, Moses. And he said, Here am I. *Exodus* 3:4. (This recalls God calling out to Jacob in a dream. See GOD, ENCOUNTERS WITH.)

11 Put off thy shoes from off thy feet, for the place whereon thou standest is holy ground. *Exodus* 3:5.

12 I am come down to deliver them out of the hands of the Egyptians, and to bring them up out of that land unto a good land and a large, unto a land flowing with milk and honey. *Exodus* 3:8.

1 God said unto Moses, I AM THAT I AM. *Exodus* 3:14.

2 Thus saith the Lord God of Israel, Let my people go. *Exodus* 5:1.

3 Ye shall no more give the people straw to make brick, as heretofore: let them go and gather straw for themselves. *Exodus* 5:7. (Bricks made of mud or clay, usually mixed with straw or other vegetable matter, were the most common building material in the ancient biblical world. The Hebrews were required to produce a quota of bricks for the Pharaoh, and here he makes the job harder by forcing them to gather their own straw.)

4 The river shall bring forth frogs abundantly, which shall go up and come into thine house, and into thy bedchamber, and upon thy bed, and into the house of thy servants, and upon thy people, and into thine ovens, and into thy kneading troughs. *Exodus* 8:3. (This is the second of the ten plagues inflicted on the Egyptians. In order, they were: 1) the rivers and streams were turned to blood, and the fish died; 2) the frogs swarmed; 3) lice and then 4) flies appeared in great numbers; 5) the cattle died; 6) an epidemic of boils afflicted people and animals; 7) a hailstorm ruined crops; 8) clouds of locusts covered the land; 9) Moses called down three days of darkness; 19) the death of the firstborn.)

5 The Lord said unto Moses, Stretch out thine hand toward heaven that there may be darkness over the land of Egypt, even darkness which may be felt. *Exodus* 10:21.

6 All the firstborn in the land of Egypt shall die. *Exodus* 11:5.

7 I will pass through the land of Egypt this night, and will smite all the firstborn in the land of Egypt, both man and beast; and against all the gods of Egypt I will execute judgment: I am the Lord. *Exodus* 12:12.

8 There was a great cry in Egypt; for there was not a house where there was not one dead. *Exodus* 12:30.

See also EXODUS; PASSOVER.

MUSIC

9 The noise of them that sing I do hear. *Exodus* 32:18.

10 Write ye this song. *Deuteronomy* 31:19. (A song and a poem are essentially the same.)

11 Awake, awake, Deborah: awake, awake, utter a song. *Judges* 5:12. (Deborah, one of the great figures of the Old Testament, was a prophetess and "judge," that is, a wartime leader. Here, in a song of triumph, she celebrates victory over the Canaanite commander Sisera.)

12 The spirit of the Lord came upon Gideon, and he blew a trumpet. *Judges* 6:34.

[1] The women came out of all cities of Israel, singing and dancing, to meet King Saul, with tabrets, with joy, and with instruments of music. *I Samuel* 18:6. (A tabret is a small drum, like a tamborine.)

[2] David and all the house of Israel played before the Lord on all manner of instruments made of fir wood, even on harps, and on psalteries, and on timbrels, and on cornets, and on cymbals. *II Samuel* 6:5. (A similar passage is at *I Chronicles* 13:8. The people of Canaan and surrounding regions were famous for their musical accomplishments. A musical parade is described at *Psalms* 68:25: "The singers went before, the players on instruments followed after; among them were the damsels playing with timbrels.")

[3] The people piped with pipes, and rejoiced with great joy. *I Kings* 1:40. (Solomon has just become king.)

[4] Sing unto the Lord, all the earth. *I Chronicles* 16:23.

[5] I will sing unto the Lord, because he hath dealt bountifully with me. *Psalms* 13:6.

[6] Praise the Lord with the lyre, make melody to him with the harp of ten strings! Sing to him a new song, play skillfully on the strings, with loud shouts. *Psalms* 33:2–3, RSV.

[7] God has gone up with a shout, the Lord with the sound of a trumpet. *Psalms* 47:5.

[8] I call to remembrance my song in the night: I commune with mine own heart. *Psalms* 77:6.

[9] Sing aloud to God our strength; shout for joy to the God of Jacob! Raise a song, sound the timbrel, the sweet lyre with the harp.
Blow the trumpet at the new moon. *Psalms* 81:1–3, RSV.

[10] O sing unto the Lord a new song. *Psalms* 96:1. (See also *Isaiah* 42:10.)

[11] Make sweet melody, sing many songs, that thou mayest be remembered. *Isaiah* 23:16.

[12] Awake and sing. *Isaiah* 26:19.

[13] Ye shall have a song . . . and gladness of heart. *Isaiah* 30:29.

[14] Use not much the company of a woman that is a singer, lest thou be taken with her attempts. *Ecclesiasticus* 9:4.

[15] Sing a song of praise, bless the Lord in all his works.
Magnify his name, and show forth his praise with the songs of your lips, and with harps. *Ecclesiasticus* 39:14–15.

1 Speaking to yourselves in psalms and hymns and spiritual songs, singing and making melody in your heart to the Lord. *Ephesians* 5:19.

See also DAVID; GOD, PRAISING.

MYSTERY

2 That which is far off, and exceeding deep, who can find it out? *Ecclesiastes* 7:24.

3 We speak the wisdom of God in a mystery. *I Corinthians* 2:7.

See also DARKNESS; SECRETS.

NAMES

1 I know thee by name, and thou hast found grace in my sight. *Exodus* 33:12. (God to Moses.)

2 I have redeemed thee, I have called thee by thy name; thou art mine. *Isaiah* 43:1. (God to the Israelites.)

NATURE

3 While the earth remaineth, seedtime and harvest, and cold and heat, and summer and winter, and day and night shall not cease. *Genesis* 8:22.

4 The heaven and the heaven of heavens is the Lord's thy God, the earth also, with all that therein is. *Deuteronomy* 10:14.

5 The tree of the field is man's life. *Deuteronomy* 20:19.

6 Blessed of the Lord be his [Joseph's] land, for the precious things of heaven, for the dew, and for the deep that coucheth beneath,

And for the precious fruits brought forth by the sun, and for the precious things brought forth by the moon,

And for the chief things of the ancient mountains, and for the precious things of the lasting hills,

And for the precious things of the earth and fulness thereof. *Deuteronomy* 33:13–16.

7 Thou shalt be in league with the stones of the field: and the beasts of the field shall be at peace with thee. *Job* 5:23.

8 Ask now the beasts, and they shall teach thee; and the fowls of the air, and they shall tell thee:

Or speak to the earth, and it shall teach thee; and the fishes of the sea shall declare unto thee. *Job* 12:7–8.

9 The earth is the Lord's, and the fulness thereof; the world, and they that dwell therein. *Psalms* 24:1. (Quoted in part by Paul at *I Corinthians* 10:26.)

10 The earth is full of the goodness of the Lord. *Psalms* 33:5.

11 The pastures are clothed with flocks; the valleys also are covered over with corn; they shout for joy, they also sing. *Psalms* 65:13.

12 The earth is full of thy [the Lord's] riches. *Psalms* 104:24.

13 I lift up mine eyes to the hills. *Psalms* 121:1.

[1] The earth abideth for ever. *Ecclesiastes* 1:4. (The entire passage is given at VANITY).

[2] The profit of the earth is for all: the king himself is served by the field. *Ecclesiastes* 5:9.

[3] The desert shall rejoice, and blossom as the rose. *Isaiah* 35:1. (The exact identity of the flower is uncertain. In the Revised Standard Version, the translation is "crocus": "The wilderness and the dry land shall be glad, the desert shall rejoice and blossom; like the crocus it shall blossom abundantly, and rejoice with joy and singing." *Isaiah* 35:1–2, RSV. *Harper's Bible Dictionary* suggests that the flower may be *Narcissus tazetta,* of the lily family; it grows wild in arid regions of the Holy Land.)

[4] The Lord looked upon the earth, and filled it with his blessings. *Ecclesiasticus* 16:29.

[5] For the earth bringeth forth fruit of herself; first the blade, then the ear, after that the full corn in the ear. *Mark* 4:28. (The Revised Standard Versions uses *grain* instead of *corn.* Corn actually is a hybrid that must be cultivated.)

[6] Every creature of God is good. *I Timothy* 4:4.

See also ANIMALS; CREATION; ENVIRONMENT; EVENING; FARMING; GARDENS AND FLOWERS; HEAVENS AND SKY; LIFE'S WONDERS; MORNING; OCEAN AND SEA; SEASONS; STARS; WEATHER.

NEIGHBOR

[7] You shall not remove your neighbor's landmark. *Deuteronomy* 19:14, RSV.

[8] Do not plan evil against your neighbor who dwells trustingly beside you. *Proverbs* 3:29, RSV.

[9] He who belittles his neighbor lacks sense, but a man of understanding remains silent. *Proverbs* 11:12, RSV.

[10] Withdraw thy foot from thy neighbor's house; lest he be weary of thee, and so hate thee. *Proverbs* 25:17.

[11] Better is a neighbor that is near than a brother far off. *Proverbs* 27:10.

[12] Bear not hatred to thy neighbor for every wrong. *Ecclesiasticus* 10:6. (The number of biblical warnings against feuding with neighbors suggest that the irritations of community life must have been every bit as keen then as now.)

[13] Be faithful to thy neighbor in his poverty, that thou mayest rejoice in his prosperity. *Ecclesiasticus* 22:23.

1 Thou shalt love thy neighbor as thyself. *Mark* 12:30–31. (More at TEN COMMANDMENTS.)

NEWS

2 I will do a thing in Israel, at which both the ears of every one that heareth it shall tingle. *I Samuel* 3:11. (The Lord is speaking to the young Samuel.)

3 Good news refreshes the bones. *Proberbs* 15:30 RSV.

4 As cold waters to a thirsty soul, so is good news from a far country. *Proverbs* 25:25.

5 How beautiful upon the mountains are the feet of him that bringeth good tidings, that publisheth peace. *Isaiah* 52:7.

6 A wonderful and horrible thing is committed in the land. *Jeremiah* 5:30.

7 Publish, and conceal not. *Jeremiah* 50:2.

See also TALK.

NEW THINGS

8 There is no new thing under the sun. *Ecclesiastes* 1:9. (More at ENNUI.)

9 Behold, I will do a new thing. *Isaiah* 43:19. (God speaks. The author of *Ecclesiastes*—see the quote above—has been corrected by a higher authority. Also, "New things do I declare: before they spring forth I tell you of them." *Isaiah* 42:9.)

10 Neither do men put new wine into old bottles. *Matthew* 9:17. (Jesus answering disciples who asked why they did not have to fast while the Pharisees fasted. The answer means that Jesus has brought a new faith, with new ways.)

NIMROD

11 He was a mighty hunter before the Lord. *Genesis* 10:9.

NOAH AND THE ARK

12 And the Lord said, I will destroy man whom I have created from the face of the earth; both man, and beast, and the creeping thing, and the fowls of the air; for it repenteth me that I have made them.
But Noah found grace in the eyes of the Lord. *Genesis* 6:7–8.

13 Noah was a just man and perfect in his generations, and Noah walked with God. *Genesis*. 6:9.

[1] And God said unto Noah, The end of all flesh is come before me; for the earth is filled with violence through them; and, behold, I will destroy them with the earth.

Make thee an ark of gopher wood. *Genesis* 6:13–14. (Gopher wood has not been definitely identified.)

[2] I, even I, do bring a flood of waters upon the earth. *Genesis* 6:17.

[3] And of every living thing of all flesh, of every creeping thing of the earth after his kind, two of every sort shall come unto thee, to keep them alive. *Genesis* 6:21.

[4] I will cause it to rain upon the earth forty days and forty nights. *Genesis* 7:4.

[5] There went in two and two unto Noah into the ark. *Genesis* 7:9.

[6] And the dove came in to him in the evening; and, lo, in her mouth was an olive leaf pluckt off. *Genesis* 8:11.

[7] The Lord said in his heart, I will not again curse the ground any more for man's sake. *Genesis* 8:21.

[8] And God blessed Noah and his sons, and said unto them, Be fruitful, and multiply, and replenish the earth. *Genesis*. 9:1.

[9] I do set my bow in the cloud, and it shall be for a token of a covenant between me and the earth. *Genesis* 9:13. (In Hebrew a single word denotes both a rainbow and a warrior's bow.)

NONVIOLENCE

See PACIFISM

NOTORIETY

[10] Israel shall be a proverb and a byword among all people. *I Kings* 9:7. (The last part of a warning from God to Solomon on what will happen if his people fail to keep his commandments. Also at *II Chronicles* 7:20.)

[11] A curse, and an astonishment, and an hissing, and a reproach. *Jeremiah* 29:18.

[12] We are made a spectacle unto the world. *I Corinthians* 4:9.

OBEYING

See GOD, OBEYING AND SERVING

OCCULT, THE

1 Thou shalt not suffer a witch to live. *Exodus* 22:18. (At *Leviticus* 20:27, death is specified for a wizard as well. As far as we know, however, there were no witch hunts or executions of witches or wizards in biblical times.)

2 Do not turn to mediums or wizards. *Leviticus* 19:31, RSV.

3 There shall not be found among you any one that maketh his son or his daughter to pass through the fire, or that useth divination, or an observer of times, or an enchanter, or a witch.

Or a charmer, or a consulter with familiar spirits, or a wizard, or a necromancer. *Deuteronomy* 18:10–11. (See also *II Kings* 17:17.)

4 Seek me a woman that hath a familiar spirit, that I may go to her, and enquire of her. *I Samuel* 28:7. (This is Saul speaking. The woman with the "familiar spirit" was the Witch of Endor. After getting Saul to promise that he would not punish her as a witch, she raised the spirit of the dead prophet Samuel, who foretold that on the morrow Saul would be killed and his army defeated by the Philistines.)

See also DEVILS.

OCEAN AND SEA

5 Deep calleth unto deep. *Psalms* 42:7. (The underworld ocean calls to the psalmist's cast-down soul.)

6 Thy [God's] way is in the sea, and thy path in the great waters, and thy footsteps are not known. *Psalms* 77:19. (This refers both to God's triumph over the original ocean of chaos and his division of the Red Sea.)

7 Yonder is the sea, great and wide, which teems with things innumerable, living things both small and great. *Psalms* 104:25, RSV.

8 They that go down to the sea in ships, that do business in great waters;

These see the works of the Lord, and his wonders in the deep. *Psalms* 107:23–24.

9 They mount up to the heavens [on stormy waves], they go down again to the depths. *Psalms* 107:26.

10 They reel to and fro, and stagger like a drunken man, and are at their wit's end. *Psalms* 107:27.

1 There is sorrow on the sea. *Jeremiah* 49:23.

2 I saw as it were a sea of glass mingled with fire. *Revelation* 15:2.

See also SHIPS.

OLD AGE

3 Thou shalt go to thy fathers in peace; thou shalt be buried in a good old age. *Genesis* 15:15. (God to Abraham.)

4 Thou shalt rise up before the hoary head, and honor the face of the old man. *Leviticus* 19:32.

5 His eye was not dim, nor his natural force abated. *Deuteronomy* 34:7. (Description of Moses at the time of his death at age 120.)

6 Thou art old and stricken in years. *Joshua* 13:1. (The Lord to Joshua.)

7 Thine age shall be clearer than the noonday; thou shalt shine forth, thou shalt be as the morning. *Job* 11:17.

8 With the ancient is wisdom; and in length of days understanding. *Job* 12:12.

9 Multitude of years should teach wisdom. *Job* 32:7.

10 I have been young, and now am old. *Psalms* 37:25.

11 Cast me not off in the time of old age; forsake me not when my strength faileth. *Psalms* 71:9.

12 When I am old and greyheaded, O God, forsake me not. *Psalms* 71:18.

13 We spend our years as a tale that is told.

The days of our years are threescore years and ten; and if by reason of strength they be fourscore years, yet is their strength labor and sorrow; for it is soon cut off, and we fly away. *Psalms* 90:9–10. (The passage is clearer in the Revised Standard Version, where it begins, "Our years come to an end like a sigh." The *Book of Common Prayer* reads: "We bring our years to an end, as it were a tale that is told. The days of our age are threescore and ten; and though men be so strong that they come to fourscore years, yet is their strength then but labor and sorrow; so soon passeth it away, and we are gone.")

14 Grandchildren are the crown of the aged. *Proverbs* 17:6, RSV.

15 The years draw nigh when thou shalt say, I have no pleasure in them . . .

Fears shall be in the way, and the almond tree shall flourish, and the grasshopper shall be a burden, and desire shall fail: because man goeth to his long home, and the mourners go about the streets. *Ecclesiastes* 12:1, 5. (From a poignant passage, calling upon the reader to remember God and rejoice while young, before age takes its course. See *Ecclesiastes* 12:1–7. Some also at YOUTH and DEATH.)

1 Miss not the discourse of the elders. *Ecclesiasticus* 8:9.

2 As the clear light is upon the holy candlestick; so is the beauty of the face in ripe age. *Ecclesiasticus* 26:17.

OLD WAYS

See PAST, THE

OPPORTUNITY

3 Observe the opportunity. *Ecclesiasticus* 4:20.

OPPRESSION

4 My father also chastised you with whips, but I will chastise you with scorpions. *I Kings* 12:14. (The term *scorpion* can refer to a whip made of leather and spikes, as well as to the animal. Scorpions appear a number of times in the Bible as symbols of suffering and evil. The speaker here is Rehoboam, son of Solomon, responding to advice to reduce forced labor and taxes. His harsh government quickly led to a revolt of ten northern tribes, which were henceforth known as Israel. The tribes of Judah and later Benjamin allied themselves with Rehoboam and the house of David, forming the kingdom of Judah. This revolt ended the unification of the tribes of Israel that had begun under Saul. See also REVOLT.)

5 Trust not in oppression, and become not vain in robbery: if riches increase, set not your heart upon them. *Psalms* 62:10.

6 Envy thou not the oppressor, and choose none of his ways. *Proverbs* 3:31.

7 Rob not the poor, because he is poor: neither oppress the afflicted in [at] the gate. *Proverbs* 22:22. (The afflicted, or handicapped, often begged near the gates of a city or at the gate of a farm or townhouse.)

8 Like a roaring lion or a charging bear is a wicked ruler over a poor people.

A ruler who lacks understanding is a cruel oppressor; but he who hates unjust gain will prolong his days. *Proverbs* 28:15–16, RSV.

9 Surely oppression maketh a wise man mad. *Ecclesiastes* 7:7.

10 What mean ye that ye beat my people to pieces, and grind the faces of the poor? *Isaiah* 3:15.

11 He looked for judgment [justice], but behold oppression; for righteousness, but behold a cry. *Isaiah* 5:7.

1 He [God] . . . will hear the prayer of the oppressed. *Ecclesiasticus* 35:13.

See also GOVERNMENT; POVERTY AND HUNGER; POWER.

ORDER

2 Set thine house in order. *II Kings* 20:1. (Also at *Isaiah* 38:1. and *II Esdras* 14:13.)

3 Let all things be done decently and in order. *I Corinthians* 14:40.

PACIFISM

1 Whosoever shall smite thee on thy right cheek, turn to him the other also. *Matthew* 5:39.

PARABLES

2 He spoke many things unto them in parables. *Matthew* 13:3.

3 The disciples came, and said unto him, Why speakest thou unto them in parables?

. . . Because it is given unto you to know the mysteries of the kingdom of heaven, but to them it is not given. *Matthew* 13:10–11. (Jesus to his disciples. "Who hath ears to hear, let him hear," he told them. *Matthew* 13:9. But he went on to warn that many have been dulled by worldly and sinful concerns.) See also *Mark* 4.

See also GOOD SAMARITAN; PRODIGAL SON.

PARANOIA

4 I hear the whispering of many—terror on every side!—as they scheme together against me, as they plot to take my life. *Psalms* 31:13, RSV.

See also FEAR.

PARENTS

5 Honor thy father and thy mother: that thy days may be long upon the land which the Lord thy God giveth thee. *Exodus* 20:12. (The Fifth Commandment.)

6 He that smiteth his father, or his mother, shall surely be put to death. *Exodus* 21:15.

7 He that curseth his father, or his mother, shall surely be put to death. *Exodus* 21:17. (Almost the same words appear at *Leviticus* 20:9. The threat is somewhat more indirect at *Proverbs* 20:20: "Whoso curseth his father or his mother, his lamp shall be put out in obscure darkness." The penalty may seem primitive, but in Connecticut's Code of Laws from 1650, death was ordered for children who cursed, hit, or stubbornly disobeyed their parents. Exceptions were granted in the case of parents who had been negligent or cruel.)

8 Hear the instruction of thy father, and forsake not the law of thy mother. *Proverbs* 1:8. (See also *Proverbs* 6:20.)

1 Despise not thy mother when she is old. *Proverbs* 23:22.

2 The fathers have eaten a sour grape, and the children's teeth are set on edge. *Jeremiah* 31:29 (Also at *Ezekiel* 18:2, and discussed in *Ezekiel* 18. The point is that under God's law, the proverb shall no longer hold. Each person shall be judged for himself or herself alone. "The son shall not bear the iniquity of the father." *Ezekiel* 18:20.)

3 As is the mother, so is her daughter. *Ezekiel* 16:44.

4 Be joyful, O thou mother, with thy children. *II Esdras* 2:30.

5 My son, help thy father in his age, and grieve him not as long as he liveth. *Ecclesiasticus* 3:12. (Most of this chapter of *Ecclesiasticus* urges honoring one's parents. It is recommended reading for adolescents.)

See also CHILDREN; MARRIAGE.

PASSOVER

6 This month [Nissan] shall be unto you the beginning of months; it shall be the first month of the year to you. *Exodus* 12:2.

7 They shall eat the flesh [of a lamb] in that night, roast with fire, and unleavened bread; and with bitter herbs they shall eat it. *Exodus* 12:8.

8 Ye shall eat it in haste; it is the Lord's passover. *Exodus* 12:11.

9 I will pass through the land of Egypt this night, and will smite all the firstborn in the land of Egypt, both man and beast. *Exodus* 12:12.

10 When I see the blood, I will pass over you. *Exodus* 12:13. (God has told the Jews to mark their doorways with the blood of the lamb that they are to eat that night.)

11 This day shall be unto you for a memorial; and ye shall keep it a feast unto the Lord throughout your generations. *Exodus* 12:14. (For a detailed description of the celebration of Passover, see *II Chronicles* 35:1–19.)

12 They kept the feast of unleavened bread seven days, making merry before the Lord. *I Esdras* 7:14. (The happiest Passover in the Bible, after the restoration of the Temple in 520 to 515 B.C.)

See also FEASTS, RELIGIOUS; MOSES AND THE EGYPTIANS.

PAST

13 Remember ye not the former things, neither consider the things of old. *Isaiah* 43:18.

14 Ask for the old paths, where is the good way, and walk therein, and ye shall find rest for your souls. *Jeremiah* 6:16. (The Revised Standard

Version reads, "Look and ask for the ancient paths, where the good way is; and walk in it, and find rest for your souls.")

1 Your fathers, where are they? And the prophets, do they live forever? *Zechariah* 1:5.

See also HISTORY.

PATIENCE

2 By long forbearing is a prince persuaded. *Proverbs* 25:15.

3 The patient in spirit is better than the proud in spirit. *Ecclesiastes* 7:8.

4 Blessed is he that waiteth. *Daniel* 12:12.

5 Woe unto you that have lost patience. *Ecclesiasticus* 2:14.

6 In your patience possess ye your souls. *Luke* 21:19.

7 Let us run with patience the race that is set before us. *Hebrews* 12:1.

8 Be patient therefore, brethren, unto the coming of the Lord. Behold, the husbandman waiteth for the precious fruit of the earth, and hath long patience for it, until he receive the early and latter rain. *James* 5:7.

See also JOB.

PAUL

9 Saul, yet breathing out threatenings and slaughter against the disciples of the Lord, went unto the high priest. *Acts* 9:1. (A dramatic portrait of the young Paul, a devoted Pharisee and a zealous persecutor of the early Christians. *Saul* and *Paul* are Aramaic and Roman versions of the same name.)

As he journeyed, he came near Damascus: and suddenly there shined round about him a light from heaven:

And he fell to the earth, and heard a voice saying unto him, Saul, Saul, why persecutest thou me?

And he said, Who art thou, Lord? And the Lord said, I am Jesus whom thou persecutest: it is hard for thee to kick against the pricks. *Acts* 9:3–5.

10 He is a chosen vessel unto me, to bear my name before the Gentiles, and kings, and the children of Israel. *Acts* 9:15. (God speaking of Paul.)

11 And immediately there fell from his eyes as it had been scales. *Acts* 9:18. (The Revised Standard Version reads, "Immediately something like scales fell from his eyes and he regained his sight.")

12 I have set thee to be a light of the Gentiles. *Acts* 13:47. (Paul and Barnabas quoting the Lord's description of their mission.)

1 I am a man which am a Jew of Tarsus, a city in Cilicia, a citizen of no mean city. *Acts* 21:39.

2 Is it lawful for you to scourge a man that is a Roman, and uncondemned? *Acts* 22:25. (Paul asserting his rights under Roman law to a Roman officer who has him in custody.)

3 I am a Pharisee, the son of a Pharisee. *Acts* 23:6. (Paul goes on to point out that the doctrines of the Pharisees concerning the existence of spirits and the possibility of resurrection are similar to those of the disciples of Jesus.)

4 I am not mad . . . but speak forth the words of truth and soberness. *Acts* 26:25.

5 Last of all he [Jesus] was seen of me also, as of one born out of due time.
For I am the least of the apostles, that am not meet to be called an apostle, because I persecuted the church of God.
But by the grace of God I am what I am. *I Corinthians* 15:8–10.

See also APOSTLES AND DISCIPLES.

PEACE

6 The Lord shall fight for you, and ye shall hold your peace. *Exodus* 14:14.

7 I will give you peace in the land, and ye shall lie down, and none shall make you afraid. *Leviticus* 26:6.

8 The Lord is peace. *Judges* 6:24, RSV. (This is the name of the altar Gideon built to God. In the King James Version, it is given as *Jehovah-shalom.*)

9 Go in peace. *Judges* 18:6.

10 Peace be with thee. *Judges* 19:20.

11 Judah and Israel dwelt safely, every man under his vine and under his fig tree. *I Kings* 4:25.

12 Be content with your glory, and stay at home. *II Kings* 14:10, RSV. (Advice from King Jehoash of Israel to King Amaziah of Judah, who had challenged him to war. Amaziah did not listen. Jehoash was victorious and plundered Jerusalem. Amaziah was killed by conspirators in revolt against him.)

13 Seek peace, and pursue it. *Psalms* 34:14.

14 He [God] makes wars cease to the end of the earth; he breaks the bow, and shatters the spear, he burns the chariots with fire! *Psalms* 46:9, RSV.

15 Righteousness and peace have kissed each other. *Psalms* 85:10. (More at SALVATION.)

1 When a man's ways please the Lord, he maketh even his enemies to be at peace with him. *Proverbs* 16:7.

2 It is an honor for a man to cease from strife. *Proverbs* 20:3.

3 Better is a handful with quietness, than both the hands full with travail and vexation of spirit. *Ecclesiastes* 4:6.

4 They shall beat their swords into plowshares, and their spears into pruning hooks: nation shall not lift up sword against nation, neither shall they learn war any more. *Isaiah* 2:4. Also *Micah* 4:3. (This will happen in the "last days," after God has judged among the nations. In *Joel* 3:10, the people are called upon to beat their plowshares into swords, pruning hooks into spears for a final battle with the forces of evil. See under WAR.)

5 The wolf also shall dwell with the lamb, and the leopard shall lie down with the kid; and the calf and the young lion and the fatling together; and a little child shall lead them.

And the cow and the bear shall feed; their young ones shall lie down together: and the lion shall eat straw like the ox.

And the sucking child shall play on the hole of the asp, and the weaned child shall put his hand on the cockatrice den.

They shall not hurt nor destroy in all my holy mountain: for the earth shall be full of the knowledge of the Lord, as the waters cover the sea. *Isaiah* 11:6–9. (Isaiah describes here the idyllic peace that will prevail in the reign of the promised Davidic king, or Messiah. A cockatrice is a mythological serpent, supposedly able to kill with a glance. In the Revised Standard Version, however, *cockatrice* is replaced by *adder*.)

6 The whole earth is at rest, and is quiet: they break forth into singing. *Isaiah* 14:7. (This is the peace to come after the destruction of Babylon; *they* refers to the surviving people of Israel.)

7 Lord, thou wilt ordain peace for us. *Isaiah* 26:12.

8 The work of righteousness shall be peace. *Isaiah* 32:17.

9 There shall be peace and truth in my days. *Isaiah* 39:8. (Spoken by Judah's King Hezekiah. Praised in the Bible for his piety, Hezekiah is also criticized for dealing with the Babylonians in an attempt to relieve the weight of Assyrian rule in the region. Isaiah warns him that one day his kingdom will be conquered by Babylon, and Hezekiah answers, essentially, that at least in his own days peace will prevail. In *II Kings* 20:19, Hezekiah asks Isaiah: "Is it not good, if peace and truth be in my days?" In modern terms, Hezekiah might be accused of appeasement.)

10 Peace, peace to him that is afar off, and to him that is near, saith the Lord. *Isaiah* 57:19.

11 Saying, Peace, peace; when there is no peace. *Jeremiah* 6:14 and 8:11. (Here Jeremiah mocks those who say that all will be well, while he preaches that God will punish Israel with war and destruction.)

1 They shall sit every man under his vine and under his fig tree; and none shall make them afraid. *Micah* 4:4. (See also *I Maccabees* 14:12.)

2 Blessed are the peacemakers: for they shall be called the children of God. *Matthew* 5:9. (From the Sermon on the Mount.)

3 Guide our feet into the way of peace. *Luke* 1:79. (More at SALVATION.)

4 Peace I leave with you, my peace I give unto you: not as the world giveth, give I unto you. Let not your heart be troubled, neither let it be afraid. *John* 14:27.

5 Live in harmony with one another. *Romans* 12:16, RSV.

6 If it be possible, as much as lieth in you, live peaceably with all men. *Romans* 12:18.

7 Let us therefore follow after the things which make for peace. *Romans* 14:19.

8 The peace of God, which passeth all understanding, shall keep your hearts and minds through Christ Jesus. *Philippians* 4:7.

See also CONFLICT; PACIFISM; SALVATION; WAR.

PENALTIES

See LAW: PUNISHMENTS AND PENALTIES

PENTECOST

9 Suddenly there came a sound from heaven as of a rushing mighty wind, and it filled all the house where they were sitting.
And there appeared unto them cloven tongues like as of fire, and it sat upon each of them.
And they were filled with the Holy Ghost, and began to speak with other tongues. *Acts* 2:2–4. (This happened at the time of Pentecost, also called Shavuot, or the Feast of Weeks. See FEASTS. At this moment the disciples were transformed from frightened survivors to bold missionaries.)

10 Every man heard them speak in his own language. *Acts* 2:6.

PEOPLE, THE

11 Thou knowest the people, that they are set on mischief. *Exodus* 32:22. (The Revised Standard Version reads, "You know the people, that they are set on evil." Aaron, speaking to his brother Moses, is excusing himself for making an idol, the golden calf. He says that the people pressured him to do it.)

12 Thou shalt not curse the people: for they are blessed. *Numbers* 22:12. (God to Balaam, who was being importuned by King Balak to curse the Israelites, whom Balak feared.)

1 The people shall rise up as a great lion, and lift up himself as a young lion. *Numbers* 23:24, (Balaam warns King Balak that the Israelites cannot be deterred by a curse or anything else—see quote above—for God is with them.)

2 All the people arose as one man. *Judges* 20:8. (This is in response to the brutal killing of a Levite's concubine. See under CRIME.)

3 Comfort ye, comfort ye my people, saith your God. *Isaiah* 40:1.

4 Surely the people is grass. *Isaiah* 40:7. (The passage begins "All flesh is grass," which will fade and wither when the Lord breathes upon it.)

5 When he [Jesus] saw the multitudes, he was moved with compassion on them, because they fainted, and were scattered abroad, as sheep having no shepherd. *Matthew* 9:36.

See also HUMAN BEINGS; MEEK, THE; POPULATION; REVOLUTION.

PERSEVERANCE

6 The bricks are fallen down, but we will build with hewn stones: the sycamores are cut down, but we will change them into cedars. *Isaiah* 9:10. (The cedar is far more handsome than the biblical sycamore [mulberry fig], and its wood is more durable.)

7 You were wearied with the length of your way, but you did not say, It is hopeless; you found new life for your strength, and so you were not faint. *Isaiah* 57:10, RSV.

8 I have fought a good fight, I have finished my course, I have kept the faith. *II Timothy* 4:7.

See also BEGINNING AND ENDING; COMMITMENT.

PETER

9 Whom say ye that I am? [Jesus to his disciples].

And Simon Peter answered and said, Thou art the Christ, the Son of the living God.

And Jesus answered and said unto him: Blessed art thou Simon Barjona: for flesh and blood hath not revealed it unto thee, but my Father which is in heaven.

And I say also unto thee, That thou art Peter, and upon this rock I will build my church; and the gates of hell shall not prevail against it.

And I will give unto thee the keys of the kingdom of heaven: and whatsoever thou shalt bind on earth shall be bound in heaven: and whatsoever thou shalt loose on earth shall be loosed in heaven. *Matthew* 16:15–19. (The central passage upon which Christian clergy base their spiritual authority. Here Jesus gives Simon the new name of Peter, meaning "rock," and conveys to him supernatural powers. The name *Barjona* means "son of Jonah" or "son of John.")

1 This night before the cock crow, thou shalt deny me thrice. *Matthew* 26:34. (Jesus to Peter at the LAST SUPPER. Peter vehemently denies it, saying, "Though I should die with thee, yet will I not deny thee." *Matthew* 26:35. But he did deny him three times while Jesus was being interrogated. Then the cock crowed.)

2 And Peter remembered the word of Jesus . . . And he went out, and wept bitterly. *Matthew* 26:75.

3 Peter saith unto him [Jesus], Lord, thou shalt never wash my feet. Jesus answered him, If I wash thee not, thou hast no part with me.

Simon Peter saith unto him, Lord, not my feet only, but also my hands and my head. *John* 13:8–9. (Peter at his most impulsive and lovable. Jesus in washing the feet of his disciples, and instructing them to do the same for each other, thus gives in his last hours with them a model of the humility and love appropriate among his followers. Washing of the feet is performed by the Pope as part of the Holy Week ceremonies.)

PHYSICAL FITNESS

4 The race is not to the swift, nor the battle to the strong. *Ecclesiastes* 9:11. (More at LUCK.)

5 Strengthen ye the weak hands, and confirm the feeble knees. *Isaiah* 35:3. (Or for those who prefer a more contemporary translation, the Revised Standard Version runs, "Strengthen the weak hands, and make firm the feeble knees.")

6 If thou hast run with the footmen, and they have wearied thee, then how canst thou contend with horses? *Jeremiah* 12:5.

PLEASURE

See HAPPINESS; HEDONISM

POETRY

See MUSIC

PONTIUS PILATE

7 Have thou nothing to do with that just man. *Matthew* 27:19. (Pilate's wife warns him not to condemn Jesus. She has had troubling dreams.)

8 He [Pilate] took water, and washed his hands before the multitude, saying, I am innocent of the blood of this just person. *Matthew* 27:24. (Recently an inscription was found in Caesaria bearing the name *Pilate,* the first evidence other than the gospels of the historical existence of this Roman governor.)

See also TRUTH.

POOR, THE

See HAVES AND HAVE NOTS; MEEK, THE; POVERTY AND HUNGER; RICH AND POOR

POPULATION

1 There is no end of all the people. *Ecclesiastes* 4:16.

2 When goods increase, they are increased that eat them. *Ecclesiastes* 5:11.

3 Thou hast multiplied the nation, and not increased the joy. *Isaiah* 9:3.

POVERTY AND HUNGER

4 Thou shalt not harden thine heart, nor shut thine hand from thy poor brother:

But thou shalt open thine hand wide unto him, and shalt surely lend him sufficient for his need. *Deuteronomy* 15:7–8.

5 Thine heart shall not be grieved when thou givest unto him. *Deuteronomy* 15:10.

6 The poor shall never cease out of the land. *Deuteronomy* 15:11.

7 You shall not oppress a hired servant who is poor and needy . . .

You shall give him his hire on the day he earns it, before the sun goes down. *Deuteronomy* 24:14–15, RSV. (See also *Leviticus* 19:13.)

8 He [the Lord] raiseth up the poor out of the dust, and lifteth up the beggar from the dunghill, to set them among princes. *I Samuel* 2:8. (This theme runs throughout the Bible; it is echoed, for example, by Mary in the Magnificat, *Luke* 1:46–55. It was not always well received by those of established wealth or position.)

9 He [God] saveth the poor from the sword . . . and from the hand of the mighty.

So the poor hath hope. *Job* 5:15.

10 The needy shall not always be forgotten: the expectation of the poor shall not perish for ever. *Psalms* 9:18. (The Revised Standard Version concludes "the hope of the poor shall not perish forever.")

11 Blessed is he who considers the poor. *Psalms* 41:1, RSV.

12 The Lord heareth the poor. *Psalms* 69:33.

13 I am poor and needy, and my heart is stricken within me.

I am gone, like a shadow at evening; I am shaken off like a locust.

My knees are weak through fasting; my body has become gaunt.

I am an object of scorn to my accusers; when they see me, they wag their heads. *Psalms* 109:22–25, RSV.

1 The fallow ground of the poor yield much food, but it is swept away through injustice. *Proverbs* 13:23, RSV.

2 He that hath mercy on the poor, happy is he. *Proverbs* 14:21.

3 He who oppresses a poor man insults his Maker, but he who is kind to the needy honors him. *Proverbs* 14:31, RSV. (See also *Proverbs* 17:5.)

4 He who hath pity upon the poor lendeth unto the Lord. *Proverbs* 19:17.

5 Whoso stoppeth his ears at the cry of the poor, he also shall cry himself, but shall not be heard. *Proverbs* 21:13.

6 To the hungry soul every bitter thing is sweet. *Proverbs* 27:7.

7 He that giveth unto the poor shall not lack: but he that hideth his eyes shall have many a curse. *Proverbs* 28:27.

8 A righteous man knows the rights of the poor; a wicked man does not understand such knowledge. *Proverbs* 29:7, RSV.

9 The poor man's wisdom is despised, and his words are not heard. *Ecclesiastes* 9:16.

10 They that be slain with the sword are better than they that be slain with hunger: for these pine away, stricken through for want of the fruits of the field. *Lamentations* 4:9.

11 Defraud not the poor of his living, and make not the needy eyes to wait long. *Ecclesiasticus* 4:1.

12 Reject not the supplication of the afflicted; neither turn away thy face from a poor man. *Ecclesiasticus* 4:4.

13 Ye have the poor always with you. *Matthew* 26:11. *John* 12:8 reads, "The poor always ye have with you; but me ye have not always.")

See also MEEK, THE; MISFORTUNE; MONEY; OPPRESSION; RICH AND POOR.

POWER

14 I will break the pride of your power; and I will make your heaven as iron, and your earth as brass. *Leviticus* 26:19.

15 The bows of the mighty men are broken. *I Samuel* 2:4.

16 How are the mighty fallen! *II Samuel* 1:19. (At *II Samuel* 1:25, "How are the mighty fallen in the midst of the battle." Both are from David's lamentation upon hearing of the deaths of King Saul and Jonathan.)

17 Power belongs to God. *Psalms* 62:11, RSV.

18 Put not your trust in princes. *Psalms* 146:3.

19 The king's wrath is as the roaring of a lion; but his favor is as dew upon the grass. *Proverbs* 19:12.

1 Doth the crown endure to every generation? *Proverbs* 27:24. (Part of a passage in praise of herding and farming, as opposed to seeking money or power. See FARMING.)

2 Where the word of a king is, there is power: and who may say unto him, What doest thou? *Ecclesiastes* 8:4.

3 Curse not the king, no not in thy thought; and curse not the rich in thy bedchamber: for a bird of the air shall carry the voice, and that which hath wings shall tell the matter. *Ecclesiastes* 10:20.

4 Strive not with a mighty man, lest thou fall into his hands. *Ecclesiasticus* 8:1.

5 He that is today a king, tomorrow shall die. *Ecclesiasticus* 10:10.

6 Riches and strength lift up the heart. *Ecclesiasticus* 40:26.

7 The devil . . . showeth him all the kingdoms of the world, and the glory of them;

And saith unto him, All these things will I give thee, if thou wilt fall down and worship me. *Matthew* 4:8–9. (The last temptation the devil offers to Jesus in the wilderness.)

8 There is no power but of God: the powers that be are ordained of God. *Romans* 13:1.

9 The kingdom of God is not in word, but in power. *I Corinthians* 4:20.

See also AMBITION; GOVERNMENT; GREATNESS; MONEY; OPPRESSION; REVOLUTION; SUCCESS.

PRAISING GOD

See GOD, PRAISING

PRAYER

10 Be not rash with thy mouth . . . God is in heaven, and thou upon earth: therefore let thy words be few. *Ecclesiastes* 5:2.

11 Call unto me, and I will answer thee. *Jeremiah* 33:3.

12 When thou prayest, thou shall not be as the hypocrites are: for they love to pray standing in the synagogues and in the corners of the streets, that they may be seen of men. Verily I say unto you, They have their reward. *Matthew* 6:5.

13 When ye pray, use not vain repetitions, as the heathen do

. . . For your Father knoweth what things ye have need of, before ye ask him. *Matthew* 6:6–8.

1 Whatsoever ye shall ask in prayer, believing, ye shall receive. *Matthew* 21:22.

2 Two men went up into the temple to pray; the one a Pharisee, and the other a publican.

The Pharisee stood and prayed thus with himself, God, I thank thee, that I am not as other men are, extortioners, unjust, adulterers, or even as this publican. *Luke* 18:10–11 (See below for the more acceptable prayer.)

3 The publican, standing afar off, would not lift up so much as his eyes unto heaven, but smote upon his breast, saying, God be merciful to me a sinner. *Luke* 18:13.

4 Ask, and ye shall receive, that your joy may be full. *John* 16:24.

5 Pray without ceasing. *I Thessalonians* 5:17.

6 The effectual fervent prayer of a righteous man availeth much. *James* 5:16.

See also PRAYERS; PRAYERS OF THANKS.

PRAYERS

7 I pray thee, if I have found grace in thy sight, show me now thy way, that I may know thee. *Exodus* 33:13. (Moses to God.)

8 I beseech thee, show me thy glory. *Exodus* 33:18. (From the same passage quoted above.)

9 O Lord God, remember me, I pray thee, and strengthen me, I pray thee, only this once, O God. *Judges* 16:28. (Samson calls to God to restore his strength so that he may pull down the temple on the Philistines.)

10 The Lord our God be with us, as he was with our fathers: let him not leave us, nor forsake us. *I Kings* 8:57.

11 Oh that thou wouldst bless me and enlarge my border, and that thy hand might be with me, and that thou wouldst keep me from harm so that it might not hurt me! *I Chronicles* 4:10, RSV. (Jabez, a leader of the tribe of Judah, voices an ever-popular prayer for more property and better protection. God favored him and "granted what he asked.")

12 Thine, O Lord, is the greatness, and the power, and the glory . . . thine is the kingdom. *I Chronicles* 29:11.

13 Remember me, O my God, for good. *Nehemiah* 13:31. (And elsewhere.)

14 Have mercy upon me, and hear my prayer. *Psalms* 4:1.

15 How long wilt thou forget me, O Lord? for ever? *Psalms* 13:1.

1 Keep me as the apple of the eye, hide me under the shadow of thy wings. *Psalms* 17:8. (For a note on biblical apples, see under CHOSEN PEOPLE, *Deuteronomy* 32:10.)

2 Be not far from me; for trouble is near. *Psalms* 22:11.

3 The Lord is my shepherd, I shall not want. *Psalms* 23:1. (The entire Psalm is given at GOD'S PROVIDENCE.)

4 Hear my prayer, O Lord, *Psalms* 39:12.

5 Deliver me from mine enemies, O my God. *Psalms* 59:1. (See also GOD, ENEMIES AND WAR.)

6 Make haste, O God, to deliver me; make haste to help me, O Lord. *Psalms* 70:1.

7 Bow down thine ear, O Lord, hear me: for I am poor and needy. *Psalms* 86:1.

8 O my God, take me not away in the midst of my days. *Psalms* 102:24.

9 Out of the depths have I cried unto thee, O Lord. *Psalms* 130:1.

10 Deliver me, O Lord, from the evil man; preserve me from the violent man. *Psalms* 140:1.

11 O Lord, be gracious unto us; we have waited for thee; be thou our arm every morning, our salvation also in the time of trouble. *Isaiah* 33:2.

12 Incline thine ear, O Lord, and hear; open thine eyes, O Lord, and see. *Isaiah* 37:17.

13 O Lord, hear; O Lord, forgive; O Lord, hearken and do. *Daniel* 9:19.

14 In the beginning was the Word, and the Word was with God, and the Word was God. *John* 1:1. (More at JESUS.)

See also GOD; BLESSINGS; LORD'S PRAYER; MARY; JESUS: PASSION AND DEATH; PRAYERS OF THANKS.

PRAYERS OF THANKS

15 O Lord my God, I will give thanks unto thee forever. *Psalms* 30:12.

16 It is a good thing to give thanks unto the Lord. *Psalms* 92:1.

17 From thee cometh victory, from thee cometh wisdom, and thine is the glory, and I am thy servant. *I Esdras* 4:59. (Zerubbabel thanking the Lord for giving him the wit to win a contest held before King Darius I. As the reward, the king allowed him to go to Jerusalem to rebuild the Temple and granted many other favors to the Jews.)

PREDESTINATION

See SALVATION

PRESS, THE

See NEWS

PRIDE

1 I know thy pride, and the naughtiness of thine heart. *I Samuel* 17:28.

2 The man of haughty looks and arrogant heart I will not endure. *Psalms* 101:5, RSV.

3 When pride cometh, then cometh shame [disgrace]: but with the lowly is wisdom. *Proverbs* 11:2.

4 The Lord will destroy the house of the proud. *Proverbs* 15:25.

5 Every one that is proud in heart is an abomination to the Lord. *Proverbs* 16:5.

6 Pride goeth before destruction, and a haughty spirit before a fall. *Proverbs* 16:18.

7 Seest thou a man wise in his own conceit? There is more hope of a fool than of him. *Proverbs* 26:12.

8 A man's pride shall bring him low. *Proverbs* 29:23.

9 The daughters of Zion are haughty, and walk with stretched forth necks and wanton eyes, walking and mincing as they go, and making a tinkling with their feet. *Isaiah* 3:16. (The Lord is speaking and he has punishment in mind. To begin, "The Lord will smite with a scab the crown of the head of the daughters of Zion, and the Lord will discover [lay bare] their secret parts." *Isaiah* 3:17. The next five verses set out a fascinating list of the ornaments and other belongings the Lord will take away. The passage concludes with an onslaught of disease and destruction.)

10 Thus saith the Lord, Let not the wise man glory in his wisdom, neither let the mighty man glory in his might, let not the rich man glory in his riches:

But let him that glorieth glory in this, that he understandeth and knoweth me. *Jeremiah* 9:23–24.

11 Exalt not thyself, lest thou fall. *Ecclesiasticus* 1:30.

12 Pride is hateful before God and man. *Ecclesiasticus* 10:7.

13 Pride is the beginning of sin. *Ecclesiasticus* 10:13. (A statement of the theological doctrine that pride is the greatest sin and the one from which all others spring. The sin causing the damnation of Satan, and the original sin in the garden of Eden, are instances of pride, of creatures wishing to be equal to God.)

14 Pride was not made for men, not furious anger for them that are born of a woman. *Ecclesiasticus* 10:18.

15 He hath scattered the proud in the imagination of their hearts. *Luke* 1:51. (From the Magnificat. See MARY.)

1 Let him that thinketh he standeth take heed lest he fall. *I Corinthians* 10:12.

See also BOASTING; LUCIFER.

PRIESTS

See CLERGY

PRISONS

See LAW: PUNISHMENTS AND PENALTIES

PRODIGAL SON

2 The younger son gathered all together, and took his journey into a far country, and there wasted his substance with riotous living. *Luke* 15:13.

3 I will arise and go to my father, and will say unto him, Father, I have sinned against heaven, and before thee,

And am no more worthy to be called thy son: make me as one of thy hired servants. *Luke* 15:18–19. (The prodigal son after a miserable spell as a swine herder.)

4 When he was yet a great way off, his father saw him, and had compassion and ran, and fell on his neck, and kissed him. *Luke* 15:20.

5 Bring hither the fatted calf, and kill it; and let us eat, and be merry:

For this my son was dead, and is alive again; he was lost, and is found. *Luke* 15:23–24.

PROMISED LAND

See CANAAN; ZION

PROMISES

6 Better is it that thou shouldest not vow, than that thou shouldest vow and not pay. *Ecclesiastes* 5:5.

PROPERTY

7 Woe unto them that join house to house, that lay field to field, till there be no place, that they may be placed alone in the midst of the earth! *Isaiah* 5:8. (The Lord promises to lay desolate such grand estates.)

8 Set not thy heart upon thy goods. *Ecclesiasticus* 5:1.

9 Soul, thou hast much goods laid up for many years; take thine ease, eat, drink, and be merry.

But God said unto him, Thou fool, this night thy soul shall be required of thee. *Luke* 12:19–20. (From the parable of the rich fool, who laid up all the abundance of his crops for himself, without regard for his neighbors or for God.)

1 Distribution was made unto every man according as he had need. *Acts* 4:35. (The earliest Christians sold their land and houses and shared the proceeds among each other. A certain Ananias, however, secretly held back part of the price of a possession he had sold. Peter rebuked him, saying, "Thou has not lied unto men, but unto God," [Acts 5:4] and Ananias fell dead. Three hours later, his wife lied on the same subject, and also fell dead.)

2 Set your affection on things above, not on things on the earth. *Colossians* 3:2.

3 We brought nothing into this world, and it is certain we carry nothing out. *I Timothy* 6:7.

See also MONEY.

PROPHETS

4 Thy God will raise up unto thee a Prophet from the midst of thee. *Deuteronomy* 18:15. (The prophets were the medium through which God spoke.)

5 I heard the voice of the Lord, saying, Whom shall I send, and who will go for us? Then said I, Here am I; send me. *Isaiah* 6:8. (This is from the great passage—*Isaiah* 6:1–10—in which Isaiah sees God on his throne with his seraphim, and God calls upon him to become a prophet. See also under ANGELS and GOD, ENCOUNTERS WITH.)

6 The voice of him that crieth in the wilderness, Prepare ye the way of the Lord, make straight in the desert a highway for our God.

Every valley shall be exalted, and every mountain and hill shall be made low: and the crooked shall be made straight, and the rough places plain. *Isaiah* 40:3–4. (This is the role of the prophet—to prepare the people for the coming of the Lord. For Christians, the one who cries in the wilderness is John the Baptist, preparing the way for Christ.)

7 I have multiplied visions, and used similitudes, by the ministry of the prophets. *Hosea* 12:10.

8 Your sons and your daughters shall prophesy, your old men shall dream dreams, your young men shall see visions. *Joel* 2:28.
(This is one of the signs that the Lord's Judgment Day is approaching.)

9 Beware of false prophets, which come to you in sheep's clothing, but inwardly they are ravening wolves. *Matthew* 7:15.

10 A prophet is not without honor, save in his own country, and in his own house. *Matthew* 13:57.

11 He spoke by the mouth of his holy prophets, which have been since the world began:

That we should be saved from our enemies, and from the hand of all that hate us. *Luke* 1:70–71.

1 We know in part, and we prophesy in part.
But when that which is perfect is come, then that which is in part shall be done away. *I Corinthians* 13:9–10. (From the chapter in praise of charity. See also VISION and CHARITY, CHRISTIAN.)

See also ELIJAH; JEREMIAH; JOHN THE BAPTIST.

PROVIDENCE

See GOD'S PROVIDENCE

PRUDENCE

2 O simple ones, learn prudence. *Proverbs* 8:5, RSV. (See the passage on the ant, also from *Proverbs*, under ANIMALS.)

3 I wisdom dwell with prudence. *Proverbs* 8:12.

4 Like a gold ring in a swine's snout is a beautiful woman without discretion. *Proverbs* 11:22, RSV.

5 A prudent man conceals his knowledge. *Proverbs* 12:23, RSV.

6 The prudent shall keep silence in that time: for it is an evil time. *Amos* 5:13.

7 Be in peace with many: nevertheless have but one counselor of a thousand. *Ecclesiasticus* 6:6.

8 Then shall the kingdom of heaven be likened unto ten virgins . . .
And five of them [the ten virgins] were wise, and five were foolish. *Matthew* 25:1–2. (The wise virgins wait for their bridegroom, carrying lamps that have oil. The foolish virgins have to go and buy oil, and while they are in the shop the wedding takes place without them. The moral is to be prepared always, "for ye know neither the day nor the hour wherein the Son of man cometh." *Matthew* 25:13. See also JUDGMENT DAY.)

9 Make to yourselves friends of the mammon of unrighteousness. *Luke* 16:9.

10 All things are lawful for me, but all things are not expedient. *I Corinthians* 10:23.

See also CAUTION; SILENCE; WISDOM.

PUBLIC OPINION

11 Woe unto you, when all men shall speak well of you! *Luke* 6:26.

PUNISHMENT See LAW: PUNISHMENTS AND PENALTIES; OPPRESSION

PURIM

1 They should make them days of feasting and joy, and of sending portions to another, and gifts to the poor. *Esther* 9:22. (The reference is to Purim, the feast celebrating the victory of Esther and her foster father, Mordecai, over the wicked Haman, who intended to kill all the Jews in Persia on a day chosen by lots. *Purim* is Hebrew for "lots." Traditionally, three-cornered pastries, *hamantaschen*, are served; they resemble the three-cornered hat Haman is supposed to have worn).

See also FEASTS, RELIGIOUS.

QUESTIONING GOD

See GOD, QUESTIONING

QUIET

1 Better is a dry morsel with quiet than a house full of feasting with strife. *Proverbs* 17:1, RSV.

2 Their strength is to sit still. *Isaiah* 37.

3 In quietness and in confidence shall be your strength. *Isaiah* 30:15.

4 Study to be quiet. *1 Thessalonians* 4:11.

See also PEACE.

RAIN

See WEATHER

RANK

1 The disciple is not above his master, nor the servant above his lord. *Matthew* 10:24.

2 The dogs eat of the crumbs which fall from their masters' table. *Matthew* 15:27.

3 Whosoever shall exalt himself shall be abased; and he that shall humble himself shall be exalted, *Matthew* 23:12. (See also MEEK, THE and REVOLUTION.)

See also RESPECT.

REALITY

4 Thou hast showed thy people hard things: thou hast made us to drink the wine of astonishment. *Psalms* 60:3.

REASON

5 Come now, and let us reason together. *Isaiah* 1:18. (This was a favorite quote of President Lyndon B. Johnson.)

6 Let reason go before every enterprise, and counsel before every action. *Ecclesiasticus* 37:16.

REDEMPTION

See ATONEMENT; SALVATION

REFORM

7 Let the wicked forsake his way, and the unrighteous man his thoughts. *Isaiah* 55:7.

8 Amend your ways and your doings. *Jeremiah* 7:3 and 26:13.

9 When the wicked man turneth away from his wickedness . . . and doeth that which is lawful and right, he shall save his soul alive. *Ezekiel* 18:27.

See also REPENTANCE.

REGRET

10 I have played the fool, and have erred exceedingly. *I Samuel* 26:21. (King Saul to David.)

1 A broken and a contrite heart, O God, thou wilt not despise. *Psalms* 51:17.

REJECTION

2 The stone which the builders refused is become the head stone of the corner. *Psalms* 118:22.

3 A wounded spirit who can bear? *Proverbs* 18:14.

4 He is despised and rejected of men. *Isaiah* 53:3. (From the verses on God's suffering servant. See under SERVANT OF GOD.)

5 All that pass by clap their hands at thee; they hiss and wag their head. *Lamentations* 2:15.

6 I was a derision to all my people. *Lamentations* 3:14.

7 Whosoever shall not receive you, nor hear your words, when ye depart out of that house or city, shake off the dust of your feet. *Matthew* 10:14. (Jesus to his disciples.)

8 The one shall be taken, and the other left. *Matthew* 24:41.

9 First must he suffer many things, and be rejected of this generation. *Luke* 17:25.

10 He came unto his own, and his own received him not. *John* 1:11. (The whole of this opening hymn of the gospel of John is given at JESUS.)

See also LONELINESS.

RELIABILITY

11 That which is gone out of thy lips thou shalt keep and perform. *Deuteronomy* 23:23.

12 Winnow not every wind, and go not into every way.
Be steadfast in thine understanding; and let thy word be the same. *Ecclesiasticus* 5:9–10.

See also COMMITMENT.

RELIGION

13 Behold, to obey is better than to sacrifice, and to hearken than the fat of rams. *I Samuel* 15:22. (In other words, the spirit of religion counts more than the forms.)

14 Bring no more vain oblations; incense is an abomination unto me. *Isaiah* 1:13. (God, speaking through his prophet, warns he will not listen to hypocritical prayers. What he wants is simple: "Cease to do evil." *Isaiah* 1:16.)

1 I hate, I despise your feast days. *Amos* 5:21 (Another rejection of the formalities of religion. The passage concludes with, "But let judgment run down as waters." Amos 5:24; see under JUSTICE AND FAIRNESS.)

2 Man shall not live by bread alone, but by every word that proceedeth out of the mouth of God. *Matthew* 4:4. (Jesus in the wilderness to the devil, who is tempting him.)

3 [The house] fell not: for it was founded upon a rock. *Matthew* 7:25. (This is the house built by the wise man in one of the parables. Jesus explains that the wise man is one "who heareth these sayings of mine, and doeth them." *Matthew* 7:24. Later, at *Matthew* 16:18–19, Jesus gives to his disciple Simon the nickname *Peter*, meaning "rock." He is the rock upon which the new religion is to be founded.)

4 The kingdom of heaven is like unto a net, that was cast into the sea, and gathered of every kind. *Matthew* 13:47.

5 Where two or three are gathered together in my name, there am I in the midst of them. *Matthew* 18:20. (Jesus to his disciples.)

6 If thou wilt be perfect, go and sell that thou hast, and give to the poor, and thou shalt have treasure in heaven: and come and follow me. *Matthew* 19:21. (Jesus to the young man with "great possessions," who wished to do more than just keep the Commandments. But this was too much for the young man to give up, and "he went away sorrowful." *Matthew* 19:22.)

7 Go ye therefore, and teach all nations, baptizing them in the name of the Father, and of the Son, and of the Holy Ghost:

Teaching them to observe all things whatsoever I have commanded you: and lo, I am with you always, even unto the end of the world. Amen. *Matthew* 28:19–20. (The resurrected Jesus speaking to the disciples at Galilee. These verses conclude the gospel according to Matthew.)

8 Other sheep I have, which are not of this fold: them also I must bring, and they shall hear my voice; and there shall be one fold, and one shepherd. *John* 10:16.

9 I will not leave you comfortless: I will come to you. *John* 14:18. (Jesus speaking farewell to the apostles before his death.)

10 Men of Athens, I perceive that in all things ye are too superstitious. ["Too superstitious" is better translated "very religious," as in the Revised Standard Version.]

For as I passed by, and beheld your devotions, I found an altar with this inscription, TO THE UNKNOWN GOD. Whom therefore ye ignorantly worship, him I declare unto you.

God that made the world and all things therein, seeing that he is Lord of heaven and earth, dwelleth not in temples made with hands;

Neither is worshiped with men's hands, as though he needed any thing, seeing he giveth to all life, and breath, and all things. *Acts* 17:22–25. (From Paul's sermon to the Athenians. See also GOD and EQUALITY.)

1 Almost thou persuadest me to be a Christian. *Acts* 26:28. (King Agrippa to Paul.)

2 As we have many members in one body, and all members have not the same office:

So we, being many, are one body in Christ, and every one members one of another. *Romans* 12:4–5.

3 Him that is weak in the faith receive ye, but not to doubtful disputations. *Romans* 14:1. (The message is to avoid religious arguments and show a welcoming spirit.)

4 God hath chosen the foolish things of the world to confound the wise; and God hath chosen the weak things of the world to confound the things which are mighty. *I Corinthians* 1:27. (The message of this chapter is that while "the Jews require a sign, and the Greeks seek after wisdom" [1:22], the religion founded by the rejected, crucified Christ is more powerful than the wisdom or learning of either.)

5 We are laborers together with God: ye are God's husbandry, ye are God's building. *I Corinthians* 3:9.

6 [God] hath made us able ministers of the new testament; not of the letter, but of the spirit: for the letter killeth, but the spirit giveth life. *II Corinthians* 3:6.

7 Put on the new man [in the image of God] . . .

Where there is neither Greek nor Jew, circumcision nor uncircumcision, Barbarian, Scythian, bond nor free, but Christ is all, and in all. *Colossians* 3:10–11.

8 Have nothing to do with godless and silly myths. *I Timothy* 4:7, RSV. (The King James Version reads, "Refuse profane and old wives' fables.")

9 Pure religion . . . is this, To visit the fatherless and widows in their affliction, and to keep himself unspotted from the world. *James* 1:27.

See also CHURCH; CLERGY; GOD, WORSHIPING; HEAVEN; PRAYER; SALVATION.

RELIGIOUS FEASTS

See FEASTS, RELIGIOUS

REPENTANCE

10 Repent ye: for the kingdom of heaven is at hand. *Matthew* 3:2. (Spoken by John the Baptist. In *Matthew* 4:17, Jesus himself repeats the message.)

1 I say unto you, there is joy in the presence of the angels of God over one sinner that repenteth. *Luke* 15:10. (The conclusion of the parable of the woman with ten pieces of silver, who loses one of them. This is the middle parable in this chapter, between the parable of the one lost sheep and that of the PRODIGAL SON. See also SIN AND SINNERS.)

2 The goodness of God leadeth thee to repentance. *Romans* 2:4.

See also REFORM; REGRET; SIN.

REPUTATION

3 A good name is rather to be chosen than great riches. *Proverbs* 22:1. (Also, "A good name is better than precious ointment." *Ecclesiastes* 7:1.)

4 A good name endureth forever. *Ecclesiasticus* 41:13.

RESISTANCE

5 Resist the devil, and he will flee from you. *James* 4:7. (For military resistance, see the last quote at WAR.)

RESPECT

6 Render therefore to all their dues: tribute to whom tribute is due; custom to whom custom; fear to whom fear; honor to whom honor. *Romans* 13:7.

7 Honor all men. Love the brotherhood. Fear God. Honor the king. *I Peter* 2:17.

See also RANK.

RESPONSIBILITY

8 Am I my brother's keeper? *Genesis* 4:9. (Cain to the Lord after murdering Abel. In almost all religious and ethical systems, the answer to the question, of course, is yes.)

9 Rescue those who are being taken away to death; hold back those who are stumbling to the slaughter.

10 If you say, "Behold we did not know this," does not he who weighs the heart perceive it? *Proverbs* 24:11–12, RSV.

11 Unto whomsoever much is given, of him shall be much required: and to whom men have committed much, of him they will ask the more. *Luke* 12:48.

1 He that is a hireling . . . seeth the wolf coming, and leaveth the sheep, and fleeth . . .
The hireling fleeth, because he is a hireling, and careth not for the sheep. *John* 10:12–13.

2 Your blood be upon your own heads. *Acts* 18:6.

3 Every one of us shall give account of himself to God. *Romans.* 14:12.

4 Every man shall bear his own burden. *Galatians* 6:5.

5 If any provide not for his own, and specially for those of his own house, he hath denied the faith, and is worse than an infidel. *I Timothy* 5:8.

See also MISFORTUNE (for what one should do for the poor and unlucky).

RESULTS

6 By their fruits ye shall know them. *Matthew* 7:20 (From the passage in the Sermon on the Mount in which Jesus warns against false prophets. But how can one tell the false from the true? "A good tree cannot bring forth evil fruit, neither can a corrupt tree bring forth good fruit," Jesus says [*Matthew* 7:18].)

See also ACTIONS.

RESURRECTION OF JESUS See JESUS, RESURRECTION OF

RESURRECTION OF THE DEAD

7 I will open your graves, and cause you to come up out of your graves. *Ezekiel* 37:12. (From the vision of the valley of bones. The dead represent defeated Israel. Here God promises to restore the nation. See also BODY.)

8 In the resurrection they [people] neither marry, nor are given in marriage, but are as the angels of God in heaven. *Matthew* 22:30.

9 Thou fool, that which thou sowest is not quickened, except it die. *I Corinthians* 15:36.

10 Behold, I show you a mystery; We shall not all sleep, but we shall all be changed.
In a moment, in the twinkling of an eye, at the last trump: for the trumpet shall sound, and the dead shall be raised incorruptible, and we shall be changed.
For this corruptible must put on incorruption, and this mortal must put on immortality. *I Corinthians* 15:51–53.

See also SALVATION.

RETALIATION

See LAW: PUNISHMENTS AND PENALTIES; PACIFISM; VENGEANCE

REVELATION

1 The secret things belong unto the Lord our God: but those things which are revealed belong unto us and to our children for ever. *Deuteronomy* 29:29.

2 He revealeth the deep and secret things: he knoweth what is in the darkness, and the light dwelleth with him. *Daniel* 2:22.

3 The people which sat in darkness saw great light. *Matthew* 4:16. (Matthew speaks of the people of Galilee, where Jesus began his mission.)

4 There is nothing covered, that shall not be revealed; and hid, that shall not be known. *Matthew* 10:26.

See also SECRETS.

REVOLT

5 To your tents, O Israel. *I Kings* 12:16. (The response of the people to King Rehoboam's "whips and scorpions" announcement. See under OPPRESSION.)

6 We fight for our lives and our laws. *I Maccabees* 3:21. (The great Judas Maccabeus rallying his outnumbered troops in battle against the Syrians. See also the last quote under WAR.)

See also REVOLUTION.

REVOLUTION

7 Every valley shall be exalted, and every mountain and hill shall be made low. *Isaiah* 40:4. (One of numerous passages in the Bible in which God ordains the downfall of the powerful and proud and the rise of the poor and meek. This message is common to both Old and New Testaments. The quote here from *Isaiah*, for example, follows the famous reference to "the voice of him that crieth in the wilderness, Prepare ye the way of the Lord," a mission adopted by John the Baptist.)

8 A sword, a sword is sharpened. *Ezekiel* 21:9. (The dramatic beginning of a revolution announced by God through Ezekiel. See also below.)

9 Remove the diadem, and take off the crown: this shalt not be the same: exalt him that is low, and abase him that is high.

I will overturn, overturn, overturn it: and it shall be no more, until he come whose right it is. *Ezekiel* 21:26–27.

1 The houses of ivory shall perish, and the great houses shall have an end. *Amos* 3:15.

2 My people is risen up as an enemy. *Micah* 2:8.

3 Think not that I am come to send peace on earth: I came not to send peace, but a sword. *Matthew* 10:34. (A verse difficult to reconcile with the Christ's injunctions to love one's enemies and turn the other cheek. See LOVE and PACIFISM. But it is consistent with the revolutionary message of Christianity. Jesus was preaching a new religion and calling for a new way of life. Contemporaneously, the anti-Roman religious group known as the Zealots espoused more violent revolutionary ideas; the Pharisees represented a more conservative position, emphasizing the justice to come in the afterlife.)

4 Many that are first shall be last; and the last shall be first. *Matthew* 19:30. (See also *Matthew* 20:16 at HEAVEN.)

See also DESTRUCTION; MEEK, THE; REVOLT.

RICH AND POOR

5 A rich man's wealth is his strong city; the poverty of the poor is their ruin. *Proverbs* 10:15, RSV.

6 The poor is hated even of his own neighbor: but the rich hath many friends. *Proverbs* 14:20.

7 Better is little with the fear of the Lord, than great treasure and trouble herewith. *Proverbs* 15:16.

8 The rich ruleth over the poor, and the borrower is servant to the lender. *Proverbs* 22:7.

9 A rich man is wise in his own eyes, but a poor man who has understanding will find him out. *Proverbs* 28:11, RSV.

10 The poor man is honored for his skill, and the rich man is honored for his riches. *Ecclesiasticus* 10:30.

11 The rich man hath done wrong, yet he threateneth withal: the poor is wronged, and he must entreat also.

If thou be for this [the rich man's] profit, he will use thee: but if thou have nothing, he will forsake thee. *Ecclesiasticus* 13:3–4. (Most of this chapter is devoted to the comparison of rich and poor. Very little has changed in two thousand years.)

12 A rich man beginning to fall is held up of [by] his friends: but a poor man being down is thrust also away by his friends. *Ecclesiasticus* 13:21.

13 When a rich man speaketh, every man holdeth his tongue, and look, what he saith, they extol it to the clouds: but if the poor man speak, they say, What fellow is this? *Ecclesiasticus* 13:23.

1 There was a certain rich man, which was clothed in purple and fine linen, and fared sumptuously every day:

And there was a certain beggar named Lazarus, which was laid at his gate full of sores,

And desiring to be fed with the crumbs which fell from the rich man's table: moreover the dogs came and licked his sores. *Luke* 16:19–21.

2 The beggar died, and was carried by angels into Abraham's bosom. *Luke* 16:22.

3 Send Lazarus, that he may dip the tip of his finger in water, and cool my tongue; for I am tormented in this flame. *Luke* 16:24. (The prayer of the rich man in hell, who sees Lazarus in heaven.)

See also HAVES AND HAVE NOTS; MONEY; POVERTY AND HUNGER; POWER; RICHES.

RICHES

4 Once in three years came the navy of Tharshish, bringing gold, and silver, ivory, and apes, and peacocks. *I Kings* 10:22. (In the reign of Solomon, the people of Israel traded widely. Tharshish, or Tarshish, is mentioned several times in the Bible. It was evidently a wealthy sea-trading city, but its identity is not clear. Tarsus in Asia Minor is a possibility. The biblical verse quoted here is the basis of the following lines in John Masefield's "Cargoes": "Quinquireme of Nineveh from distant Ophir/Rowing home to haven in sunny Palestine,/With a cargo of ivory,/And apes and peacocks,/ Sandalwood, cedarwood and sweet wine." At *Isaiah* 23:1, the destruction of Tarshish is prophesied: "Howl, ye ships of Tarshish; for it is laid waste." In this chapter, Tarshish is described as an island city, apparently in the Aegean.)

5 The king [Solomon] made silver and gold at Jerusalem as plenteous as stones. *II Chronicles* 1:15.

6 Hezekiah had exceeding much riches and honor: and he made himself treasuries for silver, and for gold, and for precious stones, and for spices, and for shields, and for all manner of pleasant jewels;

Storehouses also for the increase of corn, and wine, and oil; and stalls for all manner of beasts, and cotes for flocks. *II Chronicles* 32:27–28.

7 All thy garments smell of myrrh, and aloes, and cassia, out of the ivory palaces. *Psalms* 45:8. (These fragrant spices, greatly prized in ancient world, were used, among other purposes, to sweeten a bridal chamber. The person addressed here is probably King Ahab, at his marriage to Jezebel. See also MARRIAGE.)

8 Thy cheeks are comely with rows of jewels, thy neck with chains of gold. *Song of Solomon* 1:10.

1 Thou hast been in Eden the garden of God; every precious stone was thy covering, the sardius, topaz, and the diamond, the beryl, the onyx, and the jasper, the sapphire, the emerald, and the carbuncle, and gold. *Ezekiel* 28:13. (The jewels here represent the glory of Tyre. Sardius, a deep orange-red chalcedony, is sometimes called carnelian. In *Revelations* 21:10 it represents the glory of the new Jerusalem. A carbuncle is any of several deep-red gems, sometimes a garnet.)

2 In the hand of God is the prosperity of man. *Ecclesiasticus* 10:5.

3 The merchandise of gold, and silver, and precious stones, and of pearls, and fine linen, and purple, and silk, and scarlet, and all thyine wood, and all manner vessels of ivory, and all manner vessels of most precious wood, and of brass, and iron, and marble.

And cinnamon, and odors, and ointments, and frankincense, and wine, and oil, and fine flour, and wheat, and beasts, and sheep, and horses, and chariots, and slaves, and souls of men. *Revelation* 18:12–13. (The riches of Babylon, on the day of its destruction at the end of the world.)

See also MONEY; RICH AND POOR.

RIDDLES

4 Out of the eater came something to eat. Out of the strong came something sweet. *Judges* 14:14, RSV. (A riddle set by Samson based on once having found a swarm of bees and honey in the carcass of a lion that he had killed. He set the riddle to 30 young Philistine men, guests at his marriage to a Philistine woman. The prize for answering is to be 30 pieces of fine linen and 30 garments. The men threaten Samson's wife, saying they will burn down her father's home unless she finds out the answer for them. Samson is infuriated at having been cheated and announces, "If you had not ploughed with my heifer, you would not have found out my riddle." *Judges* 14:18. This is the beginning of the struggle between Samson and the Philistines.)

5 Son of man, put forth a riddle. *Ezekiel* 17:2. (God is addressing the prophet Ezekiel.)

RIGHTEOUSNESS

See VIRTUE

ROUTINE

See ENNUI

SABBATH

1 And on the seventh day God ended his work which he had made; and he rested on the seventh day from all his work which he had made.

And God blessed the seventh day, and sanctified it. *Genesis* 2:2,3. (See also *Exodus* 20:11, which reads, "The Lord blessed the sabbath day, and hallowed it.")

2 The Lord hath given you the sabbath. *Exodus* 16:29. (*Sabbath* comes from Hebrew *shabbat*, meaning "to cease, to desist.")

3 The people rested on the seventh day. *Exodus* 16:30.

4 Remember the sabbath day, to keep it holy. [The Fourth Commandment.]
Six days shalt thou labor, and do all thy work:
But the seventh day is the sabbath of the Lord thy God. *Exodus* 20:8–10.

5 Whosoever doeth my work in the sabbath day, he shall surely be put to death. *Exodus* 31:15. (God to Moses.)

6 What man shall there be among you, that shall have one sheep, and it fall into a pit on the sabbath day, will he not lay hold on it, and lift it out? *Matthew* 12:11. (Jesus in answer to Pharisees who, seeking evidence against him, had asked him. "Is it lawful to heal [the sick] on the sabbath days?" *Matthew* 12:10. This is among the more popular passages in the Bible, providing an authoritative excuse for sometimes breaking rules.)

7 The sabbath was made for man, and not man for the sabbath. *Mark* 2:27.

See also FEASTS, RELIGIOUS.

SABBATICAL YEAR

8 Six years thou shalt sow thy land, and shalt gather in the fruits thereof:

But the seventh year thou shalt let it rest and lie still; that the poor of thy people may eat; and what they leave the beasts of the field shall eat. In like manner thou shalt deal with thy vineyard, and with thy oliveyard. *Exodus* 23:10–11. (Also after seven years, bondservants were to be released and debts were to be forgiven or suspended. See *Jeremiah* 34:16–17 for how seriously this was meant.)

See also JUBILEE YEAR.

SAINTS

9 Precious in the sight of the Lord is the death of his saints. *Psalms* 116:15.

1 Grace and mercy is to his saints, and he hath care for his elect. *Wisdom of Solomon* 3:9.

SALVATION

2 I have waited for thy salvation, O Lord. *Genesis* 49:18.

3 Fear ye not, stand still, and see the salvation of the Lord. *Exodus* 14:13. (Moses during the flight from Egypt. In the Revised Standard Version, the translation is "stand firm," rather than "stand still.")

4 The Lord is my strength and song, and he is become my salvation. *Exodus* 15:2. (More at EXODUS. See also *Isaiah* 12:2 at GOD for a similar passage.)

5 How then can man be justified with God? *Job* 25:4.

6 Lord, who shall abide in thy tabernacle? who shall dwell in thy holy hill? *Psalms* 15:1.

7 Surely his salvation is nigh them that fear him; that glory may dwell in our land.

Mercy and truth are met together; righteousness and peace have kissed each other.

Truth shall spring out of the earth; and righteousness shall look down from heaven. *Psalms* 85:9–11.

8 This is the day which the Lord hath made. *Psalms* 118:24.

9 With joy shall ye draw water out of the wells of salvation. *Isaiah* 12:3.

10 A man shall be as a hiding place from the wind, and a covert from the tempest; as rivers of water in a dry place, as the shadow of a great rock in a weary land. *Isaiah* 32:2. (The passage refers to a great and righteous king who will rule after Israel's enemies are destroyed. Such passages are usually interpreted by Christians to refer to the coming of Christ. See also MESSIAH.)

11 Fear not: for I have redeemed thee, I have called thee by thy name; thou art mine. *Isaiah* 43:1.

12 The redeemed of the Lord shall return, and come with singing unto Zion. *Isaiah* 51:11.

13 I the Lord am thy Savior and thy Redeemer, the mighty One of Jacob. *Isaiah* 60:16.

14 He [the Lord] hath clothed me with the garments of salvation, he hath covered me with the robe of righteousness. *Isaiah* 61:10.

15 Behold, thy salvation cometh. *Isaiah* 62:11.

16 The harvest is past, the summer is ended, and we are not saved. *Jeremiah* 8:20.

1 It is good that a man should both hope and quietly wait for the salvation of the Lord. *Lamentations* 3:26.

2 After two days he will receive us: in the third day he will raise us up, and we shall live in his sight. *Hosea* 6:2.

3 There be many created, but few shall be saved. *II Esdras* 8:3.

4 Strait is the gate, and narrow is the way, which leadeth unto life, and few there be that find it. *Matthew* 7:14.

5 Blessed be the Lord God of Israel; for he hath visited and redeemed his people. *Luke* 1:68.

6 Thou [John the Baptist] shalt go before the face of the Lord to prepare his ways:

To give knowledge of salvation unto his people by the remission of their sins,

Through the tender mercy of our God; whereby the dayspring from on high hath visited us,

To give light to them that sit in darkness and in the shadow of death, to guide our feet into the way of peace. *Luke* 1:76–79. (This passage is known as the Canticle of Zechariah.)

7 Lord, now lettest thy servant depart in peace . . .
For mine eyes have seen thy salvation,
Which thou hast prepared before the face of all people;
A light to lighten the Gentiles, and the glory of thy people Israel. *Luke* 2:29–32. (Simeon when the infant Jesus is brought to him in the temple.)

8 I am the door. *John* 10:9. (More at JESUS.)

9 I came not to judge the world, but to save the world. *John* 12:47.

10 What must I do to be saved?

. . . Believe in the Lord Jesus, and you will be saved, you and your household. *Acts* 16:30–31, RSV. (The question is put by a jailer in Philippi to his prisoners Paul and Silas after an earthquake had miraculously freed them from prison and fetters.)

11 Whom he did foreknow, he also did predestinate to be conformed to the image of his Son, that he might be the firstborn among many brethren.

Moreover whom he did predestinate, them he also called: and whom he called, them he also justified: and whom he justified, them he also glorified. *Romans* 8:29–30. (Paul wrestles often with the issues of predestination versus free will, without reaching entirely clear conclusions. Scholars, however, say that he meant predestination to be seen as a promise, a source of hope, rather than as a reason to despair.)

12 Who shall bring any charge against God's elect? It is God who justifies. *Romans* 8:33, RSV.

1 Now is the accepted time; behold, now is the day of salvation. *II Corinthians* 6:2.

2 Work out your own salvation with fear and trembling.
For it is God which worketh in you both to will and to do of his good pleasure. *Philippians* 2:12–13.

3 These are they which came out of great tribulation, and have washed their robes, and made them white in the blood of the Lamb. *Revelation* 7:14.

4 They shall hunger no more, neither thirst any more; neither shall the sun light on them, nor any heat.
For the Lamb which is in the midst of the throne shall feed them, and shall lead them unto living fountains of waters: and God shall wipe away all tears from their eyes. *Revelation* 7:16–17.

See also ATONEMENT; GOD; HEAVEN; JESUS; JUDGMENT DAY; MESSIAH; PEACE; RELIGION; SERVANT OF GOD; SPIRITUAL BIRTH.

SAMARITAN

See GOOD SAMARITAN

SAMSON

5 If I be shaven, then my strength will go from me, and shall become weak, and be like any other man. *Judges* 16:17.

See also PRAYERS; RIDDLES; WAR.

SATAN

See DEVIL

SAUL

See PAUL

SAUL, KING

See DAVID; SAUL AND JONATHAN

SAUL AND JONATHAN

6 Saul and Jonathan were lovely and pleasant in their lives, and in their death they were not divided: they were swifter than eagles, they were stronger than lions. *II Samuel* 1:23. (David here laments the death in battle of Saul, his enemy but also his king and former mentor, and Saul's son Jonathan, David's beloved friend.)

See also DAVID AND JONATHAN.

SCAPEGOAT

See ATONEMENT; SERVANT OF GOD

SCIENCE

1 I applied mine heart to know, and to search, and to seek out wisdom, and the reason of things. *Ecclesiastes* 7:25.

2 God hath made man upright; but they have sought out many inventions. *Ecclesiastes* 7:29.

3 Their work was as it were a wheel in the middle of a wheel. *Ezekiel* 1:16. (These wheels appear in the prophet's vision of four multi-faced cherubim, each associated with a wheel. The wheels are far from strictly mechanical [the outer rims are full of eyes], but they do resemble spoked chariot wheels, with rims, a fairly late development in the history of the wheel. Wheels symbolize power in the Bible, for chariots were both dreaded instruments of war and vehicles for kings in ceremonial appearances. There were wheels on the Temple court lavers [*I Kings* 7:30–33] and on the thrones described in *Daniel* 7:9 and *I Enoch* 14:18.)

4 He hath given me certain knowledge of the things that are, namely, to know how the world was made, and the operation of the elements:

. . . the alterations of the turnings of the sun and the change of the seasons:

The circuits of years, and the positions of stars:

The natures of living creatures, and the furies of wild beasts: the violence of winds, and the reasonings of men; the diversities of plants, and the virtues of roots. *Wisdom of Solomon* 7:17–21. (This speech, attributed to Solomon, reflects Greek culture in approximately the first century B.C. Scholars believe this book was written by an Alexandrian Jew a few decades before the birth of Christ.)

5 O Timothy, keep that which is committed to thy trust, avoiding profane and vain babblings, and oppositions of science falsely so called. *I Timothy* 6:20.

See also DOCTORS AND MEDICINE; STARS.

SEA

See OCEAN AND SEA

SEASONS

6 While the earth remaineth, seedtime and harvest, and cold and heat, and summer and winter, and day and night shall not cease. *Genesis* 8:22.

7 I will give you rain in due season, and the land shall yield her increase, and the trees of the field shall yield their fruit. *Leviticus* 26:4.

8 To every thing there is a season. *Ecclesiastes* 3:1. (The full text is at LIFE.)

9 Lo, the winter is past, the rain is over and gone;

The flowers appear on the earth; the time of the singing of birds is come, and the voice of the turtle is heard in our land.

The fig tree putteth forth her green figs, and the vines with the tender grape give a good smell. Arise, my love, my fair one, and come away. *Song of Solomon* 2:11–13.

1 The desert shall rejoice, and blossom as the rose. *Isaiah* 35:1

SECRETS

2 The secret things belong unto the Lord our God. *Deuteronomy* 29:29. (More at REVELATION.)

3 He [God] knoweth the secrets of the heart. *Psalms* 44:21.

4 Stolen waters are sweet, and bread eaten in secret is pleasant. *Proverbs* 9:17.

5 He who goes about as a tablebearer reveals secrets, but he who is trustworthy in spirit keeps a thing hidden. *Proverbs* 11:13, RSV.

6 Woe to those who hide deep from the Lord their counsel, whose deeds are in the dark, and who say, "Who sees us? Who knows us?" *Isaiah* 29:15, RSV.

7 It is good to keep close the secret of a king. *Tobit* 12:7. (The angel Gabriel acknowledging the necessity of secrecy in government. This was written probably in the early years of the second century B.C.)

8 Let not thy left hand know what thy right hand doeth. *Matthew* 6:3. (Meant to apply to giving alms without self-advertisement [see GIVING], this line is used to urge secrecy in undertakings of all sorts.)

9 Nothing is secret, that shall not be made manifest. *Luke* 8:17. (See also *Matthew* 10:26.)

10 This thing was not done in a corner. *Acts* 26:26. (Paul using a proverbial expression to deny that there is anything secret about his mission or message.)

See also GOSSIP; MYSTERY; REVELATION; TALK.

SEEING

See BODY; VISION; WISDOM

SELF-ACCEPTANCE

See IDENTITY

SELF-CONTROL

11 He that hath no rule over his own spirit is like a city that is broken down, and without walls. *Proverbs* 25:28.

12 Their strength is to sit still. *Isaiah* 30:7.

1 Keep thy sorrow to thyself, and bear with a good courage that which hath befallen thee. *II Esdras* 10:15.

SELF-ESTEEM

2 He that is evil to himself, to whom will he be good? *Ecclesiasticus* 14:5.

3 According to thy ability do good to thyself, and give the Lord his due offering.
Remember that death will not be long in coming. *Ecclesiasticus* 14:11–12.

SELF-RELIANCE

4 Is not my help in me? *Job* 6:13.

5 Let the counsel of thine own heart stand. *Ecclesiasticus* 37:13.

See also INDEPENDENCE; INITIATIVE.

SELF-RIGHTEOUSNESS

6 Stand by thyself, come not near to me: for I am holier than thou. *Isaiah* 65:5. (The attitude of God's people, as described by God himself, who is angry at their rebelliousness and rejection of him.)

SELF-SATISFACTION

7 The Pharisee stood and prayed thus with himself, God, I thank thee, that I am not as other men are. *Luke* 18:11. (More at PRAYER.)

SELLING

See BUSINESS

SERMON ON THE MOUNT

See BEATITUDES

SERVANT OF GOD

8 Behold my servant, whom I uphold; mine elect, in whom my soul delighteth; I have put my spirit upon him: he shall bring forth judgment to the Gentiles. *Isaiah* 42:1. (The beginning of the "servant-songs" of *Isaiah*, which include 42:1–4, 49:1–6, 50:4–9, and 52:13, to 53:12. These verses historically have been the focus of scholarly debate. Christians tend to interpret them as referring to the mission of Jesus. At *Matthew* 12:18, for example, there is a specific reference to this verse: "Behold my servant, whom I have chosen; my beloved, in whom my soul is well pleased." Jews interpret *servant* as referring to the people of Israel collectively.)

9 He is despised and rejected of men; a man of sorrows, and acquainted with grief. *Isaiah* 53:3. (Here and in the following verses, God's servant is

rejected, imprisoned, and killed. This is the portrait of "the suffering servant".)

1 He was wounded for our transgressions . . . and with his stripes we are healed.

All we like sheep have gone astray; we have turned every one to his own way; and the Lord hath laid on him the iniquity of us all.

He was oppressed, and he was afflicted, yet he opened not his mouth: he is brought as a lamb to the slaughter. *Isaiah* 53:5–7.

See also JESUS; MESSIAH.

SERVING GOD

See GOD, OBEYING AND SERVING

SEX

2 Onan . . . when he went in unto his brother's wife . . . spilled [his seed] on the ground. *Genesis* 38:9 (For refusing his duty to impregnate the wife of his dead brother, Onan is slain by God. Note that the sin of Onan, usually said to be masturbation, evidently was coitus interruptus.)

3 Thou shalt not commit adultery. *Exodus* 20:14. (The Seventh Commandment.)

4 If a man entice a maid that is not betrothed, and lie with her, he shall surely endow her to be his wife. [He shall pay her dowry and marry her.]

If her father utterly refuse to give her unto him, he shall pay money according to the dowry of virgins. *Exodus* 22:16–17.

5 Whosoever lieth with a beast shall surely be put to death. *Exodus* 22:19. (*Leviticus* 20:15 adds the proviso that the beast should be killed as well. Punishment by death of animals for wrongdoing of various sorts was specified in many legal codes well into modern times.)

6 You shall not lie with a male as with a woman; it is an abomination. And you shall not lie with any beast. *Leviticus* 18:22–23, RSV. (Among the Israelites, the rules regarding sex were stricter than those of most of the other peoples of the ancient Middle East. In this same passage, sexual relations with a menstruating woman are also cited as an "abomination" deserving exile. Most of the rules promote fertility—extremely important to a young and vulnerable nation.)

7 The adulterer and the adulteress shall be put to death. *Leviticus* 20:10. (*Adultery* in the Old Testament refers exclusively to sexual relations between a married or betrothed woman and a man not her husband or husband-to-be. In the New Testament, the definition was widened to include sexual relations undertaken by a married man with someone other than his wife. This law seems to have been enforced only rarely.)

1 The lips of a loose woman drip honey, and her speech is smoother than oil;

But in the end she is bitter as wormwood, sharp as a two-edged sword.

Her feet go down to death; her steps follow the path of Sheol [hell, the underworld];

She does not take heed to the path of life; her ways wander, and she does not know it. *Proverbs* 5:3–6, RSV.

2 Lust not after her beauty in thine heart; neither let her take thee with her eyelids [eyelashes]. *Proverbs* 6:25.

3 He that doeth it [adultery] destroyeth his own soul. *Proverbs* 6:32.

4 He goeth after her straightway, as an ox goeth to the slaughter. *Proverbs* 7:22. (The poor sinner here was severely tested, for the woman [unnamed] kissed him and said, "I have decked my bed with coverings of tapestry, with carved works, with fine linen of Egypt./I have perfumed my bed with myrrh, aloes, and cinnamon./Come, let us take our fill of love until the morning: let us solace ourselves with loves./ For the goodman is not at home, he is gone a long journey." *Proverbs* 7:16–19.)

5 A whore is a deep ditch. *Proverbs* 23:27.

6 Such is the way of an adulterous woman; she eateth, and wipeth her mouth, and saith, I have done no wickedness. *Proverbs* 30:20.

7 Let him kiss me with the kisses of his mouth: for thy love is better than wine. *Song of Solomon* 1:2. (Whether this book of the Bible should be interpreted in terms of sexual, romantic love has been an issue of historical debate. It is often given an allegorical interpretation referring to the love between God and his chosen people, or the love between Christ and his church. Scholars generally believe, however, that its inclusion in the Bible involves a recognition of the importance of physical love.)

8 My beloved is mine, and I am his: he feedeth among the lilies. *Song of Solomon* 2:16.

9 By night on my bed I sought him whom my soul loveth: I sought him, but I found him not.

I will rise now, and go about the city in the streets, and in the broad ways I will seek him whom my soul loveth. *Song of Solomon* 3:1–2.

10 I found him whom my soul loveth: I held him, and would not let him go, until I had brought him into my mother's house, and into the chamber of her that conceived me. *Song of Solomon* 3:4.

11 Thy two breasts are like two young roes [fawns]. *Song of Solomon* 4:5.

12 How fair is thy love, my sister, my spouse! how much better is thy love than wine! and the smell of thine ointments than all spices! *Song of Solomon* 4:10.

1 Thy lips, O my spouse, drop as the honeycomb: honey and milk are under thy tongue. *Song of Solomon* 4:11.

2 How fair and how pleasant art thou, O love, for delights! *Song of Solomon* 7:6.

3 They were as fed horses in the morning: every one neighed after his neighbor's wife. *Jeremiah* 5:8. (Jeremiah on the subject of his fellow citizens in Jerusalem. They "assembled themselves by troops in the harlots' houses," he tells us. *Jeremiah* 5:7.)

4 Sit not at all with another man's wife, nor sit down with her in thine arms . . . lest thine heart incline unto her. *Ecclesiasticus* 9:9.

5 Whosoever looketh on a woman to lust after her hath committed adultery with her already in his heart. *Matthew* 5:28. (In his first campaign for the presidency, Jimmy Carter admitted in a *Playboy* interview that he had been guilty of lust in his heart. This imprudent frankness caused considerable merriment, especially among journalists and Republicans.)

6 Flee fornication. *I Corinthians* 6:18.

7 Abstain from fleshly lusts, which war against the soul. *I Peter* 2:11.

See also DISSIPATION; HEDONISM; JEALOUSY; LOVE, INVITATIONS TO; SOLOMON; TEMPTATION.

SHADRACH, MESHACH, AND ABEDNEGO

See MIRACLES IN THE OLD TESTAMENT

SHEBA, QUEEN OF

See SOLOMON

SHEPHERDS

8 Pharaoh said unto his [Joseph's] brethren, What is your occupation? And they said unto Pharaoh, Thy servants are shepherds, both we, and also our fathers. *Genesis* 47:3. (Throughout the Bible, shepherds are special people, with this distinction culminating in the image of Christ as the Good Shepherd. Martin Buber points out in his book on Moses that only after becoming a shepherd among the Midianites was Moses made aware of his mission. In the *Psalms* 80:1, God himself is called "Shepherd of Israel." And in the Islamic tradition, Mohammed is supposed to have said that nobody becomes a prophet who was not first a shepherd.)

9 There remaineth yet the youngest, and, behold, he keepeth the sheep. *I Samuel* 16:11. (The first appearance of David.)

10 The Lord is my shepherd, I shall not want. *Psalms* 23:1. (The entire psalm is given at GOD'S PROVIDENCE.)

1 Rejoice with me; for I have found my sheep which was lost. *Luke* 15:6. (More at SIN AND SINNERS.)

See also FARMING; JESUS (especially the "good shepherd" verses from *John* 10); GOD'S PROVIDENCE (for God as shepherd).

SHIPS

2 The way of a ship in the midst of the sea. *Proverbs* 30:19. (The entire passage is given at LIFE'S WONDERS.)

See also OCEAN AND SEA.

SICKNESS

3 When the plague of leprosy is in a man, then he shall be brought unto the priest. *Leviticus* 13:9. (This is part of a famous passage on leprosy. Priests had various duties with respect to the care of lepers and containment of the disease. Two chapters here in *Leviticus* outline their responsibilities and give diagnostic guidelines.)

4 And it came to pass that night, that the angel of the Lord went out, and smote in the camp of the Assyrians a hundred fourscore and five thousand; and when they arose early in the morning, behold, they were all dead corpses. *II Kings* 19:35. (This catastrophe, from the Assyrian point of view, was evidently an outbreak of bubonic plague, also described by Herodotus, *Histories*, Book II, 141. It saved Jerusalem from a dangerous siege conducted by King Sennacherib in 701 B.C.)

5 He has broken my strength in midcourse; he has shortened my days. *Psalms* 102:23, RSV.

6 The whole head is sick, and the whole heart faint. *Isaiah* 1:5.

7 They are drunken, but not with wine; they stagger, but not with strong drink. *Isaiah* 29:9.

8 Why is my pain perpetual, and my wound incurable, which refuseth to be healed? *Jeremiah* 15:18.

9 All hands shall be feeble, and all knees shall be weak as water. *Ezekiel* 7:17.

10 Envy and wrath shorten life, and carefulness [worry] bringeth age before the time. *Ecclesiasticus* 30:24. (A relation between emotions and health is also noted in the previous verse: "Comfort thy heart, remove sorrow far from thee: for sorrow hath killed many." *Ecclesiasticus* 30:23.)

See also BODY; HEALTH; DOCTORS AND MEDICINE; MADNESS; PARANOIA.

SIGN OF JONAH

See GENERATIONS (*Luke* 11:29); JESUS, RESURRECTION OF (*Matthew* 12:40)

SILENCE

1 A man of understanding remains silent. *Proverbs* 11:12, RSV.

2 Even a fool, when he holdeth his peace, is counted wise: and he that shutteth his lips is esteemed a man of understanding. *Proverbs* 17:28.

See also CAUTION; GOD, SILENT; PRUDENCE; TALK.

SIMON PETER

See PETER

SIN AND SINNERS

3 Ye have sinned against the Lord: and be sure your sin will find you out. *Numbers* 32:23.

4 Remember not the sins of my youth, nor my transgressions. *Psalms* 25:7.

5 When I declared not my sin, my body wasted away through my groaning all day long. *Psalms* 32:3, RSV. (This psalm concerns confessing one's sins to God to obtain forgiveness. See also *Proverbs* 28:13, below.)

6 Cleanse me from my sin. *Psalms* 51:2.

7 I was shapen in iniquity; and in sin did my mother conceive me. *Psalms* 51:5.

8 I have gone astray like a lost sheep. *Psalms* 119:176.

9 My son, if sinners entice thee, consent thou not. *Proverbs* 1:10.

10 The way of transgressors is hard. *Proverbs* 13:15.

11 Fools make a mock at sin. *Proverbs* 14:9.

12 He that covereth his sins shall not prosper: but whoso confesseth and forsaketh them shall have mercy. *Proverbs* 28:13.

13 There is not a just man upon earth, that doeth good, and sinneth not. *Ecclesiastes* 7:20.

14 One sinner destroyeth much good. *Ecclesiastes* 9:18.

15 Though your sins be as scarlet, they shall be as white as snow; though they be red like crimson, they shall be as wool. *Isaiah* 1:18. (The Lord promises that through virtuous and pious behavior sins will be cleansed away.)

16 We like sheep have gone astray. *Isaiah* 53:6.

1 The sin of Judah is written with a pen of iron, and with the point of a diamond. *Jeremiah* 17:1.

2 The soul that sinneth, it shall die. *Ezekiel* 18:4.

3 They that sin are enemies to their own life. *Tobit* 12:10

4 Be not ashamed to confess thy sins. *Ecclesiasticus* 4:26.

5 The way of sinners is made plain [smooth] with stones, but at the end thereof is the pit of hell. *Ecclesiasticus* 21:10.

6 If thy right eye offend thee, pluck it out, and cast it from thee . . .
And if thy right hand offend thee, cut it off, and cast it from thee. *Matthew* 5:29–30. (From the Sermon on the Mount. "Offend thee" means "lead into sin." The point is that it is better to lose part of oneself than "that thy whole body should be cast into hell." *Matthew* 5:30.)

7 I am come not to call the righteous, but sinners to repentance. *Matthew* 9:13.

8 Which man of you, having a hundred sheep, if he lose one of them, doth not leave the ninety and nine in the wilderness, and go after that which is lost, until he find it?

And when he hath found it, he layeth it on his shoulders, rejoicing. *Luke* 15:4–5.

9 Rejoice with me; for I have found my sheep which was lost.

I say unto you, that likewise joy shall be in heaven over one sinner that repenteth, more than over ninety and nine just persons, which need no repentance. *Luke* 15:6–7. (The first line above is the shepherd calling to his friends and neighbors. Then Jesus draws the conclusion.)

10 Sin no more. *John* 5:14. (Jesus to the man cured at Bethesda.)

11 Go, and sin no more. *John* 8:11. (Jesus to the woman taken in adultery. More at JUDGING OTHERS.)

12 Whosoever committeth sin is the servant of sin. *John* 8:34.

13 Whose soever sins yet remit, they are remitted unto them. *John* 20:23.

14 Thou art in the gall of bitterness, and in the bond of iniquity. *Acts* 8:23. (Peter to the sorcerer Simon.)

15 The wages of sin is death. *Romans* 6:23. (More at HEAVEN.)

16 Ye are fallen from grace. *Galatians* 5:4.

17 The enemies of the cross of Christ:

Whose end is destruction, whose God is their belly, and whose glory is in their shame, who mind earthly things. *Philippians* 3:18–19.

18 Christ Jesus came into the world to save sinners; of whom I am chief. *I Timothy* 1:15. (St. Paul, of course.)

1 If we say that we have no sin, we deceive ourselves. *I John* 1:8.

See also DISSIPATION; EVIL; FAILINGS; GUILT; HELL; REFORM; REPENTANCE; SEX; TEMPTATION.

SINCERITY

2 With my whole heart and with my whole soul. *Jeremiah* 32:41.

3 Let thy life be sincere. *Ecclesiasticus* 5:11.

4 Out of the abundance of the heart, the mouth speaketh. *Matthew* 12:34.

See also FRANKNESS.

SINNERS

See SIN AND SINNERS

SISERA AND JAEL

5 Sisera [the Caananite commander] fled away on his feet to the tent of Jael the wife of Heber the Kenite . . .

And Jael . . . said unto him, Turn in, my lord, turn in to me; fear not . . .

And he said unto her, Give me, I pray thee, a little water to drink; for I am thirsty. And she opened a bottle of milk, and gave him drink, and covered him . . .

Then Jael Heber's wife took a nail of the tent, and took a hammer in her hand, and went softly unto him, and smote the nail into his temples, and fastened it to the ground: for he was fast asleep and weary. So he died. *Judges* 4:17–21. (Sisera was in flight from the armies of Deborah and Balak—see under WAR—and took refuge in a household that he thought was loyal to him. The story is told again at *Judges* 5:24–27, with the dramatic conclusion: "At her feet he bowed, he fell: where he bowed, there he fell down dead." In neither book is Jael's motive explained.)

6 The mother of Sisera looked out at a window, and cried through the lattice, Why is his chariot so long in coming? why tarry the wheels of his chariots? *Judges* 5:28. (The grief of Sisera's mother is as acute as the triumph of Deborah and the Israelites. This is one of the great Bible stories, moving and mysterious.)

SKY

See HEAVENS AND SKY

SLEEP AND SLEEPLESSNESS

7 Nights of misery are apportioned to me. *Job* 7:3, RSV.

8 The night is long, and I am full of tossing till the dawn. *Job* 7:4, RSV.

1 In peace I will both lie down and sleep. *Psalms* 4:8, RSV ("I will lay me down in peace, and take my rest." *Book of Common Prayer, Psalms* 4:9. "I laid me down and slept." *Psalms* 3:5.)

2 He giveth his beloved sleep. *Psalms* 127:2.

3 When you lie down, your sleep will be sweet. *Proverbs* 3:24, RSV.

4 Yet a little sleep, a little slumber, a little folding of the hands to sleep. *Proverbs* 6:10. (Also at *Proverbs* 24:33.)

5 Love not sleep, lest thou come to poverty. *Proverbs* 20:13.

6 The sleep of a laboring man is sweet, whether he eat little or much: but the abundance of the rich will not suffer him to sleep. *Ecclesiastes* 5:12.

7 Sleep on now, and take your rest. *Matthew* 26:45. (Jesus to Peter, James, and John the night before he dies. He had asked them to keep him company, but they kept falling asleep. See also JESUS: PASSION AND DEATH.)

SMALL THINGS

8 Who hath despised the day of small things? *Zechariah* 4:10.

9 He that condemneth small things shall fall by little and little. *Ecclesiasticus* 19:1.

10 He that is faithful in that which is least is faithful also in much: and he that is unjust in the least is unjust also in much. *Luke* 16:10.

11 There is a lad here, which hath five barley loaves, and two small fishes: but what are they among so many? *John* 6:9. (Andrew to Jesus prior to the miracle of the loaves and fishes.)

12 God hath chosen the weak things of the world to confound the things which are mighty. *I Corinthians* 1:27. (More at RELIGION.)

13 How great a matter a little fire kindleth! *James* 3:5.

SODOM AND GOMORRAH

14 Then the Lord rained upon Sodom and upon Gomorrah brimstone and fire from the Lord out of heaven. *Genesis* 19:24. (Abraham had attempted to persuade God to save these cities. See the first quote at JUSTICE AND FAIRNESS.)

15 But his [Lot's] wife looked back from behind him, and she became a pillar of salt. *Genesis* 19:26. (The site is usually identified as the southern shore of the Dead Sea, which features dramatic salt cliffs, some of which have eroded into humanlike shapes.)

SOLOMON

1 I have given thee a wise and an understanding heart. *I Kings* 3:12. (God to Solomon. See Solomon's prayer at JUDGES.)

2 And I have also given thee that which thou hast not asked, both riches, and honor: so that there shall not be any among the kings like unto thee all thy days. *I Kings* 3:13.

3 Divide the living child in two, and give half to the one and half to the other. *I Kings* 3:25. (Solomon's famous ruse for deciding which of two women before him was telling the truth. The two were harlots who lived together, and each had an infant son. When one of the babies died in the night, each claimed the remaining child as her own.)

4 King Solomon loved many strange women. *I Kings* 11:1. (*Strange* means "foreign." Among these women, according to popular tradition, was the queen of Sheba, who visited Solomon out of curiosity and found that—see below.

5 He had seven hundred wives, princesses, and three hundred concubines. *I Kings* 11:3. (Polygamy was relatively common among the Israelites, and kings often had large harems. Many of these unions were political: for example, among Solomon's wives was an Egyptian princess whose father gave Solomon the city of Gezer.)

6 When the queen of Sheba heard of the fame of Solomon, she came to prove Solomon with hard questions. *II Chronicles* 9:1. (The lady arrived with a large entourage, camels and spices, jewels and gold. Moreover, she was an irresistible conversationalist. "Thy wisdom and prosperity exceedeth the fame which I heard," she told Solomon. *I Kings* 10:7. Not surprisingly, the king gave her "all her desire," a phrase open to interpretation. In Ethiopia, legend has it that the queen bore a child by Solomon: Menelek, founder of the royal house. The emperor was called "The Lion of Judah," and the national emblem was a six-pointed star.)

See also RICHES, WISDOM.

SONG OF SOLOMON

See LOVE; LOVE, INVITATIONS TO; SEX

SORROW

See MISFORTUNE; TROUBLE; UNHAPPINESS

SOUL

7 The spirit of man is the candle of the Lord. *Proverbs* 20:27.

8 Behold, all souls are mine. *Ezekiel* 18:4. (The Lord to Ezekiel.)

9 Our spirit shall vanish as the soft air. *Wisdom of Solomon* 2:3. (This view is identified as coming from "the ungodly," and is rejected. *The Wisdom*

of Solomon is the first biblical book to promise specifically immortality of the soul.)

1 What shall it profit a man, if he shall gain the whole world, and lose his own soul? *Mark* 8:36.

2 It is the spirit that gives life, the flesh is of no avail. *John* 6:63, RSV.

See also HEAVEN; SPIRIT; SPIRITUAL BIRTH.

SPEECH

See LANGUAGE; TALK

SPEED

3 That thou doest, do quickly. *John* 13:27. (Jesus to Judas Iscariot.)

SPIRIT

4 The fruit of the Spirit is love, joy, peace, longsuffering, gentleness, goodness, faith,
Meekness, temperance. *Galatians* 5:22–23. (Here *Spirit* seems to mean both Holy Spirit and the life of the spirit, as opposed to corporal and worldly concerns.)

5 Be strengthened with might by [God's] Spirit in the inner man. *Ephesians* 3:16.

SPIRITUAL BIRTH

6 Except a man be born again, he cannot see the kingdom of God. *John* 3:3. (This and the lines below are spoken by Jesus in conversation with the Pharisee Nicodemus.)

7 Except a man be born of water and of the Spirit, he cannot enter into the kingdom of God. *John* 3:5. (This birth of the Spirit occurs through faith in Jesus Christ.)

8 Ye must be born again. *John* 3:7.

9 The wind blows where it wills, and you hear the sound of it, but you do not know whence it comes or whither it goes: so it is with every one who is born of the Spirit. *John* 3:8, RSV.

SPRING

See SEASONS

STARS

1 Canst thou bind the sweet influences of Pleiades, or loose the bands of Orion? *Job* 38:31.

2 Canst thou guide Arcturus with his sons? *Job* 38:32.

3 There is no speech, nor are there words; their [the stars'] voice is not heard;

Yet their voice goes out through all the earth, and their words to the end of the world. *Psalms* 19:3–4, RSV. (The stars exert an invisible influence that testifies to the glory of God. The concept is in harmony with contemporary physics, in which even the most distant matter in the universe influences our own world.)

4 He telleth the number of the stars; he calleth them all by their names. *Psalms* 147:4.

5 The stars shined in their watches, and rejoiced. *I Baruch* 3:34.

6 The day star arise in your hearts. *II Peter* 1:19.

7 I will give him the morning star. *Revelation* 2:28. (God promising eternal life to the faithful.)

8 And the name of the star is called Wormwood. *Revelation* 8:11. (A star that appears at the end of the world, evidently a symbol of poison and destruction.)

See also HEAVENS AND SKY.

STRANGERS AND TRAVELERS

9 I am a stranger and a sojourner with you. *Genesis* 23:4. (Spoken by Abraham as he arranges to buy a burying plot in Hebron for his wife Sarah and himself. This is the first land acquired by the Jews, and is still venerated as a holy place.)

10 I have been a stranger in a strange land. *Exodus* 2:22. (These words by Moses, are also said by Oedipus in Sophocles's *Oedipus at Colonus*. The theme of being a stranger, a wanderer, is repeated often in the Bible. It reflects not only the particular history of the Jews, but the concept that before God every person is a stranger, an alien without rights. Thus God tells the Israelites, "The land shall not be sold in perpetuity, for the land is mine; for you are strangers and sojourners with me." *Leviticus* 25:23, RSV. See also the quotes below.)

11 Thou shalt neither vex a stranger nor oppress him: for ye were strangers in the land of Egypt. *Exodus* 22:21. (See also *Exodus* 23:9. *Deuteronomy* 10:19 commands, "Love ye therefore the stranger; for ye were strangers in the land of Egypt.")

1 Ye shall have one manner of law, as well for the stranger, as for one of your own country. *Leviticus* 24:22.

2 I am a stranger with thee, and a sojourner, as all my fathers were. *Psalms* 39:12. (David is speaking.)

3 Be not forgetful to entertain strangers; for thereby some have entertained angels unawares. *Hebrews* 13:2.

See also TRAVEL.

STRENGTH

4 Thy shoes shall be iron and brass; and as thy days, so shall thy strength be. *Deuteronomy* 33:25. (A blessing of the dying Moses upon the Israelites.)

5 Be strong and of a good courage. *Joshua* 1:6. (God to Joshua; repeated at 1:9 and elsewhere.)

6 As the man is, so is his strength. *Judges* 8:21.

7 By strength shall no man prevail. *I Samuel* 2:9.

8 Is my strength the strength of stones? or is my flesh of brass? *Job* 6:12. (Job speaks of the limits of human strength; his suffering is more than he can endure.)

9 They go from strength to strength. *Psalms* 84:7.

10 Strong men retain riches. *Proverbs* 11:16.

11 The glory of young men is their strength. *Proverbs* 20:29.

12 Their strength is to sit still. *Isaiah* 30:7. (Sometimes interpreted to mean that strength lies in calmness, but actually a sarcastic reference to the Egyptians. In the Revised Standard Version, the passage runs: "Egypt's help is worthless and empty, therefore I have called her 'Ra'hab who sits still'." *Rahab* is a pejorative name for Egypt.)

13 The first wrote, Wine is the strongest.
The second wrote, The king is the strongest.
The third wrote, women are strongest: But above all things truth beareth away the victory. *I Esdras* 3:10–12. (Three guardsmen of king Darius I took part in a contest to name the strongest thing in the world and to defend that choice before the king and his nobles. The winner was Zerubbabel, who argued for truth—after making a pretty strong case for women. Instead of accepting riches as a prize, he asked permission to go to Jerusalem and rebuild the Temple. See also TRUTH; WINE; WOMEN.)

14 We then that are strong ought to bear the infirmities of the weak, and not to please ourselves. *Romans* 15:1.

15 Quit you like men, be strong. *I Corinthians* 16:13. (More at FAITH.)

See also GOD AS A SOURCE OF STRENGTH; PRAYERS (Judges 16:28); SELF-CONTROL; SELF-RELIANCE.

STUBBORNNESS

1 He stiffened his neck, and hardened his heart. *II Chronicles* 36:13. (Stiff-neckedness is a recurring problem in the Old Testament. See also CHOSEN PEOPLE. The offender here is the young king Zedekiah.)

2 A stubborn heart shall fare evil at the last. *Ecclesiasticus* 3:26.

STUPIDITY

3 A stupid man will get understanding when a wild ass's colt is born a man. *Job* 11:12, RSV.

4 A foolish woman is clamorous; she is simple, and knoweth nothing. *Proverbs* 9:13.

5 The fool shall be a servant to the wise of heart. *Proverbs* 11:29.

6 The way of a fool is right in his own eyes. *Proverbs* 12:15.

7 The simple believeth every word. *Proverbs* 14:15.

8 A fool takes no pleasure in understanding, but only in expressing his opinion. *Proverbs* 18:2, RSV.

9 A fool's mouth is his destruction. *Proverbs* 18:7.

10 Answer a fool according to his folly. *Proverbs* 26:5. (Or "Answer not a fool according to his folly." *Proverbs* 26:4. The choice is yours.)

11 As a dog returneth to his vomit, so a fool returneth to his folly. *Proverbs* 26:11.

12 Hear ye indeed, but understand not; and see ye indeed, but perceive not. *Isaiah* 6:9.

13 Make not thyself an underling to a foolish man. *Ecclesiasticus* 4:27.

14 A fool changeth as the moon. *Ecclesiasticus* 27:11.

15 The discourse of fools is irksome. *Ecclesiasticus* 27:13.

16 Ye suffer fools gladly, seeing ye yourselves are wise. *II Corinthians* 11:19.

SUCCESS

17 A gracious woman gets honor, and violent men get riches. *Proverbs* 11:16, RSV. (The King James Version reads, "strong men retain riches.")

18 The desire accomplished is sweet to the soul. *Proverbs* 13:19. (Also, "A desire fulfilled is a tree of life." *Proverbs* 13:12, RSV.)

1 For men to search their own glory is not glory. *Proverbs* 25:27.

2 I made me great works; I builded me houses; I planted me vineyards. *Ecclesiastes* 2:4. (More just below.)

3 And whatsoever mine eyes desired I kept not from them, I withheld not my heart from any joy; for my heart rejoiced in all my labor . . . and, behold, all was vanity and vexation. *Ecclesiastes* 2:10–11. (This bleak view of accomplishment and success and life in general is summed up in the opening chapter of this book of the Bible. See VANITY. The full description of success runs from 2:4 to 2:11.)

4 Many kings have sat down upon the ground; and one that was never thought of hath worn the crown. *Ecclesiasticus* 11:5.

5 In the day of prosperity there is a forgetfulness of affliction: and in the day of affliction there is no more remembrance of prosperity: *Ecclesiasticus* 11:25.

See also AMBITION; GREATNESS; WINNING.

SUCCOTH

6 Jacob journeyed to Succoth, and built him a house, and made booths for his cattle: therefore the name of the place is called Succoth. *Genesis* 33:17. (This town gave its name to the feast of Succoth, one of the feasts prescribed by the Lord in *Exodus* and elsewhere. See FEASTS, RELIGIOUS. It is also called the Feast of Booths, in memory of the booths Jacob built there—*Succoth* means "booths." It is a happy feast in honor of the harvest. A memorable celebration of the Feast of Booths is described at *Ezra* 3 and *Nehemiah* 8—at the time that Nehemiah led the rebuilding of the Temple at Jerusalem.)

7 In the fifteenth day of the seventh month, when ye have gathered in the fruit of the land, ye shall keep a feast unto the Lord seven days . . .

And ye shall take you on the first day the boughs of goodly trees, branches of palm trees . . . and willows of the brook; and ye shall rejoice before the Lord your God seven days. *Leviticus* 23:39–40.

8 Ye shall dwell in booths seven days. *Leviticus* 23:42.

See also FEASTS, RELIGIOUS.

SUFFERING

See MISFORTUNE; POVERTY AND HUNGER; TROUBLE; UNHAPPINESS.

SUFFERING SERVANT

See SERVANT OF GOD

SUN

See HEAVENS AND SKY

SURVIVAL

1 Behold, I send you forth as sheep in the midst of wolves: be ye therefore wise as serpents, and harmless as doves. *Matthew* 10:16. (Jesus to his disciples. He warns them that they will face enemies on all sides. He wants them to be bold enough to preach "upon the housetops," and wise enough to escape when need be. "When they persecute you in this city, flee ye into another." *Matthew* 10:23. In the Revised Standard Version, "harmless as doves" reads "innocent as doves.")

SWEARING

2 Thou shalt not take the name of the Lord thy God in vain. *Exodus* 20:7. (The Third Commandment. In most of the injunctions against swearing, the idea of blasphemy is linked to the evil of swearing falsely, as in giving false testimony in a judicial matter. For example, "Ye shall not swear by my name falsely, neither shalt thou profane the name of thy God." *Leviticus* 19:12.)

3 The talk of him that sweareth much maketh the hair stand upright. *Ecclesiasticus* 27:14.

4 I say unto you, Swear not at all; neither by heaven; for it is God's throne:
Nor by the earth; for it is his footstool. *Matthew* 5:34–35.

SYMPATHY

5 Rejoice with them that do rejoice, and weep with them that weep. *Romans* 12:15.

6 Who is weak, and I am not weak? Who is offended, and I burn not? *II Corinthians* 11:29.

TALENT

See ABILITY

TALK

1 Should a multitude of words go unanswered, and a man full of talk be vindicated? *Job* 11:2, RSV. (Job's "friend" Zophar to Job. Having heard Job's well-founded if lengthy complaint, Zophar now intends to set him straight.)

2 Oh that you would keep silent. *Job* 13:4, RSV.

3 Should a wise man answer with windy knowledge? *Job* 15:2, RSV.

4 He multiplieth words without knowledge. *Job* 35:16.

5 Keep thy tongue from evil, and thy lips from speaking guile. *Psalms* 34:13.

6 The words of his mouth were smoother than butter, but war was in his heart: his words were softer than oil, yet were they drawn swords. *Psalms* 55:21.

7 They have sharpened their tongues like a serpent. *Psalms* 140:3.

8 A word spoken in due season, how good is it! *Proverbs* 15:23.

9 Pleasant words are like a honeycomb, sweetness to the soul and health to the body. *Proverbs* 16:24, RSV.

10 He that hath knowledge spareth his words. *Proverbs* 17:27.

11 A fool uttereth all his mind: but a wise man keepeth it in till afterwards. *Proverbs* 29:11.

12 Seest thou a man that is hasty in his words? there is more hope of a fool than of him. *Proverbs* 29:20.

13 Be not rash with thy mouth. *Ecclesiastes* 5:2.

14 Refrain not to speak, when there is occasion to do good. *Ecclesiasticus* 4:23.

15 Honor and shame is in talk: and the tongue of man is his fall. *Ecclesiasticus* 5:13.

16 Sweet language will multiply friends. *Ecclesiasticus* 6:5.

17 He that can rule his tongue shall live without strife. *Ecclesiasticus* 19:6.

18 The heart of fools is in their mouth. *Ecclesiasticus* 21:26.

1 Who shall set a watch before my mouth, and a seal of wisdom upon my lips, that . . . my tongue destroy me not? *Ecclesiasticus* 22:27.

2 Praise no man before thou hearest him speak; for this is the trial [test] of men. *Ecclesiasticus* 27:7.

3 Many have fallen by the edge of the sword, but not so many as have fallen by the tongue. *Ecclesiasticus* 28:18.

4 Let thy speech be short, comprehending much in few words. *Ecclesiasticus* 32:8.

5 Speech finely framed delighteth the ears. *II Maccabees* 15:39.

6 Every idle word that men shall speak, they shall give account thereof in the day of judgment.

For by thy words thou shalt be justified, and by thy words thou shalt be condemned. *Matthew* 12:36–37.

7 Not that which goeth into the mouth defileth a man; but that which cometh out of the mouth, this defileth a man. *Matthew* 15:11. (One of the many biblical passages making the point that religious rules—in this case, food laws—are less important than intentions and spiritual values. See also RELIGION.)

8 Thy speech betrayeth thee. *Matthew* 26:73.

9 I am speaking in human terms, because of your natural limitations. *Romans* 6:19, RSV. (The King James Version reads, "I speak after the manner of men because of the infirmity of your flesh.")

10 I be rude in speech, yet not in knowledge. *II Corinthians* 11:6.

11 Let your speech be always with grace, seasoned with salt. *Colossians* 4:6.

12 The tongue can no man tame; it is an unruly evil. *James* 3:8.

See also FRANKNESS; GOSSIP; LANGUAGE; NEWS; SECRETS; SILENCE; STUPIDITY.

TARSHISH, OR THARSHISH

See RICHES

TAXES

13 Render therefore unto Caesar the things which are Caesar's; and unto God the things that are God's. *Matthew* 22:21. (Jesus to the Pharisees who try to trick him into saying that one should not pay tribute to the Romans.)

14 There went out a decree from Caesar Augustus, that all the world should be taxed. *Luke* 2:1.

TEMPLE

1 I have hallowed this house, which thou hast built . . . and mine heart shall be there perpetually. *I Kings* 9:3. (God to Solomon, traditionally credited with building the First Temple in the tenth century B.C. In its innermost chamber was placed the ARK OF THE COVENANT. The Temple was destroyed during the Babylonian invasion in the sixth century, but was rebuilt after a period of seventy years. Herod the Great, as part of his extraordinary building program, reconstructed the Temple on a magnificent scale.)

2 Now have I chosen and sanctified this house. *II Chronicles* 7:16. (Again, God to Solomon.)

See also CHURCH.

TEMPTATION

3 Can a man take fire in his bosom, and his clothes not to be burned?
Can one go on hot coals, and his feet not be burned? *Proverbs* 6:27–28.
(The temptation warned against here is contemplation of adultery.)

4 Thou shalt not tempt the Lord thy God. *Matthew* 4:7. (Jesus to the devil.)

5 Get thee behind me, Satan. *Matthew* 16:23. (Jesus to Peter when Peter suggested that Jesus might avoid death.)

6 Watch and pray, that ye enter not into temptation; the spirit indeed is willing, but the flesh is weak. *Matthew* 26:41. (Also "Lead us not into temptation," *Matthew* 9:13. See LORD'S PRAYER.)

7 Blessed is the man that endureth temptation: for when he is tried, he shall receive the crown of life. *James* 1:12.

See also LOVE, INVITATIONS TO; SEX.

TEN COMMANDMENTS

8 If you will obey my voice and keep my covenant, you shall be my own possession among all people; for all the earth is mine. *Exodus* 19:5, RSV. (The rules of the Covenant include the Ten Commandments and other laws and instructions. The Commandments are repeated at *Deuteronomy* 5:6–21.)

9 There were thunders and lightnings, and a thick cloud upon the mount [Mount Sinai], the voice of the trumpet exceeding loud. *Exodus* 19:16. (The location of Mount Sinai is not known. The description here suggests that it may have been a still-active volcano. The name means "Mountain of God," and is possibly related to *seneh*, the "thornbush," the "burning bush." The site now called Sinai, with a Christian monastery, has only been so identified since about the fourth century A.D.)

[1] Moses spoke, and God answered him by a voice.
And the Lord came down upon mount Sinai, on the top of the mount: and the Lord called Moses up to the top of the mount; and Moses went up. *Exodus* 19:19–20.

[2] I am the Lord thy God, which have brought thee out of the land of Egypt, out of the house of bondage.
Thou shalt have no other gods before me.
Thou shalt not make unto thee any graven image. *Exodus* 20:2–4. (The Revised Standard Version, reads, "You shall not make for yourself a graven image." These are the first two Commandments. In the New Testament, the most quoted formulation is at *Mark* 12:30–31. See below. The commandment to love God is part of a great prayer in the Jewish liturgy, *Shema Israel*. See *Deuteronomy* 6:4–7 under GOD.)

[3] Thou shalt not take the name of the Lord thy God in vain. *Exodus* 20:7. (The Third Commandment.)

[4] Remember the sabbath day, to keep it holy. *Exodus* 20:8. (The Fourth Commandment. There is more at SABBATH.)

[5] Honor thy father and thy mother. *Exodus* 20:12 (The Fifth Commandment. More quotes are at PARENTS.)

[6] Thou shalt not kill. *Exodus* 20:13. (The Sixth Commandment.)

[7] Thou shalt not commit adultery. *Exodus* 20:14. (The Seventh Commandment.)

[8] Thou shalt not steal. *Exodus* 20:15. (The Eighth Commandment.)

[9] Thou shalt not bear false witness against thy neighbor. *Exodus* 20:16. (The Ninth Commandment.)

[10] Thou shalt not covet thy neighbor's house, thou shalt not covet thy neighbor's wife, nor his manservant, nor his maidservant, nor his ox, nor his ass, nor any thing that is thy neighbor's. *Exodus* 20:17. (The Tenth Commandment.)

[11] Moses drew near unto the thick darkness where God was. *Exodus* 20:21. (More at GOD, ENCOUNTERS WITH.)

[12] Moses wrote all the words of the Lord. *Exodus* 24:4.

[13] I will give thee tables of stone, and a law, and commandments which I have written; that thou mayest teach them. *Exodus* 24:12.

[14] The glory of the Lord abode upon mount Sinai. *Exodus* 24:16.

[15] He gave unto Moses . . . upon mount Sinai, two tables of testimony, tables of stone, written with the finger of God. *Exodus* 31:18. (These were the first two stone tables. Moses broke them in anger when he discovered the people worshiping an idol, the golden calf. In *Exodus*

34:1. God instructs Moses to hew new tables and gives him the Commandments again.)

1 And he [Moses] was there with the Lord forty days and forty nights; he did neither eat bread, nor drink water. And he wrote upon the tables the words or the covenant, the ten commandments. *Exodus* 34:28.

2 Fear God, and keep his commandments: for this is the whole duty of man. *Ecclesiastes* 12:13.

3 Whosoever shall do and teach them [the commandments], the same shall be called great in the kingdom of heaven. *Matthew* 5:19. (From the Sermon on the Mount.)

4 If thou wilt enter into [eternal] life, keep the commandments. *Matthew* 19:17.

5 Thou shalt love the Lord thy God with all thy heart, and with all thy soul, and with all thy mind, and with all thy strength: this is the first commandment.

And the second is like, namely this, Thou shalt love thy neighbor as thyself. There is none other commandment greater than these. *Mark* 12:30–31. (Jesus to a scribe; the classic Christian formulation of the first two commandments, introducing explicitly the commandment to love one's neighbor. An almost identical passage is at *Matthew* 22:37–40. At *Luke* 10:27 a discussion of the commandments leads to the parable of the GOOD SAMARITAN.)

6 A new commandment I give unto you, That ye love one another. *John* 13:34.

7 If ye love me, keep my commandments. *John* 14:15. (Jesus to the apostles.)

THANKSGIVING

See PRAYERS OF THANKS

THARSHISH, or TARSHISH

See RICHES

THOUGHT

See WISDOM; WORRY

TIME AND ETERNITY

8 A thousand years in thy [God's] sight are but as yesterday when it is past, and as a watch in the night. *Psalms* 90:4.

9 Teach us to number our days, that we may apply our hearts unto wisdom. *Psalms* 90:12.

10 He [God] has put eternity into man's mind. *Ecclesiastes* 3:11, RSV.

1 That which hath been is now; and that which is to be hath already been. *Ecclesiastes* 3:15.

2 There is a time for every purpose and for every work. *Ecclesiastes* 3:17. (Better known as it appears in *Ecclesiastes* 3:1–8, given at LIFE.)

3 Our time is a very shadow that passeth away. *Wisdom of Solomon* 2:5.

4 Who can number the sand of the sea, and the drops of rain, and the days of eternity? *Ecclesiasticus* 1:2.

See also FUTURE; PAST.

TOLERANCE

5 He [God] maketh his sun to rise on the evil and on the good, and sendeth rain on the just and on the unjust. *Matthew* 5:45. (This follows and explains the command to love one's enemies. In doing so one becomes like God, who exists for the good and bad alike. See LOVE.)

6 Judge not, that ye not be judged.
For with what judgment ye judge, ye shall be judged: and with what measure ye mete, it shall be measured to you again. *Matthew* 7:1–2.

7 Judge not, and ye shall not be judged: condemn not, and ye shall not be condemned: forgive, and ye shall be forgiven. *Luke* 6:37.

See also FORGIVENESS; JUDGING OTHERS.

TRAVEL

8 Rise ye up, take your journey. *Deuteronomy* 2:24.

9 A man that hath traveled knoweth many things. *Ecclesiasticus* 34:9.

See also STRANGERS AND TRAVELERS

TROUBLE

10 Man is born unto trouble, as the sparks fly upward. *Job* 5:7.

11 Happy is the man whom God reproves. *Job* 5:17, RSV. (One of Job's irritating friends is attempting to console him. Job rejects the suggestion that he has done anything to deserve reproval.)

12 The Lord reproves him whom he loves, as a father the son in whom he delights. *Proverbs* 3:12, RSV.

13 If thou faint in the day of adversity, thy strength is small. *Proverbs* 24:10.

14 The bread of adversity, and the water of affliction. *Isaiah* 30:20.

15 I have chosen thee in the furnace of affliction. *Isaiah* 48:10.

1 Comfort all that mourn;
. . . Give unto them beauty for ashes, the oil of joy for mourning, the garment of praise for the spirit of heaviness. *Isaiah* 61:2–3.

2 I will feed them with wormwood, and make them drink the water of gall. *Jeremiah* 23:15. (See also *Lamentations* 3:19.)

3 The day of trouble is near. *Ezekiel* 7:7.

4 Gold is tried in the fire, and acceptable men in the furnace of adversity. *Ecclesiasticus* 2:5.

5 In the day of prosperity there is a forgetfulness of affliction: and in the day of affliction there is no more remembrance of prosperity. *Ecclesiasticus* 11:25.

6 The affliction of an hour maketh a man forget pleasure. *Ecclesiasticus* 11:27.

7 The whole creation groaneth and travaileth in pain together until now. *Romans* 8:22.

8 Whom the Lord loveth he chasteneth. *Hebrews* 12:6.

See also DESOLATION; DESPAIR; DESTRUCTION; JOB; LONELINESS; MISFORTUNE; REJECTION; SELF-CONTROL; UNHAPPINESS.

TRUST

See GOD, TRUST IN; TRUST, MISPLACED

TRUST, MISPLACED

9 His trust is a spider's web. *Job* 8:14, RSV.

10 Thou trustest in the staff of this broken reed. *Isaiah* 36:6.

11 Cursed be the man that trusteth in man. *Jeremiah* 17:5.

See also CAUTION.

TRUTH

12 Mercy and truth are met together. *Psalms* 85:10. (More at SALVATION.)

13 His [God's] truth shall be thy shield and buckler. *Psalms* 91:4. (A buckler is a small, round shield, carried by a handle or worn on the arm.)

14 I have chosen the way of truth. *Psalms* 119:30.

15 Women are strongest: But above all things truth beareth away the victory. *I Esdras* 3:10–12. (From a contest among three guardsmen of King Darius as to what is the strongest thing in the world. Zerubbabel, who proposed truth, with women as a close second, won the prize. See also STRENGTH and the two quotes below.)

1 The truth, it endureth, and is always strong; it liveth and conquereth for evermore. *I Esdras* 4:38.

2 Great is truth, and mighty above all things. *I Esdras* 4:41.

3 Strive for the truth unto death, and the Lord shall fight for thee. *Ecclesiasticus* 4:28.

4 Ye shall know the truth, and the truth shall make you free. *John* 8:32.

5 Pilate saith unto him, What is truth? *John* 18:38. (Jesus has just told Pilate that he came into the world to "bear witness unto the truth.")

6 By the word of truth, by the power of God. *II Corinthians* 6:7.

TYRANNY

See GOVERNMENT; OPPRESSION; POWER

UNDERSTANDING See HEARING; VISION; WISDOM

UNHAPPINESS

1 Why is thy countenance sad, seeing thou art not sick? this is nothing else but sorrow of heart. *Nehemiah* 2:2. (King Artaxerxes to Nehemiah.)

2 You will forget your misery; you will remember it as waters that have passed away. *Job* 11:16, RSV.

3 Why art thou cast down, O my soul? *Psalms* 42:5. (Also at *Psalms* 42:11, and elsewhere).

4 They that sow in tears shall reap in joy. *Psalms* 126:5.

5 Even in laughter the heart is sorrowful; and the end of that mirth is heaviness. *Proverbs* 14:13.

6 The eye is not satisfied with seeing, nor the ear filled with hearing. *Ecclesiastes* 1:8.

7 Sorrow is better than laughter: for by the sadness of the countenance the heart is made better.

The heart of the wise is in the house of mourning. *Ecclesiastes* 7:3–4.

8 Is it nothing to you, all ye that pass by? behold, and see if there be any sorrow like unto my sorrow. *Lamentations* 1:12.

9 Our song is put to silence, our rejoicing is at an end. *II Esdras* 10:22.

10 There shall be weeping and gnashing of teeth. *Matthew* 8:12. (More at HELL.)

11 My soul is exceeding sorrowful, even unto death. *Matthew* 26:38.

See also DESOLATION; DESPAIR; HAPPINESS; LONELINESS; MISFORTUNE; REJECTION; TROUBLE.

UNITY

12 Cast in thy lot among us; let us all have one purse. *Proverbs* 1:14.

13 Two are better than one; because they have a good reward for their labor.

For if they fall, the one will lift up his fellow: but woe to him that is alone when he falleth; for he hath not another to help him up. *Ecclesiastes* 4:9–10.

14 A threefold cord is not quickly broken. *Ecclesiastes* 4:12.

1 They helped every one his neighbor; and every one said to his brother, Be of good courage. *Isaiah* 41:6.

2 Can two walk together, except they be agreed? *Amos* 3:3.

See also CONFLICT; LOYALTY.

VALUE

1 Lay not up for yourselves treasures upon earth, where moth and rust doth corrupt, and where thieves break through and steal:

But lay up for yourselves treasures in heaven. *Matthew* 6:19–20.

2 Where your treasure is, there will your heart be also. *Matthew* 6:21.

3 Give not that which is holy unto the dogs, neither cast ye your pearls before swine, lest they trample them under their feet, and turn again and rend you. *Matthew* 7:6. (Casting one's pearls before swine seems an unlikely thing to do. In *The Bestiary*, T. H. White suggests that "pearls" should actually be "daisies," since the Latin *marquerite*, meaning "daisy," is very close to *margarite*, "pearl.")

4 Ye blind guides, which strain at a gnat, and swallow a camel. *Matthew* 23:24. (Jesus complaining to the scribes and Pharisees that they pay too much attention to small issues and not enough to matters of "law, judgment, mercy, and faith." *Matthew* 23:23.)

5 Prove all things; hold fast that which is good. *I Thessalonians* 5:21. (*Prove* in the sense of "test.")

VANITY

6 Vanity of vanities, saith the Preacher, vanity of vanities; all is vanity.

What profit hath a man of all his labor which he taketh under the sun?

Onc generation passeth away, and another generation cometh: but the earth abideth for ever. *Ecclesiastes* 1:2–4. (The term *Ecclesiastes* is Greek for the Hebrew *Koheleth*, meaning "one who speaks to a gathering"; the King James translation is "the Preacher." He is identified as King Solomon, but scholars believe the book dates from approximately the third century B.C., several hundred years after Solomon.)

7 All things are full of labor; man cannot utter it: the eye is not satisfied with seeing, nor the ear filled with hearing.

The thing that hath been is that which shall be; and that which is done is that which shall be done: and there is no new thing under the sun. *Ecclesiastes* 1:8–9.

8 I have seen all the works that are done under the sun; and, behold, all is vanity and vexation of spirit. *Ecclesiastes* 1:14. (*Ecclesiastes* expresses a melancholy and pessimism reminiscent of the *Rubaiyat*. In the first two chapters, the writer states that not pleasure or laughter, or learning, or work, or success can overcome the truth that all of life is fleeting and futile—all is vanity.)

1 The creature was made subject to vanity. *Romans* 8:20.

VENGEANCE

2 Thou shalt not avenge. *Leviticus* 19:18.

3 To me belongeth vengeance, and recompense. *Deuteronomy* 32:35. (God is speaking.)

4 I will render vengeance to mine enemies. *Deuteronomy* 32:41.

5 Recompense to no man evil for evil. *Romans* 12:17.

6 Vengeance is mine; I will repay, saith the Lord. *Romans* 12:19.

See also PACIFISM.

VIGILANCE

7 Let your loins be girded about, and your lights burning. *Luke* 12:35.

8 Let us watch and be sober. *I Thessalonians* 5:6.

9 Be sober, be vigilant. *I Peter* 5:8. (More at DEVIL.)

VIOLENCE

10 They shall fall by the sword; they shall be a portion for foxes. *Psalms* 63:10.

11 Preserve me from violent men. *Psalms* 140:4, RSV.

12 Violent men get riches. *Proverbs* 11:16, RSV. (The King James Version reads, "Strong men retain riches.")

13 I have trodden the winepress alone; and of the people there was none with me: for I will tread them in mine anger, and trample them in my fury; and their blood shall be sprinkled upon my garments, and I will stain all my raiment. *Isaiah* 63:3.

14 The good man is perished out of the earth: and there is none upright among men: they all lie in wait for blood; they hunt every man his brother with a net. *Micah* 7:2.

15 All they that take the sword shall perish with the sword. *Matthew* 26:52. (Jesus on the Mount of Olives to the disciple who cuts off the ear of the high priest's servant.)

See also CRIME; DESTRUCTION; EMOTIONS; EVIL; PEACE; PACIFISM; WAR.

VIRTUE

16 Can we find such a one as this is, a man in whom the Spirit of God is? *Genesis* 41:38. (Pharaoh speaking of Joseph.)

1 Asa's heart was perfect with the Lord all his days. *I Kings* 15:14. (Asa was king of Judah from 911 to 870 B.C.)

2 Deal courageously, and the Lord shall be with the good. *II Chronicles* 19:11.

3 God will not reject a blameless man. *Job* 8:20, RSV.

4 The just upright man is laughed to scorn. *Job* 12:4.

5 My righteousness I hold fast, and will not let it go: my heart shall not reproach me so long as I live, *Job* 27:6.

6 Blessed is the man that walketh not in the counsel of the ungodly, nor standeth in the way of sinners, not sitteth in the seat of the scornful.

But his delight is in the law of the Lord; and in his law doth he meditate day and night.

And he shall be like a tree planted by the rivers of water, that bringeth forth his fruit in his season; his leaf also shall not wither; and whatsoever he doeth shall prosper.

The ungodly are not so: but are like the chaff which the wind driveth away. *Psalms* 1:1–4.

7 Create in me a clean heart, O God; and renew a right spirit within me. *Psalms* 51:10.

8 The righteous shall flourish like a palm tree; he shall grow like a cedar in Lebanon. *Psalms* 92:12. (Also, "The righteous will flourish like a green leaf." *Proverbs* 11:28, RSV.)

9 Light dawns for the righteous, and joy for the upright in heart. *Psalms* 97:11, RSV.

10 In the way of righteousness is life. *Proverbs* 12:28.

11 The evil bow before the good. *Proverbs* 14:19.

12 Righteousness exalteth a nation. *Proverbs* 14:34.

13 Better is a little with righteousness than great revenues without right. *Proverbs* 16:8.

14 The wicked flee when no man pursueth: but the righteous are bold as a lion. *Proverbs* 28:1.

15 Who can find a virtuous woman? for her price is far above rubies. *Proverbs* 31:10. (The entire passage, a portrait of the ideal woman, is given at WOMEN.)

16 This is the way, walk ye in it. *Isaiah* 30:21.

17 Seek good, and not evil, that ye may live. *Amos* 5:14.

18 What doth the Lord require of thee, but to do justly, and to love mercy, and to walk humbly with thy God? *Micah* 6:8.

1 The souls of the righteous are in the hand of God, and there shall no torment touch them. *Wisdom of Solomon* 3:1. (In this book, heaven is first specifically promised to the righteous.)

2 Though they [the righteous] be punished in the sight of men, yet is their hope full of immortality.

And having been a little chastised, they shall be greatly rewarded: for God proved them and found them worthy for himself. *Wisdom of Solomon* 3:4–5. (The conclusion of the passage above. It provides an explanation of the question posed so often in the Bible: why do the wicked so often flourish at the expense of the righteous? How can God allow this?)

3 Be ye therefore perfect, even as your Father which is in heaven is perfect. *Matthew* 5:48. (From the Sermon on the Mount. This is the conclusion of the passage in which Jesus urges his followers to love even their enemies. In doing so, they will be like God, who is the Father of all people.)

4 Seek ye first the kingdom of God, and his righteousness. *Matthew* 6:33.

5 The night is far spent, the day is at hand; let us therefore cast off the works of darkness, and let us put on the armor of light.

Let us walk honestly, as in the day; not in rioting and drunkenness, not in chambering and wantonness, not in strife and envying.

But put ye on the Lord Jesus Christ, and make not provision for the flesh, to fulfil the lusts thereof. *Romans* 13:12–14.

6 Let us not be weary in well doing. *Galatians* 6:9.

7 Whatsoever things are true, whatsoever things are honest, whatsoever things are just, whatsoever things are pure, whatsoever things are lovely, whatsoever things are of good report; if there be any virtue, and if there be any praise, think of these things. *Philippians* 4:8.

8 Ye are all the children of light, and the children of the day: we are not of night, nor of darkness. *I Thessalonians* 5:5.

9 Let us, who are of the day, be sober, putting on the breastplate of faith and love; and for a helmet, the hope of salvation. *I Thessalonians* 5:8.

10 Rich in good works. *I Timothy* 6:18.

11 Do not neglect to do good and to share what you have, for such sacrifices are pleasing to God. *Hebrews* 13:16. RSV.

See also COURAGE; GENEROSITY; GIVING; GENTLENESS AND KINDNESS; HONESTY; HONOR; INNOCENCE; JOB; RELIABILITY; REPUTATION; SALVATION; WOMEN (for a portrait of the virtuous woman).

VISION

12 Eyes have they, but they see not. *Psalms* 115:5. (More at IDOLS.)

1 For now we see through a glass, darkly; but then face to face: now I know in part; but then shall I know even as also I am known. *I Corinthians* 13:12.

2 We look not at the things which are seen, but at the things which are not seen: for the things which are seen are temporal; but the things which are not seen are eternal. *II Corinthians* 4:18.

See also PROPHETS.

WAR

1 Shall your brethren go to war, and shall ye sit here? *Numbers* 32:6. (Moses to the children of Reuben and Gad.)

2 Thou shalt have a paddle upon thy weapon; and it shall be, when thou wilt ease thyself abroad, thou shalt dig therewith, and shalt turn back and cover that which cometh from thee. *Deuteronomy* 23:13.

3 When a man hath taken a new wife, he shall not go out to war. *Deuteronomy* 24:5. (Other exemptions are suggested for the man who has built a new house, planted a vineyard, or is simply afraid. *Deuteronomy* 20:5–8.)

4 The kings came and fought, then fought the kings of Canaan . . .
They fought from heaven; the stars in their courses fought against Sisera. *Judges* 5:19–20. (From the song sung by Deborah and Barak celebrating their victory over the Canaanite commander Sisera. Here the Israelites are helped by God and the heavens, or stars, for the river of Kishon floods and routes Sisera's armies. This was a major victory, the first by the Israelites against a force of chariots in the open field. Chariots were so valuable that they were counted among the possessions of God himself: "The chariots of God are twenty thousand." *Psalms* 68:17.)

5 March on, my soul, with might!
Then loud beat the horses' hoofs with the galloping, galloping of his steeds. *Judges* 5:21–22, RSV. (More of the passage quoted above. Here Sisera is in flight. For his death, see SISERA AND JAEL. For a portrait of a war horse, see ANIMALS.)

6 Have they not divided the prey; to every man a damsel or two? *Judges* 5:30.

7 A sword for the Lord and for Gideon! *Judges* 7:20, RSV. (The war cry of the Israelites under Gideon as they went into battle against the Midianites.)

8 Said they unto him, Say now Shibboleth: and he said Sibboleth: for he could not frame to pronounce it right. Then they took him, and slew him. *Judges* 12:6. (With this pronunciation test, the Gileadites under Jephthah detected and killed the Ephraimites. *Shibboleth* means "ear of corn.")

9 He smote them hip and thigh with a great slaughter. *Judges* 15:8. (Thus Samson took revenge on the Philistines for burning to death his former wife and father-in-law.)

10 With the jaw of an ass have I slain a thousand men. *Judges* 15:16. (Samson speaking of an attack on the Philistines.)

1 Be strong, and quit [acquit] yourselves like men, O ye Philistines . . . quit yourselves like men, and fight. *I Samuel* 4:9. (The Philistines were formidable warriors, called elsewhere in ancient texts Peoples of the Sea. They overwhelmed Crete and, nearly, Egypt. Later, in the period 1,000 to 600 B.C., they settled into a sophisticated, industrious, urban existence, judging from recent excavations at Ekron. This city was razed by Babylonians in 603 B.C., and the Philistines were evidently destroyed at this time. The Romans named Palestine for the biblical Philistines.)

2 The Lord saveth not with sword and spear: for the battle is the Lord's. *I Samuel* 17:47. (David taunting the heavily armed Goliath. At this time and for much of their history, the Israelites were lightly armed compared to their enemies. The Philistines, the first people in Canaan to process iron, would not allow smiths in the Israelite regions. See also DAVID AND JONATHAN and the quote from *Joel* below.)

3 How are the mighty fallen in the midst of the battle! *II Samuel* 1:25. (David's lamentation at the death of Jonathan and King Saul during battle with the Philistines on Mount Gilboa; the phrase is repeated three times in this chapter, ending, in the final verse, with "How are the mighty fallen, and the weapons of war perished!" II Samuel 1:27. With this victory, the Philistines completed the conquest of all lands formerly controlled by the Israelites. Eventually, however, David drove them back into a relatively narrow band of land along the coast.)

4 Shall the sword devour for ever? Do you not know that the end will be bitter? *II Samuel* 2:26, RSV. (Spoken by the military commander Abner, a cousin of King Saul. Abner disliked and tried to avoid violence, but was himself murdered. David mourned him deeply, saying, "There is a prince and a great man fallen this day in Israel," *II Samuel* 3:38.)

5 He teacheth my hands to war; so that a bow of steel is broken by mine arms. *II Samuel* 22:35. (David is speaking of God. But in the next verse he adds, "Thy gentleness hath made me great." A similar passage is at *Psalms* 18:34.)

6 The Lord said to me, Go up against this land, and destroy it. *II Kings* 18:25. Restated at *Isaiah* 36:10. (Here Rabshakeh, a representative of King Sennacherib of Assyria, makes a time-honored claim that God is on his side. The warning is given to emissaries of Judah's king Hezekiah.)

7 They were among the mighty men, helpers of the war.

They were armed with bows, and could use both the right hand and the left in hurling stones and shooting arrows out of a bow. *I Chronicles* 12:1–2. (These were Benjamites, supporters of David against Saul, although they were Saul's kinsmen. Others who joined David were men from Manasseh and Gad. The latter are described as "mighty and experienced warriors, expert with shield and spear, whose faces were like the faces of lions, and who were swift as gazelles upon the mountains." *I Chronicles* 12:8, RSV.)

1 The battle is not yours, but God's. *II Chronicles* 20:15.

2 He [Uzziah] made in Jerusalem engines, invented by cunning men, to be on the towers and upon the bulwarks, to shoot arrows and great stones withal. And his name spread far abroad. *II Chronicles* 26:15.

3 I will not trust in my bow, neither shall my sword save me. *Psalms* 44:6.

4 Preserve me from violent men,
Who plan evil things in their heart, and stir up wars continually. *Psalms* 140:1–2, RSV.

5 Thy men shall fall by the sword, and thy mighty in the war. *Isaiah* 3:25.

6 Go not forth into the field, nor walk by the way; for the sword of the enemy and fear is on every side. *Jeremiah* 6:25.

7 Both the great and the small shall die in this land. *Jeremiah* 16:6.

8 A sound of battle is in the land, and of great destruction. *Jeremiah* 50:22.

9 The young and the old lie on the ground in the streets: my virgins and my young men are fallen by the sword. *Lamentations* 2:21.

10 They shall march every one on his ways, and they shall not break their ranks. *Joel* 2:7.

11 Prepare war, wake up the mighty men, let the men of war draw near . . .
Beat your plowshares into swords, and your pruning hooks into spears: let the weak say, I am strong. *Joel* 3:9–10. (The opposite of the famous passage in *Isaiah*. See under PEACE. In *Joel*, this is to be the final war against the forces of evil. Throughout their history, the Jewish people were often denied arms, and many of the Old Testament battles were fought with agricultural tools used or reworked as weapons.)

12 The chariots shall rage in the streets, they shall justle one against another in the broad ways: they shall seem like torches, they shall run like the lightnings. *Nahum* 2:4. (A brilliant picture of enemy chariots overrunning a city. This is from Nahum's taunting prediction of the conquest of the Assyrian city of Nineveh—probably written several decades after the actual fall of Nineveh in 612 B.C. at the hands of the Babylonians and Medes.)

13 It is better for us to die in battle, than to behold the calamities of our people and our sanctuary. *I Maccabees* 3:59. (The great warrior Judas Maccabeus during Israel's revolt against Seleucid rule.)

See also CONFLICT; DAVID; DESTRUCTION; GOD, ENEMIES AND WAR; JOSHUA AND THE CONQUEST OF CANAAN; REVOLT; SAMSON; VIOLENCE.

WASTE

14 To what purpose is this waste? *Matthew* 26:8.

[1] Gather up the fragments that remain, that nothing be lost. *John* 6:12.

WEAKNESS

See FAILINGS; STRENGTH

WEATHER

[2] Out of the south cometh the whirlwind; and cold out of the north. *Job* 37:9.

[3] Fair weather cometh out of the north. *Job* 37:22.

[4] The voice of thy [God's] thunder was in the heaven: the lightnings lightened the world: the earth trembled and shook. *Psalms* 77:18.

[5] He [God] it is who makes the clouds rise at the end of the earth, who makes lightnings for the rain and brings forth the wind from his storehouses. *Psalms* 135:7, RSV.

[6] The north wind driveth away rain. *Proverbs* 25:23.

[7] It [the wind] whirleth about continually. *Ecclesiastes* 1:6. (The full passage is given at VANITY.)

[8] He that observeth the wind shall not sow; and he that regardeth the clouds shall not reap. *Ecclesiastes* 11:14.

[9] A day of darkness and of gloominess, a day of clouds. *Joel* 2:2.

[10] Ask rain from the Lord in the season of the spring rain. *Zechariah* 10:1, RSV.

[11] When it is evening, ye say, It will be fair weather: for the sky is red.
And in the morning, It will be foul weather today: for the sky is red and lowring. O ye hypocrites, ye can discern the face of the sky; but can yet not discern the signs of the times? *Matthew* 16:2–3. (Jesus to the Pharisees and Sadducees, using a version of our saying: "Red sun at night, sailors delight; red sun in morning, sailors take warning.")

[12] The wind blows where it wills. *John* 3:8, RSV. (More at SPIRITUAL BIRTH.)

WIND

See WEATHER

WINE AND DRINKING

[13] The man Jeroboam was a mighty man of valor. *I Kings* 11:28. (If you want to drink a Jeroboam of wine—some twelve times the size of a normal bottle—valor is required. The biblical Jeroboam also "did sin and made Israel to sin," behavior associated valorous excess.)

[14] Wine is a mocker, strong drink a brawler. *Proverbs* 20:1, RSV.

1 Who bath woe? who hath sorrow? who hath contentions? who hath babbling? who hath wounds without cause? who hath redness of eyes?
They that tarry long at the wine; they that go to seek mixed wine. *Proverbs* 23:29–30.

2 Do not look at wine when it is red, when it sparkles in the cup and goes down smoothly.
At the last it bites like a serpent, and stings like an adder. *Proverbs* 23:31–32, RSV.

3 It is not for kings to drink wine; not for princes strong drink.
Lest they drink, and forget the law. *Proverbs* 31:4–5. (Strong drink also is not for the priest or prophet. See the quote from *Isaiah* 28:7 under CLERGY.)

4 Give strong drink unto him that is ready to perish, and wine unto those that be of heavy hearts. *Proverbs* 31:6.

5 Let him drink, and forget his poverty, and remember his misery no more. *Proverbs* 31:7.

6 Woe unto them that rise up early in the morning, that they may follow strong drink; that continue until night, till wine inflame them! *Isaiah* 5:11.

7 The new wine mourneth, the vine languisheth, all the merry-hearted do sigh. *Isaiah* 24:7. (The Revised Standard Version reads, "The wine mourns, the vine languishes, all the merry-hearted sigh." This gloomy state is part of a worldwide calamity predicted in *Isaiah*. See also the quote below.)

8 There is a crying for wine in the streets; all joy is darkened, the mirth of the land is gone. *Isaiah* 24:11.

9 Thou shalt be filled with drunkenness and sorrow, with the cup of astonishment and desolation. *Ezekiel* 23:33.

10 Awake, ye drunkards, and weep; and howl, all ye drinkers of wine, because of the new wine; for it is cut off from your mouth. *Joel* 1:5. (In the Revised Standard Version, "new wine" is rendered "sweet wine.")

11 It [wine] maketh every heart rich. *I Esdras* 3:21. (This claim is made as part of a contest in which three guardsmen of King Darius debate what is the strongest thing in the world. See STRENGTH.)

12 Wine is as good as life to a man, if it be drunk moderately: what is life then to a man that is without wine? for it was made to make men glad. *Ecclesiasticus* 31:27.

13 Every man at the beginning doth set forth good wine; and when men have well drunk, then that which is worse: but thou hast kept the good wine until now. *John* 2:10. (The good wine was created by Jesus for the marriage feast in Cana. See MIRACLES OF JESUS.)

1 Drink no longer water, but use a little wine for thy stomach's sake and thine often infirmities. *I Timothy* 5:23.

See also DISSIPATION; FOOD AND DRINK.

WINNING

2 Know ye not that they which run in a race run all, but one receiveth the prize? *I Corinthians* 9:24.

3 He went forth conquering, and to conquer. *Revelation* 6:2.

See also SUCCESS.

WISDOM

4 I have given thee a wise and an understanding heart. *I Kings* 3:12. (God to Solomon. See also Solomon's prayer at JUDGES.)

5 He [Solomon] spoke three thousand proverbs: and his songs were a thousand and five. *I Kings* 4:32. (The next verse tells us that King Solomon "spake also of beasts, and of fowl, and of creeping things, and of fishes." Konrad Lorenz in *King Solomon's Ring* calls this "the oldest record of a biological lecture." It gave rise to the notion that Solomon could talk to animals. Thus Kipling's verse: "There was never a king like Solomon/ Not since the world began,/ Yet Solomon talked to a butterfly/ As a man would talk to a man.")

6 Do you limit wisdom to yourself? *Job* 15:8, RSV.

7 Where shall wisdom be found? and where is the place of understanding? *Job* 28:12. (See also *Job* 28:20.)

8 The price of wisdom is above rubies. *Job* 28:18.

9 Fear of the Lord, that is wisdom, and to depart from evil is understanding. *Job* 28:28. (The concept that wisdom is something different than what the world takes it to be is a frequent theme in the Bible, stated perhaps most powerfully by Paul. See below. The identification of wisdom with fear of God is repeated several times in the opening chapter of *Ecclesiasticus*, for example, "To fear the Lord is the beginning of wisdom." *Ecclesiasticus* 1:14. See also GOD, FEARING AND RESPECTING.)

10 A wise man will hear, and will increase learning. *Proverbs* 1:5.

11 The Lord giveth wisdom. *Proverbs* 2:6.

12 Be not wise in thine own eyes. *Proverbs* 3:7.

13 She [wisdom] is more precious than rubies: and all the things thou canst desire are not to be compared unto her.

Length of days is in her right hand; and in her left hand riches and honor. *Proverbs* 3:15–16. (*Proverbs* 8:11 reads, "Wisdom is better than rubies.")

1 Her [wisdom's] ways are ways of pleasantness, and all her paths are peace. *Proverbs* 3:17.

2 Wisdom is the principal thing; therefore get wisdom: and with all thy getting get understanding. *Proverbs* 4:7. (In the RSV, "Get wisdom, and whatever you get, get insight.")

3 I wisdom dwell with prudence. *Proverbs* 8:12.

4 I [wisdom] love them that love me; and those that seek me early shall find me. *Proverbs* 8:17.

5 Whoso findeth me [wisdom] findeth life. *Proverbs* 8:35.

6 How much better is it to get wisdom than gold! and to get understanding rather to be chosen than silver! *Proverbs* 16:16.

7 A wise man is strong. *Proverbs* 24:5.

8 In much wisdom is much grief. *Ecclesiastes* 1:18. (Pessimism and melancholy are characteristics of *Ecclesiastes*, but overall, the writer leans to the view that wisdom, although not sufficient to guarantee happiness, is nevertheless, a good thing. See the quotes below.)

9 Wisdom excelleth folly, as far as light excelleth darkness. *Ecclesiastes* 2:13.

10 Better is a poor and a wise child [youth] than an old and foolish king. *Ecclesiastes* 4:13.

11 [Do not] make thyself over wise: why shouldest thou destroy thyself? *Ecclesiastes* 7:16.

12 Wisdom is better than strength. *Ecclesiastes* 9:16.

13 Wisdom is better than weapons of war. *Ecclesiastes* 9:18.

14 I shall light a candle of understanding in thy heart, which shall not be put out. *II Esdras* 14:25. (God to Ezra.)

15 Wisdom is a loving spirit. *Wisdom of Solomon* 1:6.

16 Wisdom is glorious. *Wisdom of Solomon* 6:12.

17 The very true beginning of her [wisdom] is the desire of discipline; and the care of discipline is love. *Wisdom of Solomon* 6:17.

18 The multitude of the wise is the welfare of the world. *Wisdom of Solomon* 6:24.

19 The light that cometh from her [wisdom] never goeth out. *Wisdom of Solomon* 7:10.

1 She [wisdom] is the breath of the power of God. *Wisdom of Solomon* 7:25.

2 What is richer than wisdom, that worketh all things? *Wisdom of Solomon* 8:5.

3 To whom hath the root of wisdom been revealed? *Ecclesiasticus* 1:6.

4 He that loveth her [wisdom] loveth life. *Ecclesiasticus* 4:12.

5 If thou seest a man of understanding, get thee betimes unto him, and let thy foot wear the steps of his door. *Ecclesiasticus* 6:36.

6 Wise as serpents, and harmless as doves. *Matthew* 10:16. (For more, see under SURVIVAL.)

7 The children of this world are in their generation wiser than the children of light. *Luke* 16:8. (From the parable of the worldly-wise steward. Various interpretations have been offered, but the parable may mean simply that worldly people are wise in a worldly time. The wisdom of the children of light will not be apparent until a new order is established.)

8 I will destroy the wisdom of the wise, and will bring to nothing the understanding of the prudent. *I Corinthians* 1:19. (Paul is making the point that Christ's message, although perhaps strange to the sophisticated Corinthians, is more powerful than their form of wisdom. See also *I Corinthians* 1:27 at RELIGION.)

9 If any of you lack wisdom, let him ask of God. *James* 1:5.

10 This wisdom descendeth not from above, but is earthly, sensual, devilish. *James* 3:15.

See also GOD, FEARING AND RESPECTING; PRUDENCE; SOLOMON; STUPIDITY.

WITCHES

See OCCULT, THE

WITNESSES

See LAW: WITNESSES AND EVIDENCE

WIZARDS

See OCCULT, THE

WOMEN

11 It is better to dwell in the wilderness, than with a contentious and an angry woman. *Proverbs* 21:19. (Many of the verses on women in the Bible sound the same note. In the Old Testament, the status of women was generally low and those who chafed at domestic restraints were not usually admired. There were a few outstanding women, such as the great leader Deborah, but by and large the most a woman could aspire to was

the worthy existence described in the next quote below. In the New Testament, Mary, the mother of Jesus, is unique. But generally the lot of women is only marginally improved.)

1 Who can find a virtuous woman? for her price is above rubies.
The heart of her husband doth safely trust in her, so that he shall have no need of spoil.
She will do him good and not evil all the days of her life,
She seeketh wool, and flax, and worketh willingly with her hands.
She is like the merchants' ships; she bringeth her food from afar.
She riseth also while it is yet night *Proverbs* 31:10–15. (She also feeds the servants; buys and plants vineyards; makes candles, spins, weaves, and sews; and helps the poor.)

2 Her children arise up, and call her blessed; her husband also, and he praiseth her. *Proverbs* 31:28.

3 Give her of the fruit of her hands; and let her own works praise her in the gates. *Proverbs* 31:31.

4 Rise up ye women that are at ease; hear my voice, ye careless daughters. *Isaiah* 32:9. (Used as an epigraph by Harriet A. Jacobs in her autobiography, *Incidents in the Life of a Slave Girl,* 1861.)

5 Without women, cannot men be. *I Esdras* 4:17. (Part of a debate held before King Darius on what is the strongest thing in the world. One of the contestants, Zerubbabel, offers two ideas: women and, stronger still, TRUTH. See also the two next quotes below and STRENGTH.)

6 Have not all men more desire unto her [woman in general] than unto silver or gold, or any goodly thing whatsoever? *I Esdras* 4:19.

7 Many there be that have run out of their wits for women. *I Esdras* 4:26.

8 Forgo not a wise and good woman: for her grace is above gold. *Ecclesiasticus* 7:19.

9 All wickedness is but little to the wickedness of a woman. *Ecclesiasticus* 25:19. (We may assume here that divine inspiration was overwhelmed by some bitter experience.)

10 A silent and loving woman is a gift of the Lord. *Ecclesiasticus* 26:14.

11 Neither was the man created for the woman; but the woman for the man. *I Corinthians* 11:9. (Attempts have been made to reinterpret St. Paul to show that his view of women is more favorable than his words imply. Nevertheless, he is hardly an advocate of equal rights. See below.)

12 Let your women keep silence in the churches: for it is not permitted unto them to speak. *I Corinthians* 14:34.

13 Giving honor unto the wife, as unto the weaker vessel. *I Peter* 3:7.

See also FAMILY; GENTLENESS AND KINDNESS; HOME; LOVE; MARRIAGE; SEX.

WONDERS See LIFE'S WONDERS; MIRACLES IN THE OLD TESTAMENT; MIRACLES OF JESUS

WORD

1 In the beginning was the Word. *John* 1:1. (More at JESUS.)

See also GOD'S WORD; LANGUAGE; TALK.

WORD, GOD'S See GOD'S WORD

WORDS See LANGUAGE; TALK

WORK

2 In the sweat of thy face shalt thou eat bread. *Genesis* 3:19. (God condemns Adam to labor for his food.)

3 All the women that were wise-hearted did spin with their hands. *Exodus* 35:25.

4 Ye shall rejoice in all that ye put your hand unto. *Deuteronomy* 12:7.

5 Let them live; but let them be hewers of wood and and drawers of water. *Joshua* 9:21. (This is the judgment of Joshua and other Israelite princes upon the people of Gibeon, whose emissaries tricked them into agreeing to a peace pact.)

6 The Lord recompense thy work, and a full reward be given thee. *Ruth* 2:12.

7 Arise therefore, and be doing. *I Chronicles* 22:16.

8 Let not your hands be weak: for your work shall be rewarded. *II Chronicles* 15:7.

9 Let us rise up and build. *Nehemiah* 2:18. (The project is the new Temple in Jerusalem.)

10 Establish thou the work of our hands. *Psalms* 90:17.

11 He becometh poor that dealeth [works] with a slack hand: but the hand of the diligent maketh rich. *Proverbs* 10:4.

12 Better is a man of humble standing who works for himself than one who plays the great man but lacks bread. *Proverbs* 12:9, RSV.

13 Do you see a man skillful in his work? he will stand before kings. *Proverbs* 22:29, RSV.

1 Labor not to be rich. *Proverbs* 23:4. (The message in this passage is that one pays a high price for wealth and luxuries, which, after all, may vanish.)

2 Whoso keepeth the fig tree shall eat the fruit thereof. *Proverbs* 27:18.

3 He who tills his land will have plenty of bread, but he who follows worthless pursuits will have plenty of poverty. *Proverbs* 28:19, RSV.

4 What profit hath a man of all his labor which he taketh under the sun? *Ecclesiastes* 1:3. (The pessimism of *Ecclesiastes* extends even to the value of worthwhile work and accomplishments. This verse is from the famous opening of the book, which is given in full at VANITY.)

5 All things are full of labor. *Ecclesiastes* 1:8.

6 My heart rejoiced in all my labor. *Ecclesiastes* 2:10. (More at SUCCESS.)

7 There is nothing better than that a man should enjoy his work, for that is his lot; who can bring him to see what will be after him? *Ecclesiastes* 3:22, RSV.

8 Whatsoever thy hand findeth to do, it with thy might; for there is no work, nor device, nor knowledge, nor wisdom, in the grave, whither thou goest. *Ecclesiastes* 9:10.

9 They shall build houses, and inhabit them; and they shalt plant vineyards, and eat the fruit of them.

They shalt not build, and another inhabit; they shall not plant, and another eat . . . mine elect shall long enjoy the work of their hands. *Isaiah* 65:21 22.

10 All these [craftsmen] trust to their hands: and every one is wise in his work. *Ecclesiasticus* 38:31. (This is from a passage that begins in praise of leisure: the opportunity of leisure makes it possible for a person to study and become wise. "How can he get wisdom . . . whose talk is of bullocks?" the author asks, *Ecclesiasticus* 38:25. But in the next ten verses, the author devotes loving attention to the labors of craftsmen—carpenters, seal cutters, smiths, and potters. He concludes with the verse given below.)

11 They will maintain the state of the world, and [all] their desire is in the work of their craft. *Ecclesiasticus* 38:34. (*They* refers to craftsmen; see quote above.)

12 Work your work betimes, and in his time he [the Lord] will give you your reward. *Ecclesiasticus* 51:30.

13 Come unto me, all ye that labor and are heavy laden, and I will give you rest. *Matthew* 11:28.

14 The laborer is worthy of his hire. *Luke* 10:7.

1 I must work the works of him that sent me, while it is day: the night cometh, when no man can work. *John* 9:4.

2 Every man shall receive his reward according to his own labor. *I Corinthians* 3:8.

3 Every man's work shall be made manifest: for the day shall declare it, because it shall be revealed by fire; and the fire shall try every man's work of what sort it is. *I Corinthians* 3:13.

4 Your . . . labor of love. *Thessalonians* 1:3.

5 A workman that needeth not to be ashamed. *II Timothy* 2:15.

See also ACTIONS; FARMING; IDLENESS; LEISURE; LAZINESS; SHEPHERDS.

WORKS

See ACTIONS; GOD'S WORKS

WORLD

6 All the earth shall be filled with the glory of the Lord. *Numbers* 14:21.

7 The pillars of the earth are the Lord's, and he hath set the world upon them. *I Samuel* 2:8.

8 The nations are as a drop of a bucket, and are counted as the small dust of the balance: behold, he [God] taketh up the isles as a very little thing. *Isaiah* 40:15.

9 All nations before him [God] are as nothing. *Isaiah* 40:17.

10 Behold, I create new heavens and a new earth: and the former shall not be remembered, nor come into mind. *Isaiah* 65:17.

11 This saith the Lord, The heaven is my throne, and the earth is my footstool. *Isaiah* 66:1.

12 All that is made in the world hath a beginning and an end, and the end is manifest. *II Esdras* 9:5.

13 The world has lost his youth, and the times begin to wax old. *II Esdras* 14:10.

14 The Spirit of the Lord filleth the world. *Wisdom of Solomon* 1:7.

15 The whole world before thee is as a little grain of the balance, yea, as a drop of the morning dew that falleth down upon the earth. *Wisdom of Solomon* 11:22. (A single grain was the smallest weight used in commercial balances, or scales. The concept of the world as a microcosm has a long philosophical history, especially in the hermetic, semi-secret Neoplatonist writings of the Renaissance. In poetry, the most famous formulation is by Blake: "To see the world in a grain of sand/ And heaven in a wild flower,/ Hold infinity in the palm of your hand/ And eternity in an hour." *Auguries of Innocence.*)

1 The care of this world, and the deceitfulness of riches. *Matthew* 13:22.

2 In the world ye shall have tribulation: but be of good cheer; I have overcome the world. *John* 16:33.

3 All nations, and kindreds, and people, and tongues. *Revelation* 7:9.

4 The kingdoms of this world are become the kingdoms of our Lord and of his Christ. *Revelation* 11:15.

See also CREATION; FASHION.

WORLD, END OF

5 Many shall come in my name, saying, I am Christ; and shall deceive many.

And ye shall hear of wars and rumors of wars . . .

Nation shall rise against nation, and kingdom against kingdom: and there shall be famines, and pestilences, and earthquakes. *Matthew* 24:5–7. (Earlier, at *Matthew* 16:28, Jesus seems to say that the second coming of Christ and the establishment of his kingdom will take place within the lifetime of his disciples. This has been interpreted in various ways; for example, that Christ was referring to the establishment of Christianity.)

6 There shall arise false Christs, and false prophets, and shall show great signs and wonders. *Matthew* 24:24. (Christ speaking to his disciples of the last days of the world.)

7 Immediately after the tribulation of those days shall the sun be darkened, and the moon shall not give her light, and the stars shall fall from heaven, and the powers of the heavens shall be shaken. *Matthew* 24:29. (Subsequent verses are at JUDGMENT DAY.)

8 There was a war in heaven. *Revelation* 12:7. (More at ANGELS.)

9 I heard a voice from heaven, as the voice of many waters, and as the voice of a great thunder: and I heard the voice of harpers harping with their harps.

And they sung as it were a new song. *Revelation* 14:2–3.

10 He gathered them together into a place called in the Hebrew tongue Armageddon. *Revelation* 16:16. (The forces of good and evil are brought together for the ultimate battle. *Armageddon* is a mysterious term. It may derive from *Megiddo*, the name of a fortified city in the Mount Carmel area.)

See also DESTRUCTION; JUDGMENT DAY.

WORLD WEARINESS

See ENNUI

WORRY

1 Take no thought for your life, what ye shall eat, or what ye shall drink; nor yet for your body, what ye shall put on. Is not the life more than meat, and the body than raiment? *Matthew* 6:25. (From the passage in the Sermon on the Mount in which Jesus explains that anxiety adds nothing to life. God cares for all creatures. This includes the verse on the lilies of the field. See under GARDENS AND FLOWERS. See also the next quotes.)

2 Which of you by taking thought can add one cubit unto his stature? *Matthew* 6:27.

3 Take therefore no thought for the morrow. *Matthew* 6:34. (The meaning is that one should not be anxious. God cares for all his creatures, the birds in the air, the lilies in the field. More at FUTURE.)

WORSHIP

See GOD, WORSHIPING; RELIGION

WRITING

4 Oh that my words were now written! oh that they were printed in a book! *Job* 19:23.

5 My desire is, that the Almighty would answer me, and that mine adversary had written a book. *Job* 31:35. (In one of his columns in the *New York Times Magazine,* William Safire notes that "write an indictment" would be a better translation than "write a book"—that is, make plain what crimes Job is being punished for. But the perhaps inaccurate translation has delighted generations of readers—and writers.)

6 Of making many books there is no end. *Ecclesiastes* 12:12.

7 Write it before them in a table, and note it in a book, that it may be for the time to come for ever and ever. *Isaiah* 30:8. (God instructs the prophet to make a written record. The subject: the rebelliousness of the people of Judah.)

8 Write in a book all the words that I have spoken to you. *Jeremiah* 30:2, RSV. (God to Jeremiah. Similar to the instruction above, but here the subject is God's promise to save the surviving Jews after their defeat by Babylon.)

9 A tale out of season [is as] music in mourning. *Ecclesiasticus* 22:6.

10 It is a foolish thing to make a long prologue, and to be short in the story itself. *II Maccabees* 2:32.

11 What thou seest, write in a book. *Revelation* 1:11.

See also PARABLES.

WRITING ON THE WALL

See DESTRUCTION; MIRACLES IN THE OLD TESTAMENT

YOM KIPPUR

1 This shall be an everlasting statute unto you, to make an atonement for the children of Israel for all their sins once a year. *Leviticus* 16:34. (More detail is given at *Leviticus* 23:27–32.)

See also ATONEMENT; FEASTS, RELIGIOUS.

YOUTH

2 Thou hast the dew of thy youth. *Psalms* 110:3.

3 The glory of young men is their strength. *Proverbs* 20:29.

4 Rejoice, O young man, in thy youth. *Ecclesiastes* 11:9.

5 Remember now they Creator in the days of thy youth. *Ecclesiastes* 12:1. (The beginning of an exceptionally beautiful passage that concludes with a portrait of old age and death. See OLD AGE.)

6 It is good for a man that he bear the yoke in his youth. *Lamentations* 3:27.

7 Thou hast not remembered the days of thy youth. *Ezekiel* 16:22. (Also at *Ezekiel* 16:43.)

ZEAL

1 My zeal hath consumed me. *Psalms* 119:139.

ZION

2 Beautiful for situation, the joy of the whole earth, is mount Zion. *Psalms* 48:2. (The term *Zion* probably means "citadel" or "fortress." It is usually used in the Old Testament to refer to Jerusalem, although it is not known precisely which hill of the city is meant. The term came to be used for the Holy Land generally, and in the Middle Ages, the poet and philosopher Judah Halevy created a new genre of poetry, songs of yearning for Zion. In the New Testament, the term is used to refer to God's dwelling place, "the heavenly Jerusalem." [*Hebrews* 12:22; *Revelation* 14:1] and to the church or gospel [*I Peter* 2:6].)

3 Out of Zion, the perfection of beauty, God hath shined. *Psalms* 50:2.

4 By the rivers of Babylon, there we sat down, yea, we wept, when we remembered Zion.

We hanged our harps upon the willows in the midst thereof.

For there they that carried us away captive required of us a song; and they that wasted us required of us mirth, saying, Sing us one of the songs of Zion.

How shall we sing the Lord's song in a strange land?

If I forget thee, O Jerusalem, let my right hand forget her cunning.

If I do not remember thee, let my tongue cleave to the roof of my mouth. *Psalms* 137:1–6.

5 The people shall dwell in Zion at Jerusalem: thou shalt weep no more. *Isaiah* 30:19. (The people are those Israelites that survive the vast destruction described by Isaiah.)

6 Thine eyes shall see the king in his beauty; they shall behold the land that is very far off. *Isaiah* 33:17. (Those who survive the era of destruction called down by the Lord will be able to go to a purified Zion.)

Index

Abel: A. was a keeper of sheep, 21:1
Cain rose up against A., 21:1
Abraham: A.'s bosom, 194:2
thy name shall be A., 1:5
Absalom: O my son A., 40:20
absent: a. in body, present in spirit, 1:6
account: a. of himself to God, 191:3
accuse: not a servant, 1:7
accusers: where are thine a., 1:8
acknowledges: who a. me before men, 113:7
actions: by him a. are weighed, 79:4
Adam: God called unto A., 3:4
God caused deep sleep to fall upon A., 3:1
whatsoever A. called every living creature, 7:17
adder: deaf a., 9:3
adulterer: a. and adulteress shall be out to death, 203:7
adulterous: a. generation, 71:7
the way of an a. woman, 204:6
adultery: a. . . . in his heart, 205:5
thou shalt not commit a., 221:7
woman taken in a., 128:5
adversity: bread of a., water of affliction, 223:14
brother is born for a., 61:12
day of a., 223:13
enemy cannot be hid in a., 51:2
if a. come, 51:3
men [tried] in furnace of a., 224:4
prosperity and a. come of the Lord, 76:11
the furnace of a., 224:4
advice: do nothing without a., 2:6
take a., 4:1
affection: set a. on things above, 5:6
afflicted: a God of the a., 76:9
reject not supplication of a., 176:12
to a. pity should be showed, 151:13
affliction: a. of an hour, 224:6
day of a., 216:5
furnace of a., 223:15
afraid: be not a. of [idols], 107:3
it is I, be not a., 114:1
age: a. clearer than noonday, 164:7
face in ripe a., 165:2
he [David] died in a good old a., 40:4
aged: ordain that we become a. together, 145:6
agree: how a. kettle and pot, 32:6
agreed: except they be a., 227:2
Ahab: none like unto A., 4:10
alike: things come a. to all, 64:2
alive: I am a. for ever more, 123:7
all: a. is vanity, 228:8
a. things come alike to a., 64:2
a. things to a. men, 30:17
alms: better to give a., 73:1
do not you a. before men, 73:2
give a. accordingly, 72:9
alone: not good [to be] alone, 146:6
Alpha: I am A. and Omega, 78:13
am: a. I my brother's keeper, 21:2
before day was I a. he, 78:6
I a. that I a., 77:14
amend: a. your ways, 186:8
Anathema: let him be A., 117:1
ancient: with the a. is wisdom, 164:8
angel: a: flying, saying woe, woe, 6:8
an A. before thee, 87:14
a. of the Lord smote Assyrians, 206:4
seen the a. of the Lord face to face, 5:7
angels: a. food, 58:5
a. ministered unto him, 6:2
a. of God ascending and descending, 115:3
entertained a. unawares, 214:3
four a. on the four corners of the earth, 6:7

angels: (*continued*)
give his a. charge over thee, 5:8
his a. spirits, his ministers a flame, 6:5
joy in the presence of a., 6:4
shall send his a. with a great sound of trumpet, 6:3
anger: a. endureth but a moment, 7:3
a. is overwhelming, 7:8
fire is kindled in mine a., 6:10
nor furious a., 180:14
slow to a., 50:5
angry: a. secretly, 69:9
no friendship with a. man, 7:7
strive not with an a. man, 7:11
whosoever is a. with his brother, 7:13
anoint: arise, a. him [David], 38:9
anointed: touch not mine a., 30:10
answer: a. a fool, 215:10
a. not a fool, 215:10 (note)
soft a. turneth away wrath, 7:6
thou dost not a., 86:9
ant: go to the a. thou sluggard, 9:5
antichrist: he is a., 12:10
ants: a. are a people not strong, 9:8
anxiety: a. in a man's heart, 50:3
anxious: do not be a., 139:4
apostles: I am the least of the a., 170:5
the names of the twelve a., 10:9
appearance: judge not according to a., 12:4
man looketh on a., Lord on heart, 11:13
appetite: a man given to a., 67:4
apple: a. of his eye, 27:4
keep me as the a. of the eye, 179:1
apples: refresh me with a., 67:7
appointed: an a. time to man, 138:6
Arcturus: canst thou guide A., 213:2
arise: a. and be doing, 242:7
a. my love, 201 (cont. from p. 200)
a., shine, 154:5
a., take up thy bed, 150:1; 150:9
ark: a. of god is taken, 12:8
make thee an a., 162:1
two and two . . . into the a., 162:5
Armageddon: a place called A., 245:10
armor: a. of light, 231:5
put on the whole a. of God, 55:13
Asa: A.'s heart was perfect with the Lord, 230:1
ask: a. and it shall be given you, 109:1
a. and ye shall receive, 178:4
ass: a. said . . . what have I done unto thee, 8:2
a. saw the angel, 8:1
K. cometh . . . riding upon an a., 114:6; 148:5
thy King . . . sitting upon an a., 114:6
asses: wild a. did stand in high places, 10:5
Assyrians: in the camp of the A., 206:4
astonishment: an a. . . . among all nations, 27:3
drink the wine of a., 186:4
astray: I have gone a., 207:8
we like sheep have gone a., 207:16
Athens: men of A., 188:10
atonement: make an a. . . . once a year, 247:1
attire: a man's a., 12:2
avenge: thou shalt not a., 229:2
awake: a. and sing, 157:12

Babel: name of it called B., 14:2
babes: out of the mouth of b., 23:12
Babylon: B. is fallen, 29:5
by the rivers of Babylon, there we sat down, 248:4
bad: b. company, 70:10
Balaam: the ass said unto B., 8:2
balance: false b. is abomination, 43:8
balances: ye shall have just b., 19:11
balm: no b. in Gilead, 47:7
baptize: he shall b. you with the Holy Ghost, 14:3
baptized: I have b. you with water, 14:4
then cometh Jesus . . . unto John, to be b., 124:10

baptizing: teach all nations, b. them, 188:7
Barabbas: B. or Jesus, 120:6
they said B., 120:7
battle: b. is not yours, but God's, 235:1
b. is the Lord's, 234:2
better to die in b., 235:13
he smelleth the b. from afar off, 8:7
sound of b. is in the land, 235:8
be: b. fruitful and multiply, 34:4
beam: b. out of thine own eye, 59:6
beast: God formed every b. of the field, 7:17
man hath no preeminence above a b., 9:9
righteous man regardeth life of his b., 9:6
the mark of the b., 20:7
whosoever lieth with a b. shall be put to death, 203:5
beasts: b. shall teach thee, 159:8
four b. had each six wings, and were full of eyes, 6:6
let his portion be with the b., 144:2
the b. of the field shall be at peace with thee, 159:7
wild b. shall lie there, 29:4
beautiful: b. women without discretion, 183:4
everything b. in his time, 15:3
beauty: b. of a woman cheereth countenance, 15:8
b. of the face in age, 165:2
b. of the Lord be upon us, 15:2
commend not a man for his b., 12:1
deceived by the b. of a woman, 15:7
did trust in thine own b., 15:6
bed: rise take up thy b., 151:3
take up thy b. and walk, 150:1; 150:9
before: he is b. all things, 77:3
beg: to b. I am ashamed, 20:6
beggar: b. named Lazarus, 194:1
begin: when I b., I also make an end, 16:1
beginning: all hath a b. and an end, 244:12
b. was small, latter days great, 16:2
better the end than the b., 16:3
in the b. God created, 33:10
in the b. was the Word, 114:12
behemoth: behold now b., 8:9
believe: b. . . . and he will help, 59:10
b. in the Lord, 59:9
I [Thomas] will not b., 123:3
believed: as thou hast b., 60:1 (note)
blessed they that have not seen yet have b., 60:11
believeth: whosoever b. in him, 60:8
believing: b., ye might have life, 60:12
b., ye shall receive, 178:3
belly: out of the b. of hell cried I, 125:6
beloved: I am my b.'s, 141:5
my b. is mine, and I am his, 204:8
my b. is like a roe, 141:4
this is my b. Son, 113:1
thou art fair, my b., 145:4
Bethlehem: city of David, which is called B., 119:1
when Jesus was born in B., 117:11
betray: he is at hand that doth b. me, 16:9
one of you shall b. me, 16:7
between: how long halt ye b. two opinions, 108:1
bind: whatsoever ye shall b. on earth shall be bound in heaven, 11:4
birth: many shall rejoice at his [John the Baptist's] b., 25:3
birthright: sell me this day thy b., 112:1
bishop: the office of b., 31:2
bite: prophets that b. with their teeth, 106:11
bitter: with b. herbs, 168:7
black: I am b. but comely, 15:4
blameless: God will not reject b. man, 230:3
bless: I will b. them that b. thee, 1:2
Lord b. and keep thee, 17:2
not let thee go, except thou b. me, 16:12
oh that thou wouldst b. me, 178:11

blessed: b. above all people, 27:1
b. are the poor in spirit etc. [Beatitudes], 14:6
b. art thou among women, b. the fruit of thy womb, 146:2
b. be he that cometh in the name of the Lord, 17:8
b. . . . in the city, b. . . . in the field, 17:3
b. is the fruit of thy womb, 146:5
b. he that blesseth thee, 142:13
b. . . . when thou comest in [and] goest out, 17:4
judge none b., 96:15
more b. to give than receive, 73:7
blind: b. guides, 228:4
b. receive their sight, p. 150:4
eyes of the b. shall be opened, 148:8
if the b. lead the b., 107:7
I was b., now I see, 151:4
we grope for the wall like the b., 43:14
blood: eat b. of no flesh, 68:7
this is my b., 132:9
whoso shedeth man's b., 134:13
without shedding of b., no forgiveness, 69:7
your b. be upon your own heads, 191:2
bloodthirsty: b. hate the upright, 97:4
blossom: desert shall b. as the rose, 201:1
blot: I shall not b. out his name, 100:3 (note)
boasteth: tongue b. great things, 17:15
bodies: present your b., a living sacrifice, 18:8
body: no riches above sound b., 98:3
one b. in Christ, 189:2
this b. of this death, 18:7
This is my b., 132:9
your b. is the temple of the Holy Ghost, 18:9
bone: b. of my b., 3:1
bones: can these b. live, 18:3
dry b., 18:4
he keepeth all his b., 97:10
book: b. of life, 139:9
b. sealed with seven seals, 64:4
my desire is . . . that mine adversary had written a b., 246:5
no man was able to open the b., 64:5
oh that [my words] were printed in a b., 246:4
write in a b., 246:8; 246:11
books: of making many b. there is no end, 246:6
booths: ye shall dwell in b., 216:8
born: b. of water and of the Spirit, 212:7
b. out of due time, 170:5
except a man be b. again, 212:6
good for that man if he had not been b., 127:4
let the day perish wherein I was b., 44:1
some . . . become as though never been b., 42:11
when I was b., I drew in the common air, 52:5
ye must be b. again, 212:8
borrow: him that would b. of thee, 19:4
borrower: b. is servant to lender, 193:8
borroweth: wicked b. and payeth not, 18:12
borrowing: banqueting upon b., 19:2
bottomless: b. pit, 102:3
bow: I will not trust in my b., 235:3
set my b. in cloud, 162:9
bows: b. of the mighty are broken, 176:15
bread: b. of angels, 57:6 (note)
b. of deceit is sweet to a man, 43:10
b. of wickedness, 54:5
b. which Lord hath given, 57:6
cast b. upon waters, 72:7
eat your b. with enjoyment, 67:5
I am the b. of life, 115:8
in the sweat of thy face thou shalt eat thy b., 3:8
Jesus took b. and blessed, 132:9

bread: (*continued*)
loatheth light b., 66:4
man shall not live by b. alone, 188:2
man doth not live by b. only, 74:5
rain b. from heaven, 57:4
ravens brought him b., 49:3
breastplate: b. of faith and love, 231:9
breasts: thy b. are like young roes, 204:11
breath: [wisdom] is the b. of the power of God, 240:1
brethren: Joseph knew his b., 126:5
bribe: everyone loves a b., 29:3
brick: no more straw to make b., 156:3
bricks: b. are fallen down, 173:6
bridegroom: b. cometh, 145:9
broken: b. weed, 224:10
them that are of a b. heart, 140:10
brokenhearted: bind up the b., 135:8
brother: am I my b.'s keeper, 21:2
angry with his b. without cause, 7:13
b. in need, 73:9
b. is born for adversity, 61:12
b. offended, 61:13
b. to dragons, 124:1
do will of my Father, is my b., 79:2
first be reconciled to thy b., 7:13 (note)
shalt not hate thy b., 61:5
thy b. came with subtilty, 112:3
thy b. shall rise again, 151:8
brotherly: let b. love continue, 142:3
with b. love, 142:6
brothers: b. dwell in unity, 61:10
build: rise up and b., 242:9
burden: every man shall bear his own b., 191:4
they shall bear b. with thee, 92:7
buried: b. in a good old age, 164:3
burn: day cometh that shall burn as an oven, 129:5
bury: let the dead b. their d., 44:12
bush: b. burned with fire, 155:9
God called out of the midst of the b., 155:10
business: do your own b., 20:10
overwise in doing b., 20:1
busybodies: tattlers and b., 20:11
buyer: let not the b. rejoice, 19:10
it is naught saith the b., 19:8
by: b. their fruits ye shall know them, 191:6
byword: a proverb and a b. among nations, 162:10

Caesar: a decree from C. Augustus, 219:14
appeal unto C., 134:7
render unto C., 219:13
Cain: a mark upon C., 21:5
C. was a tiller of the ground, 21:1
C. rose up against Abel, 21:2
calamity: c. is at hand, 44:7
caldron: city is the c., 30:3
calf: fatted c., 181:5
call: c. unto me, I will answer, 177:11
called: many be c., 99:7
Calvary: the place which is called C., 121:4
came: he c. unto his own, 187:10
camel: easier for a c. to go through the eye of a needle, 153:19
Cana: marriage in C., 151:1
candle: a c. of understanding, 239:14
c., under a bushel, 94:3
carcass: wheresoever the c. is, 94:8
carefulness: c. bringeth age before the time, 206:10
carpenter: is not this the c.'s son, 113:11
carry: c. neither purse, nor scrip, 11:6
case: who states case first seems right, 134:1
cast: c. thy bread upon the waters, 72:7
why art thou c. down, 226:3
cause: unto God commit my c., 85:11
chaff: as c. before wind, 50:13
change: can the Ethiopian c. his skin, leopard his spots, 22:3
chariot: c. of fire, 49:4
clouds his c., 75:15
chariots: c. of fire, 49:4 (note)
c. shall rage in the streets, 235:12
some trust in c., 9:1

charity: c. edifieth, 22:5
c. shall cover multitude of sins, 23:2
c. suffereth long and is kind . . . beareth all things, 22:6
c. never faileth, 22:6
follow after c., 23:1
greatest of these is c., 22:7
[if I] have not c., I am become as sounding brass, 22:6
charming: c. never so wisely, 9:3
chastise: I will c. you with scorpions, 165:4
cheek: smite thee on thy right c., 167:1
cheerful: God loveth c. giver, 73:8
cherub: rode upon a c., 65:6
child: a little c. shall lead them, 24:7
a poor and a wise c., 239:10
c. left to himself, 24:11
divide the living c. in two, 211:3
even a c. is known by his doings, 2:1
Jesus called a little child unto him, 24:14
joy that a c. is born, 25:5
she saw the child [Moses], 155:5
the c. [Jesus] grew and waxed strong, 119:3
train up a c., 24:3
unto us a c. is born, 147:10
when I was a c. I spake as a c., 25:6
withhold not correction from the c., 24:1
childish: I put away c. things, 25:6
children: as arrows are in the hand . . . so are c., 23:15
beware of thine own c., 24:12.
c. are an heritage, 23:14
c. have rebelled against me, 24:6
c. of God, 106:1
c. of light, 231:8; 240:7
c. of pride, 9 (note, cont. from p. 8)
c. of this world, 240:7
except as ye become a little c., 24:14
give me c., 23:4
her c. arise up and call her blessed, 241:2
in sorrow thou shalt bring forth c., 3:7
instead of thy fathers, thy c., 23:13
multitude of unprofitable c., 24:10
provoke not your c., 25:7
suffer the little c. to come unto me, 25:2
their c. dance, 23:11
woe to rebellious c., 24:8
choose: c. life, 25:9 (note)
chosen: ye have not c. me, but I have c. you, 11:8
Christ: C. is all, and in all, 189:7
C. our passover, 122:5
if C. be not risen, 123:5
now is C. risen, 123:6
one body in C., 189:2
to live is C., 139:7
Christian: almost persuadest me to be a C., 189:1
Christs: false C., 245:6
church: how shall he take care of the c., 31:4
upon this rock I shall build my c., 173:9
circumcised: every man child shall be c., 28:10
cities: c. of the plain, 1:3
c. shall be laid waste, 78:11
the waste c., 29:8
city: c. is full of violence, 36:7
c. of confusion, 29:6
c. set on a hill, 94:3
he beheld the c. and wept, 30:6
how doth the c. sit solitary, 30:2
how is the faithful c. become a harlot, 29:3
in the c. is desolation, 29:7
look not around in streets of the c., 30:4
no continuing c., 100:1
this city is the caldron, 30:3
this c. shall remain forever, 30:1
tumult of the c., 8:4
violence and strife in the c., 29:1
what c. is like unto this c., 30:7
clap: all c. their hands at thee, 187:5

clay: feet of c., 59:3
shall c. say, what makest thou, 85:9
we are the c., 105:10
clean: c. thing out of unclean, 53:9
create in me a c. heart, 230:7
he that hath c. hands, 103:4
ways of man c. in own eyes, 79:7
cleansed: what God hath c., 68:9
cleave: c. unto his wife, 3:1
c. unto the Lord, 83:3
cleaveth: a man . . . c. unto his wife, 145:5
clothing: scribes which love long c., 31:6
cloud: c. of the Lord, 12:7
fly as a c., 66:2
he led them with a c., 56:4 (note)
rideth a swift c., 66:1
clouds: a day of c., 236:9
he . . . makes the c. rise, 236:5
who maketh the c. his chariot, 65:7
clovenfooted: c., shall ye eat, 68:4
coat: c. of many colors, 125:8
cock: before the c. crow, thou shalt deny me, 174:1
come: I c. quickly, 130:1
I will c. again, 99:11
what is to c., I know not, 70:14
comfort: c. all that mourn, 224:1
c. ye my people, 173:3
comforters: miserable c., 70:11
comforteth: as one whom his mother c., 88:11
commandment: a new c. I give unto you, 141:12
commandments: fear God and keep his c., 222:2
I will give thee . . . c., 221:13
keep my c., 222:7
keep the c., 222:4
commend: into thy hands, I c. my spirit, 121:7
company: bad c., 70:10
compassion: Lord is full of c., 76:10
complain: I will c., 69:8
conceive: thou shalt c., 97:9
concubine: c. . . . divided her . . . into twelve pieces, 35:12
concupiscence: the wandering of c., 47:5
condemn: c. not, 223:7
neither do I c. thee, 128:7
confess: be not ashamed to c., 208:4
confound: foolish things to c. the wise, 189:4
conies: c. are a feeble folk, 9:8
conquering: he went forth c., 238:3
conscience: a c. void of offense, 109:5
consecrate: c. yourself . . . to the Lord, 17:1
content: I have learned . . . to be c., 96:16
contrite: a broken and c. heart, 187:1
corn: c. shall make the young men cheerful, 67:9
neighbor's standing c., 62:8
corner: this thing was not done in a c., 201:10
correction: withhold not c. from the child, 24:1 (note)
corrupt: earth also was c., 53:3
corruption: c. thou art my father, 41:11
cost: which of you [does not count] the c., 20:5
counsel: ask c. of all that are wise, 4:7
c. of thine own heart, 202:5
if this c. be of men, 90:4
counsellor: have but one c., 183:7
counsellors: in abundance of c. is safety, 93:3
in multitude of c. is safety, 4:4
counsels: c. and knowledge, 4:5
countenance: c. sign of changing of the heart, 12:3
heart . . . changeth his c., 50:8
merry heart maketh cheerful c., 50:4
courage: bear with a good c. that which hath befallen, 202:1
be of good c., 33:4
be ye of good c., 33:1
courageously: deal c., 230:2
courts: a day in thy c., 75:10
c. of the Lord, 98:7

covenant: c. between me and thee, 33:6
c. with thee and with Israel, 33:7
the words of the c., the Ten Commandments, 221:1
covered: nothing c. that shall not be revealed, 33:9
covet: thou shalt not c. thy neighbor's house, wife, etc., 221:10
craft: their desire is in the work of their c., 243:11
created: by him were all things c., 35:4
God c. man, 2:10
God c. the heaven and the earth, 33:10
thou hast c. all things, 35:5
creation: whole c. groaneth, 224:7
Creator: remember thy C. in the days of thy youth, 247:5
creature: every creature is good, 160:6
God created . . . every living c., 34:3
let the earth bring forth the living c., 34:5
creatures: houses shall be full of doleful c., 29:4
crimes: land is full of bloody c., 36:7
crooked: c. cannot be made straight, 59:2
cross: come down from the c., 120:12
enemies of the c. of Christ, 208:17
he that taketh not his c., 113:8
crown: c. of glory, 100:2
c. of thorns, 120:9
doth the c. endure, 177:1
fear of the Lord is c. of wisdom, 82:10
crownest: c. the year with goodness, 75:9
crucified: let him be c., 120:8
they c. him, 120:10
cruel: c. man hurts himself, 72:3
cruelty: dark places, habitations of c., 38:6
crumbs: c. which from masters' table, 186:2
c. from rich man's table, 194:1
cry: I c. out of wrong, 109:2
cup: let this c. pass from me, 119:6
my c. runneth over, 88:7
this c. is the new testament, 132:12
curious: be not c., 36:11
curse: a c., an astonishment, an hissing, 162:11
c. God and die, 44:1
thou shalt not c. the people, 172:12
cursed: c. be the day wherein I was born, 44:1
cursing: mouth filled with c., 54:1

Damascus: he came near D., 169:9
danced: David d. before the Lord, 39:9
danger: prudent man sees d., 37:4
Daniel: brought D. and cast him [to] lions, 37:5
D. convicted them of false witness, 136:3
D. was taken up out of the den, 37:8
dark: in the d. they dig through houses, 36:3
the d. places of the earth, 38:6
darkness: d. is not d. to thee, 89:3
d. over the land of Egypt, 156:5
d. was upon the face of the deep, 37:9
d. which may be felt, 37:10
dwell in the thick d., 38:3
he made d. pavilions, 38:2
how great that d., 55:5
in the d. they dig through houses, 36:3
men loved d., 55:9
people in d. saw great light, 79:13
the terrors of the deep d., 38:5
the thick d. where God was, 80:8
the treasures of d., 38:7
walked in d., have seen great light, 27:6

daughter: d. lieth at the point of death, 150:10
d. of the Pharaoh, 155:4
father waketh for the d., 24:13
hearken, o d., 144:6
daughters: d. of men were fair, 15:1
d. of Zion are haughty, 180:9
the horseleach hath two d. crying give, give, 24:5
ye careless daughters, 241:4
David: D. came to Saul, 38:11
D. danced before the Lord, 39:9
D. his ten thousands, 39:5
D. . . . played before the Lord on all manner of instruments, 157:2
D. saw a woman washing herself, 40:1
D. . . . took a stone, 39:3
D. took the lyre, 38:12
King D. was old, 40:3
Saul said to D. . . . thou are but a youth, 39:2
day: d. cometh that shall burn as an oven, 129:5
ye know neither the d., 183:8
d. is at hand, 154:6
d. of darkness and of gloominess, 236:9
d. of the Lord cometh, 128:11
d. of the Lord is at hand, 128:10
d. which the Lord hath made, 197:8
sufficient unto the d. evil thereof, 70:15
the d. star, 213:6
days: d. consumed like smoke, 44:4
d. of feasting and joy, 184:1
my d. are swifter than weaver's shuttle, 138:7
our d. on earth are as a shadow, 138:3
teach us to number our d., 222:9
dead: blessed are the d., 43:5
let the d. bury their d., 113:4
thou shalt not curse the d., 151:12
when d. is at rest, let remembrance rest, 42:10
deaf: d. adder, 9:3
death: a covenant with d., 54:12
d. better than bitter life, 42:9
d. hath no more dominion, 43:1
d. in the pot, 67:1
d. will not be long in coming, 202:3
God made not d., 42:7
he that smiteth man [that dies] shall be put to d., 135:1
his name that sat on him was D., 43:4
last enemy is d., 43:2
let me die the d. of the righteous, 40:8
life and good, d. and evil, 25:9
O d. where is thy sting, 43:3
shadow of d., 38:4
step between me and d., 41:1
swallow up d. in victory, 42:3
through envy of the devil came d., 42:8
valley of the shadow of d., 88:7
wages of sin is d., 208:15
way of life, way of d., 25:10
Deborah: Awake, awake, D., 156:11
debts: be not one . . . who becomes surety for debts, 153:3
forgive us our debts, 140:7
deceit: bread of d. is sweet, 43:10
decision: multitudes in the valley of d., 129:3
deeds: d. slack and remiss, 2:5
terrible in glorious d., 84:3
deep: d. calleth unto d., 163:5
maketh d. to boil, 9 (note,. cont. from p. 8)
that which is far off and exceeding d., 158:2
deliver: d. me from mine enemies, 179:5
d. me from the evil man, 179:10
d. them out of the hands of the Egyptians, 155:12
I [Judas] will d. him unto you, 127:3
make haste, o God, to d. me, 179:6
den: d. of thieves, 28:7
denies: whoever d. me before men, 113:7

deny: thou shalt d. me thrice, 174:1
yet I will not d. thee, 174:1 (note)
depart: d. in peace, 42:14
depths: they go down again to the d., 163:9
out of the d. have I cried, 179:9
derision: I was a d., 187:6
desert: d. shall rejoice, and blossom, 160:3
found him in a d. land, 27:4
desire: d. accomplished is sweet, 215:18
d. fulfilled, 215:18
his heart's d., 96:6
more d. unto [women] than unto silver and gold, 241:6
desired: whatsoever mine eyes d., 216:3
desolate: flocks are made d., 63:6
desolation: in the city is left d., 29:7
desolations: the d. of many generations, 29:8
despised: he is d. and rejected, 202:9
destroy: d. the righteous with the wicked, 44:5
go up against this land and d. it, 234:6
I will d. man whom I have created, 161:12
not to d. but to fulfill, 113:2
destroyeth: he [an adulterer] destroyeth own soul, 204:3
destroys: he d. . . . blameless and wicked, 44:9
destruction: d. cometh, 45:1
wide the gate, leadeth to d., 101:8
devil: d. . . . a roaring lion, 46:6
d. showed him all the kingdoms of the world, 46:1
envy of the d. came death, 42:8
resist the d., 46:5
serpent called the D., 46:7
ye are the father of the d., 55:10
devils: d. besought him, 46:8
he casteth out d., 46:8 (note)
dew: the d. of heaven, 16:11
die: d. because we have seen God, 80:12
d. in peace, 42:5
d. like men, 41:14
d. the death of the righteous, 40:8
great and small shall d. in this land, 235:7
if a man d. shall he live again, 41:10
not quickened except it d., 191:9
we must needs d., 41:3
why d. before thy time, 47:3
dies: when he d., will carry nothing away, 152:8
diet: care of meat and d., 67:10
dieth: how d. the wise man, 41:15
man d. and wasteth away, 41:9
dig: I cannot d., 20:6
diligent: the hand of the d. maketh rich, 242:11
disciple: d. is not above his master, 186:1
discipline: beginning of [wisdom] is desire of d., 239:17
discord: continually sowing d., 54:6
discouraged: neither be d., 33:2
discovereth: d. deep things, 38:4
disputations: doubtful d., 189:3
divided: kingdom d., house d., 32:7
their heart is d., 108:2
divination: d. . . . or an enchanter, or a witch, 163:3
do: all that the Lord hath spoken, we d., 83:7
d. that to no man which thou hatest, 91:8
d. thou likewise, 91:7
if they d. these things in a green tree, 55:8
that thou doest, d. quickly, 212:3
what shall I do., 20:6
whatsoever God hath said, d., 83:6
whatsoever thy hand findeth to d., d. with thy might, 243:8
whatsoever ye would that men should d. to you, 92:1

do: (*continued*)
whosoever shall d. and teach them [10 commandments] shall be great, 222:3
doctrine: every wind of d., 31:8
doers: be ye d. of the word, 2:9
dog: as d. returneth to vomit, fool returneth to folly, 215:11
living d. better than dead lion, 139:3
dogs: d. licked the blood of Naboth, 4:11
doing: arise . . . and be d., 242:7
weary in well d., 231:6
doings: even a child is known by his d., 2:1
dominion: d. over fish of the sea, over every creeping thing, 2:10
thou hast given him d., 105:1
door: I am the d., 116:5
I stand at the d. and knock, 117:7
doorkeeper: rather be a d. in house of God, 75:10
doubt: wherefore didst thou d., 60:4
doubtful: d. disputations, 189:3
dove: the d. came in to him in the evening, 162:6
the soul of thy turtle d., 109:3
wings like a d., 52:11
downsitting: knowest my d., and uprising, 86:14
dragons: brother to d., companion to owls, 124:1
habitation of d., 10:3
dream: d. of Pharaoh, 126:3
d. . . . through multitude of business, 48:3
d. which made me afraid, 48:5
Joseph dreamed a d., 126 (cont. from p. 125)
old men d. dreams . . . young men . . . see visions, 182:8
prophet that hath a d., 48:4
dreamer: this d. cometh, 126:1
dreams: d. lift up fools, 103:11
your old men shall dream d., 182:8
drink: erred through strong d., 30:11
give strong d. unto him ready to perish, 237:4
let him d., 237:5
strong d. a brawler, 236:14
woe unto them [who] follow strong d., 237:6
drunkard: d. and glutton . . . come to poverty, 47:2
drunkards: awake, ye d., and weep, 237:10
drunken: they are d., but not with wine, 206:7
drunkenness: thou shalt be filled with d., 237:9
dry: d. bones, 18:4
dust: all turn to d. again, 41:16
d. thou art, 3:8
enemies shall lick the d., 50:14
shake off the d. of your feet, 187:7
shall the d. return to the earth, 42:2

eagle: doth the e. mount up at thy command, 8:8
I bear you on e.'s wings, 87:13
like an e. that stirs up its nest, 88:1
way of an e. in the air, 140:1
eagles: mount up with wings as e., 77:10
ear: bow down thine e., O Lord, 179:7
e. tests words, 132:2
give e., O heavens, 84:4
incline thine e., O Lord, 179:12
the hearing e., 17:17
ears: who hath e. to hear, 167:3 (note)□
e. . . . shall tingle, 161:2
earth: e. abideth for ever, 160:1
e. bringeth forth fruit, 160:5
e: full of the goodness of the Lord, 159:10
e. full of thy riches, 159:12
e. given to the wicked, 53:8
e. is my footstool, 244:11
e. is the Lord's, 159:9
e. shall be filled with the glory of God, 244:6

earth: (*continued*)
e. was corrupt, 53:3
God called the dry land E., 34:2
going the way of all the e., 40:9
hangeth the e. upon nothing, 34:8
hurt not the e., 51:13
let the e. fear the Lord, 82:6
let the e. rejoice, 96:9
Lord looked upon the e., 160:4
O e., e., 89:6
pillars of the e. are the Lord's, 244:7
profit of the e., 160:2
the foundations of the e., 124:3
while the e. remaineth, 159:3
whole e. is at rest, 171:6
earthy: first man is . . . e., 106:2
ease: woe to them that are at e., 101:4
east: e. of the garden of Eden, 4 (cont. from p. 3)
eat: e., drink and be merry, 101:2
e., drink, tomorrow we die, 101:3
e. in Egypt freely, 66:3
e., O friends, 104:1
e. your bread with enjoyment, 67:5
every man should e. and drink, and enjoy, 100:13
forced to e., vomit, 67:13
nothing better than [to] e. and drink, 139:1
she gave me of the tree and I did e., 3:5
that shall ye e., 68:4
eaten: hast e. bless the Lord, 66:5
eater: out of the e. came something to eat, 195:4
eating: moderate e., 67:12
ecce: e. homo, 122:2
Eden: east of the garden of E., 4 (cont. from p. 3)
garden in E., 49:1
thou hast been in E., 195:1
egg: taste in white of e., 67:2
Egypt: a great cry in E., 156:8
a new king in E., 155:1
brought us forth out of E., 56:3
darkness over the land of E., 156:5
firstborn in E. shall die, 156:5
[food] which we did eat in E., 66:3
I will pass through the land of E., 156:7
out of E. have I called my son, 118:3
seven years of plenty throughout E., 126:4
Egyptian: he [Moses] slew the E., 35:8
Egyptians: E. made the children of Israel to serve, 155:2
Lord overthrew E., 56:7
elders: miss not discourse of the e., 165:1
elect: God's e., 198:12
he hath care for his e., 197:1
mine e., 202:8
Elijah: E. went up by a whirlwind, 49:4
I will send you E., 49:6
mantle of E., 49:5
Emmanuel: (see also **Immanuel**): they shall call his name E., 117:10
end: all hath a beginning and an e., 244:12
better is the e., 16:3
he that endureth to the e., 16:5
I will also make an e., 16:1
let me know my e., 41:13
remember the e., 16:4
endureth: he that e. to the end, 16:5
enemies: delivered thine e., 81:8
deliver me from mine e., 179:5
e. are the men of his own house, 51:1
e. shall lick the dust, 50:14
love your e., 51:5
make thine e. thy footstool, 81:13
saved from mine e., 81:12
enemy: e. be hungry, give him bread, 50:16
e. cannot be hid in adversity, 51:2
hast thou found me, mine e., 4:9
when your e. falls, 50:15

engines: he made in Jerusalem e., 235:2
enjoy: eat and drink and e., 100:13
e. the good of all his labors, 100:13
enmity: let e. cease, 51:4
enriched: liberal man will be e., 72:6
ensign: an ensign to the peoples, 148:3
envy: e. and wrath shorten life, 206:10
e. slayeth the silly one, 52:1
who [can] stand before e., 52:2
Esau: E. was a cunning hunter, 111:8
escape: hasten my e., 52:12
escaped: e. with the skin of my teeth, 52:8
eternity: he put e. into man's mind, 34:12 (note)
who can number the days of e., 223:4
Eve: E. . . . mother of all living, 3:9
evening: shadows of the e., 53:1
event: one e. to all, 64:1
evidence: faith is . . . e. of things not seen, 61:3
evil: an e. and adulterous generation, 71:7
be not afraid, they cannot do e., 107:3
call e. good, good e., 54:11
cease to do e., 187:14 (note)
deliver me from the e. man, 179:10
deliver us from e., 140:7
e. bow before the good, 230:11
e. for e., 229:5
e. with both hands earnestly, 19:7
hate the e., 55:3
heart of men is full of e., 144:1
he maketh sun to rise on e., 223:5
he that is e. to himself, 202:2
I make peace, create e., 35:2
imagination of man's heart, e. from his youth, 104:10
life and good, death and e., 25:9
not follow multitude to do e., 53:4
overcome e. with good, 55:12
rewarded e. for good, 108:7
shall e. be recompensed for good, 130:8
the e. which I would not, that I do, 59:7
the Lord shall preserve me from e., 88:8
this is an e. generation, 72:1
to know good and e., 3:10
ye shall be as gods, knowing good and e., 3:2
exalt: e. not thyself, 180:11
whosoever shall e. himself, 186:3
exalted: every valley shall be e., 182:6
excellent: approvest things more e., 56:1
more e. way, 56:2
expedient: not all things are e., 183:10
eye: e. for e., tooth for tooth, 135:2
e. hath not seen, nor ear heard, 83:1
e. not satisfied with seeing, 226:6
e. of a needle, 153:19
his e. was not dim, 164:5
if thy right e. offend thee, 208:6
light of the body is e., 18:5
mine e. affecteth mine heart, 18:2
mote in thy brother's e., 59:5
see e. to e., 52:3
the seeing e., 17:17
eyes: e. of Lord, brighter than sun, 87:2
e. they have but see not, 231:12
his e. stealthily watch for the hapless, 54:1
his e. were as a flame, 117:5
mine e. have seen the King, 81:6
my son . . . the light of mine e., 24:9
there fell from his e. scales, 169:11
face: Lord spake unto Moses f. to f., 80:10
Moses hid his f., 80:6
seen God f. to f., 111:5
thou canst see my f., 80:11
fair: how f. and pleasant art thou, 205:2
thou art all f., my love, 15:5

faith: abideth f., hope, charity, 22:7
f. as a grain of mustard seed, 60:5
f. hath made thee whole. 60:3
f. is substance of things hoped for, 61:3
f. without works is dead, 61:4
fight the good fight of f., 61:1
great is thy f., 150:8
I have kept the f., 173:8
not found so great f., 60:1
O thou of little f., 60:4
stand fast in the f., 60:13
thy f. hath saved thee, 60:7
we walk by f., 60:14
ye of little f., 149:8
faithful: be f. unto death, 143:4
f. in that which is least, 210:10
faithless: be not f., 60:10
f. and perverse generation, 71:8
fall: go not . . . wherein thou mayest f., 22:2
take heed lest he f., 181:1
fallen: how are the mighty f., 234:3
false: a f. balance, 43:8
beware of f. prophets, 182:9
f. Christs and f. prophets, 245:6
f. report, 103:1
thou shalt not bear f. witness, 221:9
thou shalt not raise f. report, 133:8
familiar spirits: a consulter with f.s., 163:3
women that hath a f.s., 163:4
famine: seven years of f. 126:4
the sword, the f., the pestilence, 44:12
famous: praise f. men, 94:1
far: be not f. from me, 179:2
fashion: f. of this world passeth, 63:10
fat: thou art waxen f., 66:6
fate: one f. comes to all, 64:1
father: all [have] one f., 52:4
call no man your f., 79:2
every gift . . . cometh from the F., 77:4
F., forgive them, 121:5
F., I have sinned, 181:3
F., into thy hands . . . my spirit, 121:7
f. of a fool, 24:2
f. of many nations, 1:4
hear the instruction of thy f., 167:8
help thy f. in his age, 168:5
he that curseth his f. or mother, 167:7
he that smiteth his f. or mother, 167:6
his f. had compassion, 181:4
honor thy f. and mother, 167:5
I must be about my F.'s business, 119:4
in my F.'s house, many mansions, 99:10
lad cannot leave his f., 23:6
Lord, are our f., 79:1
no man knoweth the son but the F., 113:9
our F. which art in heaven, 140:7
the f. waketh for the daughter, 24:13
whosoever shall do the will of my F., 79:2
would not listen to voice of their f., 23:8
your F. knoweth what things ye need, 177:13
fathers: f. have eaten a sour grape, 168:2
f., provoke not your children, 25:7
f. shall not be put to death for the children, 135:5
instead of thy f., thy children, 23:13
visiting iniquities of f. upon children, 78:2
your f., where are they, 169:1
fatness: f. of earth, 16:11
fatted: f. calf, 181:5
faults: cleanse . . . secret f., 59:1
fear: earth f. the Lord, 82:6
f. and trembling, 64:8
f. came upon me, 64:7
f. day and night, 64:6
f. is on every side, 235:6
f. not, 33:11

fear: (*continued*)
f. not them which kill the body, 45:9
f. not for I am with thee, 77:11
f. of the Lord driveth away sins, 82:11
f. of the Lord is beginning of love, 82:12
f. of the Lord is beginning of wisdom, 82:4 (note)
f. of the Lord is crown of wisdom, 82:10
f. of the Lord is wisdom, 82:4
f. the Lord, 82:3
God hath not given spirit of f., 50:10
I will not f. man, 33:5
Moses said f. not, 80:8
secret with them that f. him, 82:5
thou shalt f. the Lord thy God, 82:2
unto you that f. my name, 82:8
you will not f. terror of the night, 64:9
feareth: blessed man that f. the lord, 82:7
whoso f. the Lord shall not fear, 82:13
fears: f. shall be in the way, 164:15
fearful: woe to f. hearts, 108:3
feast: a f. is made for laughter, 67:6
a f. unto the Lord, 168:11, 216:7
a f. by ordinance forever, 65:3
a f. of fat things, 67:8
f. of harvest, 65:4
f. of ingathering, 65:4
f. of unleavened bread, 65:4; 168:12
f. unto the Lord, 65:2
I hate, despise your feast days, 188:1
the king made a f., 103:16
three times keep a f. in the year, 65:4
when thou makes a f., call the poor, 73:5
when ye have gathered the fruit, ye shall keep a f., 216:7
feasting: days of f. and joy, 184:1
feeble: all hands shall be f., 206:9
feet: f. . . . of clay, 59:3
not my f. only, but also my hands and head, 174:3
fell: I f. at his feet as dead, 117:6
few: f. and evil the days of my life, 138:2
fiftieth: hallow the f. year, 127:2
fig: every man under his vine and f. tree, 170:11; 172:1
they sewed f. leaves together, 3:3
whoso keepeth the f. tree, 243:2
fight: good f. for you against enemies, 81:11
f. the good f., 61:1
I have fought the good f., 173:8
Lord shall f. for you, 170:6
they shall f. every one, 32:5
we f. for our lives and laws, 192:6
filthy: f. lucre, 31:3
findeth: whoso f. me, f. life, 239:5
finger: f. of God, 80:7
fingers: f. of a man's hand wrote . . . upon the wall, 149:3
finished: it is f., 122:3
fins: f. and scales, shall ye eat, 68:6
fire: after the f., a voice: 81:3
a little f. kindleth, 210:3
can a man take f. in his bosom, 220:3
not good fruit, cast into the f., 101:7
they walked in the midst of the f., 149:5
through f. and water, 37:2
when thou walkest through the f., 149:2 (note)
firmament: f. showeth handiwork, 100:7
God made the f., 34:1
lights in the f., 100:5
first: f. shall be last, 193:4
I am the f., the last, 78:7
firstborn: f. in Egypt shall die, 156:6
smite all the f. in the land of Egypt, 166:7
fish: f. to swallow up Jonah, 125:5
f. vomited out Jonah, 125:7
fishers: I will make you f. of men, 10:8

flattereth: him that f. with his lips, 65:5
flee: f. as a bird, 52:10
flesh: all f. consorteth according to kind, 105:15
all f. is grass, 18:1
one f., 3:1; 145:8
sat by f. pots, 57:3
the f. is of no avail, 212:2
the f. is weak, 220:6
the f. lusteth gainst the Spirit, 18:11
they were but f., 105:3
flock: he shall feed his f., 88:10
I will feed my f., 89:1
ye my f., 89:2
flocks: know state of thy f., 63:1
flood: f. of waters upon the earth, 162:2
flower: let no f. of spring pass, 101:5
fly: f. as a cloud, 66:2
f. away as a dream, 52:9
follow: come and f. me, 188:6
folly: a fool returneth to his f., 215:11
fool: answer a f. according to his folly, 215:10
answer not a f. according to his folly, 215:10 (note)
as it happeneth to the f., 138:11
f. changeth as the moon, 215:14
father of a f. hath no joy, 24:2
f. hath said . . . there is no God, 12:9
f. lifteth up voice with l., 133:7
f. shall be servant to the wise, 215:5
f.'s mouth is his destruction, 215:9
f. takes no pleasure in understanding, 215:8
f. uttereth all his mind, 218:11
I have played the f., 186:10
laughter of the f., 133:6
way of a f., 215:6
whosoever shall say, thou f., 7:13
foolish: f. son a sorrow, 23:16
f. son is ruin, 61:14
f. things to confound the wise, 189:4
make not thyself an underling to f. man, 215:13
fools: discourse of f. is irksome, 215:15
heart of fools is in the house of mirth, 101:1
heart of f. is in their mouth, 218:18
suffer f. gladly, 215:16
foot: lest thou dash thy f. against a stone, 5:8
footmen: if thou hast run with f., 174:6
footstool: e. is my f., 244:11
make enemies thy f., 81:13
forbearing: by long f. is prince persuaded, 169:2
forget: how long wilt thou f. me, Lord? 178:15
forgive: Father, f. them, 121:5
f. and ye shall be f., 223:7
how oft shall my brother sin and I f. him, 69:3
f. thy neighbor, 69:1
forgiven: her sins are f., 141:10
former: remember not the f. things, 168:13
fornication: flee f., 205:6
forsaken: my God, why hast thou f. me, 44:3; 120:14
fortress: Lord, my f., 76:4
forty: f. days and f. nights, 162:4
f. years in the wilderness, 58:4
fought: they f. from heaven, 233:4
found: hast thou f. me, O mine enemy, 50:11
foundations: the f. of the earth, 124:3
foxes: a portion for f., 229:10
little f., 9:10
fragments: gather up the f., 236:1
frankincense: gold, f., and myrrh, 118:1
frantic: be not . . . f., 102:12
free: I was f. born, 69:10
freely: f. received, f. give, 73:3
friend: a faithful f. is a defense, 70:4
a faithful friend is a medicine, 70:5
f. cannot be known in prosperity, 70:7
get f., prove him first, 70:3

friend: (*continued*)
forsake not an old f., 70:6
f. in name, 70:12
f. loveth all times, 70:1
he who withholds kindness from a friend, 69:11
lover and friend [are] far from me, 140:2
not ashamed to defend f., 70:8
friends: f. of the mammon of unrighteousness, 183:9
a man that hath f., 70:2
lay down his life for his f., 70:9
frogs: river shall bring forth f. abundantly, 156:4
fruit: blessed is the f. of thy womb, 146:5
earth bringeth forth f., 160:5
good tree cannot bring forth evil f., 191:6
she took the f. thereof and did eat, 3:3
fruitful: be f. and multiply, 2:10
be ye f. and multiply, 23:3
fruits: by their f. ye shall know them, 191:6
f. of the valley, 71:1
fugitive: a f. and a vagabond, 21:3
fulfill: not to destroy but to f., 113:2
fulfilled: till all be f., 102:5
fury: f. is not in me, 7:9
sway of his f., 7:10

gall: g. of bitterness, 208:14
galloping: with the g., g., of his steeds, 8:3
garden: g. eastward in Eden, 49:1
g. of nuts, 71:1
tree of life also in . . . the g., 49:2
gardens: plant g., 102:11
garment: if I may but touch his g., 150:2
garments: g. of gladness, 31:5
thy g. smell of myrrh, aloes, 194:7
gate: strait is the g., 198:4
this is the g. of heaven, 112:7
wide is the g. . . . that leadeth to destruction, 101:8
Gath: tell it not in G., 39:8
gathered: where two or three are gathered, 188:5
gave: I was hungry and you g. me food, 73:3
generation: one g. passeth, another g. cometh, 228:6
evil and adulterous g., 71:2
evil g., 72:1
faithless and perverse g., 71:8
g. of vipers,. 71:6
perverse g., 23:7
stubborn and rebellious g., 71:3
generations: dwelling place in all g., 75:11
Gentiles: a light of the G., 169:12
gentleness: g. made me great, 72:2
get: g. thee behind me, Satan, 220:5
g. thee hence, Satan, 91:2
ghost: Jacob . . . yielded up the g., 111:7
man giveth up the g., 41:9
she hath given up the g., 42:4
giants: g. in the earth, 104:9
Gibeon: sun, stand thou still upon G., 127:1
Gideon: G. blew a trumpet, 156:12
sword for the Lord and for G., 223:7
gift: every good g., every perfect g., 77:4
g. for the Lord, 30:8
neglect not gift that is in thee, 1:1
take no g., 19:5
Gilead: balm in G., 47:7
give: freely g., 11:1
g. of thy bread to hungry, 72:10
g. to him that asketh, 19:4
more blessed to g. than receive, 73:7
given: much g., much required, 190:11
giver: God loveth cheerful g., 73:8
gives: g. freely, grows richer, 72:6
givest: heart shall not be grieved when thou g., 175:5
glad: I will be g. in the Lord, 96:10
gladness: garments of g., 31:5

glass: through a g. darkly, 232:1
glean: let me g. and gather, 62.5 (note)
glory: all earth filled with the g. of the Lord, 244:6
g. of the Lord endure, 86:7
g. of the Lord revealed, 86:8
g. to God in the highest, 119:2
king of g., 86:6
one star differeth from another in g., 94:4
show me thy g., 178:8
these were the g. of their times, 94:2
thy g., O Israel, is slain, 44:8
to search their own g. is not g., 216:1
vain g., 94:5
gnashing: g. of teeth, 101:9; 102:1
gnat: strain at a g., 228:4
go: g. and do thou likewise, 91:7
g. and sin no more, 128:7
g. and the Lord be with thee, 17:6
g. in peace, 17:7
I g. the way of all earth, 23:10
whither thou goest I will g., 140:9
goats: g. on the left, 129:8
God: a G. of knowledge, 79:4
a G. of the afflicted, 76:9
a G. of thc living, 76:15
a jealous G., 74:8
canst thou find out G., 85:12
curse G. and die, 44:1
die, because we have seen G., 80:12
doorkeeper in the house of G., 75:10
finger of G., 80:7
from everlasting to everlasting thou art G., 75:11
G. and mammon, 83:14
G. called unto him out of the bush, 155:10
G. created man, 2:10
G. created the heaven and earth, 33:10
G. formed every beast of the field, 7:17
G. goeth to fight for you, 81:11
G., gracious and merciful, 75:1
G. hath blessed thee, 87:16
G., I cry by day, 86:9
G., I will give thanks unto thee, 179:15
G. is a consuming fire, 74:3
G. is a spirit, 91:4
G. is in heaven, thou upon earth, 177:11
G. is light, 80:1
G. is love, 77:5
G. is merciful G., 87:6
G. is my salvation, 75:18
G. is our refuge and strength, 75:7
G. is not mocked, 87:4
G. is our G. . . . even unto death, 83:5
G. is with thee, 87:12
G. is my strength and power, 77:6
G. is thy refuge, 88:3
G. loveth cheerful giver, 73:8
G. made not death, 42:7
G. mighty and terrible, 74:6
G., no respecter of persons, 76:18
G. of peace be with you, 17:12
G. saw everything he had made, 34:7
G. shall bring every work into judgment, 79:8
G. shall wipe away all tears, 199:4
G. spake unto Israel, 111:6
G. will come with a strong hand, 76:3
G. will we serve, 83:9
good to praise G., 85:3
he is our G. and we are the people of his pasture, 91:1
he is the living G., 76:7
I . . . am a jealous God, 78:2
I am the Lord thy G., 221:2
if G. be for us, 77:1
I have seen G. face to face, 111:5
it is God which worketh in you, 199:2
I . . . will be their G., 26:7
I will be to you a G., 26:5
I would seek unto G., 85:11

God: (*continued*)
kingdom of G. is not in word, 177:9
kingdom of G. is within you, 76:14
know that I am G., 78:4
my G., my G., why hast thou forsaken me, 44:3, 120:14
my soul thirsts for G., 86:2
no G. beside me, 78:8
no man hath seen G., 76:16
none good but . . . G., 76:12
obey my voice, I will be your G., 83:13
seek first the kingdom of G., 231:4
separate us from the love of G., 87:5
sing praises unto G., 84:11
the breath of the power of G., 240:1
the finger of G., 80:7
the Lord our G. is one Lord, 74:4
there is no G., 12:9
the thick darkness where G. was, 80:8
they saw the G. of Israel, 80:9
this was the son of G., 121:3
thou art the son of G., 114:2
thou shalt love the Lord thy G., 82:14, 222:5
to them that love G., 82:18
what G. hath cleansed, 68:9
what hath G. wrought, 26:11
whatsoever G. doeth, 90:2
whatsoever G. hath said, 83:6
who so great a G., 84:12
with G. all things are possible, 76:13
word of G. (see under **word**)
gods: g. are come in the likeness of men, 11:10
thou shalt have no other g., 221:2
thou shalt not revile the g., 92:8
goest: whither thou g., I will go, 140:9
going: g. the way of all the earth, 40:9
gold: g. become dim, 153:11
g., and frankincense, and myrrh, 118:1
g. hath been ruin of many, 153:17
g. is tried in the fire, 224:4
judgment of the Lord more desired than g., 79:6
silver and g. have I none, 73:6
golden: g. bowl, 42:2
Golgotha: a place called G., 121:4
Gomorrah: upon Sodom and upon G., 210:14
good: all things work together for g., 82:18
behold, it was very g., 34:7
do g. to thyself, 202:3
g. news from a far country, 161:4
g. news refreshes, 161:3
g. tidings, 161:5
g. tree cannot bring forth evil, 191:6
hold fast that which is g., 228:5
I am the g. shepherd, 116:7, 116:8
love the g.,55:3
[none] doeth g. and sinneth not, 207:13
none g. but God, 76:12
seek g., 230:17
the evil bow before the g., 230:11
the g. man is perished, 229:14
the g. that I would I do not, 59:7
to know g. and evil, 3:10
ye shall be as gods, knowing g. and evil, 3:2
goodness: g. and mercy shall follow me, 88:7
praise Lord for his g., 84:14
thou crownest the year with thy g., 75:9
goods: set not they heart upon g., 181:8
when g. increase, 175:2
gospel: preach the g. to every creature, 11:5
preach the g. to the poor, 114:10
grace: g. did much more abound, 93:9
g. of the Lord Jesus Christ be with you all, 17:13
thou hast found g. in my sight, 154:8
ye are fallen from g., 208:16
gracious: g. woman gets honor, 215:17
grain: him who holds back g., 67:3
grandchildren: g. . . . crown of the aged, 61:11

grass: all flesh is g., 18:1
g. withereth, flower fadeth, 89:5
his days are like g., 105:4
grave: I will ransom them from the power of the g., 42:6
[Lazarus] had lain in the g. four days, 151:7
O g., where is thy victory, 43:3
your g. in ripe old age, 41:7
graven image: thou shalt not make any g.i., 221:2
graves: I will open your g., 191:7
great: every g. matter they shall bring unto thee, 92:7
g. men not always wise, 93:10
seekest thou g. things for thyself, 5:3
greater: g. love hath no man, 142:1
greatness: thine, O Lord, is the g. and power, 178:12
greedy: g. for unjust gain, 19:16
g. of filthy lucre, 31:3
g. to add money to money, 153:14
he who is g. . . . makes trouble, 94:6
green: g. pastures, 88:7
I am like g. olive tree, 87:8
if they do these things in a g. tree, 55:8
spreading himself like a g. bay tree, 54:2
grope: thou shalt g. at noonday, 32:8
we g. for the wall, 43:14
gulf: great g. fixed, 102:2

ha ha: saith amongst trumpets h. h., 8:7
hail: h. [Mary], 146:2
hair: long h. is a glory to her, 18:10
hairs: h. of head numbered, 87:3
halt: the h. and the blind, 104:3
hand: h. stretched out to receive, 94:7
let not left h. know what r. hand doeth, 73:2
right h. glorious in power, 81:10
thy right h. shall hold me, 88:9
whatsoever thy h. findeth to do, 243:8
handmaid: h. of the Lord, 146:4
hands: he that hath clean h., 103:4
he [Pilate] washed his h., 174:8
happeneth: as it h. to the fool, so to me, 138:11
one event h. to them all, 64:1
time and chance h. to them all, 143:8
happy: h. the man whom God reproves, 223:11
hard: is anything too h. for the Lord, 77:13
things that are too h., 5:5
harden: thou shalt not h. thine heart, 175:4
harlot: the faithful city become an h., 29:3
harlots: h.[1] houses, 205:3 (note)
harmless: h. as doves, 217:1
harmony: live in h., 172:5
harps: we hanged our h. upon the willows, 248:4
hart: as h. longs for flowing stream, 86:2
harvest: h. is plenteous, 63:7
hate: h. evil, love good, 55:3
I h. with perfect hatred, 97:1
six things doth the Lord h., 54:7
thou shalt not h. thy brother, 61:5
hath: from him that h. not, 97:5
unto everyone that h., 97:5
hatred: h. stirs up strife, 97:2
he that hideth h., 97:3
haughty: do not be h., 106:8
h. spirit before a fall, 180:6
man of h. looks, 180:2
he: h. is before all things, 77:3
h. is my refuge and my fortress, 75:12
h. is risen, 122:9
h. is wise, mighty, 75:3
h. of whom I spake, 115:1
h. only is my rock, 75:8
h. raiseth up the poor, 175:8
h. saveth the poor, 175:9
h. seeth from everlasting, 89:4
h. shall come as the rain, 76:8

he: (*continued*)
h. shall feed his flock, 88:10
h. shall judge among nations, 79:9
h. that cometh in the name of the Lord, 17:8
h. that is not with me, 143:2
h. wounds, but binds up, 75:2
I am h., 78:6
heal: h. the sick, 11:1
healed: my servant shall be h., 149:6
health: h. above all gold, 98:2
hear: be swift to h., 98:6
h., O Israel, 74:4
who hath ears to h., 98:5
heard: I am not h., 109:2
heart: a broken and contrite h., 187:1
as he thinketh in his h., 50:6
a stubborn and rebellious h., 27:10
a stubborn h., 215:2
a wise and understanding h., 211:1
counsel of thine h., 202:5
eye affecteth mine h., 18:2
h. changeth his countenance, 50:8
h. carry you away, 49:8
h. deviseth his way, 75:16
h., full of evil and madness, 144:1
h. is deceitful, 105:11
h. is divided, 108:2
h. rejoiceth in the Lord, 82:16
h. was hot, 50:1
he hardened his h., 215:1
he that trusteth his own h., 50:7
his h.'s desire, 96:6
keep your h. with vigilance, 50:2
let not your h. be troubled, 65:1
merry h., cheerful countenance, 50:4
merry h. doeth good, 96:12
merry h. hath a continual feast, 96:11
my h. panted, 64:12
out of abundance of the h., the mouth speaketh, 209:4
prepare thine h., 86:1
sorrow of the h., 50:4
sound heart is life of flesh, 98:1
them that are of a broken h., 140:10
with my whole h. and whole soul, 209:2
hearts: Lord searches all h., 86:11
Lord trieth h., 75:17
heaven: except ye become as children, shall not enter kingdom of h., 24:14
gate of heaven, 112:7
great is your reward in h., 15 (cont. from page 14)
h. and the h. of heavens, 159:4
h. is my throne, earth my footstool, 244:11
kingdom of h. is at hand, 99:4
kingdom of h. is like a mustard seed, 99:5
kingdom of h. is like a net, 188:4
kingdom of h. is like unto a treasure, 99:6
man can receive nothing except from h., 76:17
new h. and a new earth, 244:10
treasures in h., 99:2
heavens: let the h. be glad, 96:9
the h. declare the glory of God, 100:7
the h. shall be rolled . . . as a scroll, 44:11
the h. were opened, 81:7
hell: h. hath enlarged herself, 101:6
out of the belly of h., 125:6
thou [Lucifer] shalt be brought down to h., 143:6
help: is not my h. in me, 202:4
none to h., 140:4
very present h., 75:7
helped: they h. every one his neighbor, 227:1
help meet: I will make him a h. m., 2:13
hem: touch the h. of his garment, 150:7
herbs: bitter h., 168:7
dinner of h., 141:1
heritage: goodly h., 61:8
Herod: H. . . . was troubled, 117:11
hewers: h. of wood and drawers of water, 242:5

Hezekiah: H. had exceeding much riches, 194:6
hide: why dost thou h. thyself, 85:6
why dost thou h. thy face, 85:7
woe to those who h. from the Lord, 201:6
highways: go out into the h. and hedges, 104:4
go ye therefore into the h., 104:2
hills: mine eyes to the h., 159:13
him: in h. we live and move, 76:19
with h. is wisdom and strength, 75:4
Hip and thigh: he smote them h. and t., 233:9
hireling: the h. fleeth, 191:1
hiss: they h. and wag their head, 187:5
hold: ye shall h. your peace, 170:6
holier: I am h. than thou, 202:6
Holofernes: she came to . . . H.'s head, 36:8
holy: h., h., h., is the Lord of hosts, 6 (cont. from p. 5)
h., h., h., Lord God Almighty, which was, and is, 6:6
the place . . . is h. ground, 155:11
Holy Ghost: he shall baptize you with the H.G., 14:4
receive ye the H.G., 11:9
they were filled with the H.G., 18:9
we have not heard whether there be any H.G., 14:5
your body is the temple of the H.G., 18:9
home: God gives desolate a h., 102:6
man goeth to his long h., 42:2
man who strays from his h., 102:10
show piety at h., 25:8
stay at home, 170:12
honest: forceful are h. words, 103:3
honor: h. all men, 190:7
h. shall uphold the humble, 103:6
h. thy father, mother, 221:5
stain in thine h., 103:6
honored: h. in their generations, 94:2
hook: my h. in thy nose, 86:10 (note)
hope: hope deferred, 103:8
h. of the ungodly, 103:10
h. to the end, 103:14
prisoners of h., 103:9
thou art my h., 88:12
we are saved by h., 103:13
what is my strength that I should h., 44:2
who . . . believed in h., 103:12
hopeless: you did not say, it is h., 173:7
horror: h. overwhelms me, 64:8
horse: behold, a pale h., 43:4
hast thou given the h. his strength, 8:5
h. prepared against . . . battle, 8:3
horseleach: the h. hath two daughters, 24:5
horses: loud beat the h.'s hoofs, 8:3
some trust chariots, some in h., 9:1
they were as fed h., 205:3
hospitality: given to h., 104:5
hour: h. your Lord doth come, 129:2
the h. is at hand, 120:2
watch with me one h., 119:6
house: be not as a lion in thy h., 102:12
better quiet than a h. full of strife, 102:8
by wisdom a h. is built, 102:9
h. divided against itself, 32:7
h. of merchandise, 28:8
h. of mirth, 101:1
h. of the Lord, 28:3
h. of prayer for all peoples, 28:5
if a man know not how to rule his own h., 31:4
I have chosen and sanctified this h., 220:2
I have hallowed this h., 220:1
in my Father's h., many mansions, 99:10
my h. shall be a h. of prayer, 28:7
set thine h. in order, 41:5
woe to them that join h. to h., 181:7
houses: build ye h., 102:11
they dig through h., 36:3

houses: (*continued*)
they shall build h., 243:9
h. of ivory shall perish, great h. shall end, 193:1
how: h. are the mighty fallen, 234:3
howl: h. ye, the day of the Lord is at hand, 128:10
human: speaking in h. terms, 219:9
humble: h. thyself, 106:6
prayer of the h., 106:7
he that shall h. himself, 186:3
humbly: walk h. with thy God, 230:18
humility: before honor is h., 106:5
hunger: slain with sword better than slain with h., 176:10
they shall h. no more, 199:4
hungry: he hath filled the h., 97:6
I was h. and you gave me food, 73:3
to h. soul, bitter is sweet, 176:6
hunter: a mighty h., 161:11
husband: Esau was a cunning h., 111:8
h. shall rule over thee, 3:7
Husbandman: h. waiteth for the precious fruit, 63:9
hypocrite: the joy of the h., 53:10
what is the hope of the h., 106:10
hypocrites: do not sound a trumpet, as the h. do, 73:2
h.!, whited sepulchres, 106:12
scribes and Pharisees, h., 106:12

I: behold I come quickly, 130:1
here am I, send me, 182:5
I am a stranger and a sojourner, 213:9
I am fearfully, wonderfully made, 105:6
I am God, 78:4
I am he, 78:6
I am he that liveth, 123:7
I am holier than thou, 202:6
I am meek and lowly in heart, 113:10
I am not as other men, 178:2
I am poor and needy, 175:13
I am that I am, 77:14
I am the Alpha and the Omega, 78:13
I am the bread of life, 115:8
I am the door, 116:5
I am the first and last, 78:7
I am the good shepherd, 116:7; 116:8
I am the light of the world, 116:3
I am the Lord, 78:8
I am the Lord thy God, 221:2
I am the resurrection and the life, 60:9
I am the vine, 116:18
I am the way, 116:17
I am thy shield, thy reward, 77:12
I am what I am, 107:1
I am with thee, will keep thee, 112:5
I am with you always, 188:7
I and my Father are one, 116:11
I bore you on eagles' wings, 87:13
I even I am he, 78:3
I have been a stranger in a strange land, 213:10
I know my own, 116:8
I know the things [in] your mind, 87:1
I know thy abode, 86:10
I lay down my life for the sheep, 116:9
I make peace, create evil, 35:2
I must be about my father's business, 119:4
I shall not be moved, 75:8
it is I, be not afraid, 114:1
I was hungry and you gave me food, 73:3
I will be with thee, 88:4
I will be his father, 88:5
I will come again, 99:11
I will feed my flock, 89:1
I will seek my sheep, 88:13
yet a little while I am with you, 121:8
idle: they learn to be i., 20:11

idleness: i. teacheth evil, 107:2
idols: i. of silver, i. of gold, 107:6
i. of the heathen, 107:5
i. like scarecrows, 107:3
ignorant: be not i. of any thing, 108:6
image: God created man in his own i., 2:10
thou shalt not make any graven i., 221:2
imagination: i. of man's heart, 104:10
Immanuel: a virgin shall call his name I., 107:8
immortal: God created man to be i., 105:14
immortality: mortal must put on i., 191:10
the treasure of i., 98:9
yet is their hope full of i., 231:2
increase: when goods i., 175:2
inherit: he shall i. the wind, 102:7
they shall i. the land, 27:9
inheritance: good man leaveth an i., 153:1
iniquity: bond of i., 208:14
I was shapen in i., 207:7
injustice: do no i. in judgment, 133:9
instruction: he who heeds i., 4:3
fools despise i., 137:3
let your soul receive i., 137:1
poverty and shame to him that refuseth i., 137:5
instruments: David . . . played . . . on all manner of i., 157:2
interpretations: i. belong to God, 48:2
inventions: they have sought out many i., 200:2
iron: whose stones are i., 21:7
Israel: beauty of I. is slain, 41:2
God spake unto I. in . . . the night, 111:6
hear, O I., 74:4
I. shall be a proverb and a byword, 162:10
I. then shall dwell in safety, 21:8
I will dwell among children of I., 26:7
the Lord shall smite I., 27:5
thy name shall be no more Jacob but I., 111:4
Jacob: God said . . . J., J., 111:6
J. loved Rachel, 111:1
J. served seven years for Rachel, 111:2
J. . . . wrestled with a man, 111:3
J. . . . yielded up the ghost, 111:7
Jael: J. . . . said, turn in my lord, fear not, 209:5
J. . . . smote the nail into his temples, 209:5
jaw: with the j. of an ass have I slain 1,000, 233:10
jealous: he is a j. God, 74:8
I . . . am a j. God, 78:2
jealousy: ear of j. heareth all things, 112:10
j. is the rage of a man, 112:9
Jehovah: by J. was I not known, 78:1
J. is everlasting strength, 77:9
in the name of the Lord J. is everlasting strength J.-shalom, 74:9
Jeroboam: J. was a mighty man, 236:13
Jerusalem: I will rejoice in J., 29:9
new J., 129:11
pray for the peace of J., 28:2
silver and gold at J. as plenteous as stones, 194:5
Jeshurun: J. waxed fat, 66:6
Jesse: son of J. the Bethlehemite, 38:10
rod out of the stem of J., 148:1
Jesus: J., author and finisher of our faith, 117:2
J. called a little child unto him, 24:14
J. Christ the same . . . forever, 117:3
J. increased in wisdom and stature, 119:5
J. . . . walking on the sea, 150:6
J. wept, 151:9
J. . . . yielded up the ghost, 121:2
put ye on the Lord J. Christ, 231:5

Jesus: (*continued*)
this is J. THE KING OF THE JEWS, 120:11
thou shalt call his name J., 117:9
jewels: thy cheeks are comely with rows of j., 194:8
Jezebel: J . . . painted her face, 5:1
Job: a man whose name was J., 123:8
the Lord answered J. out of the whirlwind, 124:1
blessed latter end of J., 124:4
the patience of J., 124:5
John: I J. . . . was on the isle, Patmos, 124:6
give me J. Baptist's head in a charger, 125:1
J. the Baptist, preaching in the wilderness, 124:8
man sent from God, whose name was J., 115 (cont. from p. 114)
Jonah: a great fish to swallow up J., 125:5
it vomited out J., 125:7
Jonathan: J. . . . gave [his robe] to David, 40:6
my brother J. 40:7
Saul and J. were lovely, 199:6
soul of J. was knit with the soul of David, 40:5
Jordan: the people passed clean over J., 126:8
Joseph: I am J. your brother, 126:6
Israel loved J., 125:8
J. dreamed a dream, 126 (cont. from p. 125)
J. knew his brethren, 126:5
J. my son is still alive, 126:7
J. said, am I in place of god, 68:10
the angel of the Lord appeared to J. in a dream, 118:2
they stript J. out of his coat, 126:2
Joshua: J. said unto the people, shout, 126:9
journey: take your j., 223:8
joy: fullness of j., 75:5
j. cometh in morning, 96:7
shout for j., 96:8
the sons of God shouted for j., 96:5
joyfulness: j. prolongeth days, 98:4
jubilee: the 50th year . . . shall be a j., 127:2
Judah: the rivers of J. shall flow with waters, 129:4
Judas: J. said, is it I, 127:4
judge: an understanding heart to judge thy people, 128:1
go not to law with a j., 128:3
how long will you j. unjustly?, 130:5
I came not to j. the world, 198:9
I j. no man, 128:8
I will be no j. of such matters, 93:7
j. of all the earth, 130:2
j. not . . . condemn not, and . . . forgive, 223:7
j. not that ye be not judged, 128:4
j. not for man but for the Lord, 128:2
Lord shall j. ends of the earth, 79:5
Lord was with the j., 127:6
O that I were a j., 127:7
judgement: every work into j., 79:8
let j. run down as waters, 130:9
judgements: j. of the Lord are true, 79:6
judges: Lord raised up j., 127:6
judgest: wherein thou j. another, 128:9
just: a j. weight and balance, 103:5
blessings upon the j., 130:6
have nothing to do with that j. man, 174:7
he that ruleth must be j., 93:1
just, upright man is laughed to scorn, 230:4
that which is j. shalt thou follow, 130:3
justified: how can a man be j. with God, 197:5

keep: I am with thee, and will k. thee, 112:5
keeper: am I my brother's k., 21:2
kettle: how agree the k. and . . . pot, 32:6

keys: k. of the kingdom of heaven, 173:9
kid: do not seethe a k. in its mother's milk, 68:8
kill: I k. and make alive, 78:3
intendest thou [Moses] to k. us, 155:8
thou shalt not kill, 221:6
kind: all flesh consorteth according to k., 105:15
be ye k. to one another, 69:6
who is k. benefits himself, 72:3
kindly: Lord deal k. with you, 17:5
kindness: withholds k. from friend, 69:11
king: a new k. in Egypt, 155:1
art thou the K. of the Jews, 120:5
blessed be the K. that cometh, 114:11
curse not the k., 177:3
God save the k., 92:12
k. shall reign in righteousness, 148:4
k. that faithfully judges the poor,. 93:2 (note)
k.'s wrath, 176:19
no k. had any other beginning, 52:5
no k. in Israel, 92:10
shall see the k. in his beauty, 248:6
thy k. cometh . . . upon an ass, 114:6; 148:5
today a k., tomorrow die, 177:5
we will have a k., 92:11
where word of a k. is, is power, 177:2
wise k. scattereth the wicked, 93:4
kingdom: except ye become as children, shall not enter k. of heaven, 24:14
k. of God, in power, 177:9
k. of God is within you, 76:14
k. of heaven is at hand, 99:4
k. of heaven is like a grain of mustard seed, 99:5
k. of heaven is like unto treasure, 99:6
k. of heaven is like unto a net, 188:4
seek first the k. of God, 231:4
thine is the k., 86:5
thine is the k., power, glory, 140:7
thy k. come, 140:7
what can he [David] have more but the k. 39:5
kingdoms: devil . . . showed him [Jesus] all the k., 177:7
man . . . that did shake k., 143:7
kings: k. came and fought, 233:4
many k. have sat upon the ground, 216:4
not for k. to drink wine, 237:3
kiss: let him k. me, 142:11
whomsoever I shall k. . . . hold him fast, 120:3
kissed: he came to J. and k. him, 120:4
know: I k. my own, my own k. me, 116:8
I k. thy abode, 86:10
k. things come into your mind, 87:1
to k. and to search, 200:1
to k. good and evil, 3:10
to k. wisdom, to k. madness and folly, 58:6
we did not k., 190:10
we k. in part, 183:1
knowing: ye shall be as gods, k. good and evil, 3:2
knowledge: a God of k., 79:4
he hath given me k. of the things that are, 200:4
k. puffeth up, 137:14
k. that thou hast not, 137:10
people destroyeth for lack of k. 137:9
prudent man conceals k., 183:5
who increaseth k., increaseth sorrow, 137:6
windy k., 218:3
wise lay up k., 137:4

labor: all things are full of l., 228:7
come unto me all ye that l., 243:13
l. not to be rich, 243:1
l. of love, 244:4

labor: (*continued*)
my heart rejoiced in l., 243:6
reward according to l., 244:2
what profit hath a man of all of his l., 228:6
laborer: l. worthy of his hire, 243:14
laborers: harvest plenteous, l. few, 63:7
l. together, 189:5
laboring: sleep of a l. man is sweet, 210:6
ladder: he dreamed, and behold a ladder, 112:4
labors: glorious is the fruit of good l. 2:4
[the dead] may rest from their l., 43:5
lad: the l. cannot leave his father, 23:6
lamb: behold the L. of God, 115:2
brought as a l. to the slaughter, 203:1
where is the l. for a burnt offering, 109:9
white in the blood of the l., 199:3
wolf also shall dwell with the l., 171:5
lame: l. walk, 150:4
lamp: thou art my l., 79:10
word is a l. unto my feet, 79:12
land: God bringeth thee into a good l., 21:7
he who tills his l., 243:3
l. flowing with milk and honey, 21:6
l. is defiled, 51:7
l. is mine, 51:8
l. mourns, 51:11
l. of corn and wine, 21:8
l. will yield increase, 62:9
shalt see l. . . . shalt not go thither, 58:3
six years sow l. . . . seventh year . . . let it rest, 62:4
thy seed I will give this l., 26:2
ye shall not pollute the l., 51:9
landmark: remove not the ancient l., 133:12 (note)
shall not remove neighbor's l., 133:12
language: confound the l. of all the earth, 14:2
every man heard . . . in his own l., 172:10
sweet l. will multiply friends, 218:16
whole earth was of one l., 132:1
last: the l. shall be first, 99:7; 193:4
the l. state is worse, 55:6
laugh: God hath made me to l., 133:1
he that sitteth in the heavens shall l., 133:3
laughter: excessive l., 12:2
feast is made for l., 67:6
fill your mouth with l., 133:2
fool lifteth up his voice with l., 133:7
l., it is mad, 133:4
l. of the fool, 133:6
law: a l. unto themselves, 134:8
God forbid we forsake the l., 134:4
go not to l. with a judge, 128:3
his delight is in the law of the Lord, 230:6
if any man sue thee at the l., 134:5
I will put my l. in their hearts, 28:1 (note)
no l., no transgression, 134:9
one jot or tittle shall in no wise pass from the law, 102:5
one manner of l. [for all], 133:10
the l. is good, 134:12
the l. is light, 133:13
the Lord will magnify the l., 134:2
trusteth in the l., 134:3
ye go to l. with one another, 134:10
lawful: all things are l. for me, 183:10
l. for me to do what I will, 134:6
lawlessness: l. takes away lives, 133:14
lawyers: woe to you l., 136:6
Lazarus: a certain beggar named L., 194:1
L., come forth, 151:10
man . . . named L., 151:5
send L., 194:3

Leah: L. was tender eyed, 111:1
learn: l. to do well, 130:7
learning: l. doth make thee mad, 137:13
wise man will . . . increase l., 238:10
least: I am l. in my father's house, 106:4
faithful in that which is l., 210:10
the l. of these my brethren, 114:8
leaven: a little l., 68:2
leaves: green l., some fall, some grow, 71:5
left: let not l. hand know what right doeth, 73:2
Legion: my name is L., 46:9
leisure: wisdom . . . cometh by . . . leisure, 138:1
lend: l. not unto him that is mightier, 19:1
lend him sufficient for his need, 175:4
lendeth: he l. and tomorrow . . . ask it again, 19:3
length: l. of days is in her [wisdom's] right hand, 239 (cont. from p. 238)
leopard: can . . . the leopard [change] his spots, 22:3
l. shall lie down with the kid, 171:5
leper: there came a l., 149:6
leprosy: when the plague of l. is in a man, 206:3
let: l. my people go, 156:2
l. there be light, 33:10
l. us now praise famous men, 94:1
letter: l. killeth, spirit giveth life, 189:6
leviathan: draw out l. with a hook, 8:10
l. king over children of pride, 9 (note, cont. from p. 8)
lewd: l. fellows of the baser sort, 55:11
liars: all men are l., 105:5
liberal: l. man will be enriched, 72:6
lie: a man accustomed to l., 43:13
ye shall not . . . l. to one another, 103:2
you shall not l. with a male, 203:6
lies: no man who utters l. . . . in my presence, 43:6
with l. ye made the righteous sad, 43:12
you whitewash with l., 33:8
life: all a man hath will he give for l., 138:5
book of l., 139:9
choose l., 25:9 (note)
few and evil the days of my l., 138:2
he that findeth l. shall lose it, he that loseth l. shall find it, 113:8
he that loseth l. for my sake, 146:1
he that loveth [wisdom] loveth l., 240:4
I am come that they might have l., 116:6
I am the bread of l., 115:8
I am the resurrection and the l., 60:9
I hated l., 138:12
I loathe my l., 138:8
I lay down my l., 121:9
l. and good, death and evil, 25:9
one entrance into l., 52:6
strait gate, narrow way which leadeth unto l., 198:4
take no thought for your l., 246:1
thou shalt give l. for l., 135:2
way of l. and way of death, 25:10
what is your l., 139:8
light: a l. of the Gentiles, 169:12
and the l. shineth in the darkness, 115 (cont. from p. 114)
everlasting l., 79:15
God is light, 80:1
he was a burning, shining l., 125:3
I am the l. of the world, 116:3
let there be l., 33:10
l. is sweet, 100:10
l. [of wisdom] never goeth out, 239:19
put on the armor of l., 231:5
the light shineth in the darkness, 115 (cont. from p. 114)
the Lord is my l., 79:11
the people . . . have seen a great l., 79:3

light: (*continued*)
to give l. to them that sit in darkness, 198:6
wiser than children of l., 240:7
ye are children of l., 231:8
ye are the l. of the world, 94:3
yet a little while the l. is with you, 116:15
lights: l. in the firmament, 100:5
lilies: l. of the field, 71:2
lion: l. hath roared, 10:7
lions: angel . . . shut the l.' mouths, 37:7
cast him into the den of l., 37:5
my soul is among l., 37:1
the l. had mastery of them, 37:8 (note)
went in haste unto the den of l., 37:6
young l. suffer want, 9:2
young l. roar after their prey, 9:4
lips: flattereth with his l., 65:5
he that shutteth his l. is deemed a man of understanding, 207:2
that which is gone out of thy l., 187:11
thy l. drop as the honeycomb, 205:1
little: a l. while, ye shall not see me, 121:8
better is l., 193:7
despise not one of these l. ones, 25:1
l. one shall become 1,000, 147:2
whoso shall offend one of these l. ones, 24:14
live: because I l., ye shall l., 123:1
in him we l. and move, 76:19
I would not l. for ever, 138:8
we shall l. in his sight, 198:2
liveth: none of us l. to himself, 139:6
living: a God of the l., 76:15
l. dog better than dead lion, 139:3
Lo: L. the winter is past, 200:9
loaves: five barley l., 210:11
five l. and two fishes, 150:5
locusts: hath the l. eaten, 63:5
l. and wild honey, 124:9
l. have no king, 9:8
lodging: l. place of wayfaring men, 52:13
loins: let your l. be girded, 229:7
lonely: I am like a l. bird, 140:3
long: l. prologue, short story, 246:10
Lord how l., 85:8
Lord: all that the L. hath spoken, 83:7
anything too hard for the L., 77:13
a whirlwind of the L., 76:5
blessed the man that feareth the L., 82:7
blessed the man that trusteth the L., 90:12
bless ye the L., 85:4
cleave unto the L., 83:3
eyes of the L., 87.2
fear of the L. driveth away sins, 82:11
fear of the Lord is a crown of wisdom, 82:10
fear of the Lord is the beginning of his love, 82:12
fear of the L. is the beginning of wisdom, 82:4 (note)
fear of the L. is wisdom, 82:4
fear the L. and serve him, 82:3
good to give thanks to the L., 179:16
he is L. of Lords, 117:8
he that cometh in the name of the L., 17:8
holy is the l. of hosts, 6 (cont. from p. 5)
I am the L., that is my name, 78:5
I am the L., there is none else, 78:8
I the L. am thy Savior, 197:13
I will call upon the L., 81:12
I will praise thee O L., 84:9
I will sing unto the L., 56:9
let the earth fear the L., 82:6
let us go into the house of the L., 28:3
L., art our father, 79:1
L., how excellent thy name, 84:8
L., how long, 85:8
L., none like thee, 84:2
L., thou hast been our dwelling place, 75:11

Lord: (*continued*)
L., why dost thou cast me off, 85:7
love the L., 82:17
magnify the L., 84:10
make a joyful noise unto the L., 84:13
make melody to L., 84:5
my heart rejoiceth in the L., 82:16
my soul longs for the courts of the L., 98:7
not everyone that saith L., L. shall enter heaven, 99:3
O L., be gracious, 179:11
O L., my strength, 76:4
O L., none like thee, 84:7
O L. of hosts, 90:10
O L., hear, forgive, 179:13
O L., thou hast searched me, 86:14
O L., thou lover of souls, 87:11
praise the L. for his goodness, 84:14
praise ye the L. from the heavens, 84:15
prosperity and adversity come of the L., 76:11
secret things belong unto the L., 192:1
seek the L., 77:7
serve the L. with all your heart, 83:10
serve the L. with gladness, 83:12
six things doth the L. hate, 54:7
surely the L. is in this place, 112:6
the day of the L. is at hand, 128:10
the day of the L. cometh, 128:11
the eyes of the L., 87:2
the glory of the L. shall be revealed, 86:8
the glory of the L. shall endure, 86:7
the judgments of the L., 79:6
the L. also will be a refuge, 88:6
the L. be with thee, 17:6
the L. bless thee and keep thee, 17:2
the L. deal kindly with you, 17:5
the L. directeth his steps, 75:16
the L. gave, and L. hath taken away, 90:1
the L. God, merciful and gracious, 74:2
the L. . . . give thee peace, 17:2
the L. heareth the poor, 175:12
the L. is a consuming fire, 74:3
the L. is a man of war, 81:9
the L. is full of compassion, 76:10
the L. is good, 75:14
the L. is good unto them that wait, 86:4
the L. is my defense, 74:10 (note)
the L. is my helper, 33:5
the L. is my light and my salvation, 79:11
the L. is my rock, 74:10
the L. is my shepherd, 88:7
the L. is my strength and shield, 77:8.
the L. is my strength and song, 56:9
the L. is peace, 74:9 (note)
the L. is righteous, 74:11
the L. is risen, 122:10
the L. is the King of glory, 86:6
the L. is with you, 83:4
the L. knoweth the thoughts of men, 86:13
the Lord of hosts, 86:6
the L. our God be with us, 178:10
the L. reigneth, 75:13
the L. reproves him whom he loves, 223:12
the L. rideth a swift cloud, 66:1
the L. searches all hearts, 86:11
the L. shall be thy everlasting light, 79:15
the L. shall cover him, 88:2
the L. shall fight for you, 170:6
the L. shall judge the ends of the earth, 79:5
the L. shall judge his people, 130:4
the L. shall preserve thee from all evil, 88:8
the L. shall reign for ever, 74:1
the L. shall rule over you, 92:9
the L. sitting upon a throne, 5:9

Lord: (*continued*)
the L. spake unto Moses, 80:10
the L. thundered, 81:2.
the L. trieth hearts, 75:17
the L. weighteth spirits, 79:7
the L. will be a refuge, 88:6
the L. will destroy the house of the proud, 180:4
the L. will lighten my darkness, 79:10
the L. will magnify the law, 134:2
the mercy of the L. is from everlasting to everlasting, 87:10
the secret of the L., 82:5
the spirit of the L. filleth the world, 244:14
the will of the L., 64:3
the works of the L. are exceeding good, 90:3
they are a gift for the L., 30:8
thine, O L., is the greatness, 86:5
thou shalt fear the L., 82:2
thou shalt love the L., thy God, 82:14; 222:5
thou shalt not tempt the L., 220:4
thy right hand O L. is become glorious, 81:10
trust in the L., 90:9
trust ye in the L. forever, 90:11
what L. saith, 83:8
when a man's ways please the L., 171:1
who hath known the mind of the L., 77:2
who is like unto thee, O L., 84:3
who is on the L.'s side, 83:2
whom the L. loveth he chasteneth, 224:8
whoso feareth the L., 82:13
why stand afar off O L., 85:6
works of the L. are good, 90:3
ye shall not tempt the L., 82:1

lost: I will seek that which is l., 89:1

lot: cast in thy l. among us, 226:12

Lot: L. dwelled in cities of the plain, 1:3
remember L.'s wife, 45:4

loud: a l. voice in the morning, 17:10

love: affectioned with brotherly l., 142:3
arise my l., 201 (cont. from p. 200)
bands of l., 141:2
better a dinner with herbs where l. is, 141:1
everlasting l., 141:6
God is l., 142:7
good to them that l. God, 82:18
greater l. hath no man, 122:1
how fair is thy love, 204:12
I have loved thee with an everlasting l., 141:6
labor of l., 244:4
let brotherly l. continue, 142:6
l. better than wine, 142:11
l. covers all offenses, 140:11
l. . . . in deed and in truth, 73:9
l. is the fulfilling of the law, 142:5
l. one another, 141:12; 142:4
l. the Lord with all thy heart, soul, might, 74:4
l. thy neighbor, 222:5
l. your enemies, 141:8
no fear in l., 142:6
[nothing] shall separate us from the l. of God, 87:5
sick with l., 67:7
such as be faithful in l. shall abide with him, 90:13
take our fill of l., 142:10
the l. of Christ, 116:19
them that l. him be as the sun, 82:15
thou hast left thy first l., 142:7
thou shalt l. the Lord thy God, 82:14, 222:5
thy l. to me was wonderful, 40:7
ye are my disciples, if ye have l. one to another, 11:7

loved: behold, how he l. him, 151:9
he l. them unto the end, 116:16
she l. much, 141:10

lover: l. and friend far from me, 140:2
thou lover of souls, 87:11

lovers: thy l. have forgotten thee, 140:5
loveth: I found him whom my soul l., 204:10
I sought him whom my soul l., 204:9
he that l. [wisdom] l. life, 240:4
whom the Lord l. he chasteneth, 224:8
low: every mountain shall be made l., 192:7
loyalty: what is desired is l., 142:14
Lucifer: L., son of the morning, 143:5
lucre: filthy l., 31:3
Luke: L., the beloved physician, 47:13
lukewarm: thou art l., 146:8
lust: lust not after her beauty in thine heart, 204:2
lusts: abstain from fleshly l., 205:7
lying: hate and abhor l., 43:7
l. lips are abomination, 43:9
lyre: David took the l., 38:12
praise the Lord with the l., 157:6

mad: I am not m., 170:4
made: all things were m. by him, 114:12
God saw everything he had m., 34:7
I am fearfully and wonderfully m., 105:6
m. heaven and earth, 76:6
madness: m. is in their heart, 144:1
to know m. and folly, 58:6
magnify: m. the Lord, 84:10
my soul doth m. the Lord, 146:6
maid: m. is not dead but sleepeth, 150:3
mammon: cannot serve God and m., 83:14
mammon of unrighteousness, 183:9
man: a m. in whom the Spirit of God is, 229:16
a m. of strife, a m. of contention, 112:11
a m. shall be a hiding place from the wind, 197:10
a m. wise in his own conceit, 180:7
as for m., his days are like grass, 105:4
behold the m., 122:2
be strong, shew thyself a m., 23:10
day that God created m., 104:8
first m. is . . . earthy, 106:2
God created m. in his own image, 2:10
God formed m. of the dust, 2:11
happy the m. God reproves, 223:11
in the image of God made he m., 134:13
I will destroy m. whom I have created, 161:12
I will not again curse the ground for m.'s sake, 162:7
m. doth know his time, 42:1
m. doth not live by bread only, 74:5
m. goeth to his long home, 42:2
m. hath no preeminence above a beast, 9:9
m. is born unto trouble, 223:10
m. shall not live by bread alone, 180:2
m. that did shake kingdoms, 143:7
m. that is born of a woman, 104:12
m. that is a worm, 104:13
never m. spoke like this m., 116:2
the just, upright m., 230:4
the m. that feareth the Lord, 82:7
the new m., 189:7
thou art the m., 94:10
way of a m. with a maid, 140:1
what is m. that thou art mindful of him, 105:1
what is m. that thou dost make so much of him, 104:11
what manner of m. is this, 113:5
when I became a m. I put away childish things, 25:6
manger: she . . . laid him in a m., 119:2
manna: did eat m. forty years, 57:7
manners: evil communications corrupt good m., 70:10 (note)
mansions: in my father's house are many m., 99:10
mantle: m. of Elijah, 49:5
many: m. are called, few chosen, 99:7

march: m. on, my soul, 233:5
they shall m. every one, 235:10
mark: I press toward the m., 31:9
Lord set a m. upon Cain, 21:5
m. of the beast, 20:7
marriage: m. in Cana, 151:1
marry: better to m. than to burn, 145:11
in the resurrection they neither m., 191:8
Martha: woman named M., 145:12
Mary: fear not, M., 146:3
M. hath chosen that good part, 145:12
Mary Magdalene: came M.M. and the other Mary, 122:7
masters: no man can serve two m., 143:1
measure: what is the m. of my days, 41:13
with what m. ye mete, 128:4
measured: who hath m. the waters, 35:1
meat: strong m. belongeth to [the old], 68:3
meats: excess of meats, sickness, 67:14
meddles: he who m. in a quarrel, 20:9
meddling: fool will be m., 20:8
medicines: Lord hath created m., 47:9
mediums: do not turn to m., 163:2
meek: blessed are the m., 14:6
m. and lowly in heart, 113:10
m. and quiet spirit, 106:9
mysteries are revealed unto the m., 147:3
the m. shall inherit the earth, 147:1
melody: make m. to Lord, 84:5
make sweet m., 157:11
memorial: some have no m., 42:11
this day shall be a m., 168:11
men: all m. have one entrance into life, 52:6
m. of like passions with you, 11:11
quit yourselves like m., 234:1
mene: m. m., 45:2
merchandise: house of m., 28:8
m. of gold, silver, precious stones, 195:3
merchant: m. . . . loveth to oppress, 19:12
merchants: m. are princes, 19:9
thou hast multiplied thy m., 19:14
mercies: tender m. of the wicked, 9:6
merciful: be ye m., 147:8
blessed are the m., 14:6
mercy: great is his mercy, 87:9
have m. upon me, 178:14
he that hath m. on the poor, 176:2
his m. endureth, 87:7
m. and truth are met together, 197:7
m. . . . from everlasting to everlasting, 87:10
m. is seasonable, 147:6
m., not sacrifice, 78:12
merry: m. heart . . . continual feast, 96:11
m. heart doeth good, 96:12
m. heart, cheerful countenance, 50:4
messenger: I will send my m., 124:7
Michael: M. and his angels fought against the dragon, 6:9
midwives: m. feared God, 148:6
mighty: how are the m. fallen, 234:3
strive not with m. man, 177:4
the bows of the m. men, 176:15
the m. from their seats, 97:6
they were among the m. men, 234:7
mile: whosoever shall compel thee to go a m., 134:5
milk: a land flowing with m. and honey, 21:6
not seethe kid in mother's m., 68:8
millstone: better than a m. were hanged about his neck, 24:14
mind: a sound m., 50:10
who hath known the m. of the Lord, 77:2
ministers: m., a flame of fire, 6:5
miracles: where be all his m., 80:2
mirth: heart fools in house of m., 101:1
I commend mirth, 101:2
miserable: m. comforters are ye, 70:11

misery: you will forget m., 226:2
misfortune: contempt for m., 151:14
mites: she threw in two m., 73:4
money: be not greedy to add m. to m., 153:14
he that hath no m., come, 72:8
love of m. is the root of all evil, 154:3
m. answereth all things, 153:10
thy m. perish with thee, 154:1
moneychangers: Jesus . . . overthrew the tables of the m., 20:3
month: this m. shall be the beginning of months, 168:6
morning: a loud voice early in the m., 17:10
give him the m. star, 213:7
m. stars sang together, 96:5
morrow: take no thought for the m., 70:15
Moses: a new name, Moses, 155:6
he gave unto M. . . . two tables of testimony, 221:15
M. drew near unto the thick darkness, 80:8
M. hid his face, 80:6
M. . . . smote the rock, 58:1
M. stretched out his hand over the sea, 56:5
M. was 120 years, 154:11
M. was very meek, 154:9
M. wrote all the words of the Lord, 221:12
murdered against M., 57:2
not a prophet like unto M., 154:12
the Lord spake unto M., 80:10
then sang M., 56:9
mote: m. . . . in brother's eye, 59:5
mother: as the m., so the daughter, 168:3
behold thy m., 146:7 (note)
be joyful, o thou m., 168:4
despise not thy m. when old, 168:1
forsake not the law of the m., 167:8
he that curseth his father or m., 167:7
he that smiteth his father or m., 167:6
honor thy father and m., 167:5
m. of all living, 3:9
who is my m., 62:2
mother in law: go not empty unto m., 61:7
mount: a thick cloud upon the m., 220:9
the Lord called Moses up to . . . the m., 221:1
mountains: m. shall drop down new wine, 129:4
m. skipped like rams, 148:7
mount Sinai: (note) 220:9
gave unto Moses . . . upon m. S., 221:15
Lord abode upon m. S., 221:14
Lord came down upon m. S., 221:1
mourn: blessed are they that m., 14:6
comfort all that m., 224:1
mourning: into the grave unto my son m., 23:5
mouth: be not rash with thy m., 218:13
his m. is filled with cursing, 54:1
out of thine own m., 136:5
set a watch before my m., 219:1
that which cometh out of the m. defiles, 219:7
your own m. condemns you, 95:1
mouths: out of the m. of babes and sucklings, 23:12
they have m., but they speak not, 107:4
moved: I shall not be m., 75:8
much: m. given, m. required, 190:11
multitudes: m., m., in the valley of decision, 129:3
saw the m., was moved with compassion, 173:5
murderer: a m. from the beginning, 36:9
m. rising with the light, 36:2
m. shall be put to death, 136:1
murderers: soul is wearied because of m., 36:6

mustard: faith as a grain of m. seed, 60:5
my: m. God, why hast thou forsaken me, 44:3; 120:14
myrrh: thy garments smell of m. and aloes, 194:7
mysteries: given unto you to know the m. of the kingdom of heaven, 167:3
m. are revealed to the meek, 147:3
mystery: wisdom of God in a m., 158:2
myths: godless and silly m., 189:8

nail: Jael . . . smote the n. into his temples, 209:5
naked: I was n. and ye clothed me, 73:3
n. . . . and were not ashamed, 3:1
n. came I . . . n. shall I return, 138:4
n. shall he return, 105:8
who told thee that thou wast n., 3:4
name: exalt his n., 85:3
excellent is thy n., 84:8
gathered together in my n., 188:5
good n. better than precious ointment, 190:3 (note)
good n. endureth forever, 190:4
good n. rather to be chosen than riches, 190:3
I have called thee by n., 197:11
I know thee by n., 154:8
I will not blot out his n., 100:3 (note)
n. of the Lord thy God in vain, 221:3
whatsoever Adam called [a] creature, that was the n., 7:17
names: n. of the twelve apostles, 10:9
narrow: n. is the way which leadeth unto life, 198:4
nation: I will make of thee a great n. [also at Jacob], 26:2
n. shall rise against n., 245:5
righteousness exalteth a n., 230:12
thou hast multiplied the n., 175:3
nations: all n. before God are as nothing, 244:9
all n. and kindreds, 245:3
before him shall be gathered all n., 129:8
God hath made of one blood all n., 52:7
he shall judge among the n., 79:9
teach all n., baptizing them, 188:7
the n. are as a drop of a bucket, 244:8
the n. shall be subject to me, 5:4
natures: n. of living creatures, 200:4
naughtiness: bewitching of n., 47:5
the n. of thine heart, 39:1
Nazarene: called a N., 118:5
near: thou art n., 81:5
neck: he stiffened his n., 215:1
need: brother in n., 73:9
unto every man according to n., 182:1
needy: n. shall not always be forgotten, 175:10
poor and n., 175:13
neighbor: bear not hatred to thy n., 160:12
be faithful to n. in poverty, 160:13
better a n. that is near, 160:11
corn of thy n., 62:8
debate thy cause with thy n., 32:4
do not plan evil against n., 160:8
forgive thy n., 69:1
he who belittles his n., 160:9
love thy n. as thyself, 222:5
n.'s landmark, 160:7
who is my n., 91:7 (note)
withdraw foot from n.'s house, 160:10
neither: n. death, nor life, nor angels, 87:5
new: I will do a n. thing, 161:9
n. heavens and a n. earth, 244:10
n. wine into old bottles, 161:10
no n. thing under sun, 228:7
put on the n. man, 189:7
news: good n. from a far country, 161:4
good n. refreshes, 161:3

night: n. of pleasure turned into fear, 64:12
n. is far spent, 154:6
n. is long, 209:8
no n. there, 100:4
nights: n. of misery apportioned to me, 209:7
Nineveh: arise, go to N., 125:4
Noah: God blessed N., 162:8
N. was a just man, 161:13
noise: make joyful n., 84:13
noli: n. me tangere, 123:2
none: none to help, 140:4
nostrils: blast of thy n. waters were gathered, 57:1
not: n. my will, but thine, 83:15
nothing: there is n. too hard for thee, 76:6
we brought n., we carry nothing out, 182:3
now: that which hath been is n., 223:1
number: n. of thy days, 97:7
who can n. the sand, 223:4
nurtured: a man well n., 67:11

obey: o. my voice, 220:8
to o. better than to sacrifice, 83:11
oblations: bring no more vain o., 187:14
old: ask for the o. paths, 168:14
beauty of o. men, 105:7
buried in good o. age, 164:3
cast me not off in o. age, 164:11
have been young, now am o., 164:10
honor . . . the o. man, 164:4
keep the o. and young within thy walls, 152:1
o. and greyheaded, 164:12
o. and stricken in years, 164:6
o. men shall dream dreams, 48:6
olive: in her mouth was an o. leaf, 162:6
Onan: O. . . . spilled [his seed] on the ground, 203:2
one: God hath made of o. blood all nations, 52:7
have we not all o. father, 105:13
not so much as o., 56:8
o. flesh, 3:1; 145:8
o. fold., o. shepherd, 188:8
o. God created us, 52:4
o. shall be taken, 187:8
open: o. rebuke better, 4:6
opinions: how long . . . between two o., 108:1
opportunity: observe the o., 165:3
oppressed: prayer of the o., 166:1
oppression: behold o., 165:9
trust not o., 165:3
o. maketh a wise man mad, 165:7
oppressor: envy not the o., 165:4
order: done decently and in o., 166:3
house in o., 41:5
our: o. Father which art in heaven, 140:7
out: o. of the eater, something to eat, 195:4
o. of the mouths of babes and sucklings, 23:12
overcome: o. evil with good, 55:12
overcometh: to him that o., 100:3
overturn: I will o., o., 192:9
overwise: be not o. in doing business, 20:1
own: he came unto his o., 187:10
ox: as an o. goeth to the slaughter, 204:4
o. knoweth his owner, 10:1

pain: whole creation . . . in p. together, 224:7
why is my pain perpetual, 206:8
pale: behold a p. horse, 43:4
palm: took branches of p. trees, 116:14
palmerworm: p. hath left locust eaten, 63:5
panic: sudden p., 64:10
parables: spake many things in p., 167:2
why speakest thou in p., 167:3
paradise: thou shalt be with me in p., 121:6
part: we know in p., prophecy in p., 183:1

partridge: as the p. sitteth on eggs, 10:6
pass: heaven and earth shall p. away, 114:7
I will p. over you, 168:10
my words shall not p. away, 114:7
passions: men of like p. with you, 11:11
passover: Christ our p., 122:5
it is the Lord's p., 168:8
pastors: p. according to mine heart, 30:13
pastures: green p., 88:7
p. are clothed with flocks, 159:11
paths: ask for the old p., 168:14
patience: in p. possess ye your souls, 169:6
run with p., 169:7
the p. of Job, 124:5
you that have lost p., 169:5
patient: be p., brethren, 169:8
p. in spirit better than proud, 169:3
woe unto you that have lost p., 169:6
Patmos: the isle . . . P., 124:6
Paul: P. said, I was free born, 69:10
pavilions: he made darkness p., 38:2
paweth: he p. in the valley, 8:6
peace: all her [wisdom's] paths are p., 239:1
be in p. with many, 183:7
depart in p., 42:14
follow things which make for p., 172:7
God of peace be with you, 17:12
go in p., 17:7; 170:9
guide our feet into the way of p., 172:3
hold your p., 170:6
I am for p., 32:2
I came not to send p., 193:3
I make p., 35:2
I will give you p., 170:7
Lord, thou wilt ordain p., 171:7
p. be to this house, 17:11
p. be within thy walls, 17:9
p. be with thee, 170:10
p., good will toward men, 119:2
p. I leave with you, 172:4
p., p. to him that is afar off, 171:10
p. which passeth all understanding, 172:8
righteousness and p. have kissed, 197:7
saying, p., p., 171:11
seek p., 170:13
the Lord . . . give thee p., 17:2
the Lord is p., 74:9 (note); 170:8
the Prince of P., 147:10
there shall be p. and truth, 171:9
thou shalt die in p., 42:5
work of righteousness shall be p., 171:8
peaceably: live p. with all men, 172:6
peacemakers: blessed are the p., 14:6
pearls: p. before swine, 228:3
Peniel: Jacob called the name of the place P., 111:5
people: all the p. arose, 173:2
a wise and understanding p., 26:14
comfort ye my p., 173:3
how long will this p. provoke me, 26:10
I shall set the p. in order, 5:4
it is a stiffnecked p., 26:8
I will take you to me for a p., 26:5
let my p. go, 156:2
my p. is risen as an enemy, 193:2
no end of all the p., 175:1
the p. are set on mischief, 172:11
the p. is grass, 173:4
the p. shall rise as a lion, 26:11
the p. that walked in darkness, 79:13
the p. which sat in darkness,
they shall be my p., 28:1
thou shalt not curse the p., 172:12
thy p. shall be my p., 140:9
what shall I do unto this p., 57:8
ye beat my p. to pieces, 165:8
ye shall be my p., 26:9
peoples: an ensign to the p., 148:3
perfect: Asa's heart was p. with the lord, 230:1
be ye therefore p., 231:3

perverse: faithless and p. generation, 71:8
p. generation, 23:7
persecute: when they p. you in this city, 217:1 (note)
persecuted: blessed are they which are p., 15 (cont. from p. 14)
person: worthless p., 54:6
persuaded: fully p. in his own mind, 32:10
Peter: P. remembered the word of Jesus, 174:2
rise, P., 68:9 (note)
thou art P., 173:9
Pharisee: a P. and a publican, 178:2
I am a P., son of a P., 170:3
the P. prayed thus, 178:2
Pharisees: scribes and P., hypocrites, 106:12
the righteousness of the scribes and the P., 99:1
Pharaoh: the daughter of the P., 155:4
the dream of the P. is one, 126:3
Philistine: David . . . smote the P., 39:3
David . . . stood over the P., 39:4
physician: fall into hand of the p., 47:10
honor a p., 47:8
is there no p. there, 47:7
Luke, the beloved p., 47:13
p., heal thyself, 47:12
whole need not a p., 47:11
physicians: worthless p., 47:6
pierced: whom they have p., 122:4 (note)
piety: learn first to show p. at home, 25:8
Pilate: P. saith, what is truth, 225:5
pillar: p. of cloud, . . . p. of fire, 56:4
she became a p. of salt, 210:15
pillars: the p. of the earth are the Lord's, 244:7
piped: people p. with pipes, 157:3
pit: bottomless p., 102:3
they . . . cast him [Joseph] into a p., 126:2
whoso diggeth a p., 2:2
pitch: he that toucheth p., 55:4
pity: he had no p., 94:10 (note)
who hath p. unto the poor lendeth to Lord, 176:4
planted: I have p. . . . but God gave the increase, 63:8
pleasure: he that loveth p. shall be poor, 100:11
make a test of p., 100:12
Pleiades: canst thou bind the influences of P., 213:1
plow: no one who puts his hand to the p. and looks back, 31:7
plowshares: swords into p., 171:4
p. into swords, 171:4 (note)
pollute: ye shall not p. the land, 51:9
poor: better the life of a p. man, 108:4
blessed are the p. in spirit, 14:6
blessed he who considers the p., 175:11
defraud not p. of living, 176:11
fallow ground of the p., 176:1
giveth unto p. shall not lack, 176:7
he raiseth up the p., 175:8
he saveth the p., 175:9
he shall judge the p., 93:2
he that hath hath mercy on the p., 176:2
he who hath pity upon the p., 176:4
he who oppresses a p. man, 176:3
I am p. and needy, 175:13
Lord heareth the p., 175:12
p. man honored for his skill, 193:10
p. man is thrust away by his friends, 193:12
p. man's wisdom despised, 176:9
p., yet making many rich, 31:1
pretends to be p., 152:12
rob not the p., 165:5
sell that thou hast and give to the p., 188:6
the p. always with you, 176:13

poor: (*continued*)
the p. and the maimed, 104:3
the p. is hated, 193:6
the p. shall never cease, 175:6
the rights of the p., 176:8
thou hast been a strength to the p., 76:2
whoso stoppeth ears at cry of the p., 176:5
with righteousness shall he judge the p., 148:2
ye . . . grind the faces of the p., 165:8
possible: with God all things are p., 76:13
pottage: feed me . . . that same red pottage, 111:9
Jacob gave Esau p. of lentiles, 112:2
potter: hath not the p. power, 85:10
poverty: neither p. nor riches, 153:20
power: all this p. will I give thee, 46:1
give not . . . p. over thee while thou livest, 108:5
no p. but of God, 177:7
p. belongs to God, 176:17
pride of your p., 176:14
praise: I will p. thee, 84:9
let another man p. thee, 17:14
p. and exalt him, 85:4
p. famous men, 94:1
p. him heavens of heavens, 15:84
p. him with trumpet, psaltry, harp, timbrel, dance, 85:1
p. the Lord with the lyre, 157:6
p: ye the Lord, 84:15
sing a song of p., 157:15
pray: p. without ceasing, 178:5
two men went into temple to p., 178:2
watch and p., 220:6
when ye p., use not repetitions, 177:13
prayed: the Pharisee p. thus, 178:2
prayer: hear my p., 179:4
house of p. for all peoples, 28:5
whatsoever ye ask in p., 178:1
prayest: when thou p., be not as hypocrites, 177:12
preach: p. good tidings to the meek, 30:12
p. the gospel, 11:5
p. the gospel to the poor, 114:10
precept: p. upon p., 137:8
precious: p. things of heaven . . . p. fruits . . . p. things of the earth, 159:6
every p. stone was thy covering, 195:1
predestinate: he also did p., 198:11
prepare: p. ye the way of the Lord, 182:6
present: p. in spirit, 1:6
press: p. toward the mark, 31:9
pretends: one man p. to be rich, another p. to be poor, 152:12
prey: have they not divided the p., 233:6
pride: children of p., 9 (note, cont. from p. 8)
I will break the p. of your power, 176:14
p. goeth before destruction, 180:6
p. is the beginning of sin, 180:13
p. is hateful, 180:12
p. shall bring him low, 180:8
p. was not made for men, 180:14
thy p. and naughtiness of heart, 39:1
when p. cometh, then cometh shame, 180:3
priest: a faithful p., 30:9
like people, like p., 30:14
p. and prophet have erred, 30:11
revilest thou God's highest p., 30:16
priests: ye shall be a kingdom of p., 26:6
prince: the P. of Peace, 147:10
princes: not trust in p., 176:18
prison: opening of the p., 135:8
prisoner: hear the groaning of the p., 135:6
prize: one receiveth the p., 238:2
profane: p. and vain babblings, 200:5

profit: if thou be for his p. he will use thee, 193:11
what shall it profit a man, 212:1
what p. hath a man of all his labor, 243:4
prologue: long p., short story, 246:10
prophesy: sons and daughters shall p., 182:8
prophet: beware of false p., 182:9
G. will raise up a P., 182:4
p. is not without honor, 182:10
p. that hath a dream, 48:4
prophets: by the mouth of his holy p., 182:11
false p., 182:9; 245:6
prosperity: day of p., 216:5
friend cannot be known in p., 70:7
in the hand of God is p. of man, 195:2
p. and adversity come of the Lord, 76:11
p. within thy palaces, 17:9
proud: he hath scattered the p., 180:15
p. in heart, an abomination, 180:5
the Lord will destroy house of the p., 180:4
proverbs: he spake 3,000 p., 238:5
provide: if any p. not for his own, 191:5
provoke: how long will this people p. me, 26:10
prudence: I wisdom dwell with p., 183:3
learn p., 183:2
prudent: p. man conceals knowledge, 183:5
p. man sees danger, 37:4
the p. shall keep silent, 183:6
psalmist: sweet p. of Israel, 38:12 (note)
publican: the p. . . . smote upon his breast, 178:3
publish: p., conceal not, 161:7
punishment: p. greater than I can bear, 21:4
pure: blessed are the p. in heart, 14:6
unto the p. all [is] p., 109:6
purse: let us all have one p., 226:12
pursuits: worthless p., 47:1

quails: q. . . . covered camp, 57:5
quarrel: he who meddles in a q. not his own, 20:9
queen: the q. of Sheba, 211:6
quickly: do q., 212:3
quiet: better a dry morsel with q., 185:1
study to be q., 20:10
quietness: better a handful with q., 171:3
in q. thy strength, 185:3
quo: q. vadis, 46:10

raca: whoever shall say, r., 7:13
race: r. not to the swift, 143:8
Rachel: Jacob loved R., 111:2
R. weeping for her children, 118:4
rage: I know thy . . . r. against me, 86:10
rain: ask r. from the Lord, 236:10
early and latter r., 63:9
hath the r. a father, 34:10
he shall come as the r., 76:8
r. in due season, 200:7
r. upon the earth 40 days, 162:4
raisins: sustain me with r., 67:7
ravens: r. brought him bread, 49:3
reading: do you understand what you are r., 137:12
reap: shalt not wholly r., 62:5
reason: I applied mine heart to know . . . the r. of things, 200:1
let us r. together, 186:5
let r. go before every enterprise, 186:6
rebellious: a stubborn and r. generation, 71:3
a stubborn and r. heart, 27:10
rebuke: open r., 4:6
r. a wise man, 4:2
receiveth: he that r. me, r. him, 113:6
he that r. you, r. me, 11:2

redeemed: hath visited and r. his people, 198:5
I have r. thee, 197:11
r. of the Lord shall return, 197:12
redeemer: Lord, our r., 79:1
my R. lives, 90:7
reel: they r. to and fro, 163:10
refuge: God is our r. and strength, 75:7
God is thy r., 88:3
he is my r. and my fortress, 75:12
r. from the storm, 76:2
the Lord will be a r., 88:6
rejected: despised and r., 187:4
r. of this generation, 187:9
rejoice: let the earth r., 96:9
let the heart of them r., 96:3
r. in all that you put your hand unto, 242:4
r. in every good thing, 96:1
r., O ye nations, 96:2
r. with them that r., 217:5
rejoicing: our r. is at an end, 226:9
religion: pure r. is this, 189:9
remained: r. not one of them, 56:8
remember: Lord God, r. me, 178:9
r. me, o my God, 178:13
r. not the former things, 168:13
remembrance: no enduring r., 102:4
this do in r. of me, 132:10; 132:11
remit: whose sins ye r., 208:13
remnant: a r. of them shall return, 27:7
render: r. to all their dues, 190:6
r. unto Caesar, 219:13
repeateth: he that r. a matter, 92:3
repent: r. not, 2:6
r. ye, 189:10
repentance: God leadeth thee to r., 190:2
repenteth: joy . . . over one sinner that r., 190:1
reproves: Lord r. him whom he loves, 223:12
the man whom God r., 223:11
rescue: r. those who are being taken away to death, 190:9
resist: r. the devil, 190:5
respect: ye shall not r. persons in judgment, 133:11
respecter: God is no r. of persons, 76:18
rest: I will give thee r., 87:15
the weary be at r., 41:6
whole earth is at r., 171:6
resurrection: I am the r. and the life, 60:9
in the r. they neither marry, 191:8
return: he shall not r. to me, 41:4
revealed: nothing that shall not be r., 33:9
revealeth: he r. the deep and secret things, 192:2
reward: he shall r. every man according to his works, 129:6
I am thy exceeding great r., 77:12
Lord r. him according to his works, 2:8
they have their r., 73:2
your r. in heaven, 15 (cont. from p. 14)
rewarded: r. evil for good, 108:7
they shall be greatly r., 231:2
ribs: r. which God had taken from man, made he a woman, 3:1
rich: curse not the r., 177:3
he that maketh haste to be r., 153:6
it [wine] maketh every heart r., 237:11
labor not to be r., 243:1
one man pretends to be r., 152:12
r. in good works, 231:10
r. man beginning to fall, 193:12
r. man is wise in his own eyes, 193:9
r. man shall hardly enter the kingdom of heaven, 153:19
the r. hath many friends, 193:6
the r. ruleth over the poor, 193:8
when a r. man speaketh, 193:13
riches: great r. is come to nought, 154:4
he that getteth r. and not by right, 10:6
he hath swallowed down r., 152:6

he heapeth up r., 152:7
he that trusteth in his r., 152:11
hidden r. of secret places, 38:7
I have given thee . . . r. and honor, 211:2
neither poverty nor r., 153:7
r. and strength lift heart, 177:6
r. are not for ever, 153:5
r. lost in a bad venture, 153:9
r. make themselves wings, 153:4
r. profit not in day of wrath, 152:9
strong men retain r., 214:10
watching for r. consumeth the flesh, 153:16

riddle: put forth a r., 195:5

ride: r. on the high places, 66:6

righteous: lies ye have made . . . the r. sad, 43:12
death of the r., 40:8
light dawns for the r., 230:9
righteousness and peace have kissed, 197:7
sold the r. for silver, 19:13
souls of the r. are in the hand of God, 98:10
the Lord is r., 74:11
the r. shall flourish, 230:8
when r. are in authority, 93:5
wilt thou destroy the r., 44:5

righteousness: better a little with r., 230:13
r. and peace have kissed, 197:7
r. as a mighty stream, 130:9
r. exalteth a nation, 230:12
r. I hold fast, 230:5
r. of the scribes and Pharisees, 99:1
way of r. is life, 230:10
with r. shall he judge the poor, 148:2

righteousnesses: r. are as filthy rags, 105:9
work of r. shall be peace, 171:8

rights: righteous man knows r. of poor, 176:8

riotous: r. living, 181:2

rise (see also **arise**): many . . . r. up against me, 50:12
r. take up thy bed, 151:3
r. up, my love, 142:12
thy brother shall r., 151:8

risen: he is r., 122:9
if Christ be not r., 123:5
now is Christ r., 123:6
the Lord is r., 122;10

robbers: r. prosper, 36:1

rock: he is my r. and my salvation, 75:8
he is the r., 74:7
it was founded upon a r., 188:3
Lord is my r., 74:10
smite the r., 57:9
upon this r. I shall build my church, 173:9

rod: r. of iron, 93:8
r. out of the stem of Jess, 148:1
spares the r., 24:1

Roman: a man that is a R., 170:2

root: r. of all evil, 154:3

rose: I am the r. of Sharon, 141:3

rosebuds: crown ourselves with r., 101:5

rule: he that hath no r. over own spirit, 201:11
I will not r. over you, 92:9
r. with a rod of iron, 93:8

ruler: thou shalt not curse the r., 92:8
wicked r., 165:6

rulers: r. of thousand, r. of hundreds, 92:6

ruleth: he that r. must be just, 93:1

run: if thou hast r. with the footmen, 174:6

sabbath: and it [a sheep] fall into a pit on the s. day, 196:6
Lord hath given you the s., 196:2
remember the s. day, 196:4
the s. was made for man, 196:7
whosoever doeth work in the sabbath shall be put to death, 196:5

sacrifice: the s. of fools, 28:4
to obey better than s., 83:11

sad: why is thy countenance s., 226:1
saints: precious to the Lord is death of his s., 196:9
grace and mercy is to his s., 197:1
salt: eaten without s., 67:2
if the s. hath lost its taste, 105:16 (note)
s. of the earth, 105:16
she became a pillar of s., 210:15
salvation: call upon him for s., 82:17
garments of s., robe of righteousness, 197:14
God is my s., 75:18
his s. is nigh to them that fear him, 197:7
I have waited for thy s., 197:2
man should hope and wait for s., 198:1
mine eyes have seen thy s., 198:7
my rock and my s., 75:8
now is the day of s., 199:1
see the s. of the Lord, 197:3
the Lord . . . is become my s., 197:4
thy s. cometh, 197:15
wells of s., 197:9
work out your own s., 199:2
Samaritan: a certain S., 91:6
Samuel: Lord called S., S., 81:1
sanctuary: let them make me an s., 12:5
sapphire: paved work of s. stone, 80:9
Satan: get thee behind me, S., 220:5
get thee hence, S., 91:2
I saw S. fall like lightning, 46:2
S., whence comest thou, 45:7
satisfied: eye not s. with seeing, 226:6
satyrs: s. shall dance there, 29:4
Saul: David came to S., 38:11
S. and Jonathan were lovely, 199:6
S. eyed David, 39:6
S., S., why persecutest thou me, 169:9
S. has slain his thousands, 39:5
S. was afraid of David, 39:7
S., yet breathing out threatenings, 169:9
singing and dancing, to meet king S., 157:1
save: himself he cannot s., 120:13
not to judge the world but to s., 198:9
the Son of man is come to s. [what] was lost, 114:5
saved: few shall be s., 198:3
we are not s., 197:16
what must I do to be s., 198:10
scab: smite with a s. the crown of the head, 180:9 (note)
scales: there fell from his eyes . . . s., 169:11
scapegoat: s. . . . into the wilderness, 12:11
scatter: Lord shall s. thee, 27:3
s. them beyond the river, 27:5
science: oppositions of s., 200:5
scorpions: I will chastise you with s., 165:4
scribes: beware of the s., 106:13
s. and Pharisees, hypocrites, 106:12
s. in long clothing, 31:6
the righteousness of the s. and the Pharisees, 99:1
scriptures: mighty in the s., 30:15
search the s., 16:10
sea: a s. of glass, 164:2
go down to s. in ships, 163:8
sorrow on the s., 164:1
thy way is in the s., 163:6
yonder is the s., 163:7
seals: seven s., 64:4
searching: by s. find God, 85:12
season: to every thing there is a s., 139:2
secret: good to keep close s. of a king, 201:7
nothing is s., 201:9
s. things belong unto the Lord, 192:1
secrets: he knoweth the s. of the heart, 201:3
see: except I shall s. the print of the nails, 123:3
I s. him not, 81:4
men have desired to s. those things which ye s., 11:3
s. through a glass darkly, 232:1

seed: his s. shall inherit the earth, 105:2
I will make thy s. as the dust, 26:4
morning sow thy s., 63:2
the s. is rotten, 63:6
to thy s. I give this land, 26:3
seeds: divers s., 62:7
s. fell by the way, 59:8
seedtime: s. and harvest . . . shall not cease, 159:3
seek: s. and ye shall find, 109:1
those that s. me [wisdom] early shall find me, 239:4
ye shall s. me and find me, 86:3
ye shall s. me and shall not find me, 121:8
seeth: he s. from everlasting to everlasting, 89:4
sentence: s. . . . not executed speedily, 135:7
sepulchre: no man knoweth of his s., 154:10
sepulchers: whited s., 106:12
seraphims: above it stood the s., 6 (cont. from p.7)
serpent: s. . . . upon thy belly shalt thou go, 45:6
that old s. called the Devil, 46:7
the s. beguiled me, 3:6
the s. said unto the woman, 3:2
the s. was more subtil, 45:5
way of s. upon a rock, 140:1
servant: accuse not a s., 1:7
behold my s. . . . mine elect, 202:8
cast the unprofitable s. into outer darkness, 20:4
s. not above his lord, 186:1
thou good and faithful s., 99:8
you shall not oppress hired s., 175:7
serve: cannot s. God and mammon, 83:14
God will we s., 83:9
no man can s. two masters, 143:1
s. him in sincerity, 82:3
s. him with a perfect heart, 83:10 (note)
s. the Lord with all your heart, 83:10
s. the Lord with gladness, 83:12
set: s. thine house in order, 41:5
seven: s. other spirits, 55:6
s. seals, 64:4
s. years of plenty, s. years of famine, 126:4
seventh: God blessed the s. day, 196:1
people rested on the s. day, 196:3
the s. good kine are s. years, 126:3
the s. year, 196:8
seventy: until s. times seven, 69:3
shadow: days on earth are as s., 138:3
s. of death, 38:4
valley of the s. of death, 88:7
shadows: s. of the evening, 53:1
Shadrach, Meschach, and Abednego: S., M., and A. came forth of the fire, 149:2
shake: m. that did s. kingdoms, 143:7
s. off the dust of your feet, 187:7
share: s. what you have, 231:11
shaven: if I be s., my strength will go, 199:5
she: s. gave me of the tree, 3:5
Sheba: when the queen of S. heard of the fame of Solomon, 211:6
sheep: all we like s. have gone astray, 203:1
having one hundred s., 208:8
he [David] keepeth the s., 38:8
I have found my s. which was lost, 208:9
I will seek out my s., 88:13
lay down my life for the s., 116:9
lost s. of the house of Israel, 114:3
other s. which are not of this fold, 188:8
s. on his right hand, 129:8
Sheol: down to S., 41:8
shepherd: feed his flock like a s., 88:10
I am the good s., 116:7, 116:8.
Lord is my s. 88:7
one fold, one s., 188:8
shepherds: s. . . . keeping watch, 119:2
thy servants are s., 205:8

Shibboleth: say now S., 233:8
shield: my strength and s., 77:8
shine: arise, s., 154:5
ship: way of a ship, 140:1
ships: they that go down to the sea in s., 163:8
shoes: s. shall be iron and brass, 214:4
the latchet of whose s. I am not worthy to unloose, 114:9
whose s. I am not worthy to bear, 14:3
show: s. me not thy way, 178:7
s. me thy glory, 178:8
sick: heal the s., 11:1
the whole head is s., 206:6
whom thou lovest is s., 151:6
sickness: death better than . . . continual s., 42:9
I will take s. away, 97:7
Lord will take away all s., 97:8
side: who is on Lord's s., 83:2
signs: s. and wonders, 149:4
silence: let all the earth keep s. before him, 28:6
the prudent shall keep s., 183:6
silent: man of understanding remains s., 207:1
oh that you would keep s., 218:2
silver: he that loveth s., 153:8
neither their s. nor their gold, 153:12
s. and gold have I none, 73:6
sold the righteous for s., 19:13
the pieces of s., 127:5
the s. cord be loosed, 42:2
the s. in mine and the gold is mine, 153:13
thirty pieces of s., 16:6
your s. has become dross, 29:3 (note)
simple: the s. believeth every word, 215:7
sin: cleanse me from my s., 207:6
depart from all s., 82:9
fools mock at s., 207:11
go and s. no more, 128:7
if we say we have no s., 209:1
s. no more, 208:10
s. of Judah, 208:1
they that s. are enemies to life, 208:3
wages of s., 208:15
when I declared not my s., 207:5
where s. abounded, 93:9
whosoever commiteth s., 208:12
your s. will find you out, 207:3
Sinai: see mount Sinai
sincere: let thy life be s., 209:3
sing: awake and s., 157:12
I will s. unto the L., 56:9
noise of them that s., 156:9
s. aloud to God our strength, 157:9
s., o heavens, 96:14
s. praises unto G., 84;11
s. psalms unto him, 84:6
s. unto Lord, 84:6
singer: woman that is a s., 157:14
singing: s. and making melody, 158:1
sinner: joy . . . over one s. that repenteth, 208:9
one s. destroyeth much good, 207:14
sinners: I am come to call . . . s. to repentance, 208:7
if s. entice thee, 207:9
s., of whom I am chief, 208:18
the way of s. is made plain, 208:5
sinneth: soul that s. shall die, 208:2
sins: fear of the Lord driveth away s., 82:11
he is the propitiation for our s., 117:4
her s. are forgiven, 141:10
he that covereth his s. shall not prosper, 207:12
remember not the s. of my youth, 207:4
though your s. be as scarlet, 207:15
thy s. be forgiven thee, 69:2
whose s. ye remit, they are remitted, 208:13
Sisera: mother of S. looked out at a window, 209:6
S. fled away into the tent of Jael, 209:5

skillful: man s. in his work, 242:13
skin: s. of my teeth, 52:8
slain: s. upon the high places, 39:8
sleep: he giveth his beloved s., 210:2
how long wilt thou s., o sluggard, 136:8
I will lie down and s., 210:1
love not s., 210:5
s. on now, 210:7
sound s., moderate eating, 67:12
the s. of a laboring man, 210:6
yet a little s. a little slumber, 210:4
your s. will be sweet, 210:3
sleepeth: maid is not dead but s., 150:3
slept: I laid me down and s., 210:1
slippery: way be dark and s., 50:13
slothful: s. man, 136:9
s. man saith, there is a lion, 137:1
slow: s. of speech, and of a s. tongue 154:2
sluggard: how long wilt thou sleep, o s., 136:8
go to the ant, thou s., 9:5
s. will not plow, 136:10
small: he that contemneth s. things, 210:9
the day of s. things, 210:8
smite: s. the rick, 57:9
smote: he s. them hip and thigh, 233:9
sober: be s., be vigilant, 229:9
let us, of the day, be s., 231:9
watch and be sober, 229:8
Sodom: the Lord rained upon S. and Gomorrah brimstone, 210:14
soft: a s. answer, 7:6
sold: they s. the righteous for silver, 19:13
Solomon: even S. in all his glory, 71:2
S. loved many strange women, 211:4
son: Absalom, my s. 40:2
all men should honor the S., 115:6
behold thy s., 146:7
every s. ye shall cast into the river, 155:3
foolish s. is ruin to father, 61:4
foolish s. is sorrow to mother, 23:16
he gave his only begotton S., 115:4
I care for nothing my s., since I let thee go, 24:9
my s., be wise, 24:4
my s. mourning, 23:5
my s. was dead, and is alive again, 181:5
no man knoweth the S. but the Father, 113:9
no more worthy to be called thy s., 181:3
S., all I have is thine, 25:4
the Father loveth the S., 115:5
the S. of man coming in a cloud, 129:10
the S. of man hath not where to lay his head, 113:3
the S. of man is come to save, 114:5
the younger s. [went] into a far country, 181:2
this is my beloved S., 113:1
this was the S. of God, 121:3
thou art the S. of God, 114:2
thou hast not withheld thy s. . . . from me, 110:1
wise s., foolish s., 23:16
wise s. hears his father's instruction, 23:17
song: a new s., 157:10
awake, utter a s., 156:11
Lord is my strength and s., 56:9
my s. in the night, 157:8
O sing . . a new s., 157:10
s. put to silence, 226:9
sung a new s., 245:9
write ye this s., 156:10
ye shall have a s., 157:13
songs: his s. were a thousand and five, 238:5
sons: am I not better than ten s., 144:5
s. of the living god, 105:12
sorrow: any s. like unto my s., 226:8
in s. thou shalt bring forth children, 3:7
keep sorrow to thyself, 202:1
s. is better than laughter, 226:7

sorrow: (*continued*)
s. of the heart, 50:4
s. shall flee, 96:13
sorrowful: even in laughter heart is s., 226:5
my soul is exceeding s., 226:11
soul: gain the whole world and lose his s., 212:1
fear him . . . able to destroy . . . s., 45:9
I found him whom my s. loveth, 204:10
I sought him whom my s. loveth, 204:9
his s. shall dwell at ease, 105:2
my s. is among lions, 37:1
my s. is exceeding sorrowful, 226:11
s. weary of life, 138:8
this night thy s. shall be required, 181:9
souls: all s. are mine, 211:8
thou lover of s., 87:11
sow: s. beside all waters, 63:4
soweth: whatsoever a man s., shall he reap, 2:7
spares: he who s. the rod, 24:1
speak: be slow to s., 98:6
Lord saith, I s., 83:8
praise no man before thou hearest him s., 219:2
refrain not to speak, 218:14
when all men shall s. well of you, 183:11
speaking: s. in human terms, 219:9
spear: with a s., pierced his side, 122:4
spectacle: we are made a s. unto the world, 11:12
speech: by s. wisdom known, 132:5
great plainness of s., 132:8
I [Moses] am slow of s., 154:7
let thy s. be short., 219:4
rude in s., not in knowledge, 219:10
s. betrayeth thee, 219:8
s. finely three, 219:5
s. with grace, 219:11
spider: s. . . . is in king's palaces, 9:8
spin: women who were wise hearted did s., 242:3
spirit: a man in whom the S. of God is, 229:16
a wounded s., 187:3
God is a S., 91:4
no man . . . hath power . . . to retain the s., 41:17
our s. shall vanish, 211:9
the flesh lusteth against the S., and the S. against the flesh, 18:11
the fruit of the S. is love, joy, 212:4
the letter killeth, the S. giveth life, 189:6
the s. gives life, 212:2
the S. in the inner man, 212:5
the s. is willing, 220:6
the s. of man is the candle of the Lord, 211:7
the s. of the Lord filleth the world, 244:14
the S. of the Lord is upon me, 114:10
the s. shall return to God who gave it, 42:2
spirits: seven s. more wicked, 55:6
star: gave him the morning s., 213:7
I saw a s. fall from heaven, 102:3
one s. differeth from another in glory, 94:4
s. called Wormwood, 213:8
s. out of Jacob, 26:13
s., which they saw in the east, 118 (cont. from 117)
the day s. arise, 213:6
stars: he telleth the number of the s., 213:4
morning s. sang, 96:5
s. in their courses fought against Sisera, 233:4
s. shined in their watches, 213:5
steadfast: be s. in thine understanding, 187:12
steal: thou shalt not s., 221:8
ye shalt not s., 103:2
stiffnecked: a s. people, 26.8
stolen: s. waters are sweet, 201:4

stone: almost ready to s. me, 57:8
let him first cast a s., 128:6
not one s. upon another, 45:3
stone which the builders refused, 187:2
the s. sunk into his forehead, 39:3
this s., which I have set for a pillar, 112:8
stones: in league with the s. of the field, 159:7
stork: the s. knoweth her appointed times, 10:4
story: short in the s. itself, 246:10
strait: s. is the gate, 198:4
stranger: I am a s. and a sojourner, 213:9
I am a s. with thee, 214:2
I have been a s. in a strange land, 213:10
one law . . . for the stranger, as for your own, 133:10
surety for a s., 152:10
strangers: entertain s., 104:6
ye were s. in Egypt, 213:11
straw: s. to make brick, 156:3
strays: man who s. from home, 102:10
streets: look not around thee in the s., 30:4
strength: a s. to the poor, needy, 76:2
as the man is, so is his s., 214:6
by s. shall no man prevail, 214:7
glory of young men is s., 214:11
God is my s., 77:6
go from s. to s., 214:9
he has broken my s., 206:5
he [the horse] rejoiceth in his s., 8:6
in Jehovah is everlasting s., 77:9
in quietness, s., 185:3
is my s. the s. of stones, 214:8
out of the mouths of babes and sucklings . . . s., 23:12
riches and s. lift heart, 177:6
seek his s., 77:7
s. is to sit still, 214:12
the Lord is my s., 56:9
the Lord shall renew their s., 77:10
strengthen: s. me . . . only this once, 178:9
s. ye the weak hands, 174:3
strife: a man of s., a man of contention, 112:11
honor to cease from s., 171:2
stripes: forty s. he may give him, 135:4
strive: go not hastily to s., 32:4
s. not without cause, 32:3
s. not with a mighty man, 177:4
s. not with an angry man, 7:11
strong: be s., 234:1
be s. and of good courage, 214:5
be s. and quit yourselves like men, 214:15
s. men retain riches, 214:10
we that are s., 214:14
strongest: the first wrote wine is the s., 214:13
stubborn: a s. and rebellious generation, 71:3
a s. and rebellious heart, 27:10
a s. heart shall fare evil, 215:2
study: much s. is a weariness, 137:7
stupid: s. man will get understanding when colt born a man, 215:3
Succoth: Jacob journeyed to S., 216:6
sue: if any man will s. thee, 134:5
suffer: s. fools gladly, 215:16
s. many things, 187:9
sufficient: little is s., 67:11
s. unto the day is the evil thereof, 70:15
summer: thou hast made s., 34:11
sun: a pleasant thing to behold the s., 100:10
shall the s. be darkened, 245:7
s., stand thou still, 127:1
the s. also ariseth, 100:9
the s. is as a bridegroom, 100:8
the s. of righteousness, 82:8
the s. shall be darkened, 128:11
swear: s. not at all, 217:4
ye shall not s. by my name falsely, 217:2 (note)
sweareth: them that s. much, 217:3

sweat: in the s. of thy face shalt thou eat bread, 3:8
swine: devils . . . into herd of s., 46:8
s. is unclean, 68:5
sword: [all] are fallen by the s., 235:9
a s., a s. is sharpened, 192:8
a s. for the Lord and for Gideon, 233:7
came not to send peace but a s., 193:3
every man's s. against his brother, 32:1
every man's s. against his fellow, 32:1
send the s., famine, pestilence, 44:12
shall the s. devour for ever, 234:4
s. without . . . terror within, 44:6
the Lord saveth not with the s. and spear, 234:2
they shall fall by the s. 229:10
they that take the s., shall perish with the s., 229:15
thy men shall fall by the s., 235:5
swords: beat ploughshares into s., 171:4 (note)
beat s. into ploughshares, 171:4

tabernacle: glory of the Lord filled the t., 12:6
who shall abide in thy t., 197:6
tables: I will give thee t. of stone, 221:13
take: t. me not away in the midst of my days, 179:8
tale: spend our years as t. that is told, 164:13
t. out of season, 246:9
talebearer: thou shalt not go as a t., 92:2
words of a t. are as wounds, 92:4
talk: honor and shame is in t., 216:15
t. not of other men's lives, 92:5
tangere: noli me t., 123:2
tarry: t. all night, 103:15
Tarshish: (See **Tharshish.**)
Tarsus: a Jew of T., 170:1
taste: the t. of it was like wafers, 57:6 (note)
tattlers: t. and busybodies, 20:11
taxed: a decree . . . that all the world be t., 219:14
teach: t. us to number our days, 222:9
teaching: may my t. drop as rain, 84:4
tears: god will wipe away t., 42:3
they that saw in tears, 226:4
teeth: the skin of my t., 52:8
gnashing of t., 101:9; 102:1
tell: t. it not in Gath, 39:8
temper: man of quick t., 7:4
tempest: there arose a great t. in the sea, 149:8
temple: the t. of God is holy, 28:9
tempt: thou shall not t. the Lord, 220:4
ye shall not t. the Lord, 82:1
temptation: blessed is the man that endureth t., 220:7
enter not into t., 220:6
lead us not into t., 140:7
tender: the t. mercies of the wicked, 9:6
tenth: give the t., 112:8
tents: goodly are thy t., 26:15
to your t., O Israel, 192:5
terror: not fear the t. of night, 64:9
t. on every side, 167:4
the t. within, 44:6
terrors: t. of deep darkness, 38:5
testify: your own lips t. against you, 95:1
thanks: good thing to give t. unto the Lord, 179:16
Tharshish: the navy of T., bringing gold and silver, 194:4
that: t. which hath been is now, 223:1
they: t. know not what they do, 121:5
thief: t. in the night, 36:10
t. is better than man . . . accustomed to lie, 43:13
t. [who] is hungry, 36:5
thieves: fell among t., 91:5
thing: no new t. under the sun, 228:7
the t. that hath been, 51:6

things: all t. come alike, 64:2
desire to see those t. ye see, hear those t. ye here, 11:3
seek not t. that are too hard, 5:5
set affection on t. above, not t. on earth, 5:6
six t. doth the Lord hate, 54:7
three t. which are too wonderful for me, 140:1
t. which are seen, t. which are not seen, 232:2
whatsoever t. are true [etc.], think on these t., 231:7
thinketh: as he t. in his heart, 50:6
thirst: if any man t., 116:1
thirty: t. pieces of silver, 16:6
Thomas: T., because thou hast seen me, thou hast believed, 123:4
thorn: t. in the flesh, 109:7 (note)
thorns: crown of t., 120:9
t. in your sides, 109:7
thou: t. art near, O Lord, 81:5
t. art the man, 94:10
t. hast been a strength, 76:2
t. hast made heaven and earth, 76:6
t. sayest, 120:5
t. shalt have no other gods, 221:2
t. shalt love . . . God, 222:5
t. shalt love thy neighbor, 222:5
t. shalt not . . . [Ten Commandments], 221–222
thought: take no t. for the morrow, 246:3
take no t. for your life, 246:1
[who] by taking t. can add one cubit, 246:2
thoughts: knoweth t. of man, 86:13
my t. not your t., 78:9
three: t. days and t. nights in the heart of the earth, 122:6
t. things too wonderful, 140:1
threefold: t. cord not quickly broken, 226:14
thunder: thy t. was in the heaven, 236:4
thundered: the Lord t., 81:2
thunders: t. and lightnings, and cloud upon the mount, 220:9
tidings: him that bringeth good t., 161:5
t. of great joy, 119:2
till: sent him forth . . . to t. the ground, 62:3
tills: who t. his land, 62:11
time: an appointed t. to man on earth, 138:6
a t. for every purpose and work, 223:2
a time to be born, die, etc., 139:2
a t. to every purpose under heaven, 139:2
die before thy t., 47:3
man does not know his t., 42:1
my t., is at hand, 42:13
swallow observe the t. of their coming, 10:4
t. and chance happeneth to all, 143:8
t. is a very shadow, 223:3
today: t. thou shalt be with me in paradise, 121:6
tomorrow (see also **morrow**): boast not of t., 70:13
t. we shall die, 101:3
tongue: be not hasty in thy t., 2:5
death and life in power of the t., 132:3
he that can rule his t., 218:17
keep thy t. from evil, 218:5
many have fallen by swords, but not so many as by t., 219:3
the t. is a little matter, 17:15
the t. . . . is an unruly evil, 219:12
tongues: they have sharpened their t., 218:7
though I speak with the t. of men and angels, 22:6
t. of fire, 172:9
to speak with other t., 172:9
touch: t. me not, 123:2
t. not, taste not, 134:11
tower: build us a city and a t., 14:1
train: t. up a child, 24:3
transfigured: and was t. before them, 114:4

transgressors: way of t. is hard, 207:10
trap: he that setteth a t., 2:2
travelled: man that hath t., 223:9
treasure: t. that is hoarded, 153:15
where your t. is, there will your heart be, 228:12
treasures: give thee the t. of darkness, 38:7
lay not up t. upon earth, 228:1
lay up t. in heaven, 99:2
tree: a green olive t., 87:8
good t. cannot bring forth evil fruit, 191:6
he shall be as a t., 90:12
she gave me of the t., 3:5
take also of the t. of life, 3:10
the t. of life, 3:10
the t. of life [in paradise], 100:3
the t. of the field is man's life, 159:5
the t. of the knowledge of good and evil, 2:12, 49:2
tremble: all the inhabitants of the land t., 129:2
trembling: drunken dregs of t., 64:13
fear and t., 64:8
trespass: for all manner of trespass, 135:3
triumphed: he hath t. gloriously, 56:9
trouble: day of t. is near, 224:3
how are they increased that t. me, 109:8
man is born unto t., 223:10
they are not in t. as other men, 54:4
true: whatsoever things are t., 231:7
trump: at the last t., 191:10
trumpet: blow the t. at the new moon, 157:9
Gideon blew a t., 156:12
if the t. give an uncertain sound, 137:2
praise him with the sound of the t., 85:1
the sound of a t., 157:7
trumpets: the priests blew with the t., 126:9
trust: blessed are they that put their t. in him, 90:8
in him will I t., 75:12
they put t. in him shall understandeth truth, 90:13
t. in the Lord, 90:9
t. is a spider's web, 224:9
t. ye in the Lord forever, 90:11
t. ye not in a friend, 22:1
yet will I t. in him, 90:6
trusteth: blessed is man that t. in thee, 90:10
curseth be man that t. in man, 224:11
trustworthy: who is t. keeps a thing hidden, 201:5
truth: by the word of t., 225:6
great is the t., 225:2
his t. shall be thy shield, 224:13
I have chosen way of t., 224:14
mercy and t. are met together, 197:7
speak every man t., 106:3
strive for t., 225:3
there is no t. in him, 46:3
there shall be peace and t., 171:9
the t. shall make you free, 225:4
t. beareth away victory, 224:15
t. endureth, 225:1
t. shall spring out of the earth, 197:7
t. beareth the victory, 224:15
what is t., 225:5
tumult: t. of the city, 8:4
turn: t. to him the other [check] also, 167:1
turtle: voice of the t., 200:9
turtledove: the soul of thy t., 109:3
two: can t. walk together, 227:2
no man can serve t. masters, 143:1
t. are better than one, 226:13
t. of every sort shall come unto thee, 162:3
t. and t. unto Noah, 162:5

unbelief: help thou my u., 60:6
unclean: man of u. lips, 81:6
understand: hear ye indeed, but u. not, 215:12
understanding: get u., 239:2
man of u., 240:5

understanding (*continued*)
peace which passeth all u., 172:8
u. heart to judge thy people, 128:1
ungodly: the hope of the u., 103:10
the u. are like the chaff, 230:6
unleavened: the feast of u. bread, 65:4; 168:12
u. bread, and with bitter herbs, 168:7
unprofitable: cast the u. servant into outer darkness, 20:4
upright: the bloodthirsty hate the u., 97:4
usurer: thou shalt not be a u., 152:3
Uz: a man in the land of Uz [Job], 123:8

vagabond: a fugitive and a v., 21:3
vain: knoweth v. men, 86:12
valley: every v. shall be exalted, 149:1
v. of decision, 129:3
v. of the shadow of death, 88:7
vanity: all is v., 228:8
creature subject to v., 229:1
v. of vanities, 228:6
vengeance: I will render v., 229:4
to me belongeth v., 229:3
v. is mine, 229:6
vessel: a chosen v., 169:10
weaker v., 241:13
victory: from thee cometh v., 179:17
vigilant: be sober, be v., 46:6
vine: every man under his v. and fig tree, 170:11, 172:1
I am the v., 116:18
vinegar: sponge filled with v., 121:1
vineyard: shalt not glean v., 62:6
not sow v. with divers seeds, 62:7
wellbeloved hath a v., 63:3
violence: v. and strife in the city, 29:1
wine of v., 54:5
violent: v. men get riches, 229:12
preserve me from v. men, 229:11
vipers: generation of v., 71:6
virgin: a v. shall be with child, 117:10
a v. shall conceive, 107:8
virgins: kingdom of heaven likened unto ten v., 183:8
virtuous: v. women is a crown to her husband, 145:1
who can find v. woman, 241:1
vision: where the is no v., 93:6
visions: I have multiplied v., 182:7
v. of God, 81:7
young men shall see v., 182:8
voice: a still small v., 32:9
a v. from heaven, 245:24
blesses his neighbor with a loud v., 17:10
their [stars'] v. goes out through all the earth, 213:3
v. of one that crying in the wilderness, 124:8
v. of the turtle, 200:9
vow: better thou shouldest not v., 181:6

wages: w. of him that is hired, 152:4
w. of sin, 208:15
wail: I will w. and howl, 144:3
wailing: w. and gnashing of teeth, 102:1
wait: good unto them that w., 86:4
waiteth: blessed is he that w., 169:4
walk: w. humbly with thy God, 230:18
walking: Jesus . . . w. on the sea, 150:6
wall: the wall [of Jericho] fell down flat, 126:10
wrote . . . upon the plaister of the w., 149:3
war: a w. in heaven, 6:9
he teacheth my hands to w., 234:5
prepare w., 235:11
shall your brethren go to war, 233:1
the Lord is a man of w., 81:9
they are for w., 32:2
they [shall not] learn w. any more, 171:4
when a man hath a new wife, he shall not go to w., 233:3
wars: he makes w. cease, 170:14
w. and rumors of w., 245:5

wash: if I w. thee not, 174:3
thou shalt never w. my feet, 174:3
washed: he [Pilate] w. his hands, 174:8
waste: it shall lie w., 51:12
to what purpose this w., 235:14
watch: w. and be sober, 229:8
w. and pray, 220:6
w. with me, 119:6
w. with me one hour, 119:6
w. ye therefore, 129:9
watchman: w., what of the night, 37:3
water: bid me come unto thee on the w., 150:6 (note)
there shall come w. out of it, 57:9
we are as w. spilt, 41:3
w. out of the wells of salvation, 197:9
waters: I have healed these w., 51:10
let the w. bring forth abundantly, 34:3
w. may come again upon Egyptians, 56:6
w. were divided, 56:5
way: I am the w., 116:17
show me now thy w., 178:7
the w. of an eagle in the air, w. of serpent, w. of a ship, w. of a man with a maid, 140:1
the w. of life and the w. of death, 25:10
this is the w., 230:16
wayfaring: lodging place of w. men, 52:13
ways: when a man's w. please the Lord, 171:1
weak: God hath chosen the w. things, 210:12
let not your hands be w., 242:8
rescue the w. and needy, 152:1
who is w., and I am not w., 217:6
weaker: w. vessel, 241:13
wealth: my power . . . hath gotten me this w., 152:5
thou hast w. if thou fear God, 82:9
w. hastily gotten, 152:13
w. is his strong city, 193:5
w. maketh many friends, 153:2
weapon: paddle upon the w., 233:2
weather: fair w. cometh out of the north, 236:3
fair w., for the sky is red, 236:11
weaver: days swifter than w.'s shuttle, 138:7
weep: w. with them that w., 217:5
weepeth: she w. in the night, 140:6
weeping: w. and gnashing of teeth, 101:9
w. may endure for a night, 96:7
weighed: w. in the balances . . . found wanting, 59:4
weight: just w. and balance, 103:5
whales: God created great w., 34:3
what: w. hath God wrought, 26:11
whatsoever: w. things are true [etc.], 231:7
wheel: w. in the middle of a w., 200:3
whips: w. . . . scorpions, 165:4
whirleth: it w. about continually, 236:7
whirlwind: Elijah went up by a w., 49:4
they shall reap the w., 2:3
w. of the Lord, 76:5
Lord answered Job out of the w., 124:2
out of the south cometh the w., 236:2
whispering: w. of many, 167:4
white: his raiment was w. as snow, 122:8
w. in the blood of the lamb, 199:3
whited: w. sepulchres, 106:12
whitewash: w. with lies, 33:8
whither: w. goest thou, 46:10
w. thou goest, I will go, 140:9
who: w. hath woe, w. hath sorrow, 237:1
whole: w. heart and w. soul, 209:2
whore: w. is a deep ditch, 204:5
whoredom: w. and wine, 47:4
why: w,. art thou cast down, 226:3
w. dost thou stand afar off, 85:6

wicked: be not over much w., 47:3
earth is given . . . the w., 53:8
God is angry with the w., 53:12
let the w. forsake his way, 186:7
no peace . . . unto the w., 55:1
put not thy hand with the w., 135:9
seven spirits more w., 55:6
tender mercies of the w., 9:6
the triumphing of the w. is short, 53:10
the w. are estranged from the womb, 54:3
the w. . . . cut off in darkness, 53:6
the w. flee when no man pursueth, 95:2
the w. shall not be unpunished, 54:9
when the w. man turneth away from wickedness, 186:8
w. . . . spreading himself like a green bay tree, 54:2
wise king scattereth the w., 93:4
why do the w. live, 53:11
wickedness: bread of w., 54:5
ploughed w., 55:2
what w. is this, 53:5
w. of a woman, 241:9
w. of man was great, 53:2
w. proceedeth from wicked, 53:7
wide: w. is the gate . . . that leadeth to destruction, 101:8
widow: a certain poor w., 73:4
city . . . how is she become as a w., 30:2
do right to the w., 152:2
ye shalt not afflict any w., 151:11
wife: cleave unto his w., 3:1
every one neighed after his neighbor's w., 205:3
grace of a w., 145:7
if a man entice a maid . . . he shall endow her to be his w., 203:4
w. . . . fruitful vine, 61:9
live joyfully with w. whom thou lovest, 145:3
man cleaveth unto w., 145:5
man [with] a new w., shall not go to war, 144:4
sit not with another man's w., 205:4
rejoice with w. of thy youth, 144:7
thou shalt not covet thy neighbor's w., 221:10
w.'s quarreling, 61:14
w., the weaker vessel, 241:13
who finds a w., finds a good thing, 145:2
whosoever putteth away his w., 145:10
wild: he will be a wild man, 110:2
wilderness: in the waste howling w., 27:4
in the w. a lodging place, 52:13
wander in the w. forty years, 58:2
will: not my own w., but the w. of the Father, 115:7
not my w., but thine, 83:15
thy w. be done, 120:1
w. of the Lord, 64:3
wind: every w. of doctrine, 31:8
he that observeth the w., 236:8
inherit the w., 102:7
north w. driveth away rain, 236:6
they have sown the w., 2:3
the w. blows where it wills, 212:9
wings of the w., 65:7
winnow not every w., 187:12
winds: w. and sea obey him, 113:5
windy: w. knowledge, 218:3
wine: a crying for w., 237:8
do not look at w. when it is red, 237:2
drink the w. of astonishment, 186:4
drink w. with merry heart, 67:5
new w., 67:9
new w. into old bottles, 161:10
new w. mourneth, 237:7
they have no w., 151:2
they that tarry long at the w., 237:1
thou hast kept the good w. until now, 237:13
use a little w., 238:1
whoredom and w., 47:4
w. is a mocker, 236:14
w. is as good as life, 237:12
w. maketh merry, 67:6
w. maketh glad heart, 62:10

wine: (*continued*)
w. of violence, 54:5
w. when it is red, 237:2
winepress: trodden w. alone, 229:13
wings: walketh upon w. of wind, 65:7
w. like a dove, 52:11
w. of morning, 88:9
winter: Lo, the w. is past, 200:9
thou hast made summer and w., 34:11
wisdom: by w. a house is built, 102:9
do you limit w. to yourself, 238:6
fear of Lord is w., 238:9
get w., 239:2
how much better is w. than gold, 239:6
if you lack w., 240:9
in much w. is much grief, 137:6
I will destroy w., 240:8
I w., dwell with prudence, 183:3
price of wisdom is above rubies, 238:8
the Lord giveth w., 238:11
the root of wisdom, 240:13
this w. is earthly, sensual, 240:10
thy w. and prosperity exceedeth thy fame, 211:6 (note)
what is richer than w., 240:2
where shall w. be found, 238:8
w. excelleth folly, 239:9
w. is a loving spirit, 239:15
w. is better than rubies, 239 (note, cont. from p. 238)
w. is better than strength, 239:12
w. is better than weapons of war, 239:12
w. is glorious, 239:16
w. of God in a mystery, 158:2
w. that is hid, 153:15
with the ancient is w., 164:7
wise: ask counsel of [the] w., 4:7
a w. and understanding heart, 238:12
a w. and understanding people, 26:14
be not w. in thine own eyes, 238:12
[do not] make thyself over wise, 239:11
he is w., mighty, 75:3
let not the w. man glory in his wisdom, 180:10
man w. in his own conceit, 180:7
I have given thee a w. and understanding heart, 211:1
the multitude of the w., 239:18
there came w. men from the east, 117:11
walketh with w. men, 69:12
w. as serpents, harmless as doves, 217:1
w. child [better than] foolish king, 239:10
w. man is strong, 239:7
w. man will hear, 238:10
w. son hears father, 23:17
w. son makes a glad father, 23:16
wiser: children of this world w. than children of light, 240:7
witch: shalt not suffer w. to live, 163:1
with: he that is not w. me, is against me, 143:2
witness: an unrighteous w., 135:9
false witness against thy neighbor, 221:9
single w. shall not prevail, 136:2
wives: he had 700 w., 211:5
woe: angel . . . saying w., w., w., 6:8
who hath w., who hath sorrow, 237:1
wolf: the w. also shall dwell with the lamb, 171:5
woman: a brawling w., 102:8 (note)
a contentious and angry w., 240:11
a silent and loving woman, 241:10
a virtuous w., 241:1
beauty of a w. cheereth, 15:8
deceived by the beauty of a w., 15:7
enmity between thee and the w., 45:6
foolish w. is clamorous, 215:4
forgo not a wise and good w., 241:8
gracious w. gets honor, 215:17
if a w. have long hair, 18:10
lips of loose w. drip honey, 204:1
neither was man created for w., 241:11

woman: (*continued*)
virtuous w. is a crown, 145;1
who can find a virtuous w., 241:1
wickedness of w., 241:9
w., behold thy son, 146:7
w. . . . gave me of the tree, 3:5
w. in travail has sorrow, 25:5
w. that is a singer, 157:14
w. without discretion, 183:4
women: blessed art thou among w., 146:2
out of their wits for w., 241:7
rise up ye w., 241:4
without w. men cannot be, 241:5
w. keep silence in the churches, 241:12
w. . . . singing and dancing, 157:1
wonderful: things which are too w. for me, 140:1
w. and horrible thing, 161:6
word: be doers of the w., 2:9
earth, hear the w. of the Lord, 89:6
every idle w., 219:6
every w. that proceedeth out of the mouth of God, 89:7
good w. makes him glad, 50:3
in the beginning was the W., 114:12
thy w. is a lamp unto my feet, 79:12
w. better than a gift, 132:6
w. burned like a lamp, 49:7
w. fitly spoken is like apples of gold, 132:4
w. spoken in due season, 218:8
w. of God grew, 89:8
w. of God is quick, 89:9
w. of God shall stand forever, 89:5
w. of the Lord endureth, 89:10
Word was made flesh, 115 (cont. from p. 114)
words: a question of w. and names, 93:7
by w. justified, by w. condemned, 136:4
he multiplieth w., 218:4
he that hath knowledge spareth his w., 218:12
let thy w. by few, 117:10
man that is hasty in his w., 218:12
my w. shall not pass away, 114:7
pleasant w. like a honeycomb, 218:9
should a multitude of w. go unanswered, 218:1
the ear tests w., 132:2
w. smoother than butter, 218:6
work: every one is wise in his w., 243:10
if this . . . w. be of men, 90:4
man should enjoy his w., 243:7
man skillful in his w., 242:12
man's w. shall be made manifest, 244:3
the Lord recompense thy w., 242:6
w. of our hand, 242:10
w. the works of him who sent me, 244;1
w. your w., 243:12
your w. shall be rewarded, 242:8
workman: that needeth not be ashamed, 244:5
works: all the w. done under the sun, 228:5
her own w. praise her, 241:3
I made me great w., 216:2
man . . . who works for himself, 242:12
rich in good w., 231:10
spirit of the Lord filleth the world, 244:14
the Lord reward him according to his w., 2:8
w. of the Lord are good, 90:3
world: all that is in the w. hath a beginning and an end, 244:12
care of this w., 245:1
children of this w. . . . wiser than children of light, 240:7
he hath set the w. in their heart, 34:12
I have overcome the w., 245:2
kingdoms of this w., 245:4
not to judge the w., but to save the w., 198:9
the w. has lost his youth, 244:13
the w. knew him now, 115 (cont. from p. 114)
whole w. is as a little grain of the balance, 244:15

world: (*continued*)
w. has lost his youth, 244:13
worm: w., my mother and sister, 41:11
wormwood: I will feed them with w., 224:4
star called W., 213:8
worship: let us w. and bow down, 91:1
thou shalt w. the Lord, 91:3
worthless: a w. person, a wicked man, 54:6
w. pursuits, 47:1
worthy: not w. that thou shouldest come under my roof, 149:7
wounded: a w. spirit, 187:3
wounds: w. but binds up, 75:2
wrath: envy and w. shorten life, 206:10
king's w. as roaring of lion, 176:19
let not the sun go down on your w., 7:14
slow to w., 7:5
soft answer turneth away w., 7:6
through w. of the Lord . . . land darkened, 44:10
w. brings punishment, 7:2
w. is cruel, 7:8
w. killeth foolish man, 7:1
w. worketh not righteousness, 7:15
wrestle: we w. against principalities, 55:13
wrestled: Jacob w. a man, 111:3
wretched: w. man that I am, 18:7
write: w. in a book, 246:8; 246:11
w. in a book all the words I have spoken, 246:8
w. it before them in a table, 246:7
writing: put all in w., 20:2
the w. that was written [on the wall], 45:2
wrought: what hath God w., 26:11

year: hallow the fiftieth y., 127:2
the seventh y., 196:8
years: a thousand y. in thy sight, 222:8
few and evil the days of the y. of my life, 138:2
forty y. in wilderness, 58:4
threescore y. and 10, 164:13
y. as a tale that is told, 164:13
y. come to end like a sigh, 138:9 (note)
y. draw nigh . . . no pleasure in them, 164:15
y. should teach wisdom, 164:9
young: glory of y. men is strength, 247:3
have been y., now old, 164:10
y. and old shall lie in the streets, 235:9
y. men shall see visions, 48:6
youngest: there remaineth yet the y., 38:8
youth: bear the yoke in his y., 247:6
not remembered the days of thy y., 247:7
rejoice young man in thy y., 247:4
thou hast the dew of thy y., 247:2

zeal: z. hath consumed me, 248:1
Zion: daughters of Z. are haughty, 180:9
joy of the whole earth is mount Z., 248:2
out of Z. the perfection of beauty, 248:3
the people shall dwell in Z., 148:5
we wept when we remembered Z., 248:4
woe to them at ease in Z., 101:4